Ethnic Medicine in the Southwest

Edited and With an Introduction by
Edward H. Spicer

Eleanor Bauwens *Margarita Artschwager Kay*
Mary Elizabeth Shutler *Loudell F. Snow*

The University of Arizona Press
Tucson, Arizona

Although the informants in this book granted the authors permission to quote them, they did not want to be identified. Fictitious names, therefore, have been used throughout.

Third printing 1981

THE UNIVERSITY OF ARIZONA PRESS

Manufactured in the U.S.A.

Library of Congress Cataloging in Publication Data

Ethnic medicine in the Southwest.

Bibliography: p.
Includes index.
1. Folk medicine – Southwest, New. I. Spicer, Edward Holland, 1906–. II. Bauwens, Eleanor.
[DNLM: 1. Ethnic groups – United States. 2. Folklore. WZ309 E84]
GR109.E86 615′.882′0979 76-62553
ISBN 0-8165-0636-1
ISBN 0-8165-0490-3 pbk.

Contents

FIGURES

About the Authors

EDWARD H. SPICER, editor of this book as well as contributing author, has been a professor of anthropology at the University of Arizona since 1950. Early in his career he headed the Community Analysis Section of the War Relocation Authority in Washington, D.C., and for more than thirty years has dedicated much of his time to teaching, writing and research on the American Indians of the Southwest including the Yaquis, one of whose communities is discussed in this volume. He is past president of the American Anthropological Association and has been recipient of numerous honors and awards including the 1976 Malinowski Award given by the Society for Applied Anthropology.

LOUDELL F. SNOW, assistant professor of anthropology and community medicine, College of Osteopathic Medicine, Michigan State University, contributes to this book the study entitled "Popular Medicine in a Black Neighborhood," in the course of which she was supported by the Danforth Foundation. Identifying with her informants as "rural people in an urban setting," she attributes much of her success in gathering information for this study to the knowledge she holds in common with them about "weather signs, planting by the almanac, quilting, making soap, making garden, canning and butchering." She received her Ph.D. in anthropology from the University of Arizona in 1971.

MARGARITA ARTSCHWAGER KAY first became interested in the medical anthropology of Spanish-speaking people as a student of public health nursing in San Francisco where she worked with many Central Americans. Subsequent work as a visiting nurse in New York's East Harlem, where she came in contact with the Puerto Rican and Cuban populace, as well as research done in Mexico, Arizona and New Mexico, have intensified her interest in the field. The author holds a Ph.D. in anthropology from the University of Arizona where in 1972 she became assistant professor of nursing and associate in community medicine.

MARY ELIZABETH SHUTLER has been chairman of the Department of Anthropology at Washington State University, Pullman, since 1975. She received her master's degree in anthropology from the University of Arizona in 1958, the year she began her research on the curing beliefs and practices of an Arizona Yaqui community. She received her Ph.D. in anthropology from the same university in 1967 and since then has done extensive research, writing and field work involving the New Hebrides island group and their inhabitants.

ELEANOR BAUWENS, an assistant professor of nursing at the University of Arizona, Tucson, since 1974, is a graduate of St. Mary's Hospital School of Nursing, Tucson. She received her M.A. and Ph.D. degrees in anthropology from the University of Arizona in 1970 and 1974 respectively. She is a member of the Committee for Nursing and Anthropology, Society for Medical Anthropology, and is author of several published papers.

• • •

The authors of this volume wish to express appreciation to the many informants whose contributions to these studies were an invaluable resource, and to Keith Basso, Harry T. Getty, James Officer, Edward H. Spicer, and Thomas Weaver of the Department of Anthrolopogy, University of Arizona, for their encouragement and assistance in the various research projects. Finally, words of thanks go to Raymond Thompson, head of the Department of Anthropology, University of Arizona and Director of the Arizona State Museum, as well as to the University of Arizona Press for effecting publication of this book.

Southwestern Healing Traditions in the 1970s: an Introduction

Edward H. Spicer

Southwestern Healing Traditions in the 1970s: an Introduction

Edward H. Spicer

THE PRACTICE OF MEDICINE, according to whatever tradition in whatever society, is an art which makes use of a body of specialized knowledge for the maintenance of health and the treatment of disease. In complex societies where several cultural traditions flourish, practitioners are, whether they admit it or not, in competition with one another. In complex societies like our own, there is never a single homogeneous tradition guiding the medical arts. At least as many healing traditions exist as there are peoples with different ethnic backgrounds. In the United States distinctive beliefs and practices about medicine characterize the surviving Indian groups such as the Navajos; the Mexican Americans maintain medical arts with deep historical roots in the cultures of both hemispheres; Blacks have developed some beliefs of their own in the course of their long separate experience; and all of these exist in the midst of a variety of curing practices stemming out of the many ethnic traditions of Europe and even of Asia.

The practice of medicine is complicated not only by these varied ethnic contributions, but also by the fact that medical knowledge and the medical arts are never static. New traditions keep coming into existence as this extremely dynamic area of life continues to develop. One need only follow the best-seller lists of books over a period of years to be aware of the continual succession of new ideas which gain followings in the field of medicine. To consider these as unimportant fads is to miss their importance as indicators of the state of the medical arts. They are frequently, as in the case of diets, expressions of developing traditions growing out of dissatisfactions with the medicine practiced by graduates of our medical schools. From these and other sources which will be discussed later in this volume grow innovations which produce a variety of medical practices in our modern societies.

Thus the society in which a graduate of a medical school in the United States, or France, or Mexico, or India begins to practice his art exhibits a medley of medical traditions. He has been taught to believe that his body of knowledge is the one true source of successful treatment of disease. He is, however, in the midst of millions of people who have not been through the rigorous discipline of Western medical training which led to his understanding of human disease. All around him among his patients are people who without taking much thought about the matter are quite comfortable in beliefs about curing which are incompatible with what the young graduate believes. They are inclined to repose their faith in those techniques which work. They also are much more intensely aware than is the new graduate of the various failures of physicians to effect cures in specific cases. All around him also are people who have grown up in the awareness of several different medical traditions – Chinese herb doctors, touch therapy, the efficacy of a rosary or a "sing," and a host of others. There are also people who may be as certain as the young physician that there is only one true medical tradition, but that it is one with which he is not familiar. The fact is that the world of human illness which the hopeful young practitioner sets out to relieve does not conform to the image of suffering people waiting to be informed of, and thence to use, the techniques and the logic of what the young graduate has become accustomed to call "modern" or "scientific" medicine. The real world is a world of many medicines and there are in it tens of thousands of practitioners who do not believe in "scientific medicine" as a universal cure-all. The environment in which the new practitioner begins to practice, to which he must adapt, is complex, with a history of many medical traditions out of which his own beliefs and practices have emerged.

It is the purpose of this volume to contribute to the understanding of that environment and perhaps to aid somewhat the process of adaptation. Basic to such understanding is a clear conception of what we are talking about. We have already used such terms as "modern medicine" and "scientific medicine," two labels which are a great source of confusion, and we have introduced without adequate discussion as yet a concept of "medicines," which may be confusing to anyone who has been taught that only graduates of accredited medical colleges practice medicine and that all other practitioners are dealing in something that is not worthy of the name of medicine. Let us begin by making a distinction between the body of knowledge which a practitioner uses and the art which he or she employs in treating persons. There is a body of knowledge about human health and disease which has been steadily growing in Europe and the Western world and is now known all over the world in some degree. It has accumulated with the impetus of the use of the scientific method in medical laboratories connected with clinics and hospitals.

This coherent body of knowledge in which holders of the M.D. or D.O. degree are grounded, we may call "scientific medicine." However, it must be understood that physicians do not practice a body of knowledge when they treat patients; they practice the art of medicine, making as much use as they can, according to their abilities, of the body of scientific knowledge. These physicians we may speak of as practicing Western medicine; they do not practice scientific medicine, which is carried on in the laboratories although with constant reference to what practitioners do in clinics and hospitals. If we call the practice of medicine in close contact with scientific medical knowledge "modern medicine" as is often done, then we open ourselves to thinking in very narrow terms. What is modern today will be old, or old-fashioned, or ancient some time hence. "Modern" is a label which has no permanent referent, and it is apparent that the cumulation of scientific medical knowledge is a permanently ongoing process. The employment of the scientific method in this accumulation is a phenomenon of the Western world with its origins in ancient Greece and Western Europe. It seems appropriate, then, that we call this special kind of practice "Western medicine." We shall abandon entirely the use of the term "modern medicine," because we do not wish to use labels which confuse a passing phase with a permanent process.

Then what of the other medicines to which we have alluded above? There is a strong tendency to speak of those medical traditions which exist in present-day societies, but which are out of touch with Western medicine, as "folk medicine." This label may have connotations which are either good or bad, that is, of desirability or undesirability. Medical traditions which are regarded as survivals from more or less primitive conditions and are seen as on their way out are usually labelled "folk." It is also true, however, that some practices – such as the use of apple cider vinegar – are labelled folk medicine by advocates who regard them as highly desirable. This or other practices may be believed to embody an older wisdom which ought to be revived and made part of a system of medical practice which will then be superior in some ways to Western medical practice. Probably persons will continue to use the term "folk medicine" in the two opposite ways, for both desirable and undesirable traditions deriving from cultures which have developed separately from Western medicine. The ambiguity of the term makes it of limited use in our effort to see clearly the nature of the medical environment of our own and other present-day societies. We shall not employ it in what follows.

The term which we believe is most useful for designating those kinds of medical practice which are not focused on making the maximum use of scientific medicine is "popular medicine." An alternative term which has come into use in the 1970s may indeed turn out to be the most practical, namely, "parallel medical traditions." That is, however, somewhat awkward in such phrases as "parallel medicine" when we wish to refer to the practice of non-Western traditions. It is nevertheless useful in emphasizing a major point in our discussion; namely, that there are traditions of medical thought and practice which have developed and continue parallel with Western medicine. We shall have more to say about the "parallelness" of the various medical traditions which we find in present-day societies around the world. Meanwhile we suggest the use of "popular medicine" as a general term of contrast with Western medicine.

In this usage, each of the four kinds of medicine described in this volume is to be regarded as a variety of "popular medicine." There need be no connotation in this usage of a tradition that is on the way out, as in the case of one of the meanings of "folk." The view to be emphasized is that these traditions are maintained by ethnic and class segments in any society, rather than by the specialists engaged in scientific and Western medicine. Existing and developed among people who do not have the kind of technical training required for scientific medicine, nor the close contact with scientific medicine required for the practice of Western medicine, these traditions are of the people rather than of the scientists.

There are of course popular medicines which have developed exclusively in the Western world parallel with Western medicine. There are also Oriental and native American and African popular medicines, and many others. The four medical traditions which are sketched in this volume are good examples of the many varieties of popular medicine to which they more or less conform. Much more comparative study is required. Our effort here is focused on merely sketching some outstanding features of local (which may turn out to be regional) medical environment.

The most obvious characteristic of the people who participate in the belief and practice presented here is that they differ according to ethnic group. There are very clear differences among the traditions according to whether they are employed by Blacks, by White Anglos, by Mexican Americans, or by Yaqui Indians. We have chosen therefore to present them as ethnic varieties of popular medicine. This should not, however, close our eyes to the possibility of variations in socio-economic conditions as major influences. All four are low-income groups and probably all four are on that basis classifiable as lower class segments of the general population. We do believe nevertheless that the beliefs and practices described here are not confined to lower class persons. Study is required with reference to determining to what extent the beliefs and practices described characterize also middle-class persons of the four ethnic groups. On the supposition that isolation from Western medicine, or as we say opportunity for health care, is directly correlatable with income and class position, one might suppose that we have identified varieties of medicine which are class determined. But it is that very assumption which needs to be examined. We suggest that the choices involved in using or not using Western medicine are not wholly class determined and that continuing popular ethnic traditions related to subcultural systems in our society are of importance in differential usage of Western medicine. Some of these subcultural factors may become apparent as we examine the varieties of popular medicine in this volume.

The four popular medicines singled out for description are presented as ethnic varieties largely because each seems fairly clearly associated with people whose differing historical experience has led to a distinct sense of ethnic identity. It appears also that the distinctive characteristics of each are specifically connected with their historical background. The relation between particular medical traditions and the history of an ethnic people has not yet been adequately investigated, but certain relationships will become obvious in what follows. A good beginning has been made in these four studies, all of which evolved from dissertations completed at the University of Arizona. Of the four ethnic medical systems presented here, only one has been treated extensively by other anthropologists – that of the Spanish-speaking people. Although the data for the survey on a Yaqui community were collected in 1958-59, the information is still relevant in 1976 as curing practices and beliefs have not changed markedly since that time.

The medical beliefs and practices of the low income Blacks of what the author has called the "Martin Hill Neighborhood" are characterized by an intimate connection with religious belief. Running through most of the cases and the comments of informants is evidence of a definite belief in the intervention of God in human affairs and specifically in matters of disease and health. God both confers health and brings sickness. The sense of divine punishment, of retribution for sin, is strong, even though this by no means is believed to be the only cause for illness and disease. But if a most general cause can be identified it is transgression of God's will, or that is to say, sin. This cause operates through the assistance and connivance of the devil, Satan, but its presence as an attack on individual well-being is there by virtue of the all-powerful character of God, of the divine providence. This view of sickness appears to be the general background of most practices concerning curing. Sin is in a person, attacking his well-being, and must be driven out for the attainment of health. It is driven out most generally through, again, divine intervention. That is, individuals through a mystical experience acquire the power to cure, to drive out the sin which causes the illness. Through the laying on of hands, through prayer, through the use of prayer cloths, and through various exercises of faith, a person is made well. The power to aid a person who is ill is a result of a mystical preparation and a divine relationship. The divine power is understood to flow constantly and may flow through the hands of the curing minister and through the patient, driving out the evil. Disease is thus seen as part of a system of relationships with the divine supernatural, a system which is reinforced by attendance at church, by association with others who have the same beliefs, and by repeated revivals of faith in recurring group rites associated with the church.

The system of belief in divine interventions is by no means the whole of the Black medical tradition. It is linked with a parallel set of beliefs concerning the need for maintaining a harmony with nature. "Nature" is not sharply differentiated from God and the divine system, but is probably conceived as a part of it. The terms in which it is thought about come from sources such as almanacs, like MacDonald's, but also from a strong oral tradition. Diagnosis of disease in this sub-system is not in terms of sin but with reference rather to the "reading of the signs," such as the phases of the moon, positions of the planets, and seasonal changes. It promotes such values as that the best medicines are "natural" ones and that the old herbal remedies (often no longer attainable from drugstores because of changes in the dominant White Anglo beliefs) are the best. This set of beliefs about man in the natural world is bound up with a special concept of the blood as an indicator of conditions of health and as an object of treatment. One needs "new blood" under some circumstances, one's blood is "used" and needs renewal, or it is thick and impure (the impurities thought of as "germs") or there is too much of it and it needs refining. The blood should be "purified" in the springtime.

It is characteristic of this medical tradition that there is apparently no elaborate specialization of knowledge. One indication of this is the strong tendency to lump together all kinds of illnesses and not to seek to identify particular ones. Accordingly, specific causes are not isolated. One falls ill and explains his or her condition in terms of having "the misery." This may be in the head or the stomach or the back or anywhere in the body. It does not matter greatly where or specifically what it may be. In one instance it may be diagnosed as having divine causes, and dealt with in the punishment-faith system, or in another it may be diagnosed as in the "natural" system and may be attributed to the state of blood.

This system of medicine is notable for its simplicity, its demands on the patient with respect to exercises of faith, and for its linkage with group rites and participation in a religious congregation.

There exists also a close relationship between curing and religious belief among the Mexican Americans described here. However, the nature of this relationship is extremely different, and this difference clearly goes deep. The conceptions of relationship with God and the supernatural differ profoundly in the two religious systems and this is reflected in the medical systems. For the Mexican Americans it is not believed that God punishes with disease; God does not visit illness on individuals. He is entreated, usually indirectly through Mary and the saints, for help and is definitely regarded as sending aid under the proper circumstances, but His punishments are reserved for the other world, not this. The result is a system of beliefs and practices that differs in very marked ways from that of the Blacks.

One gets the feeling of an elaborate and highly organized institutionalization of human-divine relationships with respect to sickness and health. Aid is constantly sought through the saints, and particular saints are associated with particular cures. This becomes apparent at the religious festivals which recur annually in the Arizona and Sonora cities and which are attended, often for specific health purposes, by the Mexican Americans, such as those whose beliefs are described in this volume. At these occasions there are always "*hábitos*" (cloth smocks) which are worn by persons who have sought the aid of a particular saint for relief from some illness or functional disorder. It is the color and type of smock which is associated with the saint, rather than a particular disease. The basic idea is that one makes a contract with the saint to wear his or her symbol if a cure occurs. This is perhaps the basic concept involved in all the entreaties to saints. They may be appealed to in other ways well established in the tradition – by a vow to perform some penance, for example; in fact the wearing of the *hábito* is conceived as a penance by the wearer, as well as an honoring of the saint. There are other long-recognized penances, such as walking great distances to a church or the shrine of a saint. Also families may construct and maintain for generations shrines to particular saints or to the Virgin Mary. In these and in the whole system of elaborately developed traditions for obtaining supernatural intervention there is an absence of emphasis on intense individual ecstasy, in contrast with the Black system. Rather the emphasis is on formal relationships which have become systematized and widely institutionalized in the course of the development of a long-existing religious tradition, which has gained the sanction of the Catholic Church and is linked with the Great Tradition of Christian theology.

However, there is, as in the case of Black popular medicine, a second aspect of medical belief and practice which, while not wholly separate from the religious linkage, seems nevertheless somewhat apart from the latter. Dr. Kay presents us with a classification of diseases which she has found to be implicit in the discussion of illness by the women with whom she became acquainted. This is a systematic and extensive classification which contrasts greatly with the lumping tendency (in terms of "the misery") among Blacks. The names of diseases are many; the general categories and sub-categories seem quite systematic. It is possible that the elaborateness of this classification is a result of the method employed by Dr. Kay and that if the same method were employed in the study of other popular medical systems, the results would be similar. This is possible, but it is more likely that there is a real difference here between Black and Mexican American popular medicine. The lumping tendency in conceptions of disease among Blacks is well established; it is part of the general approach and consistent with the dominant ideas of the system. On the other hand, the splitting and systematization of the Mexican American system is consistent with its general formalized and extensive elaboration.

The Mexican American classification makes clear some aspects of the concepts of disease which are important to the people who use it. There are not only "corporal" illnesses, but also "mental" and "moral" categories. These distinctions within the same universe of health and disease offer some contrasts with the basic concepts of present-day Western medicine. The mental illness category of non-volitional emotional disturbances is, of course, similar to the concept of mental illness in Western medicine, but it must be emphasized that this area of Western medicine has been only recently brought into relation with the established tradition after a considerable period of sharp separation between "medicine" and what is now called psychiatry. This category has existed continuously on the other hand, in the Mexican American system. However, the sub-categories in the Mexican American tradition of mental illness do not conform with those in current Western medicine, and this fact gives some cause for conflict in the attitudes of Mexican Americans. They are forced in the United States to recognize some of the traditional mental illnesses such as "susto" (fright) as "Mexican diseases," that is, as in a special category which physicians trained in Western medicine tend to dismiss as either nothing at all or else symptoms which must be interpreted in wholly different terms from the Mexican American system.

Those illnesses classified as moral in the Mexican American system are in the category of human disorders which the Western medical system insists on separating entirely from the universe of health and disease. The Mexican American system in this respect has affinities with aspects of Black popular medicine and raises the question as to the existence in popular medicine traditions of certain universals which are excluded from the developing tradition of Western medicine. Their existence emphasizes the compartmentalizing tendency of Western science with which Western medicine is closely linked. There are other, more minor, characteristics which Mexican American and Black popular medicine have in common, namely, the concern with and basic importance attached to the condition of the blood and the employment of "rubbing" or massage. As we shall see, these are also to be found in the other two systems of medicine and have been present in various phases in the development of Western medicine.

In general, Mexican American popular medicine gives the impression of a long and well-established tradition which has through the centuries received contributions from various sources. Among these were ideas of the missionaries who came to the New World who were in a position to make special and individualized contributions from the old European stock of medical practice and belief, and to use elements from the native American medical pharmacopoeia. It is no grab-bag of superstition, but a true example of a medical tradition developing parallel with Western medicine in precisely the same societies in which the latter has developed.

The overlapping similarities between Mexican American and Arizona Yaqui popular medicine are considerable. They suggest some of the processes that are constantly at work in the diffusion of beliefs and practices among the medical traditions of the world and of the dominance which one may gain with respect to another, processes which involve Western medicine as well as the other systems. Obviously the Yaqui tradition is not wholly separate from the Mexican American, but on the contrary shares many elements with it, especially practices connected with the Catholic saints and other elements of popular Catholic belief. This overlap of curing concepts would be even more apparent if the study included here had dealt with the whole of the Arizona Yaqui curing world. Dr. Shutler deliberately excluded from her study, except for brief mention, the realm of curing most closely connected with Catholic belief. A major part of the Yaqui health concern is expressed through their highly organized ceremonial activities centering around each community's church or chapel. At the time of Dr. Shutler's study a considerable portion of the males of each Arizona Yaqui settlement were participants in organized ceremonial activities as a result of promises to serve Jesus and the Virgin. The "promise," or vow, was an obligation solemnly undertaken to serve as a dancer, as a participant in religious drama, as a singer, or as a leader or assistant in the Yaqui variants of Catholic ritual. These vows were made in an effort to find aid in curing as a result of illness. The fulfillment of the vow was regarded as a devotion to Mary or Jesus in return for their assistance in curing. The vow, often also spoken of as a penance, was a major foundation of Yaqui organized religious life. The basic form of the vow and its consequences for religious ceremony in the community were introduced into aboriginal Yaqui life by Jesuit missionaries in the 1600s, but there is no doubt that there were native counterparts with which the European Christian forms fused. Yaqui health and curing cannot be understood wholly apart from this important system of religious service.

Dr. Shutler's study reveals that in addition there is an extensive set of beliefs and practices regarding health and illness which appears to have deep roots in aboriginal concepts. Unquestionably, the fundamental belief underlying and integrating the various practices which are described is the concept of *seataka.* This, as Dr. Shutler points out, may be literally translated as "flower-body," which may seem strange to Western understandings of health. Within the Yaqui world of ritual concepts it is not at all strange. There is a whole realm of thought and practice involving "flowers" which is fundamental in religious life and which in some respects resembles the Aztec conception of flowers as inextricably bound up with the highest forms of ritual expression. Among Yaquis, for example, a tradition of an ancient sacred world continues to be sung about in the ritual songs which accompany the dance of the deer, important in many celebrations accompanying the most sacred of the Christianized occasions. The "flower" of *seataka,* in short, is linked with a whole realm of religious belief which has been in large part, but not wholly, overwhelmed by the introduced Christian ceremony.

Seataka is, somewhat like the Black conception of divine love, present everywhere and may be drawn on in curing. It is the curing specialist, the *hitevi,* who commands more curing power than anyone else through the *seataka* with which he is born and which he develops by learning from others and by using it for the benefit of all who ask him for help. Again like the divine love of the Blacks which flows from curer to patient through the laying on of hands, *seataka* is a source only of good, never of evil (although there is some doubt about this among present-day Yaquis, who have been conditioned to think that anything derived from the non-Christian traditions is suspect and necessarily bad). The abundance of *seataka* inherent in the curer gives him special powers, such as the ability to divine the nature and time of events at a distance. He has command of knowledge in the world of the unseen. This is manifest in connection with his dreams and the interpretation of others' dreams. In the dream world the *hitevi* may carry on battles with witches, practitioners of black magic, and defeat them for the benefit of others as well as of himself. He may meet God in a dream and learn more about his good power. Thus, the Yaqui curer's effectiveness is based on a fairly clearly conceptualized view of what Westerners would call supernatural power, its presence in all of nature, and its uses for human benefit.

Yaqui popular medicine has, as it were, two foundations which maintain some degree of separateness. The foundation in Christian ceremonialism is in no way dependent on the *seataka* of the curing specialist, but many of its elements are an intimate and essential part of the *hitevi's* activities. The Christian prayers, for example, are employed in all steps of a cure carried out by the Yaqui curer and regarded as necessary for the efficacy of what he does. This is true even though the cures in which the prayers are appropriate are purely secular in the sense that they involve only the use of plants which so far as the research indicates have no ritual meanings or values. There is also a kind of prayer which does not consist of formal word-for-word Christian type, but is rather improvised for particular purposes. The improvised prayers nevertheless are directed toward God or toward various figures in the Christian pantheon of supernaturals.

It is interesting that the curer with whom Dr. Shutler worked most intensively was an accomplished herbalist who had a vast store of knowledge. She counted some 70 plants with which the curer was quite familiar and for which he knew various uses. He told her that a good curer ought to have knowledge of 69 different ways in which to use every herb. Perhaps this number was thought of on the spur of the moment and has no definite or traditional significance, but this statement and the evidence of the curer's actual extensive herbal knowledge are indicative of a considerable degree of systematization of curing knowledge. Moreover, the majority of the plants of which this man had knowledge were native, not European, plants. There is a contrast here with the herbal knowledge of the Mexican Americans, which rested heavily on European-introduced herbal lore, although they also used the same native herbs as the Yaquis. The intensive Yaqui adaptation to the natural environment in which they lived before the influences of European popular medicine reached them is well indicated in this kind of knowledge of native plants.

There seems to be an element of adaptability in the Yaqui medical tradition in that it rests on concepts of multiple causes for particular illnesses and consequently on the view that there are alternative cures. This suggests a flexibility which may account in part for the persistence of the Yaqui medical tradition in the face of a powerful trend toward replacement by the Mexican popular traditions.

The Anglo lower-class beliefs and practices reported in this volume cannot be regarded as representative without more intensive study. They are nevertheless indicative of a type of tradition quite distinct from the others described. Only in this variety of the four popular traditions do we find a wholly secularized medicine. As reported, there is no connection between these practices and religious belief, in contrast with Black, Mexican American, and Yaqui. In this respect the Anglo popular medicine is consistent with Western medicine generally; in both, curing and religion are quite separate aspects of culture. In other respects the Anglo medicine also shows characteristics consistent with urban Anglo culture. For example, it is fairly clear that the Anglo popular tradition is by no means a non-literate tradition. There is considerable use of current literature, much more so than in the case of the Black and apparently more than in the case of the Mexican American system. Books and magazines are often consulted with respect to dietary and "health food" aspects of the Anglo treatments. There is also reference to printed literature in connection with "reflexology." In general, the kinds of beliefs and attitudes suggest widely read publications, such as recent best-sellers like Dr. D. C. Jarvis's *Folk Medicine* and various books on diet. It should be emphasized also that TV commercials are well-known and often referred to by the people who participate in the medical tradition described by Dr. Bauwens. In short, in an important degree this popular medicine rests on the use of communications of the modern type. It cannot be regarded as a product of isolation in any simple physical sense from Western medicine.

Moreover it is also clear that the Anglo medical practices and beliefs are closely related to various classes of curing specialists who have developed with urban Anglo society. There is considerable reliance on "druggists" or pharmacists both for diagnosis and for advice in connection with treatment. The use of these specialists is carried on independently of Western medicine practitioners but also as supplementary to them. They constitute a variety of practitioner who is more available than Western type M.D.'s both with respect to convenience of time and place and also with regard to intelligibility of the language they use. In addition, other types of practitioners who are widely established in urban communities in the United States are employed. Some of these are, like the pharmacists, what Western medical practitioners would classify as sub-professionals closely linked with Western medicine generally, like the laboratory technicians and nurses who are sometimes consulted. Others have no status in connection with Western medicine standards, but are nevertheless resorted to even more generally, namely, the chiropractors and reflexologists, and probably naturopaths. All of these must be recognized as well-established medical practitioners in Western society; they are in certain ways definitely linked with the developed tradition of Western medicine. They do not seem to be disappearing, but rather to be multiplying. Their numbers and relationships to the practice of Western medicine need to be better understood. However, it appears from the comments of the persons studied as well as from studies made elsewhere that the proliferation of such practitioners rests in some degree on the recurrent and persistent dissatisfactions of people, possibly especially low-income people (although income may not be the significant factor), with the actual state of the art of Western medical practice. This sample of lower class persons repeatedly mention dissatisfaction with respect to the ability or desire of practicing physicians to communicate with them about their illnesses. This is probably related to the kind of specialization which has taken place in training for Western medical practice and must be regarded as a persisting condition, not a temporary one. There is also, as probably in the case of all medical traditions, dissatisfaction of people with failures of Western practitioners to fulfill their expectations and their hopes regarding particular cures. As people turn to other alternatives from the physicians who have not been able to provide them with hoped-for cures, they seek especially two kinds of practitioners.

There are the ones who offer alternatives through diet to what the M.D.'s prescribe. Food is a strong concern among the Anglos studied and the concept of "eating right" is a well-developed one. Published books and articles on diet not endorsed and often proscribed by M.D.'s are referred to as useful guides. This concern with foods and constant self-treatment with diets seem to characterize each of the popular medical traditions described in this volume. Another common feature which is also a source of alternative treatments among the Anglos is reliance on massage. In this connection the specialist type which has developed in Western society is the chiropractor. Anglos find a function for the chiropractor which supplements the practice of the Western medicine practitioners; in this they resemble the Yaquis and to a lesser extent the Mexican Americans and the Blacks.

There is a good deal of self-diagnosis and self-treatment. Whether this is a distinctive characteristic of this variety of popular medicine or not is not certain. It is apparently similar to what goes on in connection with the quite different practices of Mexican Americans. It may be that it is merely not emphasized in the descriptions of Black and Yaqui medicine. The self-treatment is stimulated apparently by the availability of many "patent medicines," products of commercial specialization in medical commodities in Western society generally. The elaboration of such readily available "medicines" described and advocated in their labels and recommended for various common ailments seems comparable to the complex universe of herbal remedies and salesmen for them characteristic of the religious fiesta described as part of the Mexican American system. The Anglos know, discuss, and use these various packaged "pills" and liquids. Dr. Bauwens found some 16 types of patent medicines in common use, three types of which were very commonly employed. The three most popular consisted of vitamins, aspirin-like pills, and various varieties of "stomach" medicines. The vitamins were at the top of the list and were used by most in the knowledge that M.D.'s either pooh-poohed them or recommended against them. In addition, sodium bicarbonate, salt, and Clorox were also in common use.

The self-treatment and diagnosis aspect of Anglo popular medicine included the use of what might well be called a "folk medicine" tradition within the whole system. This included the use of various "physics" (laxatives), "tonics," and sulfur and molasses (which many Anglos will recognize as a part of an earlier tradition of popular medicine preceding the great proliferation of patent medicines), as well as more esoteric specifics such as skunk fat, horseradish, and turpentine and lard. The self-treatment aspect of the Anglo system may be a characteristic and distinctive feature consistent with other aspects of the American Anglo "self-reliance" orientation in general. In this connection, it should be examined more carefully and more widely compared with other ethnic traditions, along with the distinctive secular quality of the whole system.

The medical traditions briefly described in this volume give some indication of the nature of the environment in which medical practitioners of all kinds carry on their arts. This portion of the world of culture is obviously complex and is barely suggested by the sketches of these four traditions in the ethnically heterogeneous southwestern part of the United States. Characterization of the environment of medical practice in such simple terms as "tested practice versus superstition" is not only biased from the point of view of a single system of medicine, but also wholly inadequate as a basis for understanding the nature of human health and disease.

In the light of our review of these living traditions, it is possible to see that all four have general characteristics in common. Moreover, these qualities are shared with Western medicine. In the first place, the character of each is consistent with and closely related to the nature of the subcultural whole of which it is a part. Second, each has a history and has obviously developed and continues to develop in response to human needs. Third, this development has resulted in an internal logic in each system which governs its continuing borrowing of elements and general growth. Finally, each depends for its existence on the maintenance of a faith in the fundamental tenets of the logic of each system, a characteristic which permits participants in the system to ignore rational evidence in many instances. These general characteristics may be taken as the foundation of every tradition of medicine which develops among human beings. The recognition of them provides a basis for the adaptation of medical practitioners to the environments in which they work.

It is unlikely that the environment of medical practice anywhere will become less complex, less heterogeneous. There is no indication of a general trend toward the replacement of the many medicines by any one medicine, any more than there is a general trend toward the replacement of the many religions by any one of them. Despite their many real triumphs over particular diseases, practitioners of Western medicine cannot assume an ultimate disappearance of all other medical traditions and practices. If that is the case, then it would seem that the training of practitioners of Western medicine ought to be based on a realistic conception of the environment in which practice will be carried out. The human needs and the human tendencies apparent in the whole cultural world of medicine must be taken into account in training so that the survival of Western medicine is insured.

Popular Medicine in a Black Neighborhood

Loudell F. Snow

Popular Medicine in a Black Neighborhood

Loudell F. Snow

A YOUNG MAN HAS SPENT THE NIGHT lying before the altar of a Pentecostal church, praying that God will cure him of epilepsy. A woman with a small baby sits in a pediatrician's waiting room on the other side of town. A middle-aged man struggles to start his ramshackle truck so that he may take an elderly neighbor to the county hospital, where health care is provided for the indigent. At a Spiritualist temple a woman who is a licensed practical nurse attends meditation classes so that she may learn to "visualize herself in the white light of protection." Nothing in her nursing course taught her what to do if she had been bewitched.

Despite the apparent disparities, these people share two things in common. All are Blacks living in a poor neighborhood in a Southwestern town. All have concluded that they need expert attention to restore them to good health and are behaving in accordance with this belief. Mere observation of their actions, however, is of little meaning unless the underlying causes of their behavior can be discovered. A description of the behavior alone (without knowing the cultural rules on which it is based) may even be misleading. Why does Brother Matthew go to church for a cure, while Arthur goes to the county hospital? Why does Lily take her baby to a pediatrician, when her neighbor's child is cured by its grandmother? Why does Alma feel that her illness is the result of witchcraft, and that a physician can do her no good? To what does Harry attribute his many years of ill health? To what does Olive attribute her lifetime of good health? Answers to all of these questions are found in the beliefs and values of the group. The following pages will seek to illuminate the assumptions about health and illness held by the inhabitants of the Martin Hill Neighborhood, a predominantly Black section of the community.

The medical belief system to be described here is a composite, containing elements from a variety of sources: European folklore, Greek classical medicine, the cultures of West Africa, and modern scientific medicine. These diverse threads are tied together by the tenets of fundamentalist Christianity, elements from the Voodoo religion of Haiti, and the added spice of sympathetic magic. It is not a system confined to Black Americans, however. Much of it is shared by segments of the White population, particularly those reared in poverty in the rural South. There are also striking parallels in the health beliefs of Mexican Americans in the community under study.

THE NEIGHBORHOOD

Black people have been coming to the area to live for over a century, brought here by a variety of reasons. Most of the first arrivals were employed mainly as soldiers, cowboys and cooks for mining camps.

In the early part of this century a nearby military post was turned over to a regiment of Black enlisted men and (usually) White officers. Men from the post often moved to the town to live when released from the service.

Others have come to the area for their health. Delia J.'s young daughter has asthma; Wilson E. developed TB and when told to come to a warm climate chose this town, because he had been stationed in the state during World War II; Ella May T.'s husband contracted TB in a California jail, and she brought him here before he died; Nellie J.'s husband was told to come to a lower altitude for "swelling of the glands" in his neck; Mary H.'s husband suffered from an unspecified lung disease, and it was recommended that the family move to a dry climate.

Rumored work opportunities in the West brought a number of people. Olive P. and her husband left the Midwest during the Depression to look for work in California. They stopped here, however, and never went on:

> We stopped here. My mind didn't *lead* me to go on to California. I heard about California, but I thought I'd stop here. If I didn't like it and couldn't get a job, why, if I wanted to I could make a note to get back home. I just didn't want to go on to California somehow or other. (Olive P.)

Many people came because relatives were already here. Brad L. came to visit a niece and liked it so well he sent for his family. Pearlie M. came to see her married daughter 15 years ago and is still here. Her husband is still in Texas waiting for her to come home. She thinks she may go back soon, as she misses having a garden.

A few informants had spent years of their lives in seemingly aimless wandering. A job, marriage, or ill health may cause such transient individuals to pause in one place for a few years. Loss of a job or breakup of a marriage may promote another move. Some, both men and women, are in town now but will move on when the spirit moves them:

> I left home when I was 15. Traveled. I traveled different states, countries. I been all around the panhandle, Louisiana, 'round the oil field, then I went on to California. Travelin'. I just wanted to learn some of the world. I told my mother before I settle down and marry, I was gonna learn some of the world and mingle with the different peoples. Then I'd know how to treat a husband when I come to marry. And I mingled with different people. And each town I went to I did get a job, 'cause I used to send her money back all the time. I'd get a job. I'd hit a town, I wouldn't stop until I found me somethin' to do. I'd make my little money, I'd send her some and tell her not to write to me till she hear from me again. I didn't stay a place more than about three weeks or more. (Arnella L.)

Only one informant was born in the community, although some have minor children born here. Most people interviewed are from the states of Oklahoma, Kentucky, Arkansas, and Texas. By far the greatest number of people in the sample are originally from Texas. A few people were city bred, but most were raised in rural areas, on farms or in small country towns. This predominantly rural background is an important factor in the understanding of health beliefs and behaviors.

The Neighborhood was one of the first areas of the town to be occupied by Black people. It comprises about 40% of a U.S. census tract, the larger portion occupied by a Mexican American *barrio* to the west. The entire area is deteriorating physically and is losing population at a rapid rate. At the time of the study there were an estimated 350 Black people living in the Neighborhood.

The Neighborhood is a small residential backwater, which has been surrounded on all sides by urban expansion. It is bounded on three sides by major business streets and on the fourth by the tracks of the Southern Pacific Railroad. Just across the tracks lies the main business district, within easy walking distance of Neighborhood residents. To the west is the *barrio,* and to the north a small business area gives way to a newer housing development. To the east several blocks of businesses and a park separate the Neighborhood from the area where many of the Black elite live. The Neighborhood is thus effectively cut off from other residential areas on three of its four sides.

It is a poor area and part of the reason for the population loss is undoubtedly the quality of the available housing, much of which is adjudged deficient or substandard. There are many empty housing units, and some have been condemned by the town. Most of the inhabitants remaining in the district are the very young, the middle-aged, and the elderly. Young people tend to move out of the Neighborhood when they marry.

The Black segment of the population is concentrated in a central strip of 15 blocks. There is a discernible difference in the northern and southern parts of this area. In the northern third, nearly four-fifths of the dwellings are owner occupied (78.9%). The area is one of small single-family homes, typically of brightly painted stucco with flowers and grass in the front yard and a small vegetable garden in the backyard. A few homeowners also keep chickens. Nearly every home has a small front porch where the inhabitants spend a great deal of time watching the comings and goings of their neighbors. The lots are rather large and there is no sense of crowding. There are few trees, and this fact plus the presence of a number of unpaved streets and dusty empty lots gives this section of the Neighborhood a somewhat barren aspect. It is, however, quiet and peaceful.

In direct contrast are the ten blocks of the southern portion of the Neighborhood. There are fewer single-family homes in this portion, and most of these are on small lots, contributing to an impression of crowding. There are a number of crib housing units, small rectangular buildings cut into sections, each section a tiny apartment. The majority of the dwelling units are rentals, the percentage of home ownership dropping to 12.5% in this sector. As one travels toward the downtown area, the air of decay increases and some houses are virtually surrounded by a junkyard of old cars, worn-out mattresses, and discarded furniture. The few nicely kept homes are nearly all surrounded by steel chain-link fences. A number of people keep vicious looking watchdogs, and nearly everyone keeps their mailbox padlocked.

In this southern portion of the Neighborhood live most of the welfare recipients, and on their limited incomes they have little chance of obtaining adequate housing. This part of the Neighborhood, then, houses the very poor. One four-block area is particularly run down, and contains over 50% dilapidated dwellings, the greatest number of housing units, and the highest population density. In the very center there is a Neighborhood landmark, a corner grocery store. When urban renewal in the downtown area destroyed cheap housing, several bars were demolished as well. The enterprising owner of the grocery applied for a beer and wine license at that time, and the store is now the hangout of unemployed men. A sign in the window declares that no drinking is allowed on the premises, but the sidewalk outside is city property and is the scene of drinking, gambling, and frequent fights. Neighborhood residents do not blame the store owner for getting the liquor license, however. They say that everyone has the right to make a living.

In the Neighborhood there are two other small grocery stores, a barber shop, a dry-cleaning establishment, seven churches, and a center run by the Salvation Army. There is a junior high school, but primary and high-school-age students must go elsewhere to school.

Outwardly, then, the Neighborhood is somewhat drab in appearance. It is the site of small and modestly priced homes in the north, and of crowded and increasingly dilapidated homes and apartments in the south.

NEIGHBORHOOD INHABITANTS

Most investigators agree that due to discrimination and the income and educational differentials between the Black and White populations, social classes are not equivalent across racial lines. The Black upper class, for example, is much like the White upper-middle class. According to Gordon (1964:169-70), members of the Black middle class do not always vary in education, income, or occupation from the Black lower class but are different mainly in their overt emphasis on ". . . 'respectable' public behavior, stable family life, and planning for the future, either of oneself or one's children." According to such a definition it is difficult to assess the difference between the stable element in the lower class and low-income members of the middle class.

There are certainly a few middle-class families in the Neighborhood. Of the people I knew fairly well, I would unhesitatingly assign middle-class status to two couples (Brad and Lizzie L. and Bertha and Oliver A.) and to two individuals (Lillian A. and Louis W.). It is necessary to know people fairly well before making judgments of this kind, however, and doubtless a number of people I did *not* know well should be assigned middle-class status. With this reservation in mind, I would say that the majority of the people in the Neighborhood belong to the lower class. One prominent member of the community's Black elite lives with his wife in the area as well, although their grown children have moved to more affluent neighborhoods. In general, however, as the Black population of the town expanded, those middle-class families who could afford to do so moved out of the area. The middle-class families who do remain tend to be on fixed incomes and living in houses which they own. They, as well as the members of the lower class, cannot usually afford to leave the area now, and generally bemoan the changes they see in the Neighborhood:

> I'm just sick down here, it's changed! . . . Well it is 'cause those people moved down there on Mason. From over the other part of town. They had to move somewhere, and a whole lot of 'em have moved in out here! But they had to get a house where they could find one. This here was a nice district in here till different people was movin' over here! It was quiet and everything over here.
>
> Most of 'em come from on the other side of town. They scattered around different places. And they find out that man sells wine, and they all just flocks there! Buys their wine and beer! This whole area in here was quiet, you couldn't hear nothin', it was quiet. You couldn't hear no cussin', you couldn't hear no kind of bad language. But now, you can hear anything! If I wasn't buyin' this house, I'd get out. (Arnella L.)

HOUSEHOLD COMPOSITION

Female-headed Households

Slightly more than half of the households in the Neighborhood are headed by women. At times during this study it seemed as if the Neighborhood was composed of nothing *but* elderly ladies; in one block alone they accounted for 13 of the 19 household heads. The status "female head-of-household," however, contains a diverse assortment of women: there is Olive P., the oldest informant, who learned herb medicine from her father and still uses it whenever possible. There are Arnella L. and Erma V., both Pentecostal evangelists. Both women believe that they have the "gift of healing" in their hands. Young Millie T., a prostitute, has a small daughter living with relatives in Kansas. She was saving her money for a bus ticket "back home," as she had not seen her child for two years. There is Freda T., whose 54-year-old son lives with her. She considers herself to be the household head since she pays the rent and gives her son spending money.

Male-headed Households

Thirty-six-year-old Jim S. is the youngest single male informant. He is divorced from his second wife and is the father of three children, whom he has not seen for several years; he does not know where they live. The oldest informant (Louis W., 71) is separated from his third wife. He hopes that she will come back to him. If not, he says, he will "have to start all over and get another woman," as he doesn't like living alone. Wilson E.'s first wife was a Mexican woman, but she left him when he spent time in prison for manslaughter. His second wife, an Indian woman, died of alcoholism a few years ago, leaving him with three small children to raise. He doesn't worry about his sons, but says he wants to live long enough to see his daughter married; otherwise he fears that she will "go out on the streets." Wilson, his friend Jack, who lives across the alley, and his next-door neighbor Arthur J. cooperate on household tasks. When I interviewed Wilson (in Jack's apartment), it was Jack's turn to cook, and a big pot of beans was simmering on the stove. When that food was gone, Jack said, it would be the turn of one of the other men to cook in *his* quarters. Directly across the alley, Harry J. shares a small house with three unrelated men. Harry pays $30 per month for his bedroom, sharing bathroom and kitchen facilities with the others. Single males head 17% of Neighborhood households.

Couple-headed Households

One-third of the households in the Neighborhood are occupied by married couples. Lily M. is the one informant who could be accorded upper-class status. Her husband is a prominent businessman in the Black community, and his office is on the periphery of the Neighborhood. During the time of the interviews, this couple was living in an apartment at the back of his office building. None of their social contacts are in the Neighborhood, however, and they were planning to buy a home in the suburbs. Other couples interviewed are more typical: Bertha and Oliver A. are retired and live in the house which they built in 1945. Their only son has made a career of the army, and plans to come back to the community upon retirement. Tom and Anna P. are also retired and own a house in the southern part of the Neighborhood. Across the street live Brad and Lizzie L. and most of their 9 children. One son is in the army, and two daughters are married and live in another part of the city. Another son has recently separated from his wife and has come back home to live with his parents.

A number of people are rearing children not their own, an adaptive response to often difficult social and economic circumstances. Such "giving away" of children, temporarily or permanently, is common. Tom and Anna P. kept an "adopted godchild" from the age of three months to 13 years, when his mother decided that she wanted him back. Pearlie M.'s landlady had a child for five years, but in that case the mother also reclaimed the child. Arnella L.'s sister "adopted" a girl of eight but gave her back to her mother a couple of years later when she became "unruly."

Anna P. "gave" her first three children to her mother to raise, just as her own mother had given away Anna and her sisters to be raised by others when the father deserted the home. Most older informants, in fact, report that when they were small, they had spent nearly as much time in other households (often that of a grandmother) as in that of their parents.

EDUCATION

The level of formal education attained by informants is somewhat low. Only one informant (Lily M.) has a college degree, and one other woman completed one year of college training. Six women have high school diplomas. Louise R. further completed a course in "beauty college," and Alma U. has been trained as a practical nurse. All other informants report only some primary schooling. None of the men in the sample had completed high school, although Jim S. finished the 11th grade before dropping out. A few informants are not sure exactly how much schooling they have had. Anna P., for example, can remember four different teachers, so guesses that she must have gone to school through the fourth grade.

Such a low educational level does not reflect a disinterest in education as much as circumstantial events in individual childhood experiences. Arnella L. went to work at the age of 11:

> When I started to work, I started washin' dishes. I wasn't old enough to cook. I worked out; I did cleanin' up and seein' after kids, y'know, the work that I could do. I started out when I was about 11 years old. They didn't put too much on me 'cause I was young. I was just glad

> that I was able to help my mother, you know, 'cause all of 'em had gone but me. I was a mother's child; I always liked to be around my mother. And I lived at home till I was got grown and got to goin' for myself. I left home when I was 15. (Arnella L.)

Oliver A. had to go to work to help his mother after the fifth grade, as his father had died. Louis W. finished the eighth grade, but his family could not afford to buy his books for high school. Often those informants raised in rural areas also were taken out of school to help with seasonal farm work.

Most informants view education as the key to better jobs and a better life, and many wish that they had had the chance to complete their schooling:

> I had to plow; I had to stay home and help my mother. In those years, if kids didn't go to school, peoples didn't care. They just let 'em run around. Now, it's the sweetest thing that they're compellin' the education! They was a little boy out here about 14, and the truant officer had to come for him. And I said to him, "Look, let me tell you sumpin'. You need to take advice from that man. That man is got his learnin'. If they had of pushed *me* through and made me get an education like they pushin' you kids today, I wouldn't have been like I am today. I'd of had well livin', and a home and ever'thing else. I would have did sumpin' with what I learnt. That truant officer is tryin' to help you learn.
>
> This is what I'm tryin' to say: you used to take a rag and soap and wash dishes, but you don't take a soap and rag no more. You have to have an education in your head, or that machine might blow up! You got to have an education to even wash dishes with a machine. You get it too hot, and that thing will blow up and pop all over you! Now you need an education to even wash dishes. Education means somethin'." That's what I told him. I think I went to school three or four years . . . But I had to help my mother make a livin', I had to start workin'. I had to stay at home and help make a crop. (Erma V.)

INCOME AND OCCUPATIONS

The occupations of Neighborhood residents reflect the low educational level, and both naturally affect income. With a few notable exceptions, the inhabitants of the Neighborhood are at the lower end of the economic continuum. One informant is a teacher, another a secretary, and a third a practical nurse. All other women are domestics, cooks, or work in a laundry. Of the men interviewed, only Jim S. is working; he has been trained as a Sanitation Aide by the County Health Department. Before retirement Tom P. was a cook, Oliver A. a porter for the Southern Pacific Railroad, and Louis W. a gardener. Others had worked as laborers. A number of men and women had worked as agricultural laborers both in the South and in this state, particularly in the cotton fields.

About one-fourth of the household heads in the Neighborhood are retired. In part this reflects the preponderance of older people in the area. Many people, however, are less than retirement age but are unable to work because of ill health and/or job-related injuries. Tom P. was working as a cook for the army when a carload of frozen meat pinned him against a wall. His leg was broken in seven places, and he now walks with difficulty. Wilson E. was working for a construction company when he sustained a serious back injury. He is now unable to do heavy work and is afraid to have the recommended surgery on his spine. Bertha A. was working in a restaurant when her hand was caught in a salad maker and badly mangled.

Those people who are working often earn very little. They lack the education and specialized job skills necessary to secure good-paying jobs. The mechanization of agriculture in recent years has cost many farm laborers their jobs as well:

> They wonder why so many people are on the welfare, why that the people have to get on the welfare. People have to get on the welfare for a certain reason. You know they taken cotton pickin' away from the people. Why, this unemployed many many thousand people. 'Cause when I come here, I come for cotton pickin'! And I picked cotton for years and years, and I could *pick* cotton!
>
> But after they put machinery in there, I mean there's no more cotton pickin'! Now they just go out and chop a little grass. They got to give the people somethin'! You got to get a livin' some kind of way. That's why so many of 'ems on there! They pushed 'em to it, they pushed 'em on there with these machineries! (Erma V.)

SOCIAL OBLIGATIONS

The most important social ties are those of kinship, followed by church membership, and Neighborhood residence. Primary obligation is to family members, regardless of where they live. Many informants have most of their social contacts with relatives living in other parts of the town. Olive P. and her sister-in-law live in different neighborhoods, but speak daily by phone. Georgia S. brings her children to be cared for by their great-grandmother. Martin G., who has a car, takes his daughter to and from work each day. Frank L. came from his home in the south part of town to stay with his sister when she was ill. Relatives living out of town may also be more important than close neighbors. Many people spend a relatively large part of their meager incomes on long distance telephone calls to family members. Anna P. and her sister Jewel W., who lives in Los Angeles, talk by phone each Saturday morning. When Arnella L. had a stroke her aunt in Texas knew something was wrong because Arnella did not telephone her for two weeks. Freda T.'s two brothers came from Arkansas by bus when she was in the hospital.

And when Lillian A. became suddenly ill, her next-door neighbor did not phone the doctor, she phoned one of Lillian's daughters in California (who arrived by plane the same night).

Even death may not intervene in family feelings, as the spirits of dead relatives are believed to maintain a lively interest in their earthbound relatives. A number of informants both young and old reported the appearance of dead relatives (usually parents) during times of stress. In such situations the dead seem to return as problem-solvers:

> I never seen my father but one time since he passed, and that was here. That's when I was tryin' to make up my mind to quit [my husband]. And I was aworryin', bein' in a strange place and wonderin' if I could make a honest *livin',* you know, by myself, bein' alone. But it wasn't that much he was doin' for me. I was good on washin' and ironin', I know I was, people praised me like that. And my mother and father come to me. They was a back porch on the house, [and] it was a dream, a vision or sumpin', I don't know what it was.
>
> But I seen 'em plain. And they come in a *truck* one night, I'll never forget it. And they brought one of these old-fashioned, big iron pots; what they used to boil they clothes in. Used to boil the clothes, y'know, before they had the washin' machines. And so they brought two tubs and two rub boards, washboards. And they had that truck piled up with bundles of clothes tied up in sheets. And they come, and they fixed the two tubs, and me and my mother was rubbin', washin' the clothes on the washboard. And my daddy had filled up the pot and was makin' the fire, puttin' more wood around the pot. *Showin'* me that I could make a livin' *washin'* and *ironin'!* That's the way I taken it. (Olive P.)

And that is what she did.

The importance of kinship ties is also underscored by the common occurrence of fictive kinship, the ritual of making of kin out of non-kin. Liebow (1967) mentions the practice of "going for brothers," in which two men who are not brothers present themselves as if they are. As kin are more important than non-kin, such ties may be manufactured " . . . to explain, account for, or even to validate friend relationships" (Ibid.: 167). Frankel (1970: 179) also reports the existence of the "play mother" or "play sister," usually when real kin are far away. Olive P.'s next door neighbor, Alice R., asked Alice to be her "adopted mother," as her own mother was in Mississippi, and she seldom gets to see her. Olive agreed and not only calls Alice her "adopted daughter," but introduces Alice's son as "my foster grandson." When a fictive kinship tie is set up, the participants owe each other the same rights and obligations as they do "real" kin.

Church affiliation is also important, and kinship terms are commonly used among church members. That is, members of the fundamentalist Protestant churches address each other as "Brother" and "Sister," and recognize mutual obligations not extended to members of other churches or to the "unsaved." People are more likely to visit fellow church members informally than others. Crisis situations such as serious illness or a death in the family are announced from the pulpit, and church members rally around the person or family needing assistance. Such assistance may be in the form of prayers, food, household help, money, or whatever else is required.

Living in the Neighborhood itself confers little feeling of "neighborliness" except during emergencies. During a serious illness, for example, people may extend help to a person with whom they might not have dealings at other times. When Arnella L. suffered a stroke, therefore, her neighbor Willa M. suspended hostilities and she was one of the first to bring food. The illness episode provided a brief respite in what is otherwise a constant feud between the two women (Arnella had offered to brain Willa with a hoe the previous week). At worst, neighbors may be viewed with suspicion and hostility; at best, with reserve. The "good neighbor," in fact, may be a far cry from the middle-class stereotype. (In the Neighborhood the neighbor who minds his own business is valued even if his lifestyle is somewhat dubious):

> Her husband is what you call a procurer or a pimp. She said that they're married. I don't know. He has those two young girls, one is 18, the other is 17. One is the little boy's mother, and the other is the mother of the little baby. And these girls get out and hustle, you know, and give the money to him! And my neighbor, she takes care of these children [while they do it]. Now, *he's* supposed to be the *father* of these children. I'm sure she still do some prostitutin', but she don't do it as much as she did. But she takes care of the kids while the girls go out.
>
> [But] she is a real neighbor; she is a excellent neighbor. She is a good neighbor. They stay over there, and what they do over there, they never bring over *here*. They never bother me with anything. (Alma U.)

EXPOSURE AND THE LAWS OF NATURE

The beliefs to be described in the following pages are based on the premise that all phenomena, including health problems, can be classified as being "natural" or "unnatural." In general, natural happenings are those which have to do with the world as God intended it to be. Unnatural events are seen as disruptive of natural laws and therefore potentially dangerous if not downright evil.

Events may also be lumped into desirable and undesirable categories, so that illness may be seen as just another misfortune, such as loss of a job, financial problems, failure in love, and so forth. Good health, in contrast, may not be conceptually separated from other indices of good luck: money, success, a happy home, whatever one might want.

The tendency to view things in oppositions, in fact, is based on the belief that *everything* has its opposite. This is expressed in health terms by proverbs stating that there is a cure for every illness, a birth for every death, an antidote for any poison, a healing purpose for every herb.

The understanding of such an arrangement is necessary to the manipulation of events, which is not only thought possible, but is essential: the individual who makes no effort at all to guide his life is weak, exposed, and unprotected. The ability to "keep on *keepin'* on," as it is often styled, has survival value in a hostile world.

The inhabitants of the Neighborhood view the world as a battleground between opposing forces. Such factors, on both the natural and supernatural level, seem engaged in an eternal tug of war in which man is a hapless bystander. In the world of nature, the seasons themselves are in opposition, for example, and according to the almanac, March is disagreeable because there are "Warm days and cold ones, bright sunshine and terrible storms. The great struggle between Winter and Summer takes place this month, and woe to the person who is taken sick at this time, for they seldom recover" (MacDonald's 1973). Good health depends in large part upon the individual remaining in harmony with the forces of nature. Every man or woman is responsible for knowing those natural laws which govern life, as any behavioral lapse may result in illness or death. The word "exposure" is used over and over as people describe presumed causes for health problems, the implication being that the individual failed to use "mother wit" and take protective measures.

Disease causation is extremely generalized, and the idea of specificity is missing. There is no knowledge, for example, that a specific microorganism such as the measles virus causes a specific disease, measles. Illnesses may not even be given specific names – instead, they are often lumped under the term "misery," and the location noted. Thus, the individual will say, "The misery is in my head," or "stomach," or "joints," or wherever. Although informants do know the names of many illnesses, this information is essentially irrelevant. Curing techniques are dependent on causation, and what is of prime importance is to determine what *caused* the misery, not to give it a name. Illness seems to be thought of as a kind of attack upon the body by some diffuse outside force. Cold air and impurities are the dangerous agents most commonly mentioned, and the problems they cause will be described more fully later. There is complete agreement that nature is more powerful than man, however, and according to Wilson E. if a direct conflict arises, "Nature will kill you, you won't kill it." When health problems do arise as a result of failure to abide by natural laws, they are referred to as "natural" illnesses because the cause is natural.

Natural Illnesses: Environmental Hazards

Informants' views on man's place in nature are based on the assumption that everything in nature is connected, and that events can be both interpreted and directed by an understanding of these relationships. Such sympathetic magic, as it is styled, is the basis for much in popular medical beliefs and practices, and a brief description is in order. Sympathetic magic is divided into contagious and imitative magic. Contagious magic has as its basis the premise that things once joined can never be separated; the part stands for the whole. Many witchcraft practices are based on contagious magic. For example, an evildoer need only obtain a lock of the victim's hair to do harm. Imitative magic, on the other hand, is based on the assumption that like follows like, and one imitates the wished-for effect: a knife under the bed will "cut" labor pains, or rubbing rabbit entrails on the gums of a teething infant will bring the teeth in quickly, because a rabbit is quick.

In preventing natural illness it therefore becomes imperative to comprehend the direct connection between the body and such natural phenomena as the phases of the moon, the position of the planets, and the changing seasons. Such phenomena are readily observable, and good health depends in large part upon the individual's ability to read "the signs" and remain in harmony with nature.

Health in the Life Cycle

If safety lies in harmony and balance, extremes are seen as potentially dangerous. Any activity carried to excess weakens the body, and it is considered unwise to eat too much, drink too much, stay out too late and so forth (see Kay for a parallel belief among Mexican Americans).

> Lotsa times when people get sick, now take myself. . . . People can get out here and stay out all night and not take their rest, be rest broken, and just keep on doin' it, just keep on doin' it, they gonna get down! Sumpin' gonna happen! And you ain't gonna know what it is! It's your nerves, or you gonna need to be sleepy, you need to sleep, sumpin' gonna happen to ya that you gonna have to go to the doctor. And the doctor gonna tell you you gonna have to slow up. Well, you brought it on your own *self*. (Arnella L.)

This weakening of the body may not be manifest for years to come, but sooner or later the individual will have to pay the price for reckless behavior. Anna P. needs more sleep now, she says, as the ". . . older you get the tireder you get, because you didn't take your rest." One of the oldest informants in the study, on the other hand, has only seen a physician once. This occurred when she required surgery for the removal of her appendix. She attributes both her long life and her good health to the fact that she has taken care of herself:

> I feel like it's the care that they take of theirselves. That's what I think, I don't know. I feel like they exposes theirselves too much, and don't take enough care of theirself like they should. That's one reason that I can get around and do things now at my age! Now I've worked hard all my life, ever since I started at ten years old. But otherwise I've

> taken care of myself. And I never was the goin' kind! I didn't work all day, and then goin' half of the night and all like that. . . . I taken my rest and taken care of myself. (Olive P.)

Women are thought constitutionally weaker than men and are particularly susceptible to disease at certain times. This susceptibility is connected with the reproductive functions, and a woman is at risk during menstruation, immediately after an abortion, and following childbirth:

> There's somethin' about a girl gets a disease quicker than a boy. On account of her different sex. She's easy to catch, or she's eager to catch ever'thing. Because she'll get it in her breast. Different things come through the breast, through your vagina too, you know. These are two things you have a man don't have, that make you easily get sick. (Erma V.)

If women are sometimes weak due to functional bleeding and anatomical differences, however, this is somewhat offset by the power conferred upon them by fertility. This is exemplified by the folklore surrounding the pregnant woman, whose fertility is obvious. Following the principles of imitative magic, pregnant women are often asked to plant seeds, bake cakes, or make bread – any task where increase is desirable. Conversely, the menstruating woman, whose temporary non-fertility is just as patent, should avoid those occasions when her presence might have a negative effect. She should stay out of gardens and avoid cooking chores – her condition may wither the vines and spoil the food. There also are proscriptions having to do with bleeding. The pregnant woman, whose menstrual periods have ceased, must avoid helping with butchering. Her very presence might cause the meat to not "bleed out" properly, and it would then spoil. A menstruating woman, on the other hand, should not pick up a baby lest she cause it "to strain," a belief shared by Kay's Mexican American informants. Fertility is stronger than barrenness, however, and another folk belief states that a menstruating woman and a pregnant woman should not be in the same room together – such conjunction, according to one woman, may be enough to make the menstruating woman ". . . be the next one to turn up pregnant."

Strength and weakness are associated with the age as well as the sex of the individual. Babies and children are weaker than the sexually active adult, and, after the climacteric, the body gradually declines with old age. Death occurs because the body has "worn out." The unborn infant is the weakest of all, however, and is literally at the mercy of the mother-to-be's behavior. Nearly all of her actions can "mark" the infant in some way, and care must be taken to maintain a harmonious and placid lifestyle during pregnancy. Again, extremes are to be avoided, and any sort of excess is dangerous to the foetus. Food cravings, for example, are the most common explanation for birthmarks. Some informants say that the mark is the result of an unsatisfied craving. Others say that the mark is the result of the mother touching herself while she was experiencing the desire for food. In this case, the birthmark will then be located where her hand rested, and will resemble the food she wanted. Delia J.'s son has a drumstick-shaped light mark on one hand, she says, because she craved fried chicken and didn't get it. Pearlie M. says that if pregnant girls come around asking for special foods every effort is made to give it to them.

The emotional state of the pregnant woman is of prime importance to the well-being of the infant and again excess is to be avoided. Fear, sorrow, sympathy, worry – any of these can directly affect the baby. It is said that pregnant women should not go to horror movies or funerals, for example. Sometimes, of course, excitement is unavoidable:

> You know what, I had a friend one time and she were pregnant. And we were goin' along and was a hog jumped up in front of us, it was just about light. And this hog jumped up in front of us, and she slapped her hand to her ear and screamed. Did just like that. And when her baby was born, he had a pushed-up nose like a hog, and this ear was stopped up. One of his ears, it was grown together where she threw it up there and mark it. Some people say, you can't mark children, but it's a true fact. Fear marks childrens. She were frightened. So many times when you touch yourself you gotta be careful. I say to a lots of pregnant girls, "Be careful how you touch yourself, how you sit or how you do. Because you can inherit these things." That's why you should say thank God for a normal healthy baby. (Erma V.)

Worrying about a loved one with some sort of illness may also cause the baby to have the same illness:

> To my idea I feel that before the mother gets too far along *with* the baby, it will be boresome about someone in the family. I mean *burdened,* you know, and *worried.* Worries about the condition of maybe her husband or some of her in-law relatives, or maybe it's some of her close relatives. That puts it on the baby! (Olive P.)

Not all informants believe that children can be affected in this way. Lizzie L., the mother of nine, says that she does not believe it, because during her pregnancies she went to horror movies and none of her children were affected. She went on to say, however, that perhaps God knew she was ignorant and therefore protected the unborn children from her ignorance. (Informants rarely categorically denied anything. A statement might be made that they did not believe in something, witchcraft, say, or marking children. Almost always they would go on to say that it might be *possible,* but they had not experienced it.) In only two instances was the father mentioned as somehow marking the child – one woman's first grandchild, an 18-month-old toddler, reportedly walks in a "wobbly" fashion, because both parents were intoxicated at the moment of conception. Jackie K., who has been married twice, says that her younger son has a quieter disposition than his brother, because his father was an older man and more "dignified" than the father of her other child.

An awareness that there are times during the life cycle when the individual is relatively weak and the knowledge that natural phenomena may impinge on human activities is important, but not enough to guarantee good health. It is even more important to be completely familiar with the workings of the body, as these will have to be regulated throughout life. Beliefs concerning bodily components and processes reflect the centuries-old, classical humoral pathology. In this system, best known from the writings of Hippocrates, there were believed to be four major "humors" – blood, phlegm, black bile, and yellow bile. The humors were correlated with intrinsic properties of heat and cold, wetness and dryness. Good health depended upon the humors and their associated properties being kept in balance; imbalance, too much blood (and therefore heat) or an over-accumulation of phlegm (cold and wet) meant illness. Humoral pathology was popular well into the nineteenth century in American medicine. It was introduced into the slave cabins of the antebellum South, where a substantial economic investment made the health of slaves a prime concern (Shryock 1966; Postell 1951). More than a century later, remnants of this old system are still to be found among both Blacks and poor Southern Whites, passed on in true folk tradition by word of mouth.

Of the original four humors, blood and phlegm are the components which presently receive the most attention. The focus on bile has largely disappeared, other than a notion that the liver may become "germy" and should be "cleaned off" every spring. Heat is still associated with blood, which thickens to keep one warm in the winter, with fevers, and skin eruptions. Cold is associated with phlegm (usually referred to as "slime"), with damp air, and water. Phlegm is a normal bodily component associated with uncleanliness and is present in the body, according to Anna P., because "Jesus Christ made us of the slime and the dirt. A little [newborn] baby is slimy; all that stuff's in you." She also notes that this substance is sometimes to be seen in a baby's diaper.

The greatest attention, however, is focused on the blood. It is probably the most important single factor to be considered in the maintenance of good health. The state of the blood is an index of the state of the system, and may vary along several dimensions. If any general statement can be made about the blood it is that it is never static – responding to a variety of external and internal stimuli, the blood goes "up" or "down," is "thick" or "thin," "high" or "low," "clean" or "defiled," "good" or "bad."

Generation and Volume of Blood

Blood may be spoken of as "new," or "used." New blood constantly is being formed, and older blood is eliminated from the body. There is a sex differential attached to this process, and the renewal takes place during the menses for women, but must be sweated out by men.

The amount of blood in the body can increase or decrease and is most prominently affected by diet. There is an optimal amount present, however, and again extremes are dangerous. The upper extreme, "high blood," results from eating too much rich food, particularly red meat. Informants have terminologically confused "high blood" with "high blood pressure," and strokes are blamed on excess blood backing up into the brain. High blood pressure was defined by informants as ". . . too much blood, the blood goin' to your heart, to your brain or somethin' " (Letha A.), an ". . . overflowin' of blood, a cloggin' . . ." (Erma V.), and from ". . . eatin' too much and gettin' too fat, the blood goes up to your head too fast" (Bertha A). The individual is at fault, as usual, and Bertha continues ". . . but you know you can help that yourself, just don't eat all that rich food."

During the field work Arnella L. suffered what was diagnosed as a light stroke. Her own explanation was that her blood had "boiled up," giving her "blood on the brains." When I stopped by to see her she was sitting up in bed as she felt this would allow the blood to drain back down. She had thrown away the medicine prescribed for her at a community hospital, because the physician had said she would always have to take it. This did not make sense to her as she felt all she needed to do was "bring down" the blood level itself. She was therefore using a home remedy suggested by an aunt in Kentucky:

> My auntie wrote me a letter, at least my cousin did, wantin' to know what happened that I hadn't wrote to 'em since the week before Valentine's. "What's wrong? I wanted to call ya, but I didn't have no way to get ya. [She has no phone.] Mama says the reason you haven't answered, you about sick."
>
> I went and called 'em. "Auntie didn't lie. The 15th of February I was right at death's door. My blood pressure was run up so I couldn't see nothin', couldn't do nothin' but feel my way." My auntie talked, said, "Well, honey, your sight will come back, it will eventually come back. But you drink you a teaspoon of vinegar in some water and that will prevent another stroke. And keep your hand rubbed in it, in white vinegar. Take a teaspoonful of that vinegar in water, that'll thin your blood, too, that'll prevent your havin' another stroke." (Arnella L.)

Arnella's neighbor, Anna P., told me that Arnella would have been *much* better off taking a pinch of epsom salts every day for nine days. Astringent substances such as lemon juice, vinegar, and epsom salts are believed to open the pores so that the excess blood can be sweated out.

"Low blood," on the other hand, is conceptually allied with anemia, but terminologically equated with low blood *pressure*. "They say you can have *high* blood or *low* blood, and I know the low blood is not *enough* blood and they say it can make you just as sick as the high blood" (Letha A.). Arnella L. feels that the blood pressure can get so low that it is difficult for the heart to pump the blood through the body; then you need a transfusion. But manipulating the diet can solve this problem, too, and when a physician told Freda T. that her blood pressure was low, Arnella made a special trip to tell her to eat rare liver, beef broth, and beets to "build up" her blood. Erma V. is in agreement with both the definition and treatment of "low blood pressure":

> Darlin', low blood pressure is not enough blood to go through. They have to give you iron, they give you iron pills, iron tonic to build the blood. Then they give you food to eat, tell you to eat beets or liver, somethin' like that. Then some of 'em, they'll tell to drink wine. But I wouldn't drink wine, I wouldn't prefer wine. I used to be a wino myself, [and now] I don't prefer no drinks. (Erma V.)

The person with "low blood" is again at fault because he or she ate too many astringent foods. Anna P. loves pickles, but is afraid to eat them too often lest she "cut" her blood too much. It is also dangerous to take the treatments for "high blood" for too long, which explains why Arnella L. said, "Now that don't make no sense . . .", when the physician told her not to let her prescription run out. *Sangre débil,* "weak blood," is also a problem for Kay's Mexican American informants, who also attribute it to poor eating habits. They do not, however, associate anemia with low blood *pressure* (*baja presión*).

Location and Circulation of Blood

"Lotta doctors stand around on their butts laughin' at the signs," says Bertha A., "they'd do better if they paid attention." She refers to the signs of the zodiac, which do not simply predict the weather and regulate agricultural pursuits. They also affect the body, and their supposed effect on the human organism is the basis for a constant and lively practice of self-medication, dietary regulation, and behavioral modifications of various sorts. "The signs" thus may be consulted for the best times to get a haircut or a permanent wave, have teeth filled or extracted, wean babies, and have surgery.

Each day is believed ruled by one of the twelve zodiacal signs, each appearing at least once a month for two or three days at a time. Each sign is correlated with a particular part of the body and "rules" that anatomical feature: Aries controls the head, Taurus the neck, Gemini the arms, and so on. The signs change in sequence from top to bottom, starting with Aries and working downward to the feet, ruled by Pisces. There is thought to be more blood in that part of the body under control at the time, and a surgical procedure should be avoided until the sign has moved on. If this is not followed, the patient may lose too much blood, or postoperative recuperation may be delayed. It is usual, however, for minor symptoms to appear in that part of the body whose associated sign is in control – a stomachache, for example, may be considered normal during the sign of Cancer, which rules the breast and stomach. The birth sign of an individual may also foretell his or her anatomical weaknesses; the Capricorn native is inclined to diseases of the knees, for example, as Capricorn rules the knees.

Practically every household visited contains an almanac in which the changing signs of the zodiac are scanned for medical reasons as well as for weather forecasts, the proper time to plant gardens, kill weeds, and so on. Informants who use the almanac for advice (and these are by no means always those persons lacking in formal education) are quite aware that doctors do not believe in the effect of the moon, sun, and planets on human health. For those events over which they have control, such as voluntary tooth extraction or nonemergency surgery, people may choose the proper time according to the almanac, saying nothing to the dentist or physician. When the procedure is a success, credit goes to their own manipulation of the time element as well as the skill of the practitioner – the signs are as important as the scalpel or the drill.

Environmental conditions also affect the rate at which the blood circulates through the body. The blood moves faster when conditions are unsettled, when the moon is waxing, the tide is high, the weather stormy or the seasons changing. This is another very old idea, three centuries separating Sydenham's description (Dewhurst 1966: 127) of the increased incidence of a disease ". . . espetially at that season which is between spring and summer, the blood at that time from the approach of the sun being disposed to an effervescency and disorderly condition . . ." from Bertha A.'s "In the spring the seasons done made their turn; when sap go up, it makes you sick. In the fall when sap go down, it'll make you sick." In contrast the movement of the blood is more sluggish when the tide is out, the winds calm, the moon in its decrease. During the winter sap goes down into the roots of plants and there lies dormant.

Blood Purity

One of the most commonly held beliefs is that the body will become "defiled" if not incessantly purged and cleansed by the use of laxatives. The giving of laxatives starts at birth and is continued until death. The kind and amount taken depends upon the age of the individual, but this systemic purification follows the individual through the entire life cycle.

During the prenatal period impurities may build up in the foetus as mother and child are considered to share a single circulatory system. Anything present in the mother's blood is therefore also to be found in the blood of the newborn infant:

> I guess sugar's inherited for sure. Inherited down from your mother, just like TB. If your peoples die with TB, it goes through the family. Germ is still in the blood stream, it's in the blood stream. You can inherit it from your dad, or either your mother. Goes down into the blood stream. (Erma V.)

Formerly most women had their children at home, being attended by a midwife. Both the newborn infant and the mother were given catnip tea shortly after the birth took place, which drove any residual impurities from the blood of both. In infants, the fine red rash that frequently developed on the face was considered to be the impurities "coming out." The idea that it is dangerous for the baby if the rash does *not* appear is still to be found all over the United States (Snow 1974; Stekert 1971; Frankel 1970). If catnip is not available, a few drops of a commercial laxative may be used instead. The dosage is increased gradually until the child reaches adult strength at puberty, after which an adult dose should be taken weekly in order to keep the system clean. Failure to do so allows impurities and phlegm to build up and weakens the body, making it more susceptible to and less able to "throw off" illness.

The presence of systemic impurities is represented symptomatically by fever and/or rashes. Fevers, says Anna, are caused by insect bites, and insects are composed of germs. "Flies is germs, and mosquitoes." When the insect bites, some of these germs get into the blood. If you have taken proper precautions, illness may not occur, but ". . . if the system's not clean, [it] throws you into a deep sickness. Everybody's blood's not clean." When asked about fevers, she mentioned scarlet fever, yellow fever, and malaria. She does not consider that a specific insect vector exists – that malaria is transmitted by mosquitoes but not flies, for example. Any biting insect can give you any fever; the germs enter your blood and ". . . if the blood isn't purified, [it'll] come out on you."

An imbalance of heat and cold in the body may produce symptoms and is another residual belief from the humoral pathology, as is the effort to restore the balance by use of both cold and hot substances:

> And measles, you give [corn] shuck tea and ice water. You see that ice water drive the fever out, it'd come out in those little heat bumps, measles they call it. And you'd drink somethin' cold that'd drive them out. You'd break out and your face'd be plumb thick with those little things, and when they'd dry up you'd be well. And the tea you'd give mostly to 'em at night. See, that'd keep the pores open through the day if you drank tea, and you'd take more cold. But at night, they'd give it to you when you go to bed and be under cover. (Bertha A.)

Any kind of skin eruption, in fact, from diaper rash to chicken pox is likely to be blamed on ". . . something in the body trying to come out."

Symptoms caused by the presence of impurities in the body may also be seasonally variable because of the notion that they sink in the body during the winter and lie dormant until spring. "When spring comes, birds start mating. Fishes in the water start mating. The sap is rising and impurities start rising too. If your system's defiled, why you're liable to come with *anything!*" (Anna P.). Such ideas are reinforced by the almanac, which advises spring as a time to clean up: "Purify and enrich the blood and drive out all impurities with a good cathartic, and you will avoid the diseases of June" (MacDonald's 1973).

In the minds of informants impurities are now often equated with germs. Not only insects but carrion, says Anna P., are composed of germs and "the buzzard created to eat germs, God created him for that." She feels that there is so much sickness around because there are so few buzzards left to eat up this health hazard. Other neighborhood residents are not quite sure just what germs are either, and are also in disagreement about contagion. Bertha A. feels that some illnesses are "catchin," colds, for example. She says that it goes from one person to another through "sneezin' or coughin' " of germs, and that germs are "sumpin' that people have in their body; you sneeze or cough, it blows it out. When they have a disease and stuff." Lily M., who has a college degree, says that "germs and viruses" can spread some diseases, but she is unable to say what germs and viruses are. Arnella L. says that colds are "catchable," because of germs. "You know, you can pick up germs any kind of way, on your hands, pick it off a glass, anything. It ain't no certain way that you can pick up germs." When asked what she thinks germs are, however, the answer was, "Well, I couldn't tell you what germs was, because I don't know." Delia J., many years younger and much better educated, says that malaria is contagious. Everyone in her family back in Oklahoma had it at once, she says, so it must have been something that went from one person to another. She understands better than most informants that there is a causal relationship between germs and viruses ("tiny little things always in the air") and some illnesses. Her belief about malaria makes good common sense, however, and she is unlikely to question it.

Other informants are adamant in that they do *not* believe that illnesses can be transmitted from person to person. Lillian A. does not believe that colds or anything else are contagious. Freda T. says that you cannot become ill this way. She has heard people talk about germs, but she does not know what they are; she thinks that "maybe germs are just any kind of sickness." Harry J. also does not believe in contagion. He has been in the hospital a lot, "around all those other sick people," and has never "picked up" anything from anyone else. As far as he is concerned, that proves it is not possible. Olive P. says that she has heard that some things, like colds, can go from one person to another. She doesn't know if this is true or not. As to germs, she has heard a lot of talk about them, but she doesn't know exactly what they are. She thinks that they may be something like bedbugs.

Even if informants *do* understand about microorganisms and how they can cause illness, mysticism may interrupt the cause-and-effect relationship. Erma V. is a Pentecostal evangelist to whom God gave "the position" of visiting the sick. Since she has a minister's license, she has access to the hospitals, and spends each Sunday visiting the sick. She has seen germs (she was the only informant to use the term "bacteria") through the microscope at one of the hospital laboratories. She says that they are tiny creatures of different shapes, and that different kinds can cause different diseases. This reflects a fairly clear understanding. She goes on to say, however, that though she is around sick people a lot, God puts a protective barrier around her which the germs cannot penetrate – therefore she does not get sick:

> Well, yes, there is contagious disease that peoples can catch from other peoples, but I believe this about this disease: I believe that you have to be drinkin' behind them, or usin' the same, or either stayin' in the room with 'em long enough that you can get that germ. You know, that germ can fly right in the room with them. [But] you know this is the reason why I say that the Lord is good to me, and the Lord is with me – 'cause I went through all of these things and didn't catch nothin'.
>
> I visit the TB ward, they make me put on that mask, sometime I don't *put* on that mask. With the help of the Lord if you just *believe*. . . . I believe when I go in with people who are sick the *Lord* help me. I believe fully in the Lord, and I feel He's a protection for me. If it wasn't for Him, I would *take* these germs. (Erma V.)

Blood Viscosity

Blood is often spoken of as being "thick" or "thin," attributes which are dependent upon age, gender, diet, and environmental temperature. Thinner blood is associated with constitutional weakness, and the blood of babies, pre-pubescent children, females, and the elderly is relatively thin, contributing to their heightened susceptibility to illness. Blood becomes thicker at puberty and ideally remains so until the climacteric, after which it begins to thin down in the gradual decline of the body.

Blood viscosity is also affected by outside temperatures and is associated with maintaining proper body temperature. The blood thickens in the winter as a protection against cold and thins down again when outside temperatures rise. People living in warmer climates are thought to have thinner blood than those living where the winters are more severe; informants often mentioned that the years in the Southwest had thinned their blood. Heat is rarely mentioned as posing a health hazard and only a few examples were cited. Tom P. says that hot damp air (steam) is bad for you as it softens the bones. He was working as a cook for the army when he was slammed against a wall by a carload of frozen meats. The resultant seven leg fractures would not have occurred, he says, if his bones had not been so soft from years of working in steamy kitchens. Working in a laundry is thought to be unhealthy for the same reason. Lillian A. has heart disease, one of the manifestations of which is shortness of breath. But she doesn't really think there is anything wrong with her heart, though the doctor tells her there is. She believes that her most recent illness was brought on by visiting her children in hot, damp Los Angeles:

> Sometimes you have to put your head up high on a pillow, or even sit up [to breathe easily]. Sometimes it's worse. Now when I was over in Los Angeles, it was hot there at night. And I had the windows up and that smog there and that fog, it was a foggy night. I thought that dampness coming in the windows could have caused me to wheeze. (Lillian A.)

Cold damp air, however, is *always* dangerous, and its entrance into the body is the most frequently cited cause of illness. The entrance of cold into the body is blamed for upper respiratory infections, for certain degenerative diseases of old age, and with illness or death of adult women when associated with the menses, childbirth, or abortion. Thin blood has lessened protective capability, which helps explain why women and older people are especially vulnerable. In any case, individuals are usually faulted for failure to exercise "mother wit" and protect themselves by wearing warm clothing or staying inside. Exposing the body to inclement weather simply invites the entrance of cold damp air:

> Well, in other words . . . it's *exposure,* that you get sometime when you're young in your body. Through your system as you get older, it take effect . . . dampness and not takin' proper care of yourself. Goin' out in bad weather and rainy weather, you expose yourself. Pores are open. You're subject to takin' a complaint, in through the blood . . . [it] kind of grows into the system, and as you get older, it works with you. (Bertha A.)

The belief in the power of cold air to enter the body and thereby cause illness is held by virtually every informant, irrespective of age, sex, or education. It was nearly always the first thing mentioned when speaking of the causes of illness.

> There's gonna be many, many a girl wearin' these mini dresses; two or three years from now they'll be in a wheelchair. Of exposure. They

think that the teachers and the preachers and the mothers are meddlin', to tell them put on somethin' warm when they go out. But they want to go out lookin' *good,* or go out and show they bottoms and so forth. This creates sickness. (Erma V.)

Well, sometimes it's the weather conditions. Now just take for instance this time of year [November]. I can't go without my stockings. And people go around with just those sandals on, and no stockings. I see 'em with these thongs on in the wintertime. Well, I can't do that. If I get up in the morning, I try to wear these warm house shoes, but even with them on, if I don't put stockings on, by night I'm sneezing, seeming getting a cold. (Lillian A.)

Well, some of 'em will go the time like now, right now [December], the majority of the people is wearin' practically the same they wore during the hot weather! Now, you seen them things hangin' up in the bathroom there [winter underclothing]? I never think that I can go along with clothes on like I wear in the summer, the hottest weather. Now I notice these girls, now sometimes they don't even have on stockin's, nor socks, these kids goin' to school. Now that's not good for 'em! (Olive P.)

Phlegm has already been noted as a normal bodily component associated with cold, and its presence is a sure sign that cold has entered the body: "Now, just like this cough I have, now I don't really feel that it's a cold. And yet I *know* it's *cold* in there, because the main reason of the coughing, I get that little lump of phlegm or mucus in my throat, and I have to cough until I can get it out. And of course I know that's cold in there" (Lillian A.). Anna P. says that pneumonia is caused by an over-abundance of "slime" in the body. It collects in the stomach, and if the body is not regularly rid of the excess by means of laxatives, it will cause trouble. Cold air may enter the body, circulate through the blood stream and reach the stomach. There it somehow mobilizes the collected slime and causes it to rise into the chest. The next thing you know you have a pain, and pneumonia. The overabundance of slime is proven by the fact that people with pneumonia are always coughing it up.

Slowly, slowly, over years, the cold builds up in the body:

Oh yeah, I have arthritis. Here they call it arthritis, but it ain't nothin' but rheumatism. See, I worked so long, I worked a long time, and the cold settled in my joints. Standin' in the cold catchin' the buses and things. And you know how much cold you accumulate. (Ella T.)

The idea that present carelessness can cause future illness is common. It provides a convenient explanation for not only the fact that many people going out in the cold without sufficient protection do *not* get sick, but also for many of the degenerative diseases of older age. The girls in their short skirts may not suffer *today,* but the cold circulating through their blood will settle in their joints. As the body weakens with advancing age, the cold in the joints begins "to work with the body" and *voilà,* rheumatism!

> Now this here is wintertime, isn't it? If I go out here half-dressed, half-nekkid, catch a whole lotta cold, won't try to do nothin' about it, you know I'm gonna be sick! . . . I brought it on myself! . . . Lookit the girls today, walkin' around here with no clothes on. Their mini-skirts up to here. I saw some with *shorts* on yesterday. Shorts! Up to here! And poor me, I couldn't stay warm with what I had on. [It had been 82 degrees the day before.] All right! They don't *feel* it now! They young, blood's thick. But you wait until they get up 25, 30 years old, maybe 40. They gonna be crippin' along, got the rheumatism. "I'm hurtin'." They brings it all on theirselves! They exposin' theirself! They not takin' care of theirselves! They just goin' head on, just dressin', and you cain't tell 'em nothin'! More nekkid folks now than I ever seen in my life! Walkin' nekkid in the street. And when they get my age, mightn't get as old as I am, they gonna feel it. Sumpin' gonna happen to 'em! If they don't go into TB, they gonna have pneumonia; if they don't do that, they gonna have arthritis; they gonna have rheumatism. They gonna pay for it. All that cold is settlin' in their joints. . . . When they get older, they gonna feel it. They be to the place they be walkin' on crutches, sticks, and ever'thing else! (Arnella L.)

Cold and dampness are potentially dangerous to everyone but are particularly so for women who are menstruating, who have recently had an abortion, or who have just given birth. All are at risk because of vaginal bleeding, and cold, which thickens blood, might enter the body and cause the flow of blood to stop altogether. The blood must have somewhere to go, however, and if it cannot flow it will "back up" and result in a stroke or tubercular hemorrhage.

> You can be exposed before your baby gets old enough. After you have your baby. See, some people have a baby and three or four days, just up and go like that. This is exposure. This is exposure to TB. And many times people go and take abortions, keep from bein' pregnant, take abortions. This goes into TB. (Erma V.)

The notion that cold would suppress menstruation was common a century ago, as was the idea that such suppression might end in "consumption" (Pierce 1895:499). The fear that natural blood flow will be impeded is responsible for certain behavioral taboos. It is considered dangerous for women to go out or to bathe while losing blood, a belief also held by Kay's Mexican American informants.

If it is natural for women to lose blood at certain times, however, it is never so for men. Ella T. attributes the death of her first husband to a lethal combination of blood loss and damp cold:

> He died of tuberculosis. He give his sister a blood transfusion, and they took too much blood from him. He only weighed 125 pounds, and they took 300 cc's of blood from him, and that's too much blood. And you couldn't tell him nothin'. And you see, it's damp out in California, and instead of him wearin' them heavy clothes, he'd pull off them heavy drawers and go in his shirt sleeves. When he give his sister that blood transfusion, instead of wearin' them warm clothes and things, he didn't do it. Then he took that quick kind of TB. He must not have been very strong or sumpin'. And see, he's supposed to drink wine to run that blood back, and he didn't. (Ella T.)

Heat, on the other hand, opens pores and veins and promotes bleeding. Hot teas may be consumed to bring on a delayed menstrual period and sitting in a very hot bath is believed to induce abortion.

Home regimens to prevent illness are based on these ideas concerning man's place in the natural world. Illness, which is seen as a kind of attack upon the body by some outside force, can be averted by deflecting this force. Some agents in themselves are believed to have such properties, and some older informants mention that as children they were required to wear a string of garlic buds or an asafetida bag around the neck to keep sickness away. Asafetida dissolved in hot water is still used by some informants to prevent "heart trouble." One woman keeps a quart jar containing a mixture of asafetida, whiskey, and garlic buds, and she takes a teaspoonful every other day to "keep healthy." Formerly children were given ground calamus root rolled in bits of bread "to keep them from getting sick." Calamus (sweet flag) was official in the *United States Pharmacopeia* from 1820 to 1916, and in the *National Formulary* until 1950 (Vogel 1970:378). According to some older women, the fact that it is no longer available commercially explains why children are sick all the time now. Younger women are forever taking their children to the doctor, the older women say. When *their* children were young this was not so, due to the use of the good "old-timey" medicines. Substitutions may be made, however, and since calamus root is no longer available, Anna P. gave her younger children a daily vitamin pill instead. The use of laxatives is also essential to keep the body clean, and those preparations which contain "natural" ingredients, such as senna leaves, are greatly favored.

A series of purificatory rites also takes place in the spring. These start in March and usually last for nine days. According to Fred G., nine has special power because there are nine planets. It is a ritual number which has a very long history in European folklore, however, and one which is heard over and over in curing procedures. Sulfur and molasses should be taken for nine days to clean the system; castor oil (as well as the usual weekly laxative) is taken for nine days to "lubricate the system" and prevent the joints from getting stiff; sassafras or poke greens are consumed for nine days to thin the winter-thickened blood; medicine to "clean off the liver" is taken for nine days, etc. One man told me that he refuses to take all of the spring medicine that his wife recommends. One spring she hid "liver pills" in his hot cereal, but he managed to remove them when she wasn't looking. Fortunately for the body, clean up time is only once a year: "You can't take a blood tonic all the time; it would work in the blood too forcible, strip things out that you didn't want out" (Anna P.).

Precautionary measures are not always taken, of course. People *do* go out in the cold, the hot sun, and the rain; they *do* overeat, work hard, go without sleep, bathe while menstruating, go to horror movies while pregnant, and so on.

They do *not* always watch their diets; they eat too much red meat, citrus fruit, pickles, olives, and any number of other potentially harmful foods. They fail to *take* castor oil, their senna leaves and sassafras, their epsom salts, and vitamin pills. There is therefore no dearth of natural illnesses to afflict mankind. But don't blame nature if you *do* get sick, says Arnella L., because "you done done it to yourself!"

ILLNESS AS PUNISHMENT

Man is not just a child of nature, however, and unlike the plants and animals with which he shares the natural world he has a spiritual side to his being. In some instances illness may be attributed to punishment for failure to abide by the proper behavioral rules vis-à-vis God. Due to the welding of body and soul into one being, these illnesses are also considered "natural." In other instances mental disorders may be attributed to the machinations of the Devil, and these, being "unnatural", are greatly to be feared.

As in the more mundane seasonal conflict, there is also a continual battle between the forces of good and the forces of evil as personified in God and the Devil. Again, the *unprotected* man or woman is a helpless pawn in a power struggle for his or her immortal soul. "Evil influences" is a term often used to describe a state of affairs in which the Devil's invisible henchmen surround one, putting thoughts of evil deeds into the mind:

> Then there's demons. A demon is a bad spirit. You know, don't have no desire to do right. Do wrong. We have some people in the world have *never* done right. Wrong doin', that's a demon tell 'em to do that. A spirit tell you to do this and tell you to do that, that's a demon is overpowerin' the *good!* Which the Devil did tell Christ on the last day he would do that, he'd be goin' to and from seekin' the children of God. That's what he meant. (Mother D.)

Again the struggle is external to the individual, and unaided, he or she may be unable to discriminate between the adversaries:

> I keep my Bible with me at all times. This holiness [religion] is a wonderful thing, but you got to keep on prayin' fast, and you got to try to live it. Cause the Devil will step in and tell you to do a whole lot of things when you ought not to do it. But you don't know who's talkin' to you. (Arnella L.)

It will be recalled that the physical body is considered to be naturally dirty (because it is composed of a handful of dust), unless steps are taken to purify it and keep it clean. There is a parallel on the spiritual side of human nature as well, which is seen as a mixture of the good and the bad. It is the bad which must be eliminated lest the individual heedlessly present an affinity for evil:

> Evil influence mean the *Devil,* which name is Satan. He is evil, he can put evil thought in your mind. Also, the Devil can work in the frame of anyone mind, cause you to do things you don't want to do. Our body is made up of evil and of good. If we are not close to God in spirit, the Devil take control of us. God guide me each day and teach me wisdom and knowledge how to cope with my problem and people around me. Sometime I have so many burden on my shoulder, I don't know which way to turn to. I learn to work them out by talking to Jesus and forget about them, and before long He work them out because I can't do anything for myself. (Lunell N.)

It is not surprising that most informants find it impossible to separate medical beliefs from religious beliefs. Thoughts on the relationship of man to God are of consuming interest to most people. Religion is not something relegated to a few hours on Sunday; it permeates virtually all aspects of daily life. Special religious calendars provide scripture reading for each day of the year, and in many homes reading of this scripture begins the day. Thorough knowledge of the Bible is a matter of some pride, and is instilled in children at an early age. The Bible is considered the definitive source of information, and rare was the interview in which "It's in the Bible," or "The Bible tells you that," was not heard at least once. A religious rationale is provided for every aspect of health behavior from the onset of illness to its cure. The word "diagnosis" is even from the Bible, according to Anna P.

Church affiliation among blacks is closely allied with social class, and members of the lower class are more likely to belong to one of the fundamentalist Christian churches. In such churches, the teachings of God as they appear in the Bible are taken literally. For example, when I asked Delia J. why her church has their communion service in the evening instead of the morning, she replied, "The Bible calls it the Lord's *supper,* not his brunch or dinner!"

Behavior at Neighborhood churches is spontaneous, uninhibited, and infectious. Emotional outbursts punctuate prayers and sermons, and individuals may fling their arms and bodies about. Singing, accompanied by rhythmic hand clapping, is an important part of the services. Individuals rise to testify how good God has been to them, and audience and minister participate in a back and forth verbal exchange referred to as call-and-response behavior (Simpson 1970:112). Religious fervor may rise until the minister can no longer be heard over the clapping, singing, tambourine-shaking, and shouts of the faithful. It is not uncommon for someone to "fall out" (lose consciousness) during services, particularly members of Pentecostal or Holiness congregations. Far from being disapproved, such an occurrence is thought to signify the individual's strong faith, and underscores the fact that God is "working with" the individual.

There are doctrinal differences between the churches, however, which are important in health behavior. In the Baptist and Methodist churches, the prerequisite to salvation is baptism. The individual publicly declares his wish and is baptized by water (total immersion). The individual is now "saved," i.e., a member of God's elect, and a full-fledged church member. Ministers of these churches have received formal religious training and are paid a salary. There is a rather elaborate hierarchy of church functionaries: the minister, deacons, elders, ushers, robed choir, etc. There is also a Missionary Society for women whose function is partly social as well as religious. It combines the social aspect of a women's club with charitable works. The recipients of the Missionary Society's good works are the sick of the congregation. Nearly as many men as women attend services.

For adherents of the Holiness and Pentecostal churches, on the other hand, salvation is a three-step process. As in the Baptist and Methodist churches, individuals publicly declare their wish for baptism and are then baptized by water, again by total immersion. A third step is necessary, however, known as "baptism by the Holy Spirit." According to informants, this is something one must work to achieve. The supplicant kneels at the altar, praying that the Holy Spirit will descend and fill his or her heart. The congregation prays aloud, sings, claps hands, and a few people shake tambourines. The individual may resist "giving over," and everyone bends over the candidate, praying aloud and offering advice. The praying, shouting and clapping grow louder and faster until the person's heart "opens up" to admit the Holy Spirit. At this point, the individual "falls out" and may exhibit the phenomenon known as "speaking in tongues." He or she is now a full-fledged member of the church and is hereafter referred to as one of "the saints."

A fourth step may or may not take place. This occurs when God makes known to one of "the saints" that He wishes him or her to become a minister. God may publicly "work with" the individual or "the call" may come in a vision. The individual may hear God's voice. At any rate, the person so selected applies for a license, pays a small fee, and is thereafter a licensed minister. There is no training for such a position and Pentecostal ministers may have little or no formal education. It is believed that when God thus selects someone to be His minister, He also confers upon him or her the gift of healing, and healing rites are a regular part of Pentecostal religious services. Being a Pentecostal minister is not a full-time position – during the week the minister may be a janitor or a maid. A monthly "love offering" is taken up in lieu of salary. Church members come from the very lowest income level in the Neighborhood and are mainly women. Of over 50 persons present one Sunday when I attended services at a Pentecostal church, only three were men. Religious fervor at Pentecostal services is apt to be quite contagious:

> And anything I would get up and say, speak and say in that church, it would come to a showdown. I told 'em the last night I prophesized in there, I just didn't prophesy, I *predicted* it! I just got up and told 'em out of my mouth. I said, "God's gonna meet us here tonight. He gonna be strong in this buildin', so that you all think the house is on fire. There's not gonna be any blaze, but the house is just gonna be smoked up." And it was, just like I told it. I said, "Lord gonna work with the audience. When he get through workin' the audience, He gonna hit the pulpit." And when He got through workin' with those people in the audience, He come just as straight up in the pulpit and worked with the choir members. And I was singin' in the choir. They thought I was dead up there. . . . God throwed me out up there, and I just laid. Just laid like a statue. Wasn't even sayin' nothin'. Some of the members thought I was dead, and they went there and looked at me. Caught me by the arm. Somebody said to the pastor, "That's all right. She's all right, she ain't dead. Lord just workin' with her, leave her alone. She's alright." (Arnella L., a Pentecostal minister)

It has often been stated that churches play mainly a cathartic role for low-income Blacks, giving them a place where they can let off steam which cannot adequately be expressed in other ways. Certainly for many Neighborhood residents, religion provides the means of handling stressful situations. The assistant pastor at one church, who works as a domestic during the week, testified one morning how mean the White woman she works for is to her. She "turns the other cheek," however, and prays that God will soften the heart of her employer and "show her the way." In the following passage, a religious framework provides both the rationale for a racial slur and the justification for aggressive retaliation:

> When my mother were in the hospital, did I tell you about this white lady what were lightin' a cigarette? She were in the room with my mother. She was alyin' in there, and she was tryin' to find her mouth. And she couldn't find her mouth to light her cigarette. And she says,

"Hey there! Would you come and light me a cigarette?" She was a beautiful blonde, beautiful skin, beautiful. But she was all crippled up, you know.

I said, "Darlin', I don't indulge in those things; the Bible says touch not the unclean things. And dear, you don't need that nohow." She said to me, "Why, you big old black nigger! Why, you *big black nigger!* You just get your big black self out of here! I pray for myself. Get out!" And she began screamin'.

Sound like when she said, "You big black nigger," you know in my ears I heard? "Sister Erma, pray for me, cause I'm demon-possessed!" So I began to pray for her.

"Lord, rebuke this demon! This hatred! This arthritis demon!" I began to rebuke it. When I got through prayin' for her, I looked up and there was five nurses standin' to see. It's against the law to rile a patient, but darlin', it was my time to take over then. She'd been cussin' all other times, but when I got through prayin' for her she began to thank the Lord. And you know what? She got where she could use her hands; the Lord take this numb feelin's out of her.

See, it takes a person with a heart! I love people, and I know people, and I knew she was demon possessed! Many of these people today, what are goin' on with all of this racial and all of this fightin', is possessed! Demons. They're demon possessed.

Ain't no little I's and big you's – ever'body's same, ever'body's same in Christ Jesus. (Erma V.)

God is approached for help in the most mundane of everyday matters as well as during times of crisis. Dreams and "visions" are scanned for the light they are thought to throw on problems large and small. In some cases, the Deity is even employed as matchmaker:

God chose this last husband of mine. I had just give up lookin' for a good man. So one night in the summer, I just come on in the house and hooked the screen door. I got down on my knees and I says, "Lord, I is tired of lookin'. If you wants me to have a husband, You'll have to pick one out for me!" I got on in bed and that night I had a vision: They was two men standin' side by side. One was the Reverend Roberts, and he was wearin' a blue suit. The other man I had never seed before. He was wearin' a gray suit. Now I knowed the Reverend Roberts, and I didn't like him much – he was just a little old jackleg preacher. So I just went on. Four years later my white folks carried me to a party so I could meet some of my own people. And the door opened and this man walked in. I knowed 'im right away; it was the man from the vision. So we got married. And do you know, when he come to the weddin' he was wearin' a gray suit. (Anna P.)

Mother D., too, asked God to help her find a suitable mate. She had been married three times, and each husband, she says, ". . . interfered with my gift. I had to go out and heal, and they didn't understand." After she left the third husband, she asked God for His help. Two weeks later she met her present husband, Jackie C. Of him she says, "He hasn't given me a bit of trouble in 15 years!" He does all the housework and cooking, while she goes across town to her "doctor's office," and her successful curing practice. The theme of male/female hostility is often presented in a religious framework; all three women who are licensed ministers complained that men had tried to "keep them down":

> I was in this church over on the corner. I told them about the Lord had called me, [and] the Bishop told me that the Lord hasn't called a woman. This set me back, you know? And see, I heard with my own ears . . . there's many and many of women been whipped down, but they's ministers of God what will save many people. Because the ministers are tellin' 'em they can't preach, when God called 'em to preach. Why can't a woman carry the Word when Mary carried the Word nine long months, and give birth to it. And after this when He was *crucified,* Mary was there to find Jesus, she went to the tomb. He said to her, "Why weepeth thou, go in peace." When she heard that, she knew His voice. He said, "Go and tell my disciples I said meet me in Galilee." Now, Jesus give her those words to go, why can't women go and tell somethin', huh? God's the same God yesterday, today, and forever. Why can't a woman carry the word of God? You know lots of times they whup 'em down and tell 'em they got to be draped down and go and be silent. How can you? He said, "I'm gonna pour out my strength, gonna pour out my power on all folks." What is He gonna pour it out on 'em for just to be silent? No, peoples get this thing wrong. They kept me bound five years. (Erma V.)

Most women, however, passively accept the idea that women in some way deserve maltreatment. It was commonly stated that labor pains are the continuing punishment of all women, laid on because Eve tempted Adam in the Garden of Eden.

A number of informants, all women, report hearing the voice of God "just as plain as you and I are talkin' right now." As in the matchmaking, these occasions are usually those in which the individual is in a conflict situation and God is the problem-solver. Arnella L., for example, was a newly ordained evangelist in a Neighborhood church. She did not feel that the minister (male) was giving her the proper advice and guidance to help her in her new vocation. As she tells it, the problem was solved in the following way:

> It got so God wasn't pleased with sumpin' down there, I don't know what was goin' on. But I know me and another woman was standin' at the altar prayin' over some sinner, and God walked up and spoke to me just as plain as you'd walk up and speak. "Leave here!" I looked, wasn't a soul close to me! And the pastor's wife was playin' the piano, and I know it wasn't none of her! I stood there, and I looked on this side, and I looked on *this* side, and I turned around and looked behind me — wasn't a soul standin' there close to me. Wasn't nobody sayin' nothin' to

> me, just imagination! Just my ideas. I went on and sat down after we all left the altar, got in my seat, wasn't nobody close to me. God spoke to me again. Right in the same ear. He said, "I said *leave here!* You're not gettin' nowhere." I said, "Thank you, thank you, Jesus." I didn't argue with it that time! And I haven't been back since. (Arnella L.)

God is also the ultimate rescuer and may reach down and save the sinner. Erma V., who had been living the life of "a wretch undone," describes her salvation:

> I would come in and get me a dose [heroin] for the weekend, and I drank, too. "You all better give me the streets!" See, I'd have me a jug of that wine, whole jug, didn't buy no little old bottle. I'd get enough so I could get drunk! They moved, they moved, they moved, ever'body moved! Ever'body danced to my music, ever'body danced to my music! But you know, I could've gotten killed, and I thank God that He reached and got me one day 'fore it was everlastin' too late! Some of those people down there could have killed me. They could have, but they didn't.
>
> I come into the church, out of the world, and the Lord saved me and cleaned me. Even old oil pool, you got lilies growin' in a oil pool. Lily can grow up out of dirty filthy water, bloom up just as purty and bright! That's the way God can bring you out of filth, just like He do a lily. He can, He can bring you out and bloom you over all of this junk. You know, you can go out and get that lily, and the lily will smell just as good and won't have none of the scent of filth on it. Out of this dirt, out of this pool . . . . (Erma V.)

For Sister Erma, in fact, religion makes up all worldly lacks:

> I got joy; I got peace; I got ever'thing I want. There's nobody no happier than I am. I don't have no childrens; I don't have no husband; I have Jesus. He's childrens; He's husband; He's *ever'thing!* He's a great consolation to me. I'm not in no good lookin' house, but inside I'm just as rich and happy as anybody else. I don't know nobody in town no happier than I am. I don't have luxury and all, but I have a home up yonder. This home, I'm not bothered about nothin' here; I'm lookin' beyond. (Erma V.)

Whatever the denomination, religious training begins early. Infants and children are taken to church as a matter of course. In every church service which I attended, quite small children were quiet and attentive through services which often lasted for hours. (Admittedly the services were vastly more entertaining than the church services of *my* childhood.) Public "declaring for Jesus" may take place at an early age, and at one Baptist revival, children six, seven, and eight years of age came forward to ask for baptism.

Persons whose behavior is disapproved – those who use bad language, drink excessively, gamble, etc. – are perceived by churchgoers to be either "unsaved" or those who have fallen from grace and strayed from the right path. It is frequently mentioned by informants that people gamble on the sidewalk in front of the corner market on Sunday morning, and the God-fearing people on their way to church must step off the sidewalk and go around the loiterers. It is considered that children must be trained from infancy to serve God, and church attendance is a requisite in proper socialization. Ella T. says that the rise in what she calls "juvenile" (delinquency) is due to the fact that prayers are no longer allowed in the schoolroom:

> Children is not like they was. You never had no juvenile, nothin' like that back in those days. You never seed no police had nobody's child. Since they got these prayers out of the schools, it just ain't the same. They don't have prayer in the schools, and children is not the same. They took the prayers out of the schools, and there is too much strife and juvenile, and there is too much dope and stuff in the world. And there's a law you can't whup your children, and if you can't whup your children, you look for all this to happen. They got a law here you can't whup no child! But I whup mine; he never get too big for me to whup. Ever'body should know how to whup 'em without beatin' 'em and bruisin' 'em up. . . . Ever'body say he's a very sweet child, he's raised. But he's mean, he's spoiled. (Ella T.)

She went on to say that she is too nervous to put up with his meanness much longer. She has therefore told him that if he doesn't improve, she will have him sent to juvenile home where they will have a *gun* to see that he behaves himself.

Children and adolescents in trouble with the law are usually pointed out as coming from families where church attendance is lacking. The parents are blamed for not showing their children the proper way and failing to guide them in life. Lizzie L., the mother of nine children, says:

> You know, a lot of kids don't go to church. I been goin' around tryin' to get some of my neighbors to send their little kids to church. I think if the neighbors would let their kids go to church and go *themselves,* there wouldn't be quite so much trouble. They stand on the corners here, and they drink, and disrespectable, and goin' in and out of the store, they hear all of it. And if they'd just go to church, spend just one day in church, and then come home, I think the world would just be lots better off than what it is. But it's misunderstanding. I think the parents is at fault for most of it. (Lizzie L.)

As in those instances where lack of protection leaves the individual open to onslaughts of inclement weather, lack of training results in someone who does not know how to behave. The man or woman who is not "raised," who flouts behavioral rules set down by God is due for a fall, and the motif is no longer exposure, but punishment. There are striking parallels in child-rearing practices and in belief in divine punishment for sin. A stern and punishing God is equated with punishing parents, and a "whupping" is good for both body and soul. One woman says, regarding her mother and father:

> Sho, they whup me, they *whup* me! You know what I mean. They didn't whup me a lick or miss, they whup me. It done somethin' for me. And it helped me. Both of 'em; she whupped me when I was grown. (Ella T.)

Any success in life, in fact, is often attributed to the spankings of childhood:

> And when my mother died, I got a sermon from my mother's hands. Her little old hands we had folded, my sister said, "Put gloves on 'em," but I didn't want gloves on my mother's hands! I wanted a remembrance of those hands! I stood there so long I guess maybe they thought I got dumbfounded or sumpin', but to me I was drawin' a picture: to think those little old hands busted my mouth so much; them little old hands busted my bottom so much; them little old hands whupped me so much; them little old hands made a livin' for me. I thought so many things about them little old hands. If it hadn't been for them little old hands, I wouldn't a been a minister today! Those little old hands brought me so far. (Erma V.)

When one parent is physically punitive, and the other is not, in fact, credit for successful rearing is given to the stricter of the two:

> She was a wonderful mother, but she was *strict* on us. Our daddy wasn't, he'd get out and play with us just as big! And she'd get after him about it: "All right, play with a puppy, he'll lick your mouth." But that daddy, I dunno, sometime he'd scold some of us, speak short to us. Then if he scold one of us and'd [and we'd] break and cry, why, then he's gonna pet him! Him or her. Hug and kiss 'em, y'know, "Hush cryin', now, hush cryin', now, daddy didn't mean it!" and all like that. . . . We had *two* parents, but only *one* of them raised us. She sure raised us; my daddy he didn't. He *fed* us, but she raised us!" (Olive P.)

A view of punishment merited is, on the spiritual level, what illness is on the physical side of man's nature. That is, divine punishment is something you bring on yourself by failure to observe known rules. After the individual has been "saved," strict adherence to the laws of God (as written in the Bible) is required to keep the soul from sin. If the child behaves himself, the parent need not punish; if the individual avoids sin, God will not punish either:

> So many time the Lord get vexed with us when we do things. Like sickness, I would say sometimes is a whup to us, just like whuppin' a child. So many times we have to be taught a lesson, a sickness sometime bring us down to make us serve the Lord's will. Sometime we don't know to say "Thank the Lord," and we don't know how to praise the Lord and

> thank Him for things He did for us. You can invite it in yourself. If you live a real good life for God, it's just like children: if you got good children, you don't have to punish 'em. Sickness and different things comes like a whuppin', a reminder. The Lord would heal all the peoples if they would ask the Lord to heal 'em. But the people, they forget God. (Erma V.)

Like parents, God often resorts to physical means to bring the individual round to His will. When Arnella L. was being called for the ministry, she didn't want to accept, as it is so much work. But:

> Another evangelist minister, she says, "You better say yes, you better open your mouth and say yes. God is gonna knock your brains out. There is work He has got for you to do, and you won't accept it! He's callin' you for a ministry, and you won't accept it and won't open your mouth. You just keep on, you gonna get tired of Him bammin' you and boffin' you and knockin' you, you gonna say yes. . . . You better open your mouth." . . . [So I did], I got tired of 'im knockin' me out. (Arnella L.)

The commandments must be followed, but not all of them seem to be regarded as equally important. The sins of envy and greed seem to be considered far worse than the sins of the flesh. Pre- and extramarital affairs are taken rather lightly, and do not affect the individual's standing in the church. Sexual relationships are thought to be perfectly natural, and, if the spirit is willing, it is generally agreed that the flesh is weak. It should be noted, however, that members of the Pentecostal churches are *very* vehement against such behavior. Not uncommonly, however, their conversion to the church came after years in a life much "in the world." The sin which seems to be considered the worst possible is the use of foul and profane language – informants who are not overly upset at homicide get quite indignant when discussing "cursin'." Several stated that the use of such language is a sure sign that the individual is controlled or even possessed by the Devil.

At any rate, whatever *is* considered to be sinful is to be avoided. When one does sin, amendment can be made by public confession and such testimony may be a part of regular church services. Bodily mortification such as fasting is also practiced by some individuals. It is generally agreed that the life of a Christian, while rewarding, is difficult. As one Baptist minister put it, "Salvation is free, but not cheap, my friends!"

The Punishment of Sin

What happens to the individual who fails to take precautions? Most people agree that he or she is liable to be "struck down." Disobedience to the will of God may result in a "curse" or "affliction" and may take a variety of forms. Such ideas were expressed by members of the Baptist, Methodist,

Pentecostal, and Episcopalian faiths. As in the doctrine of maternal impressions, the unborn child is often the target of punishment. If a pregnant woman sees a deformed individual and laughs, for example, her child may be born with the same affliction, thereby punishing her for her lack of charity. Retardation in children is often explained as divinely inspired, and there is an attempt to see such punishments as a tangible sign of God's love:

> I feel that a lot of things that you do, when you're disobedient to God's will, that a curse or something is put on you . . . sometimes I think it could be in the form of an illness. To really say, sometime I think retarded children is a curse, and that's something you've got to go through for the rest of their life or your life. They say somewhere in the Bible about you can be whipped by many stripes. I think this person has been whipped till he has come to his knowledge of his sins and knowing that he was sinful. Then it make him a better person or made him closer to God. (Lillian A.)

This idea that the punishment will be longlasting to give the sinner time to reflect on the error of his ways is often expressed:

> Here is what can happen if you don't obey the Lord. One time my mother came down here and stayed with me, and she went over there to that church on the corner. Now, my mother never went to school, and she had never in her life taken music. But the Lord anointed her hands, and she played that piano like nobody's business! While she was playin' that music, the people would just fall out under the anointin' of her playin'! And she would not stay here and run a meetin'! She went back home. She had a stroke and laid there nine long years. Lookin' up at me, nine long years. She said to me, "Don't disobey God. When that small voice come to your ears and tell you to do sumpin'." She said, "I'm tellin' you, if Jesus tell you to do sumpin', if that small voice come in your ear, and He keep puttin' it in your mind to do sumpin', you do it. If you don't, you'll be layin' here like I am, under a curse."
>
> See, she was supposed to come back here. If she'd had that meeting, she would of saved many, many a soul down here, but she went back home. She can't obey man, she got to obey God. She felt that she was whupped. So many times when you disobey God, He whup you. He lay you down so you can think these things over. She was so *anointed,* and she turn us away, savin' souls. 'Cause many a soul could of been saved, and them souls is now lost. She could of saved the souls. I mean if we can do sumpin' for God we need to do it, but she didn't. She said to me, "Darlin', don't obey man, obey God." Those nine long years. (Erma V.)

Divine retribution may be the explanation for any occurrence, as a matter of fact, as no happening is random:

> Seem like a lot of times things come through Him like that; lot of times people will be well. And then on down the line somethin' will happen to

> him, sometimes be crippled. And then be out workin' around machinery sometimes, somethin' will explode. Cause him to lose his sight, accidental things. So many different things, for sinnin' all the time. We here in the world sin. Things gonna come upon us, unless we serve Him more. I think if we go away from Him, He might suffer some of these things to happen. (Bertha A.)

All men may be sinners, but not all sins merit such direct punishment; when queried on this point, over and over the same sins are mentioned: greed and pride. Acquisition of material goods and thinking that you are better than your neighbor are not condoned:

> Sometimes seems like you can be very prosperous and just have everything, and then all of a sudden you lose everything. But if you just get too wicked about it, then God'll bring you down to where you can see that. Through losing this, He can bring you back up again, if you have faith in Him. (Lillian A.)

Failure to share what you do have may also bring trouble:

> Well, according to the Bible, He does suffer you to be afflicted. Sometime that's the only way He can bring us down when we are so high up. And then He can remove it, just as quick as it got on you! What I mean by high up, why, some folks when they get a little something, they spendthrifty, you know. And they forget about maybe a neighbor across the street might need something. And they *could* go across and ask did they need anything! Nobody's gonna *beg,* but you could offer your services. You forget about what other people in the world might need. And He can put an affliction on you, and He can remove it just as fast as He puts it on you. (Lizzie L.)

Haughtiness and materialism meriting punishment are perhaps understandable in a neighborhood small enough to permit frequent face-to-face encounters, and one in which there is little difference in income. Punishment of the individual for appearing to think he is better than his neighbor is an effective form of social leveling, a theme which will recur in the discussion of witchcraft.

Not all informants believed that God would punish an individual by sending illness, although most of them did. The few who did disagree, however, did not do so because of disbelief of divine sanctions. The feeling seems to be that God is too good to do something like that – therefore, it could only be the work of the Devil:

> No, I don't think so, I don't think God would make you sick. I don't think that, course my religion is not like everybody's. But I don't believe God would send no sickness. But I know the Devil can put 'flictions on you, the Devil can. I always believe that God would try to take things off of you. Ever' breath we draw is 'cause God let us to live. (Ella T.)

In another instance it was not the *punishment* that was in question, but that it could take the form of illness:

> I ain't gonna put everything on God [very irate]! 'Cause I'm gonna tell you one thing, now listen. Now who said God puts sickness, God can punish you all right for some things, but He don't put anything on you! 'Cause a whole lot of things you brings on yourself! And people ought to quit tryin' to put ever'thing on God!
>
> I tell you now, here the way I look into it. Now God died; give His own life for us, for our sins. Now why'd He wanta turn around and put sumpin' on us? When He gave *His* life, died on the cross for our sins. Well, He made us; you know He taken a rib out Adam and made *us!* And when we all die and leave here, we going back to Mother Dust, that what we made out of, dust. Now how in the world God would come down and put some kind of 'fliction on *you!* People oughta quit tellin' that on God! (Arnella L.)

God can, of course, remove the affliction – but woe betide the sinner who backslides:

> Now I know a man right down here that had cancer. And they prayed for him, and the Lord really healed him. And do you know that he's back drinkin' and gamblin'? I saw him Christmas night, and I said, "You forget that good God that healed your body." This is why the Lord doesn't heal ever'body. He said, "Go in peace and sin no more unless a worser thing come upon you." Because when it come, it liable to be worser. It could be worser. I believe you can work it so that He get vexed. It's a bad thing to be whupped under a angry God. (Erma V.)

Those who do believe that God punishes also believe that the Devil may enter the picture. When the individual's behavior is considered particularly vile, it is considered that God simply steps back and lets the Devil take over:

> You should say thank God for a normal healthy baby. Because truly many many people don't have healthy children, they have abnormal children. There's a man out here had three children, and all of 'ems was deformed. 'Cause the Devil tries to afflict you with this; I dis-remember where you find it in the Bible. Sometimes people are raised up with pride so much that sometimes the Lord takes this to bring you down. When you're proud or not livin' for the Lord, [if] you get too proud, then God steps out of the way and let the Devil take over. The Devil causes these things. Then God can fix 'em. See, the Devil has never got dominion over you. He have dominion over you providin' God let him *have* dominion. God have to *let* him have dominion. (Erma V.)

Nothing can be more terrifying, of course, than abandonment by God, and if the Devil takes over the problem is no longer natural but unnatural. The ultimate is demonic possession, with the victim's body thought actually inhabited by an evil spirit. The influence of satanic forces is believed responsible for many mental disorders. "Many, many people are in the State Mental Hospital who the doctors are unable to cure," said a visiting evangelist at a Baptist revival one night. Their sickness is "the sickness of sin," and "medicine will not reach the mind nor a sin-diseased heart."

Symptoms of such illness are said to take the form of profane language which is why this so disturbs the God-fearing:

> Wrong doin', that's a demon tells 'em. Sometimes they are talkin' silly talk. Then some is radical, like cursin', you know, and sayin', "I don't believe in no God," and this and that. Ever'thing they wanna do, they wanta hurt somebody or harm somebody. (Mother D.)

Just as some natural illnesses are treated by driving the causal factors out of the body, supernaturally-caused illnesses are treated by driving the causal factor (sin) out of the soul. This is done by virtue of prayer and faith in God. Some afflictions may be cured by prayer alone – by turning, as Lewis W. says, to "Doctor Jesus." If one's faith is great enough, the illness may be lifted by divine intercession alone.

Another man told of the terrible behavior of his youth: he drank, fought, gambled, and had no regard for anyone. Finally, he was struck down by illness. His behavior had been so terrible that he had neither family nor friends willing to care for him. He was placed in an empty shed to die. He saw that he was entirely alone, and that he would die without a miracle. He began to pray, promising God that if he were cured, he would devote the rest of his life to His service. In a few days, he felt better and was soon well. He became a Pentecostal minister and is now famous for his preaching. Faith in God, in fact, is probably the single most important ingredient in the search for a cure.

UNNATURAL ILLNESSES: CONFLICT AND CONTROL

Man as a child of nature risks exposure to the elements. Man as a child of God risks divine punishment for transgression. But it is man the social animal who is in the greatest jeopardy, as all personal relationships are potentially dangerous. Human nature is seen as basically exploitative, and it is therefore natural for people to take advantage of others for personal gain. A survey (Rainwater 1970:69) in a federal slum housing project in St. Louis, for example, revealed that 91% of respondents agreed with the statement, "It's not good to let your friends know everything about your life, because they may take advantage of you." Nearly 70% agreed that it was unwise to trust your own relatives for the same reason. This distrust of others contributes to a view of life as a constant hustle in which an individual had *better* learn "to go for himself" as certainly others, even significant others, will not.

A third major category of illnesses may therefore be seen in the context of the individual's interactions with others in his daily life. Some of these illnesses are caused by the annoyances and worries of daily living. Others are the result of direct magical attack in the form of witchcraft. Both are considered "unnatural." They are not believed to be amenable to treatment by physicians and thus are a source of deep concern.

Worry as a Cause of Illness

Most people agree that the stresses and strains of everyday life can cause one to fall ill. Concerns over money matters are frequently mentioned in this context, which is not surprising in a group where the average income is so low:

> Peoples sit down and worry sick. Do you know some peoples worries theirselves sick? Because, "My bill, if I could pay my bill! I used to have this, and I don't now. Don't know what I'm gonna do, I can't do this." I mean worries, nervousness. Peoples have lost their mind. Right, this'll kill you. You can worry yourself to death. Over your bills and over your money. (Erma V.)

According to Mother D., a very successful Voodoo practitioner, many of her patients come to her suffering from "nervousness," and money is often the cause. These problems she describes as "mental," and considers them to be unnatural:

> . . . A person that's sick in mind, mentally sick, doctors can't find *that*. They X-ray, and they can't find it. They say, "Well, I don't see nothin'; there's nothin' wrong." And yet they *sick!* Mentally sick, sick in mind. It's a believing, you know. You can believe *hard* on something, it just come to you. I think that's the way people go *crazy!* They believe one thing too strong, and next thing you know, they flipped their wig, and they in the insane asylum. But I get people with all kinds of feeling, like some of 'em says, "I can't sleep, I can't sleep. . . . Mother why I can't sleep?" . . . They're *sick,* they're thinkin' too hard about somethin'. Their bills are worryin' them.
>
> You know how times is. Things is changed 'n everything is high. Some people get such a small wage, don't make much money, they can't make ends meet. And then it come to them when they stop still, you know. Like they'll lie down, and they get to thinkin' and it get into the mind. They're so weak, they can't throw it off. Well, next thing you know, it's daylight! (Mother D.)

Even more commonly, people are anxious in their dealings with others: husbands run around, wives nag, fathers desert children, children talk back.

People feel that they have little control over their own lives, let alone the lives of their loved ones. Thus Louis W. differentiates between "trouble" and "worry" – trouble you know what to do about, but worry is another matter:

> Seems like worry is worse than trouble. *Trouble* is when you've killed a man, and you're shuckin' through the woods tryin' to keep away from the law. You know if the law catches you, you'll get the electric chair. That's trouble.
>
> But – worry is when you're fussin' with somebody you love. Maybe it's your wife; maybe it's a brother or sister. But I'll tell you, dear, seems like you can't eat, and you can't sleep at night. No matter *what* you do, you can't forget about it. Can't get it off your mind. That's why I say that worry is worse than trouble. (Louis W.)

One's own relatives are considered more important than spouses or in-laws. A number of informants overtly stated that husbands or wives came second to parents:

> ". . . You seldom find one that really loves any woman! If they marry one, ain't gonna treat her right. I wasn't with him a bit over three years, if it was that much, before I just quit and went on back to my mama! I've had people to tell me I didn't love no man, said I had hydrant love. Said I had hydrant love, *electric* love, said I could turn it *off* and *on!* And I guess they's about right! I thought more of my mother and daddy than I did any man! (Olive P.)

The theme of hostility between the sexes reappears, and domestic strife often leads to violence. For Erma V., the discord which she saw in her mother's relationships with men as a child marred each of her own marriages:

> Mens bore me. Even my brothers. I can stand 'em so long, and after so long I get sick of 'em. My mother was treated so bad by mens, you know. And I always said when I was a little girl, "If I live, I'll never let a man whup me." And I married two mens, and I whupped *them!* I tore 'em up. That last man, I married him and stayed with 'im a month, then whupped 'im real good! I never saw 'im no more. I whupped 'im one night and opened that door and throwed 'im out. I whupped both my husbands! My stepdaddies would fight my mother. I declared for my mother, you know, that I'd never let a man whup me. I would *die* before I would let a man whup me. I meant that. And I didn't *let* no man whup me! (Erma V.)

Expectations of marriage are low and many women see men as untrustworthy exploiters of female labor:

> Mens always like to ride on a woman who's got somethin'. A woman's got a bunch of kids and a ol' farm or somethin', he knows she's gonna

> make some money or somethin' like that. And he just lay around. And it makes me sick to see a man layin' around a woman when she got kids, call hisself tryin' to court her. I think of my family, the same thing. My stepdaddy, he think, "Well, this here is a bowl, and I'll just fall right in this bowl of salad and just sit right here and eat, and I won't have to worry." (Erma V.)

Women expect men to drink, to gamble, and to desert family responsibilities when they become too onerous. Lillian A. was pregnant when her husband left her for another woman. She was not surprised. It was the sort of thing that men are apt to do, and she considered her marriage to be average:

> It was just a average thing, I guess. Just come out here and got with a wild bunch and just started chasin' around and runnin' around. Finally he left, and I felt like I was better off. To me, if you were going to live together and had to live that kind of life, it wasn't very happy for me. And after he left, I just considered it a blessing. . . . I just put my trust in God, and we just made it through somehow! But it wasn't easy. (Lillian A.)

Men, on the other hand, often view women as interested in their money-making potential, a charge which is also borne out upon occasion. Certainly, love may be less a factor than convenience. Erma V., for example, had been working as a domestic for three years. One of her more unpleasant tasks was the daily washing and ironing of the shirts worn by her employer's husband and several male boarders. She met a man, and after seeing him twice decided to marry him. As she tells it:

> Well, it's just like this: one time a man was out in a windstorm. It was just a windin', his arms was just wearin' out around a tree, trying to hold on, keep the wind from blowin' him away. He said, "I wisht there would come a earthquake!" And this other man said, "A earthquake! You don't want a earthquake!" And the first man said, "Anything for a change." And that's what I wanted, just something for a change. Better than six shirts a day, 'cause he only had one. That's why I got married to him; there wasn't that much love. I married for convenience. That's why I got this man, I didn't love him. Just anything for a change! (Erma V.)

Lana N., the divorced mother of nine, is also looking for a new husband. "A good man," she says, "someone to help with my bills." Alma U. is currently planning to marry a man she has not seen in 16 years. She sent him a Christmas card because she remembers him as a good man, and she is tired of working and having the responsibility of four children:

> I'm really tired of it, and in all the letters, he say to me he would be willin' to accept me or whatever children I had. He has a son, and he say he wouldn't be marryin' me to baby-sit his son. He wasn't married

> to *her,* but evidently they had this baby, and she gave him this child when it was seven months old. He says he hasn't even heard from her in about eight years. He has a son and his mother. He *have* to be a decent man, to care for his mother and a son. (Alma U.)

If marital relationships are often brittle, turmoil between parent and child and among siblings is common as well. When Louise R. was 14 her mother died, and Louise was sent to live with her father, whom she had not seen for years. They did not get along well, and one day he became angry at her for an impertinent remark, beat her, and told her she had until sundown to leave. She was to go to the home of an aunt in another town, a woman described by Louise as a prostitute. Her father handed her a dollar bill, her grandmother found another dollar for her, and an aunt managed to slip her 50 cents. She packed her few belongings and was put out of the house; her aunt and grandmother were not allowed to accompany her to the bus. All the neighborhood children tagged along, however, and one teenage boy walked beside her and gave her some advice which she has never forgotten: "I know you're hurtin' inside," he said, "but don't cry. Don't let him know you're hurtin'; don't let him see you cry. Someday you will be a lady. Just walk straight and be a lady now." So she walked down to the station and got on the bus. She never saw her father again. When Henry J. was nine years old his mother died and his father deserted him. Although he had several older brothers and sisters in the vicinity, none were willing to take responsibility for him. He was left to fend for himself and was allowed to live in a woodshed by a white family in return for chopping wood and other chores. Many years later Henry learned that his father had died, so he quit his job to go back home for the funeral. When I commented to Anna P. that I certainly would not attend the funeral of a man who had deserted me as a small child, she said "The Bible says 'Honor thy father and thy mother'," adding rather ominously, "and you'll live longer."

A theme common to much intra-familial strife is differential treatment of children based on variations in skin color and hair form. "Good" (i.e., light) skin and "good" hair (wavy or straight, not kinky) are valued by many parents, and the darker child may be treated with less favor. Lana N. describes the races of mankind as "God's bouquet," and explains that God did not intend discrimination based on color:

> When God create the Garden of Eden, He made beautiful animals, all colors; beautiful flowers, all colors; vegetables, all colors; fruits, all colors; people all colors. So this earth was a garden or paradise for man to work and enjoy and worship Him. Nothing wrong with all colors of people, it make the garden or world beautiful. If everyone was the same color, we would get tired of each color, so I am glad I am black. I like my color. I thank God for being able to live in His beautiful world; I like all people. In each race of people, bad and good. In each animal

> race, bad and good. So we must love everyone, hate no one regardless of the color of skin. Because every man or woman was made from Adam. We are all God's children. (Lana N.)

The skin color of a child may be used by a father who wishes to disavow paternity. This happened to Marcie T. when she became pregnant; her boy friend put off marriage until he saw the infant. When the child was born, he took one look and said, "That ain't no son of mine, he's too dark." After making this pronouncement, he disappeared and left Marcie to rear her child alone. Arguments over the skin color of the children led to violence in Erma V.'s family:

> My mother shot my daddy one time; I think I was three years old. We were in a buggy, but what it was about I really don't know, 'cause I was too little. And he told her, "Oh, you don't have sense enough to shoot me," and she just drawed that trigger and shot. And they was pickin' shots out of his hip for a long time. I guess he was just like all other mens. By mother bein' brown and my daddy bein' black. My daddy was real black, with curly hair. But one time he said wasn't none of the brown kids his, only the black ones was his. She told him, "They have a mother, and they have another blood stream than just one." But see, he didn't know no better, he was a ignorant man. He wasn't learned. If you're ignorant and unlearned, you don't know no better. So they fought quite a bit. (Erma V.)

It is against this background of ambivalence, distrust, and outright hostility that the most dreaded cause of illness may be best understood. Witchcraft is based on the premise that there are people with the ability to mobilize unusual powers, and who may use these powers to manipulate events. It is feared that such powers may be used to cause the loss of a job, the desertion of a spouse, the perfidy of a sweetheart, or to control one's own behavior in undesirable ways. Such "unnatural" powers do not follow God's laws and are therefore seen as being diabolically inspired. The terms "black magic," "rootwork," "conjuring," and "Voodoo" or "Hoodoo" are used interchangeably with witchcraft in descriptions of such activity. A "charm," a "hand," a "toby," or a "mojo" may be used to bring about the desired result. When the result is illness or bad luck, the individual is said to suffer from a "fix," a "hex," be "crossed up," or in a "crossed condition."

Voodoo

As informants most often categorize witchcraft behavior as Voodoo, a brief discussion is in order. The word itself is a corruption of a West African word for god or spirit (Metraux 1959: 27). When slaves were brought to the West Indies from Dahomey, religious beliefs were transplanted as well. Slaves in the French-owned islands were required by law to be baptized in the Roman Catholic religion. True Haitian Voodoo today is a folk religion, a syncretism of African and European beliefs. From the islands of the Indies, slaves were brought to America by their Creole masters. An attenuated form of Voodoo exists among American Blacks, and is said to be particularly strong in New Orleans. Several informants who mention Voodoo say that it originated in Louisiana, a notion reinforced by an old blues song (Oliver 1960: 162):

> You know they tell me in Louisiana there is
> hoodoos all over there, (twice)
> You know they'll do anything for their
> money, murder
> anyone I declare.
> Now Miss Hoodoo Lady, please give me a hoodoo
> hand, (twice)
> I want to hoodoo this woman of mine, I
> believe she's got another man.

The word "witch" was never used by an informant. Instead, the evildoer was always vaguely categorized as "somebody" or "people like that," or "people who know how to do that kind of thing." The act itself was usually described in vague terms as well: "puttin' sumpin' on," "putting a fix," "throwing something," and so on. Like everything else in the study, the belief in witchcraft was rationalized by some because of biblical references; according to Anna P., the word Voodoo itself is found in the Bible.

> I'm trying to think who was this in the Bible called for this woman to do this witchcraft, it's in the Bible. It's biblical. Call for 'em to call up the dead, and they would talk with the dead. All this is witchcraft. All of this is true, these wizards and this witchcraft. They got power, but God got all power. Most peoples has got this power have been saved, and the Devil steals they mind. Like some of these peoples was dancin' in the nude in the church, and havin' drinks in the church. This happened in California in a Methodist church. Well, I got all these books here, and that's *Satanic!* All of this is nothin' but witchcraft. (Erma V.)

Arnella L. says that the Devil may cause the misuse of the Bible to evil effect:

> Well, you know the Bible speaks of witchcraft. If the people know what they're doin', with the Bible, some of 'em will take the Bible and try to do somethin' to you with it. It was told to me that you could take the Bible, certain Scriptures in the Bible, kill you with it. I ain't never found out what Scripture it is, 'cause you know, I ain't interested in it. See, when I hear people talk about all that old crap, I stays my distance from 'em. See, I don't mingle with the world. Because if they talk like that, I figure they're not right. And I don't have nothin' to do with 'em, 'cause if people see you associatin' with that person, they say you doin' the same thing. That's why I don't fool with 'em. They say Capitol City is broke out with it! A woman tole me, she went up there, "Honey,

> I wouldn't stay in Capitol City!" I asked her why. "Honey, you talk about old witchcrafts, that's all you hear up there is witchcraft!" (Arnella L.)

Only two informants flatly denied any belief in witchcraft. Others, while not having firsthand knowledge of such doings, did not wish to categorically deny the possibility.

> Well, I haven't seed it, but I have heard that people can do such things. They say, "Don't fool yourself, they can." But you know, I've been here this long in the world, and I haven't run into nothin' like that yet. So I wouldn't know about that. But you hear people say it; they discuss it. (Bertha A.)

Wilson E. and his friends reported that there was a lot of that sort of thing "back home" in the South. The belief of some is selective:

> I heard that when I was a child; people comin' to your door and sprinkling things all around your door, and if you walk over it . . . but I never was a believer. I don't know, my family wasn't, and they were born in Louisiana where they say this all originated. But they didn't believe in it, which I guess made me not believe in it. But I seen some very strong believers of it. But I just never have believed in it. I feel like I could walk over everything they put outside, and it wouldn't hurt me. Onliest way I think they can make you sick, if they get something in you. Like give you something to drink or something to eat, and put some medicine or something like poison in you. (Lillian A.)

The term "poison," in fact, is sometimes used synonymously with witchcraft, and the fear of adulterated food or drink is a recurring motif. This is present in the following passage, which also indicates that *denial* of witchcraft may be as illustrative of fear as much as disbelief:

> I don't talk about witchcraft! I don't know nothin' about it, and I don't let people come and put that kind of junk on me. I don't believe nothin' about no witchcraft, I don't believe nothin' like that! I don't believe unless nobody can't get nothin' in your stomach, you're all right. If you drink water, if you get it in your stomach, you'll get sick. And I don't believe in no witchcraft! We don't think about no witchcraft, and I don't have nothin' like that in my home, and I don't talk about no witchcraft. And when people go to talkin' about all that old junk, I say they minds is crazy. And I don't believe nobody can do nothin' to you unless they get sumpin' in your stomach. You eat somethin' somebody got poison in, that's one thing if you get ahold of some. I don't know, I don't believe in witchcraft. I don't believe nobody can throw spells. . . . I don't even let nobody talk to me about it. I don't want to get my mind confused with that. (Ella T.)

The informant was so distressed that the subject was dropped at once.

The idea that someone who has power given by the Devil may be trying to harm an individual is unsettling enough, of course, but a further reason that witchcraft-caused illnesses are greatly feared is that they are not thought treatable by ordinary means – in fact, the more you go to the doctor the sicker you become:

> Well, I'll tell you what, now, when a person goes to usin' this witchcraft stuff, the doctor's can't do it no good. Ain't nothin' the doctor can do for you. The more you go to the doctor, the worse it's gonna get on you. 'Cause the doctor'll tell you quick, "You got somepin; I can't do nothin' with you." You'd have to try to find out who could cure you! But findin' it out, that's the thing! You might not know who to go to, who knows how to take it off of you! That's the way I look into it. (Arnella L.)

Mother D., who has a reputation for being able to cure illnesses caused by witchcraft, has many people come to her with such fears:

> They thinkin' evil. "Mary come to my house early in the mornin', and Mother, she came in and she looked real suspicious, looked funny, and she wanted to use my bathroom. Do you think that she come to put some bad luck on me? She wanted to use my bathroom, do you think she wanted to put something in my house that cause me to be worried? I took a headache after she left." I hear a lot of that, suspicious talk. (Mother D.)

To turn our attention to those persons who *do* believe in witchcraft, several questions must be answered. How is it done, to whom and by whom, and why?

The Techniques of Witchcraft

Witchcraft procedures reported by informants may be divided into several categories, imitative or contagious magic, the use of verbal and mental spells, and the use of poisons.

The belief that you may destroy a victim by destroying his image (imitative magic) is found worldwide, and the following anecdotes are examples of such practices:

> Tom tell me now, he's had somebody to make somebody sick. He had the peoples to steal some of the peoples clothes off of the line, and make a doll and put some of the clothes in the doll. And take this doll and whatever you want 'em sick at, you take some pins, put some pins wherever you want the pain. I said, "Is this true?" But I was talkin' to another man, a minister, and he said, "Yes, this is true." (Erma V.)

In some cases technology has provided the wherewithal for magical innovation. The use of the camera can provide a ready-made image of the intended victim. Alma U. had been backsliding from the church, but finally started going again. One night she and Arnella L. went to a revival at one of the Pentecostal churches. Members of the congregation put items of personal jewelry on the altar rail, and the evangelist used them to tell the owner something personal. Alma had put her watch on the altar rail. The evangelist picked it up, looked directly at her, and told her that she would be dead now if she had not come back to God. After the meeting she asked Arnella if she remembered the previous summer when she had been so sick – she was feeling "poorly," steadily losing weight and unable to work at her usual job as a practical nurse. One day she was in her backyard doing some gardening and happened to dig up a snapshot of herself, buried face down on one of her undergarments. On the back of the snapshot was written the day that she was to die. The spell was broken when she found the charm, but she was so frightened that she not only started attending her regular church again, but also a Spiritualist temple where training is given in avoiding witchcraft.

The use of contagious magic is also prominent so that there may be anxiety about the proper disposal of hair, nail parings, and the like. Anna P. has never had her hair done in a beauty salon, lest her hair clippings fall into the wrong hands. She notes, however, that the more intimate the connection between the substance used and the intended victim, the stronger would be the charm. The most dangerous of all are the secretions of sexual intercourse and menstrual blood. Clara S., in fact, always burns used menstrual pads because she has heard that they could be used to turn her into a snake. (The fear of being turned into an animal is paralleled by notions that animals may be magically introduced into the body, or that the individual may be forced to behave like an animal – nothing is more "unnatural," of course, than a human being who harbors, behaves as, or *becomes* an animal!)

Unlike the methods described above, spells do not utilize substances. Recitation of a verbal formula or thought of the deed alone is enough to do injury. In only three cases did an informant mention witchcraft by spell. Jim S. (age 35) says that he does not really know if witchcraft is possible or not. But he does not want to come right out and say it is *not* possible either. When he was a teenager, he often ran errands for an old woman whose legs were paralyzed. It was told that one day her phone rang and when she answered, a voice told her that she would never walk again. She never did. This story made a powerful impression on Jim, and he does not believe in taking chances. Mother D., although disavowing any real knowledge of the technique, says that:

> A lot of people, they feel like that somebody can cast spells upon them. Now there is some people, I go according to the Scriptures, there is some people that are wrong-doers, that don't believe in God, period. You know what I mean. Put it this way, they don't believe in *right!* Evil all the time. Well, I guess they could hold a thought, something like that. (Mother D.)

Finally, the use of poisonous powders or like substances may be used to effect the desired result. Three different uses were described by informants: sprinkling the substance around the doorstep, putting it in food or drink, and sprinkling the substance on sanitary napkins. In food or drink, of course, the substance enters the body. In the other instances, proximity to the victim alone is enough to produce the desired result.

Four informants mentioned the sprinkling of substances around the doorstep. The idea is that either the intended victim will walk over the substance and thus be injured, or, be *unable* to walk over it and thus be prevented from entering the home. Salt and pepper, presumably magically endowed, were mentioned as having the effect of repelling unwanted visitors.

"Doctoring" food or drink was the most commonly mentioned mode of sorcery (10 informants). Like the sprinkling of substances around the doorstep, different effects can be obtained. Of the 12 instances mentioned, one was a love charm, and the remainder were used to injure or kill. For those persons who believe in witchcraft practiced by this means, then, illness can be a time of special anxiety. When an individual falls ill, it is expected that friends and neighbors will bring food to the household. To refuse to eat the food would be tantamount to an accusation of witchcraft. To eat it, on the other hand, means taking the risk that you may be ingesting poisoned victuals.

Henry J. has solved the problem of accepting food by having nothing to do with his neighbors. He is sick a lot, he says, and if he *did* associate with people, they would be bringing him food all the time. Then he would worry about whether people were trying to make him sicker by "cookin'." This way he is lonely, but he doesn't have to worry about witchcraft.

Anna P. once knew a pretty young girl whose husband left her for an extremely ugly woman. This was considered to be unnatural behavior. It was decided that the ugly woman must have put something in his coffee to lure him from his more attractive wife. Here the idea of *control* is implicit, the feeling that someone may do something to make you behave in a way which you would not ordinarily do. If it is feared that a loved one may be lured away by a magical practice, however, this is somewhat offset by the belief that magical practices can also be used to *keep* someone from leaving:

> Well, I've heard people can take your clothes, take your menstruating [pads], or anything that you wear on your body. I heard that they could put stuff in your food, or they could come to your house and put something down for you. Yeah, I hear talk of it. Yeah, I hear about a few people, someone have control of 'em. They *do* act rather peculiar, they doesn't act normal or sensible. Well, for instance, I've heard of men fixin' their wives, and wives fixin' their husbands, stuff like that, you know. Well, if this *happen* to you, they say you would be the last person to suspect. Anyone could tell you, and you wouldn't believe it. Well

> [lowers voice], I don't know why, but I hate the thought of a person takin' control of you if they want to. (Cassie S.)

The belief is widespread that animals can be introduced into the body in food or drink. Most commonly mentioned are snakes, lizards, and toads. The eggs may be used, resulting in the presence of tadpoles in the blood or baby snakes in the stomach. Alternatively, the animal may be dried and pulverized, sprinkled in food, and then magically reconstituted in the body of the victim. Frank L. reports that a baby octopus once had to be removed from his bladder. He had been having a few drinks with another man's girl friend, and the jealous man retaliated by putting a dried octopus egg in his beer at the first opportunity.

Though most informants agree that it is possible to be made ill or killed by something put into the food, they do not agree as to the properties of the substance used. Some feel that it is simply poison; that is, it would kill anyone who ate it. Others feel that the substance will kill *only* the person for whom it was intended – anyone else could consume the adulterated food or drink with impunity. Erma V.'s grandmother was poisoned by food which harmed no one else who ate it.

> My grandmother died when I was five. . . . My grandmother went on a vacation, went down to see her sisters and brothers. And while she was down there, my great-aunt poisoned her. She ate somethin' that poisoned her system; before they could get her to the doctor, she was dead. Whatever it was she ate, it didn't kill anybody else. They think she did it on purpose, because she didn't like my grandmother. (Erma V.)

Anna P. says that poisoned food will harm only the person for whom it is intended, and tells the following story: once when they were living in Kansas, the family attended a church supper. The plates were handed to each person already filled with food. As they sat down to eat, Anna's son, Norman, who was then a small boy, decided on a childish impulse to trade plates with his mother. As the plates were switched, the cook rushed over to demand why this had been done. Anna saw this as clear proof that the plate intended for her had been poisoned, and the cook no doubt saw it as a blatant accusation of witchcraft.

Another type of poisoning mentioned occurs where the magical substance gets into or near the body by means other than ingestion. Anna's young daughter was killed by means of a powder sprinkled on a sanitary napkin. Her mother tells how it happened: Lila was young and very pretty, she had light skin and good hair. She had a devoted husband and a home which she kept "like a doll's house." Her female in-laws, however, were very jealous of her. She was planning an anniversary party and intended to invite the women even though they did not like her. A week before the party, her mother had the following dream, which was seen as a portent of the tragedy to come: the three women who were her daughter's in-laws were standing before her. One of them handed something to her. It was small, black, furry, and alive – "Somethin' like a black chick." She immediately knew that it was something evil, dropped it, and awoke with a scream. She shook her husband awake and told him that there would be trouble in their family. She telephoned her daughter at once, telling her not to invite the women to her party. Lila replied that the Bible says to forgive and invited them. On the day of the party, her sister walked into a bedroom and saw one of the women sprinkling some kind of powder into a box of sanitary napkins. Sachet, she said quickly, something to make them smell nice. Two weeks later the girl was dead. Though her daughter told her that the Bible says to forgive, Anna says that it *also* says, "Watch as well as pray." Although Anna never doubted that her daughter had been the victim of witchcraft, the fact that the women suspected were all from Louisiana was the final proof she needed. She also recalls that the mother-in-law had once offered to comb *her* hair for her, sure sign, in retrospect, of malignant intentions.

Symptoms of Witchcraft

How is the diagnosis of witchcraft made? Although there are few symptoms which may be exclusively attributed to witchcraft, the diagnosis seems usually to be based on the presence of "unnatural" symptoms, or because there can be found no other explanation for the illness.

Some symptoms are considered unnatural in themselves. Pearlie M. knew a man who, after bewitchment, "howled like a dog till he died." When Anna's daughter Lila died, ". . . her face was black, and she was foaming at the mouth and down over her clothes." In sudden deaths, the presence of such froth on the lips of a corpse is said to be a sign that the individual died without divulging something they had wished to say (Hurston 1935). The unexpected death of a person thought to be in good health may also be attributed to witchcraft.

With the interest in poisons and the widespread fear of something being put into the food, it is not surprising that various stomach ailments are interpreted as being the result of witchcraft. Such symptoms may include a bad taste in the mouth, abdominal pains, nausea, or lack of appetite. Often mentioned was unexplained weight loss, or "falling off," because it is not natural to lose weight when you are consuming the usual amount of food. Delia J. had a friend who died of mysterious causes. She had called Delia one day and asked if she believed that people could "fix" you. Delia said that she didn't know. Her friend had been sick and the doctors could not seem to find anything wrong. So she consulted a woman who told her she had been fixed by something put into her liquor. She "fell off" until she was skin and bones, says Delia, except for her face, which stayed the normal size. This unusual symptom was considered proof that the illness had be an unnatural one. Lillian A.'s cousin also felt that she had been fixed, because she always had a bad taste in her mouth and her food didn't taste right to her. She consulted Mother D., who gave her a tonic and a talk, and the symptoms ceased.

The sensation of something crawling over the skin or wriggling around in the stomach may be interpreted as the presence of animals in the body:

> I've heard of people with snakes in their body; how they got in there, I don't know. And they take 'em someplace to a witch doctor, and snakes come out. My sister, she had somethin', a snake that was in her arm. She was a young woman. I can remember her bein' sick, very sick, and someone told her about this healer in another little town. And I do know they taken her there. This thing was just runnin' up her arm. You could actually *see* it. And we would have to hold her in the bed. And someone told her about this healer, and my parents did take her there. And this actually came out of her arm. You could actually see it when she would go into one of her spells; it was in her left arm. Some woman they said didn't like her [had done it]. (Cassie S.)

Anyone who behaves in a fashion seen as "crazy" may also be seen as a possible victim of witchcraft if their actions are strikingly different from their normal behavior. Behavior symptomatic of psychosis is therefore never considered amenable to treatment by physicians, as it is seen as either the punishment for sin or the result of witchcraft.

On the other hand, the diagnosis of witchcraft seems to be made at times simply because there is no other explanation. There is little understanding of chronic disease, and it is generally considered that every illness ought to be curable in a relatively short time. Many informants reported that they expect alleviation of symptoms within two or three days after the inception of treatment. This is true both for home remedies and those of the professional practitioner. Illnesses considered chronic by physicians, e.g., diabetes or hypertension, are considered curable if the proper means is found. Lack of a cure may therefore reflect failure to try the right medicine, find the right doctor, a lack of faith, or something more ominous. If an illness has gone on for some time, therefore, and the sufferer has tried everything, then witchcraft may be the final diagnosis. A neighbor of Pearlie M. had been sick for three years without getting much better. She had been to a number of doctors, none of whom had been able to help her. After that length of time, she said to Pearlie, "One thing certain – this ain't no natural illness."

Responsibility for Witchcraft

In any group in which it is believed that witchcraft is possible, it is instructive to establish which persons are thought responsible for such deeds. Everywhere you go, says Anna P., there is someone who knows how to you," and someone who knows how to take them back off erally agreed that these powers do not rest in the same indi- gh the curer of witchcraft may be greatly feared as well. There actitioner of good and a practitioner of evil. Utilization of such present in the community rests on the continued interest in of their special powers.

r (1969: 37) has described the witch as ". . . the antithesis of the kind of person we like our neighbors to be." Although not called witches, there are people in the Neighborhood who are talked of as being especially difficult to get along with. Such people are the ones who might be suspected of evil powers. Willa J. is such a person. Ella T. (who so vehemently denies her belief in witchcraft) formerly lived in the same building and actually moved out of the Neighborhood because she was afraid of her. On one occasion Willa threw a dead cat on Arnella L.'s front porch—more accurately, Arnella *says* that it was Willa; she did not see her do it. Arnella is now wanting to sell *her* house, so that she can leave the Neighborhood.

The one behavioral trait that marks Willa and other such persons is unpredictability. At times, say the neighbors, she is perfectly friendly and speaks politely. The next time they see her, she may not speak at all or, worse still, may abuse them verbally:

> The Devil's busy, I don't care what you do. I went by a woman's house on Tuesday, comin' in. . . . And that woman standin' there, honey, she cussed me like a dog. Aw, honey, she cussed awhile out there! I just walked off and came on in the house 'cause I didn't want to hear her, see. I just leave that to her ignorance. But honey, she got out there, and she cussed me awhile! She's just hellish! See, she thinks she can do everybody like that. But I don't want to hit her, 'cause she's a sick woman, she's got heart trouble. I don't want to hit her, 'cause if I hit her, I might kill her. But you know, you get tired of takin' that. She's been doin' me that way for the past four months. I don't know what's wrong with her. So I just goes ahead on, I says, "Well, they talkin about the Devil, the Devil is sure busy." She's nothin' else but a hellion! Look like she's tryin' to make me hit her or something! But I says, "Aw, no, she ain't worth my goin' to prison for." (Arnella L.)

The use of foul and abusive language as a symptom of wrong-doing has been mentioned elsewhere. Religious people see it as a sure sign of the sinner. It may be considered, in fact, as a symptom of demonic possession. The person who habitually uses such language, therefore, is thought capable of *any* sort of deed. In a group with such strong fundamentalist Christian beliefs, it is not surprising that the practitioner of witchcraft (or one who would purchase such practices) is seen as the personification of evil and equated with the Devil. Any sort of unusual behavior may be suspect as well:

> And just like I say, Snow, I'm scared to say anything to these people! I'm scared to go around 'em. Now I was up at the store Monday. Woman walked in, old bright [light skin color] lady. She stays down here on Gerard Street. Just show you how people do you when you're not botherin' 'em! I'm standin' there by the soda water box, waitin' for my niece to get through shoppin'. This old woman walked in, just stood there and rolled her eyes at me. I says, I better watch this old sister, 'cause the way she's lookin' at me, she's liable to take me for somebody else, and haul off and hit me with sumpin', you know! She rolled her eyes at me, I kept awatchin' her. Kept lookin' at her roll her eyes at me. At last I said, "Lady, what have I did to you? Why are you rollin' your eyes at me? Have I did anything to you? Or misuse you in any kind of way? If I have, I would like for you to tell me! 'Cause I don't like for anyone to stand and roll their eyes at me like they're gonna cut me in two! I want to know what have I did to you!"
>
> "Oh, fuck ya!" I say, *"What?!"* That's the way she answered me! I says, "Don't you cuss me, 'cause I'd knock the fire from you!" And I run at her. And she hit that door, and she went out of that door.
>
> My niece says, "What's the matter with that woman?" I says, "Child, I don't know!" She says, "Why didn't you pick up a bottle and knock her out with it?" I says, "Aw, she ain't worth my gettin' trouble for."
>
> And I tell you, people now is got you crazy, you scared to go to the store, you scared to go anywhere. Scared you liable to get cussed out, you scared you liable to get hit. You don't know what's goin' on! I'm absolutely almost scared to speak to people. (Arnella L.)

The Reasons for Witchcraft

Given malevolent people and persons from whom they are able to purchase the wherewithal to work mischief, what is considered likely to bring on such actions? Two common reasons given are based on envy and sexual conflict.

The possession of anything which another person might want is considered to put the individual in a precarious position vis-à-vis others. A pretty face, a nice house, a new car, good clothes – any of these might strike envy in the heart of the beholder. Some people are just that way, says Anna P., "Just put on a few little clothes, and they get begrudged-hearted." They may not even know you. When I accepted a teaching position in another state, therefore, Anna wrote to warn me about going to social occasions and thoughtlessly accepting refreshments:

> Witchcraft is real, it can be did; you can be hypnotized. You hafta be careful where you eat and drink. Parties is not good. You know some

> ladies is looking at that man of yours. You is new there, so don't be so fast in going to parties and eating and drinking, it isn't good. (Anna P.)

That envy is commonly considered a cause for witchcraft is demonstrated rather obliquely by Pearlie's reaction to her neighbor's fear of witchcraft. When the woman confided that she was afraid her illness was not a natural one, Pearlie retaliated, "Well, I don't know why you think it's witchcraft – you're too old and ugly for anybody to be jealous of you!"

When the discussion changes from the general to the particular, however, the wrongdoer is nearly always considered to be someone from the victim's immediate social milieu: the women accused of killing Lila C. were her in-laws, and it was reported that her own husband, at their behest, refused to get help for his wife until it was too late. Alma U. does not know who took the snapshot which was used against her, but it was someone with entry to her home. A substance administered to you in your food or drink requires that someone have access to it. Frank L. says that the dried octopus egg was put into his beer when he was drinking with his usual circle of friends. And if harm is worked by use of one of the most powerful substances of all, sexual secretions, the party accused is husband or lover, mistress or wife.

Since people whose success is demonstrated by the acquisition of material goods are thought to be in danger of witchcraft, the fear of such retaliation may serve as an economic leveler. Lily M. and Lizzie L., the two women who disclaimed belief in witchcraft, attributed to God the same function. That is, individuals who are too interested in flaunting their possessions may be visited by divine wrath. Whether the fear is of a spell or the retribution of God, clearly being "higher up" than your neighbors is both socially disapproved and dangerous. Mother D. attributes most of the problems of her patients to this all-pervasive mistrust of others:

> People are in the dark. That's why they have so much trouble; they have left off *ever'*thing! They don't have any respect – no manners; they don't give honor to who honor is due. All that is left off; you don't see people doin' that no more. Because I don't think that ever get old. Anything's right, if it's a thousand years ago, it's right today. It's right to do those things. But they misjudge people, always misjudgin' somebody, they mis*judge* them! In that way it makes them have a confused mind. Lotta people. My patients, most of the ones that comes to me, they're sick in *mind* – mentally sick. (Mother D.)

Certainly there is no more graphic example of the fear and unease felt by many in their social relationships. One question must remain unanswered, however, and that is whether the resolution of conflict will take the form of violence or the more covert methods of witchcraft. When, in other words, do you shoot your rival, and when do you put an octopus egg in his beer?

PRACTITIONERS AND THEIR CURES

A variety of health practitioners is available for the prospective patient to choose among, including some not officially recognized as such in professional medical circles. Curers and their abilities differ, just as the causes of illness do. The physician is thought able to cure only illnesses caused by man's conflicts with nature. Others, such as spiritual healers, may cure both these natural diseases *and* those which represent divine punishment. Mother D., the Voodoo practitioner, and the mediums at the Spiritualist temple claim to cure illnesses in all categories: those which are the result of environmental causes, those which represent divine sanctions, and those which are the result of witchcraft practices. There is thus no clear-cut correlation between a particular ailment and any kind of practitioner. In many cases, in fact, the patient may be utilizing practitioners of various sorts simultaneously: when Alma U. was the victim of witchcraft, she went to an M.D., asked for healing prayers at her usual Pentecostal church, *and* began attending a Spiritualist temple for instruction in the avoidance and curing of witchcraft.

Divine Gifts

One theme underlies all beliefs and behaviors present in the search for a cure. This is the idea that the ability to cure – by the housewife knowledgeable about home remedies, by the physician, by the spiritual healer, by the Voodoo doctor, or by the spirits of dead relatives – is a gift from God. This gift has been bestowed upon the individual to enable him to make his way in life: God gave Bertha A. the ability to cook, and she made her living until retirement by cooking in restaurants; Carl A. is a talented amateur plumber and makes his living as a plumber's assistant; Olive P.'s gift was that of washing and ironing, enabling her to operate a hand laundry in her home. These gifts must be used, however, or God takes them away again.

This idea of divine bestowal of ability is especially well developed in those older people whose education is limited. Nearly all informants value formal education highly, but few were able to go to school more than a few years. If one does have the opportunity to go to school, these everyday gifts may be lessened:

> You know, I think about it so often at night. Bein' alone so much, you know. And I think back about things that way. You don't find youngsters now'days that has the gifts like *your* grandmother, and like elder people like my age, and older than I. Some are not as old. Well, I feel like that God knowed that we wasn't gonna have the chance that you younger generation have for school. But there's just a lot of 'em that's graduated and finished school, they don't got as much common sense as some of us elderly people, some of us don't know nothin' *about* school! Y'see, God knowed that when way back, when we was born and older people, He knowed that on and on of the younger generation, they was

> gonna have a better chance about it. And He give us *gifts,* and I feel like when God give a person a gift, He *reveals* somethin' in their mind. And sometimes you can kind of brush that gift off, and He'll come back again with it. And you keep on brushin' it off, He'll *quit!* But if you *use* that gift, feel like it *is* a gift from God, and go ahead on and cope with it, why, He'll continue. (Olive P.)

Though the better educated younger informants are less likely to credit God for their day-to-day survival, *special* abilities are usually believed to be divinely bestowed. Only one informant (Lily M.) stated that doctors are able to cure by dint of long academic training. All others, though they realize that schooling is necessary for a medical degree, believe that the ability to cure is a gift from God. This is true for all types of practitioners, as will be seen in the following examples:

Fred G.'s grandmother, Mother May, was given by God "the knowledge of all the roots and herbs." Olive P.'s father was a famous herb doctor, and was called "The Daddy of the Herbs." Although he taught all of his children how to prepare the various remedies, he himself said that he was taught by no one. His talent was a gift from God, and as such must be kept secret "so it will stay in the family." The proper cure of a difficult case was often the result of divine revelation:

> When we was small, why, he'd get a hard case of some kind. And most places where we lived was a fireplace, you know, and a chimley. And he'd take a chair, they had chairs then with shuck bottoms – do you know about them? They used to use the thick comforters, they called 'em. He'd fold one of them and spread it down . . . across in front of the fireplace on the floor. And he'd take one of them shuck-bottom chairs, and he'd turn it down with the back of it down, and he'd let the quilt come up onta that. And he'd lay down on it flat on his back, and he'd fold his arms and shet his eyes. And we knowed to be quiet. And sometime we'd be playin', you know, runnin' and runnin' and hoppin' and playin', and we'd leap over his feet.
>
> He'd leave his eyes shut, but wouldn't sleep. Ever once in awhile he'd say, "Oooooh, Lordy!" And he'd go on awhile, "Thank you, Lord!" Just like that. And he'd get up. He'd say, "Sister, you come along and go with me. The Lord showed me some more roots to dig." (Olive P.)

Bertha A. has never been to a spiritualist healer. When she is ill she either uses medicine of her own making, or goes to a doctor. She believes that spiritual healers have the power to cure, however, because the power of the Lord is revealed in different ways:

> Christ is in there. He's healin' so many different ways, given these people a healin' hand. He help them to do that. I think He does, 'cause He had the power Hisself and *He* healed. He loved man so greatly, He wanted

> man to have some of the works that He done. God love man so much, He made him in His image and ever'thing, and give him power. I think some people can heal, 'cause God give people a healin' hand; a gift of God, nobody can take it away. See, He loves ever'body, but He give some of 'em different gifts. And He give some more than He did others. (Bertha A.)

The idea that God bestows power differentially affects the individual's behavior when he or she decides to seek medical care, as will be seen later.

All informants have gone to a physician at one time or another. It is sometimes said that the Bible mentions physicians, and that God has put these people on earth as part of His plan. Pearlie M. says:

> I believe in doctors. There was doctors here when Jesus was here; the doctors are here for a purpose. [They have] a knowledge; I'll say in a word, a gift. People have these gifts. You put these gifts in practice, and they can do these things. It's from God. (Pearlie M.)

If you *don't* have the gift, however, you won't be a good doctor, no matter how much you study. Therefore, says Pearlie, "Sometimes they have to take you out from one doctor and put you under another," in order for a cure to be effected. She says that once she was in the hospital, and a doctor tried to start an intravenous feeding in her arm and "busted the vein." He called another doctor to help, and the second man inserted the needle without difficulty. While both were standing at her bedside, Pearlie said to the doctor who had been successful, "Now you's a good doctor! *Some* of these *things* around here ought to be out in the field plowing!"

One informant (Anna P.) goes so far as to say that an atheist would not be able to cure at all, irrespective of how many years he had gone to school.

The notion that the time has come to quit trying home remedies and go to a doctor is credited by some to God:

> If you should go to the doctor, I think God has directed you or your *mind,* you know, to go to the doctor. 'Cause I feel that God has given these doctors knowledge to help people and to cure them. Sometimes I feel your healing has come from both: that God has given them the *knowledge,* and that He give you the *faith.* In this doctor and in Him. (Lillian A.)

Once the decision to visit the doctor has been made, it is expected that God will help out with the diagnosis:

> Some people says, "Why do you give God credit when the doctors do [so much]?" I says, "Give God all the credit, 'cause God give men wisdom and knowledge to diagnose cases. 'Cause men didn't have sense enough to diagnose a case unless God give it to him." He had to

> go through school with God's help, for him to learn. They have to have God's help! With God's help you can do all things. How can you work with the Devil and cure somebody? It's God's will. (Erma V.)

When a cure *is* forthcoming, it is not surprising that God usually gets the thanks, not the physician:

> Well, he [the doctor] doesn't have any power; all he can do is give you the medicine that he has studied about that he feels will help you. God's the one that has got the power to cure you if you *gonna* be cured. He [God] sees fit. The doctor can only do so much. He can only do so much, that's right. My little girl, she's had the pneumonia three times. And the last time she had the pneumonia, the doctors had give her up! They said, "We did all we can do for her." And they give her up. And my husband, he sat there 14 days, watchin' over her. And he said he *prayed,* and dropped off to sleep. He woke up and all the nurses was standin' around and she was smilin' with 'em. So I know God has sumpin' to do with *anything*. You just ask Him and believe in Him. (Lizzie L.)

No matter what practitioner or combination of practitioners is utilized, then, prayer and faith are indispensable ingredients in the search for a cure. When Ella T.'s aunt had a light stroke, she was taken to the hospital, given medicine, and sent back home again. On the same day, the minister of her Pentecostal church (hence a spiritual healer) and the "saints" also were notified. That evening they arrived to pray for the sick woman. An immediate effect was noticed:

> [She also had] spiritual healing; they pray for you, and then God do the work. It did. I know she can use herself, and she couldn't use herself. And they prayed for her. They just went there, and they prayed for her. And she got up out of bed, and she walked that same evening. That child was so sick! And her blood pressure went down. I believe in doctors, too! We all believe in doctors. It coulda been the medicine and the prayer, too! They give her a big bottle of medicine. (Ella T.)

The aunt later told me that the doctors "didn't do nothin' " for her and attributes her recovery to "the saints." She says that she "felt the stroke leave" when the minister put his hand on her head and prayed. In any case, religious belief is inextricably linked with beliefs regarding health, illness, and the curing of illness.

The search for a cure for any given illness is based in part upon the individual's perception of the cause of that illness. In general, those persons who can cure the environmentally-caused illnesses, whether housewife or physician, are thought to have the least power. Spiritual healers, whose gift of healing was bestowed during a mystical experience, are thought to have more power. The spirits of the dead also are thought to be more powerful than ordinary mortals, because they can foresee the future. Those healers such as Mother D., who were *born* with the power to cure, are thought to have the most power of all. God, of course, is ultimately responsible for all cures, and may cure the individual without the intercession of a second person.

Doctors and Medicines

Those natural illnesses in which the individual has come in conflict with some agent found in nature are those which respond to the use of medicines. As medicines and their proper use can be taught to others, provided that God has given the individual the ability to learn, it is in this area that informants have the most medical information. Knowledge of herb medicines and home remedies is common, and the treatment of illness is not considered to be the province of doctors alone. Nearly all informants learned about some remedies from their parents. Many men as well as women were taught herbal medicine as children. Freda T. remembers a doctor coming only when a brother broke his leg. Bertha A. saw a doctor only once as a child, when a boil on her neck was lanced. Jim S. did not visit a doctor until he was eighteen. He went then only because he thought he had gonorrhea, and he did not want to tell his mother. Wilson E. had never seen a doctor until he was drafted into the army. Olive P. went to a doctor for the first time at the age of 82, but only after trying every home remedy she knew. Knowledge of illness and treatment thereof is not considered to be something esoteric in the hands of the few. As children, informants say, curing was in the hands of their relatives or neighbors. It was something about which everybody knew a little, and some people knew a lot.

One woman (Erma V.) is a "power doctor" or "bloodstopper." Such practitioners are quite common in the rural South and their specialty is the ability to cure hemorrhage by the recitation of a certain Scripture. The individual is supposed to be able to pass his or her ability to three members of the opposite sex who are not blood relatives. The biblical passage (Ezekiel 16:6) is spoken aloud until the bleeding stops: "And when I passed by thee, and saw thee polluted in thine own blood, I said unto thee *when thou wast* in thy blood, Live; yea, I said unto thee *when thou wast* in thy blood, Live." On one occasion Erma taught the formula to the father of a small girl hospitalized with vaginal bleeding. The child did not have to undergo surgery, reports Erma, cured instead by the verbal charm. On another occasion, a boy in the Neighborhood cut his head and was brought to Erma's house. She applied ice to the wound, at the same time reciting the above formula. When the bleeding stopped, the scripture was thought responsible, not the ice, "God sewed it up with *His* needle, darlin'!"

As the friend or neighbor with the gift of healing is thought to be just as talented as the physician with the gift of healing, it is not unusual for an individual to go to the doctor and use home remedies at the same time. In some cases ailments which the doctors have been unable to help are reportedly cured by a neighbor. Olive P., for example, has a recipe for a liniment with which she cures arthritis:

> I make up something for arthritis. And this woman what lives there at the back of me, I don't know, she'd been kinda sick, and I called her . . . She said, "Oh, I feelin' much better. Only my knees; I can't hardly walk. I have to hold onto things. My knees is painin' me."
>
> And look like sumpin' run over me, you know, like *you* turns *red!* And I says, "Well, I'll be over there right away – I'm comin' right now." And I *trotted* around here gettin' ready to go. Fastenin' up the doors and like that. I went on over there, and when I walked in, she was settin' down . . . and I just went and dropped down on my knees by her . . . and I rubbed them knees real good. And when I quit rubbin', why, she got up and said, "I'm gonna see if I can walk." And she got up, and she says, "You know, I can walk better already."
>
> So when her husband come, he said, "Well, if it's helped you *this* quick, and you gettin' around like you gettin' around, she's bound to have electricity in her. *Then,* while she was rubbin' your knees, she would have been prayin' *secretly!*" Which I was. And say, why she hasn't been bothered by them knees since! And she had been goin' to the doctor, goin' to the doctor with the pains in her knees. (Olive P.)

Many of the older informants, in fact, think that the home remedies they learned about as children are the best:

> I think it's better, if you really have tried it. Doctors a lot of times don't know anything about these home remedies. Because he study medicine and stuff, makin' his different mix. Where this home remedy wouldn't come in his mind. Likely know so much now, figure the home remedies no good. Wouldn't try it, you know, if it *was* good. Because he just write a 'scription now for some of the medicine they mix together, and give it to his patients.
>
> I believe in that, I believe in home remedies. I believe a person can mix different ingredients together and help pains, I sure does. Home remedies, some of 'em works now. But people, they depends on the doctor. Anything hurt 'im, go to the doctor. And sometime I think these doctors don't know all the time. (Bertha A.)

Not surprisingly, the best medicines are those thought to be "natural," because they are made from plants. Some informants say that they do not like to take medicines given to them by a physician, because they don't know what is in them. Although the natural herbal remedies are thought most efficacious, their use in the Neighborhood is dying out. Most of the herbs mentioned as having medicinal properties are not available because they do not grow in the Southwest. They are considered the ones "proper" for various illnesses, and it is felt to be dangerous to substitute a plant about which you know nothing. Bertha A. gives the example of the family she knows who were all poisoned by eating what they thought were edible mushrooms. She says that many plants *look* alike, but do not have the same properties. Of the various remedies mentioned by informants, 27 different plants and herbs were listed. Only a few of these are available in the area, the rest are native to other parts of the country.

The Mexican American population of the community also uses a number of herbal remedies. Kay, in her study among Mexican American women, collected a list of 27 herbs believed to have medicinal properties. In not a single instance were they the same as those mentioned by Black informants. Black informants, that is, know of only those herbs which grew "back home."

A second reason that herb use is disappearing is one that is responsible for some resentment toward physicians. Many of the plants mentioned by informants were at one time listed in either the *United States Pharmacopeia* or the *National Formulary* (Vogel 1970). Due to the chemical synthesis of drugs, however, many of these herbal remedies have now been removed from the market (Bauer 1969). When people ask for them, therefore, they are told that they are no longer available, or, in some cases, younger pharmacists may not even know what they are. Informants see this as a plot on the part of physicians to get all the money for medications. Anna P. often mentions with resentment that the pharmacist at the nearby drugstore "pretends" not to know what she is talking about when she asks for herbs and medicines which were formerly available. The same man also laughed when she once asked for buzzard grease, which offended her greatly.

Older informants sometimes wish they had reserved a supply of medicines while they were available:

> We could get it; we could get the stuff until a few years back. But we can't get things to make the liniment, cain't get stuff from the drug store to make the salve and to make the liquid drinks. You gotta get the things from the drugstore to put in that. Can't do it [now].
>
> So, that's the reason none of us know a thing about a medical doctor. We was raised up on it, and after we was married off we stayed on it. Well, if I'd have known that we couldn't have got it, I'd have brought a lot of the stuff. Yeah, I'd have had it layin' up here. I don't know. Our systems have never been poisoned up by no medical doctor. That's all we knowed, was just herb medicine. (Olive P.)

The remedies which *are* still used include various foodstuffs (poke greens, lemon, vinegar, salt, pickle or olive brine, beets, meats, grapejuice, wine, and the like) and other items found on the kitchen shelf, such as baking soda. Many patent remedies are purchased and used, especially if composed of herbs and other plant products. Many substances which are readily available may also be used as medicines, rubbing alcohol, turpentine, alum, or epsom salts, for example. When Bertha A. stepped on a rusty nail, her employer insisted that she take the afternoon off to get a tetanus shot. Instead, Bertha went home and soaked her foot in kerosene. No use paying for a shot, she said, when kerosene works just as well. *Ad hoc* combinations of ingredients may be used, as when Lunell N. takes a hot bath after a long day at work. She adds 3 tablespoons each of boric acid, epsom salts, saltpeter, baking soda, and vinegar to the water, saying that "sumpin' just told me to use it."

To sum up, many informants go to doctors mainly because they control many drugs and medicines, not because they feel the physician is superior in knowledge or training.

Faith and the Laying on of Hands

The next position in the hierarchy of healing practitioners is occupied by the spiritual healer. Just as medicines are commonly used by physicians and lay personnel in the curing of certain natural illnesses, faith itself is the prominent weapon in the arsenal of the spiritual healer.

Spiritual healing is employed in the curing of illnesses thought to be sent by God as a punishment for sin. However, a physician's prognosis of any illness as incurable may lead people to try faith healing. Informants who subscribe to this type of medical treatment can relate any number of anecdotes about the miraculous cure of persons who "the doctors had give up on":

> See, now, if you have cancer, the doctors can't cure cancer! But if they go prayin' for you, and you have lots of faith, the Lord will cure that cancer! The Lord heals a whole lot of people of things the doctors done give up! While the doctor may give you up, the Lord can come in and deliver you! Put you on your feet! Then whenever the doctor come back and examine you for that particular thing, and he don't see it, why, he'll say, "Well, I know it was there, but I don't know what become of you now!" They'll be amazed theirselves; they want to know what happened! (Arnella L.)

It was mentioned earlier that most people subscribe to the notion that human abilities are a gift from God, and that individuals have been gifted *differentially*. Some doctors are better than others, for instance. Some doctors may understand one disease, arthritis, say, quite well – but not be able to do much for heart trouble, and so on. Likewise, the person able to do spiritual healing has been given *more* power than the ordinary physician or lay practitioner. This extra power enables him or her to cure ailments beyond the ken of the M.D. Although several informants indicated a belief in spiritual healers, most persons who used such healing are members of the Pentecostal faith. Two informants, Arnella L. and Erma V., are licensed Pentecostal ministers and, hence, are thought to be endowed with the power to heal.

To recapitulate, the Pentecostal church is a Christian sect, which holds the belief that the Holy Ghost descends upon the individual in spiritual baptism. The descent of the Holy Ghost is often marked by loss of consciousness ("falling out") and "speaking in tongues." Such religious experience can occur unsought and unexpectedly, as the following anecdote illustrates: Erma V. spent many years "in the world," using narcotics, drinking, gambling, brawling, pushing drugs, and bootlegging whiskey to the Indians. She was living the life, as she puts it, of "a wretch undone." One day, however, she walked unknowingly into a prayer meeting.

> I never went to a prayer meeting like that before or after. This was the sweetest prayer meeting I ever been to in my life! We didn't sing a song, we didn't pray a prayer, we just began to praise the Lord. We was just praisin' His name. Praisin' for how good He was; what He had did for us, and what He was gonna do for us. And while we was praisin' the Lord, in this praise, a prophet would go forth. A prophet would go forth and somebody would interpetate this prophet. And when they would interpetate this prophet, we would just fall like grass! Couldn't nobody stand on his feet, ever'body would just hit the floor, just like that! They was two rooms of us, they was so many of us.
>
> And we couldn't stay up, couldn't stay on the floor! This went on for maybe two or three hours, and it was a real refresher of the soul! And if a person never *knew* the Lord, there was so many persons that day got baptized by the precious Holy Ghost. And it was just like the day of Pentecost. It would fall on ever'body there, even them that didn't know the Lord. 'Cause it would knock them down, too; them that didn't know the Lord. And when they would fall, this experience would come upon them, the experience of the Lord. The experience of the Lord is just unexplainable, you would have to have it yourself before you would know what I am talkin' about. You have to taste and see yourself. Truly God is self-experience.
>
> Well, I'll tell you. I'll tell you how I happened to go that day. There was this girl, this woman's daughter, and I was gamblin' with her. She owed me three dollars, and I went on down there for my money. I went down there to kick her or whup her for my money. She was gonna pay me or I was gonna drag her all up and down that alley! She went to get the money, and when she got there, they were havin' this prayer meeting. And she got there, and she couldn't leave! I waited and I waited, and she didn't leave; And I didn't know what was happenin' down there, and I went on down. I said to myself, "I'll go get her; I'm gonna get my money or I'll whip her this day!" I went on down to get my money.
>
> I got there, they was praisin' God; the power of God fell. And I felt so free to go in, with a welcome to go in! And as I went on in, I just lift my hands and began to praise the Lord! And when I knew anything, there I was, right in the middle of it with them, praisin' God. I know this man were up there waitin' for us to gamble, but we were praisin' God! And from then on, we didn't gamble with this man any more. I praised God from then on. (Erma V.)

Such religious experiences are not limited to members of any one church, although they are perhaps more common among the Pentecostal sects. Where such experiences are not only culturally approved but consciously sought, it is not surprising to find belief in the mystical curing of illness.

From the ranks of the "saved," God occasionally selects an individual to be a minister of His word. This selection may or may not be public, but is always dramatic. Both informants who have received "the call" did so during the unusual excitement of a religious revival.

To digress briefly, a revival is a sort of religious rite of intensification held periodically in the fundamentalist Christian churches. Religious services are held nightly for a period of some days. An outside speaker is brought in, who delivers a sermon nightly. Not being a regular member of the congregation, he calls the audience to task for taking their religion for granted, for lack of faith, for backsliding, for sinning in general. One speaker I heard began his oration in a low monotone, gradually increasing in volume and emotional intensity until I could no longer understand what was said. Verbal and emotional responses of the listeners increased concomitantly. Such revivals set the scene for sinners returning to the fold, for new conversions, for miraculous cures, and for God's selection of new ministers:

> I was called by God! Darlin', He called me one mornin', and give me my position. To visit the sick and to preach and to help save the laws. And I heard this, and I didn't believe it! I went on back to sleep, and then He woke me up again. And this mellow-toned voice, you know, waked me again. And I wasn't frightened, it wasn't a frightenin' voice, it was a *glorious* voice! I don't know whether you ever felt the Lord or not. When I felt the Lord, it just woke me up out of sleep, just seem like to touched me all over. And called me by my name: "Erma! Go ye therefore!" I said, "Yes, Lord." And I didn't believe this! When I went back to church that night, I had to tell the peoples, you know, what had happened to me that mornin'! It was one mornin' afore day. God called me to a ministry. And to visit the sick and pray for the sick, and pray for the hands that handles them, and so forth.
>
> I went to the services that night. It seemed like I had a joy all day, I couldn't *wait* till that night. They were havin' a great revival, and I couldn't wait till that night to tell all of 'em what a joy it was. And what a mellow voice that spoke to me and told me, "Go ye therefore." You know, the Lord doesn't leave you crazy, and the Spirit doesn't make a fool out of you; the Spirit makes you wise. When I come out of the world, I was *lookin'* for real people. You know what I mean? Somebody, if you tell me you love, I *believe* you love!
>
> That night, when He called me to a ministry, it meant somethin' in life to me. I mean it *meant* that I couldn't stop, wherever I go. If I went to Kansas, I went in the hospitals there, too. He gave me somethin' in my hands that I could touch the peoples that they may be healed. (Erma V.)

Arnella L., on the other hand, did not want to accept the ministry and refused to give in for a while:

> The Lord call you to do that. I don't *learn* nothin'; I was called through the Spirit of God. He work with you, and you got to say yes. A voice will call you. Well, I had to open my mouth. God done me so bad; I'm tellin' you the truth!
>
> We had a revival; we had a good meetin', Lord got to workin' in there, had me under all the chairs. I couldn't even get out from under. They had to move the chairs offa me. I asked another woman, "What did I do under them chairs? I don't know nothin' about gettin' under them chairs!"
>
> She says, "I know! You don't know when He hung you across the bannister up there in the pulpit, either do you? Your head over in the pulpit, and your heels was stickin' out to the public, and they had to cover you up. You don't know nothin' about that, either, do you? Your little behind was right to the public, and we had to get sumpin' and cover you up!" (Arnella L.)

The gift of healing is bestowed upon the individual at the time of this visible proof of divine approbation. The individual so selected then applies for a minister's license, pays a small fee, and is ready to do the Lord's work. The possession of such a license admits the bearer to any hospital. Erma V. spends each Sunday at a local hospital praying for the sick, and, when the Lord so directs, "laying on hands" to cure:

> I went to Kansas, I went in the hospitals there, too. He gave me somethin' in my hands that I could touch the peoples that they may be healed. You know what I mean? I went into a hospital there and prayed for those people. There was five womens in a room, and they all had cancer. They was to be operated on. And do you know, all those womens got well. It wasn't *me* [or, presumably, the surgery], it was just obeyin' God.
>
> You see I never lay hands until I hear that voice "Lay hands on so and so." I'll go all over the room, if the Lord never say, "lay hands," I'll never lay hands. I won't put my hands on anybody. I have to obey the Lord, whatever I'm doin'. (Erma V.)

Such laying on of hands is the curing practice most commonly mentioned. The idea seems to be that the power of God present in the healer is transmitted to the patient through the healer's hands, rather like electricity. "Holy oil," "blessed water," and "prayer cloths" also are used occasionally. The invalid is often "anointed" with oil during the laying on of hands. Water is brought to church services (Pentecostal) and blessed by the pastor. It can then be taken home and drunk during illness. Erma V. prescribes it for people as follows: "[I] mostly gives the water to people that are sick. Peoples that have kidney stones, ulcerated stomach, peoples that have sick stomach. Peoples that drink a lot, I let 'em drink it, just drink it."

In Pentecostal churches, the end of midweek night services (often Wednesday or Friday) is marked by a call for the sick to come forward to be healed:

> The sick person comes forward, and they pray for you. Anoint you with oil and pray for you. They put their hand on you, anywhere it is, they'll put it on you. Or a woman will put it on you. Anoint your forehead with oil, plus maybe your misery. If it's your stomach, a woman will go there, 'cause a man will hardly fool with no woman down around here, you know. 'Cause you know womens is so funny now, and men. And he'll [the minister] call one of the women, a evangelist [to do it]. (Arnella L.)

Those unable to attend services, however, may order "prayer cloths" by mail, as advertised by radio evangelists. The cloths are impregnated with "oil" exuded by an individual "when the Spirit is on him." The "oil" thereby obtained, presumably contains supernatural power, and the cure is effected by simply pinning the cloth anywhere on the body:

> You know, one day I was surprised. One day I was out prayin', and when I was prayin' the oil came up in my hands. One woman was prayin' there [Miracle Valley], and the oil came up in her feet and her stockin's. She walked across the floor, and they had her to get up there in this box on those cloths, and put this oil on this cloth. When peoples are sick, they can send those cloths out to different ones. It's anointed with oil from the hands. You just take it, and pin it on you. Just the contact [will cure you], just anyplace. (Erma V.)

The most spectacular cures, however, usually occur at the great public revivals. Twice a year such a revival is held at Miracle Valley, and the credible come from all over the United States to seek healing. At one of these revivals, Erma cured a small girl of heart disease:

> Oh, I got a little girl's picture here, a little girl from South Dakota. They were down there [at Miracle Valley]. . . . I got so anointed that night . . . I tell you, many people come to Miracle Valley to see me shout! 'Cause darlin', when I get really anointed of God, I feel like I'm light as you [Erma weighs 350 pounds]! I don't feel this weight; this weight ain't nowhere about me when I get anointed. I can shout as good as anybody else; I don't know nobody that can beat me shoutin'! 'Cause it's not me, it's God! 'Cause when I get really anointed, my weight's gone.
>
> I notice these people; this lady dropped her head. I said to myself, "I must encourage these people, because somebody have really told them the wrong thing." I went to 'em, and she had walked out – 'cause

they had been there two or three different times. She went through the line [for healing] that night, and she come out and say, "Well, it's gettin' close to the time for us to go home; my baby just won't get healed."

"Darlin', if God heal your baby, what would you do?" "Oh, I'd be the happiest soul!" I said, "In exchange, what would you do?" "Well, I would just be happy." I said, "Would you give God the rest of your life to serve Him, 'cause your baby could die with this enlarged heart." She said, "Well, we're Episcopalians, we just come for the baby's healin'." So I said to her, "Darlin', probably you're holdin' back on the baby's healin'. God knows that this is all you want from Him. Many times this is why people don't get healed, because they sittin' there, and they want to snatch healin' like a hamburger and walk off with it. Like a hot dog stand or sumpin'. Well, you have to give your life in exchange. God want you to promise Him sumpin'; your baby's life. Maybe He touched this child to get you to come to Him; He wants you to love Him."

So this woman said, "Well, we knew our baby was gonna get healed tonight." I said, "Darlin', don't put God on the spot. You go runnin' like a hamburger, like a hot dog stand and get your baby healed, and then run back home. Maybe you need to feed on what they're feedin' down there from the pulpit; maybe you need to eat from that pulpit, there's somethin' good up there for you. That's why the Lord is keepin' you down here longer." She said, "Well, Brother Jones prayed for my baby, but she didn't get healed." I said, "Darlin', Brother Jones not the only somebody what can lay his hands on your baby and heal that baby."

Just about that time my hands went up, the Lord anointed me, the power of God hit me and began to shout me all over that ground. And ever'body else *out* there, I mean, was shoutin'! And this little girl [the "baby"] run to me and said, "Mama, Mama, I'm healed! I can feel that I don't have it no more!" And she [the mother] laid up on my shoulder, and she said, "You don't know what you have done, you don't know what you have done!" But I'm just shoutin' away; I'm just gone in the Spirit. I just felt so good; I couldn't stop. Somethin' about the Spirit of God, I can't stop shoutin' when I want to; I have to shout till shout's gone! So I looked around and he [the father] was on this shoulder, and she was on this shoulder, and I was shoutin' away. And the little girl had me by the skirt and was just a pullin' on me, and I was just a shoutin' away.

"Don't you know what you have done? Do you know what you have done?" Well, I thought I had did somethin', you know what I mean. I thought I'd hurt somebody or somethin'. Then I began to say to the Lord, "Lord, forgive me if I did anything wrong." But I was still shoutin' away. I didn't know what was happenin', 'cause I can't see; I close my eyes on the world, and then I'm gone away in the Spirit. So I looked around, and she say, "I'm healed, I'm healed!" I said, "Praise God!" I looked around; everybody, that Spirit just went through there ever'body; ever'body *down* there was shoutin'! Just like they was inside the church. The Spirit just cut through ever'body, and ever'body began to shout. And she said to me, "Come on back in the house and let me

> take your picture." It was a colored picture, and she sent it back to me. I got it here someplace. And the little girl got healed. Little White girl. (Erma V.)

As the above recital shows, the failure of a cure to take place does not mean that the curing technique itself is at fault, or even that the healer lacks power. The individual is clearly in a bargaining position vis-à-vis the deity, and God wants something in return for favors; love, adulation, promises of various sorts. God can certainly cure anything, and if the patient is not healed, it is *his* fault, not God's.

The practice of spiritual healing may itself be dangerous to the practitioner. Arnella L., also a Pentecostal minister, has had to give up praying for the sick altogether. The events related in the preceding pages reveal the power of suggestion in such religious exercises. Arnella is so extremely suggestible that she is unable to pray for a sick person without taking on *their* symptoms – a sort of spiritual contagion:

> I don't pray for 'em though, 'cause I picks up their ailments. See, you could have something wrong with you, and I could pray for you, and I'd take it.
>
> Q. Would I get well?
>
> Yeah, you'd be all right. But I'd be sufferin'! It'd go in me! And then somebody'd have to come along and pray it out of me! Lots of times people won't accept it; it's the way you have to pray for the sick people to keep from takin' it. Reverend McBride, he stopped me from prayin' for people down there. Ever' time I'd take it. Pick it up; take it like that. And they had to come right on and pray it off of me. And so they kinda stopped me. Say, "You just quit prayin' for the sick; your body's not strong. You takes it for some reason. You just quit puttin' your hand on these people and prayin' for 'em. Cause you picks up ever' thing they got! And then *we* got to worry and pray and get it outa you!" They stopped me. (Arnella L.)

Just as medicines may drive some illnesses out of the body, it may be noted that others are seen as entities which can be "prayed out" all at once. The parallel with the exorcism of demons is inescapable:

> I've seen 'em preach demons out of 'em. I've heard demons talkin' over the loudspeaker, just like this here [points to the tape recorder]. They can put it to your mouth, and you can hear 'em talk, "I ain't comin' out! If I come out, I'm gonna get in somebody else!"
>
> Then that's when the pastor tell ever'body, "Put your hand on Bible! Ever'body get your Bible! Put one hand on the Bible and throw your hand up to God, and get to prayin'! Ever'body get back, this demon come out, gonna get on you. Get back! Get back!" They won't let you get around nobody that's got demons, 'cause you'll pick it up. They'll jump outa them and jump on you. (Arnella L.)

With the high drama present in such cures, it is little wonder that the curing techniques of the physician are relegated to everyday status. The medical profession surely has a formidable opponent in the spiritual healer.

Born With the Power to Cure

Those persons publicly selected by God for His service have more than just everyday ability. The person with the most power of all, however, is the one *born* with the gift.

Being born with a gift presupposes some pre- or immediately postnatal sign that the infant is unusual. The woman known as Mother D. was such an infant. She was born with the gift of healing, inherited in some fashion from her maternal grandmother:

> My grandmother was a woman of many gifts; she was a very gifted woman. . . . She was a wonderful healer, and then, too, she was a midwife. Oh, she was great! I can remember, when I was very small, things that she did . . .
>
> I never seen any sign of the power in my mother. My mother was more for house things. I had two brothers, they twins. And I were born behind the twins. Some people believe that twins have the gift. . . . Some people say that I have the gift, because I were born behind two twins. But I don't know; I always had the *urge* that I could cure anything. I've always felt like that.
>
> But grandmother knew before I were born. I cried three times in my mother's womb before I were born. Then she said, "That's the one! That's the one what's gonna be just exactly like me!" I was fortunate. I was born just exactly with the gift.
>
> My mother told me that I was born with power. I remember when I was five, five years old. 'Cause I never will forget the little stool which she used to use for me to lie my hands on my brothers and sisters. Her or them would have a pain; I could lie my hand on them, and their pain would leave them. She would tell me all along that I was gifted. I was born like that. From God. (Mother D.)

The idea that twins have supernatural power, and that the child born after twins has even *more* power is West African in origin (Herskovits 1938). It was transported to the New World and is an important element in Haitian Voodoo as well (Metraux 1959: 146): "Twins (*marassa*), living and dead, are endowed with supernatural power which makes them exceptional beings. . . . The child who follows twins immediately in order of birth . . . unites in its person the power of both twins and therefore can dispose of greater powers than they."

Mother D. is not only a well-known healer, but she is a spiritual leader as well, maintaining her own chapel. In a Mexican American *barrio,* about a mile from the Neighborhood, two modest unmarked stucco buildings are the site of her operation. The larger of the buildings, an old house, contains a store where oils, incenses and religious items may be purchased, a small chapel, and the home of her son, Fred G., and his wife. The chapel is a curious combination of Roman Catholic, African, and zodiacal elements. The altar table holds votive candles, a large portrait of St. Theresa of the Little Flower, statuettes of St. Martin of Porres, St. Francis of Assisi, the Infant Jesus of Prague, a pyrex bowl of water, and a large, jointed, wooden snake. Sticks of incense burn in holes in the snake's back. According to Metraux (1959), the snake is a symbol of the African serpent God, Damballah Ouedo, of West Africa and Haiti.

Mother D. is regarded by her congregation as more than an ordinary human being. She was described at one religious service I attended as ". . . A *divine* mother . . . our spiritual leader, our divine mother of all time. . . ." On one occasion I attended the regular Friday night service, at which the entire congregation was Black. At the special Sunday morning Mother's Day service, however, several Mexican American families were present as well.

Behind the combined store-chapel-home is a smaller building, an office where patients are seen. A sign on the door announces that office hours are from 9:00 to 5:00 Monday through Thursday. Inside is a waiting room containing a number of wooden benches and folding chairs and a receptionist's desk presided over by a young Black girl. There is a four-foot statue of St. Martin of Porres, patron saint of the poverty stricken, draped with many rosaries. In front of the statue burn a number of large votive candles. At the north end of the room is the office of Fred G., Mother D.'s son, who reads cards. He has a license from a School of Swedish Massage in the Midwest. He gives massages, prescribes medicines, largely herbal tea prepared by his wife in the house, and, like his mother, gives advice. He "read my vibrations" on one occasion and told me that people of African descent "have more power than White people, even *educated* ones!" He has inherited the power of healing by laying on hands from his mother. In their family, he says, at least one child in each generation has the power; it has been passed on to one of his teenage daughters.

At the south end of the room is Mother D.'s examining room, from which she periodically emerges clad in a white uniform to call in the next patient. The room contains a hospital bed, a chair, a small table covered with jars and bottles, and a number of statuettes of saints and the Virgin on shelves. She does not charge for her services, she says, but donations are accepted. These donations may be money, but whatever the patient has, ". . . a chicken, ham, sheets, and pillowcases," is acceptable.

If the congregation at the chapel is largely Black, the clientele at the office seems to be primarily Mexican American. A Papago Indian woman of my acquaintance took her small son there to have him cured of "fright." On the occasions when I have visited the office, the waiting room has never been empty. On one morning I waited three hours to speak with Mother D.

When I arrived at 9:15 A.M. there were already eight people ahead of me. During the period in which I was in the office, 21 other people were in and out, 13 women, five men, and three small children. All but one were Mexican American, and most had come to consult Mother D. Fred gave a young Black woman advice on her love life (the walls are thin, and she was so angry at her boyfriend that she was speaking very loudly). He also saw a Mexican American woman who had come to have her "prescription" refilled – after a few minutes she bore away her medicine, a quart jar of steaming tea.

Mother D. also has a minister's license from the International Universal Church, and the diploma of a Doctor of Divinity from the same organization. So she really could be called "doctor" if she wanted, she told me. She also has a certificate from a school of Swedish Massage, and a massage is included in many of her treatments. One woman told me that Mother D. had cured her of "crossed eyes" by massaging her face.

According to Mother D., her professional credentials are printed in the Bible (I Corinthians 12:4-11):

> There is a variety of gifts but always the same Spirit; there are all sorts of service to be done, but always to the same Lord; working in all sorts of different ways in different people, it is the same God who is working in all of them. The particular way in which the Spirit is given to each person is for a good purpose. One may have the gift of preaching with wisdom given him by the Spirit; another again the gift of healing, through this one Spirit; one, the power of miracles; another, prophecy; another the gift of recognizing spirits; another the gift of tongues and another the ability to interpret them. All these are the work of one and the same Spirit, who distributes different gifts to different people just as he chooses.

This same Scripture is doubtless responsible for the unanimity of opinion regarding the giving of gifts which was expressed by informants.

Mother D. has been told of her great power virtually since the day she was born, and she possesses a really superb self-confidence. Doctors can cure natural diseases and so can she, she says – but she can cure unnatural diseases as well, and they cannot. "Doctors can see so far, but I can see farther." As soon as the patient walks in the door, "the spirit" gives her the diagnosis: ". . . I have a spirit that tell me; I get it like you would say *something* told me. The spirit tell me what's wrong. It comes into my mind, subconscious mind."

Natural illnesses are treated by laying on of hands:

> No, I never been trained . . . that's one thing I know is from God . . . what I *really* have, born with, I don't know nothin', no place, nowhere. I never seen anyone like me. I've seen *healers* and what not, don't get me wrong that I'm the only healer. I've *seen* healers, seen them go

> through their procedure . . . you know, like Oral Roberts. I've seen that done, but I don't know how that's done. But I know about myself. When a person come to me, I can diagnose the case on the inside; he have gallstones, bladder infection, somethin' like that, or a tumor. I actually can diagnose a case, and I never miss. I just see it! It come in my mind; I can see it. The minute they walk in the door, they say, "What I come for, to get a treatment on my back; the doctor say it's a pinched nerve." Then I tell 'em to lie down, face down, then I put my hands on them and then I can *tell,* tell 'em, "It isn't a pinched nerve, it's arthritis" or, "rheumatic in the nerve center," or whatever it is on the body.
>
> I can put my hands on it, and then I'll work with my hands a little while. No ointment, nothin', just my plain hands. Finally, they'll say, "I don't feel anything, it's gone." Like that, y'know. And ever'body say it's a miracle. Like people [that] cain't walk. They brought several people [like that]. . . . And they say, "Mother, I don't see how you can take that man, or that woman in there, and they cain't walk." You know what they mean. I have faith in myself that they gonna walk, that I'm gonna help them . . .
>
> I don't turn down nothin'; I don't care what's wrong. I just have confidence. I tell you what; I believe in God. I believe God can do anything and everything. *That* is a high power, faith and the belief I never lose faith; I never doubt myself. I know there's nothin' I can do *without* Him, and I feel like He's with me at all times. That goes to workin', take 'em in, and you get a result. (Mother D.)

For the treatment of mental problems brought on by the stresses of daily life, she simply talks to the patient:

> There's so many sickness that can come upon a person. Well, whatever's in their mind, it control the body. Some buys too much; go downtown 'cause they can get things on credit. Well, they over*do* it! See, they get more than they can *pay* for! Then when the time come for them to pay for what they got, they don't see no way out of it, and they gets thinkin' about it and broodin' about it; they don't want to lose what they *have,* nobody does. "Where is I gonna get the money to pay this and that," and next thing, he's sick! I get a lot of people like that. And then, I'm a *counselor*; I counsel to them. And I talk to them, and they say, "Oh, Mother, I feel so much better now – I feel so strong; I feel so good!" I give 'em medicine, you know, 'cause I give it to 'em through their mind. I call that spiritual medicine. 'Cause I talk to them, and get their mind off of whatever that is amakin' them *sick*. They're not strong enough to know what's the cause of them feelin' like they feel. They doesn't, that's why they hunt somebody to advise 'em, or counsel with them. I get people like that ever'day. (Mother D.)

Regarding witchcraft, Mother D. feels that such a thing is possible; the result of a person with devilish powers "holding a thought." On the other hand, she feels that *most* of the clients who come to her thinking that they are the victims of witchcraft are simply made ill by the fear of witchcraft. In either case, her treatment is the same, to convince the client that her power, being from God, can overcome any evil:

> It's just a bad spirit, all of it's from the devil. Like they say, "Mother, am I witchcraft?"
>
> I just say, "If you *sick,* you want to be healed, believe in God! I don't care what is done to you, or what you believe is done to you. God is everything. He's all power. If you have faith in God, God can heal you. Change your thinkin', your way of thinkin'." I tell 'em they're always lookin' down, and [to] feel like lookin' up. Get their mind *up* instead of down. That'll help 'em. You just don't know how a person can be helped by counselin' with 'em. . . . Well, I *do* help people. They bring folks over here, they don't know one day from another, and in days they be right back to their right mind. I tell 'em all that I am *recommendin'* a man they call Jesus! That He can do all things . . .
>
> Anybody that believe in those things, to harm, *my* job is gettin' people to believe right! All in the world it is, no need of takin' it piece by piece. If they believin' wrong, I *know* they believin' wrong! I get some of the Scripture out and show them how Jesus were tryin' out people in the disciples and prophets *presence;* tellin' them about wrong people, like Pharisees. *They* are sorta like people are today, wrong people, wrong people, wrong thinkin' people. . . .
>
> I talk to people, get them to thinkin'. I don't know, I talk to people and *watch* them, seein' is it takin' effect. And it *is,* then I pour it on! 'Cause that's what I want, you know, I want them to believe what I'm *sayin'.* And then when they *do,* I pour it on, see. Then they get so strong! See, they gainin' all the time when I'm counselin' to 'em. . . . All of it is on the mind, bad thoughts. Whatever you *think,* well, that's what you are, you know. That's true. So many people don't know about life; they stumble and blunders. I feel *sorry* for 'em; they in the dark. They don't have no confidence, no faith in *theirself.* You have to *first* place faith in yourself; *believe* that you can do a thing. If you get enough faith, in yourself, then you can face anything. I don't care *what* it is, you can face it. . . .
>
> My intention is to go higher. *Higher* and *higher* power. I know I am. I want to demand; I want to *demand* right someday. In ever'body. I want to be strong enough to demand right . . . . I want to demand it through the powers of *God.* I tell God all the time to make people think right and make them believe in right, and *do* the right thing. Put it into they mind, into their thoughts. That's what I pray for all the time; I ask God. And then I want to be *strong* enough to make it happen . . . .
>
> I do believe in bein' strong enough to *convince* people in their own way of thinkin'; if they're thinkin' in the *wrong* way, to convince them to think in a different way. I do believe in that. And do it through *peace;* I do see peace as everlastin'. Peace is something that nothin' can blot out. I believe in love. Love is one of the greatest and one of the strongest powers on earth. Love rule the whole world, if you can learn to

> love ever'body . . . ever'thing that you do, you do in a way to try to make people *happy!*
>
> Now, that's one thing I love, too, to make people happy. I go all out the way to make someone happy. You know, feel good. Come to me cryin', in tears 'n ever'thing, then I think right quick, "What can I do to make them smile?" Then I'll go all out, and they'll smile. I don't care how burdened down; next thing you know, we'll have a big conversation and laughin' up a breeze! And that's my desire, too, that's what I do ever'day of my life. When they come to me ever'day, they leave laughin'. I don't care how heartbroken they are, how sorry, what feelin' bad they were. They go out feelin' good. Then that make me feel good. And that's my desire. My desire is for good, all way. (Mother D.)

That Mother D.'s combination of massages, teas, and folk psychotherapy fills a felt need can be assumed from the steady parade of people in and out of her office, her chapel, and her home.

THE CIRCLE OF PROTECTION: THE SPIRITS OF THE DEAD

Several miles across town is another combined dwelling and church. It is the Spiritualist temple where Alma U. went when she was the victim of witchcraft. The pastor of this church is also a woman, the Reverend Esther W. She is White, however, and unlike any of the other practitioners in the study, she is a medium. That is, she is considered to have the ability to make contact with the spirits of the dead. I attended the church on "message night," when the spirits of deceased friends and relatives utilize the medium to bring messages to members of the congregation. Hymns were sung, the Lord's Prayer recited, and after an invocation to "God the Father-Mother," the messages were delivered by the medium. Like the curing of Mother D., the ceremony incorporated a blend of the occult and the ordinary. That is, most of the communications from the "astral plane" had to do with the solving of everyday problems and worries. The spirit of a woman's dead brother promised to help her overcome her quick temper; an older woman was advised to go ahead and make a projected journey as it might be her "last chance," and so on. Underlying premises seemed to be that (1) spirits can see into the future and (2) being the spirits of each individual's own loved ones, they naturally wish to be helpful.

Although no one asked to be healed on the night I was there, I was told how it is done. The method is by laying on of hands, as in the Pentecostal churches, but there is an extra link in the chain from God to the afflicted individual. In the Pentecostal churches, the cure comes from God through the healer to the patient. In the Spiritualist belief, the cure comes from God through the spirits through the healer to the patient. Treatment can be both preventive and curative. In prevention, the individual concentrates so that the spirits will band around him. This is the "white light of protection." Illness, bad luck, witchcraft, or whatever are unable to "get through" this barrier of ghosts. If the individual is already ill, however, concentration is on "the green light of healing," and the spirits are summoned to come and remove the problem. As in all other varieties of healing in the study, the trouble, the illness, the worries, or the charm can be extracted all at once. And, as in all other varieties of healing in the study, the individual does not play a passive role, but must do his own part for the help to be most effective. In this instance he must concentrate, meditate, and do what he can to "cooperate" with the helpful spirits.

Although Alma is the only informant who sought out this type of *professional* spiritualism, other informants have mentioned that the spirits of their loved ones are near when needed. When Olive P. is troubled over something, the spirit of her deceased mother comes to spend the night in the front bedroom. When the daughter of Cassie S. had to go to the hospital for breast biopsy, Cassie saw her father's spirit:

> Now just last week, just before my daughter went in the hospital, I was so, you know how something like that can upset you. I was here in the house, just myself and my grandbaby, upstairs in the bathroom shampooin' the rug. And I felt this person behind me, and I just said, "Papa," I looked around, and he just went up [into the air] . . . never when things are all right. But whenever there's some sort of trouble if I'm *depressed* or *worried,* he'll come. (Cassie S.)

Fred G. says that he rarely has to go to the doctor. His grandmother was a talented herb doctor, and his mother gave him to this grandmother at birth. He lived with her until he was nine years old, when she died. When he is ill, he says, the spirit of his grandmother comes to him. He sees her standing before him; then she puts her hand on his forehead. At her touch he "breaks out in a sweat," and when he wakes in the morning he is cured.

Disparate though the various practitioners of the healing arts seem at first to be, they all have one thing in common. Whether physician, herb doctor, spiritual healer, Voodoo practitioner or grandmother's ghost, the ability to heal is perceived as a gift from God, and it is believed that without this gift curing practices would be futile.

Health and Illness in a Mexican American Barrio

Margarita Artschwager Kay

Health and Illness in a Mexican American Barrio

Margarita Artschwager Kay

IN A LARGE SOUTHWESTERN CITY, under a freeway ramp and sandwiched between two large, luxurious motels is a neat brick building housing a Neighborhood Health Center. It is intended to be one of a new kind of health facility, located near the people it serves, and offering an innovative service that reflects the particular illnesses, lifestyles, and wishes of its clients. At this facility probably 70 percent of the patients are Mexican American, most are poor, and some speak only Spanish. How might a health care service reflect the needs of this special clientele? During the remodeling of the center building, the planners of the Neighborhood Health Center asked me this question. The following study is my response.

What do we need to know about a people in order to tailor health care to them? We need to know what makes them sick, and what gets them well, of course. But such a question is commonly answered by an epidemiologist. He looks into another society from the outside and considers disease as a result of biological, environmental, sociological, and cultural factors. The epidemiologist's reply concentrates on the natural consequences of a lifestyle interacting with the physical environment. Cultural factors that affect biology – patterns of mating, the prenatal environment of the fetus, the episode of birth, and infant and child care practices – are taken into account. The epidemiologist looks at customs that have consequences in fertility, birth, morbidity, and mortality. In these ways he will have partially answered the question of what we need to know to tailor health care to these particular people.

But even more, we need other kinds of answers. We need to know what the people who are to be served know about illness. Particularly, we need to know what the women of that society know. We need to know women's ethnomedicine, that is, their ideas and practices concerning health and illness, because it is women who bear the major responsibilities for the health of their families.

We might refer questions of health care for Mexican Americans to the considerable literature already written on the subject (see Saunders 1954; Clark 1959; Rubel 1960; Madsen 1964), but such works will probably not be very helpful because to begin with, they report field work done 20 to 30 years ago. In the intervening years, Mexican Americans have participated increasingly in the medical system of Western science. Secondly, none of these studies has focused explicitly on women, the people who are actually the most concerned about matters of health and illness. Finally, no one has dealt with *norteños,* the people of northwest Mexico. The last point is important because most Mexican Americans of the southwestern United States descend from norteños. The ecology, prehistory, conquest, missionization and settlement of northwest Mexico were not the same as in the central plateau of Mexico. Population composition, migration, life style, and language usage differed on the frontier. And all of these factors have affected ethnomedicine profoundly, making previous studies of ethnomedicine inapplicable to the Neighborhood Health Center.

In this study we will look at a *barrio* (Mexican American neighborhood) to which I have given the pseudonym of El Jardín, where the Neighborhood Health Center is located, then at the lives of the women who live there. We will note particularly what these women say about illness, having used the techniques of ethnographic semantics to elicit this information. Let us consider the method of ethnographic semantics to see what it may tell us about the folk medicine of El Jardín.

According to Goodenough (1957), "A society's culture consists of whatever it is one has to know or believe in order to operate in a manner acceptable to its members." This knowledge comes from experience. Goodenough (1963) further shows that experience is organized in the mind in terms of classes or categories of phenomena, which are grouped in the way that they are seen to be associated. Knowledge and belief are communicated by words. And although there is a range of variation in the application of these labels and their referents, within this range there is enough agreement so that the people who use them can communicate. Thus, there are generally acceptable rules about what these labels signify. The research for this study was aimed at learning what labels, or words were used and how the people who used these words defined them. The definitions were obtained by asking how, in each case, one term differed from another because of the presence or absence of one particular feature. The labels were then grouped by including progressively more features of meaning found in common into a taxonomy.

These techniques of ethnographic semantics were used to learn words for illnesses, for cures, curers, and in fact for every aspect of culture that required explanation. Even ethnic identity came from the technique. My informants call themselves Mexicans, not Chicanas, for the latter term labels women who wish to change the very life style that is represented in this study.

Thus, for this research I concentrated on words. The reader will have to contend with both the Spanish and English words that I heard. To make reading easier, I have followed this procedure. Statements that informants made in English are separated by quotation marks. Spanish words are italicized. Standard translations of Spanish are enclosed in parentheses, as well as occasional non-standard translations that I have contrived to convey the features of meaning as faithfully as possible. The reader may ignore much of the Spanish by avoiding italicized words and attending to the parenthesized translations. He may also consult the *Southwestern Medical Dictionary* (Kay 1977).

LIFE FROM WOMEN'S POINT OF VIEW

To the Mexican American woman, the most important people are her family; in fact her very identity is defined through her family relationships. The health and happiness of family members is her principle responsibility. So if we are to learn what a woman knows about health and illness, we need to direct our attention to the social milieu that influences her ethnomedical behavior. We need to learn who she considers family, and what she does for these people.

The Mexican American woman believes that much illness is due to the way one lives. She has explicit ideas about what kinds of activity, rest, recreation, and nourishment lead to good or poor health. As the regulator of the diet and preparer of food, she is almost solely responsible for the nutrition of family members. When she thinks that someone is sick, she tries to discern what the illness might be and what care would restore health or at least give comfort. For it is the woman in the Mexican American family who will determine what should be done.

Lifestyle in El Jardín contains many cultural elements from Northwest Mexico that are renewed by regular contacts with that region. However, much of barrio culture is Anglo, and is learned in school or from newspapers and television and from contacts with institutions such as clinics, doctors' offices, banks, and stores. The Spanish-language radio stations help to bridge *norteño* and Anglo cultures.

Illustrating the culture that results from fusing these elements, we will discuss the women who were informants for this study. The women ranged in age from 22 to 78 years, in nationality from Mexican-born through third-generation American, and in schooling from none to 10 years. Sixty women were interviewed for this ethnomedical study; most of them came from four families.

FOUR FAMILIES

The first family in this study, the Garcías, have been in the United States longest. Amalia García, the oldest (89) family survivor, reminisced [author's translation]:

> Here was a desert, in the wide river ran clear water. And on the banks there were fruit trees. Further up lived the Indians: Uchis, Taris, Comanches, Malinches, and then the Aztecs, the last. And "El Tejano," the most valiant robber of them all. We arrived in 1905. It was four days from Hermosillo, with stops to change horses, for there was no train, rather a *diligencia* (coach). I was married in 1909. My husband had walked from Tomiston when it was the capital. My mother came from Guaymas, and my father from Soyopa, where he was an Imperial soldier who guarded the trains from the Indians. He had a long beard, like Maximillian.

She went on to say that when they married, they farmed her husband's father's land. Later, she and her husband bought land on the opposite side of the river, where they had a brickyard for many years and then farmed. Farming stopped in later years because the river went underground, and the water table ultimately dropped to levels that were impractical for pumping. When Doña Amalia's husband died in 1956, he divided his land, apportioning it to each of his nine surviving children. The role of family head was given to the oldest daughter. Some of the land has been further subdivided for grandchildren.

On the land adjoining the original settlement lives Doña Amalia's sister-in-law and husband's half-sister, Juana Ramírez, and her husband's half-brother, Ignacio, and his household. Born in Tubutama, Sonora, Juana came to the area as an infant and has spent all her life in El Jardín. The two old ladies remember their parents' tales of Mexico and about their seeing Geronimo and Pancho Villa.

The García family fortunes fell seriously with the Depression. Both sons and daughters stopped going to school and found work as domestics, cooks, or field hands. In turn, their children stopped attending school at an early age, with few attending high school and fewer yet finishing. Most of the men work either in construction or for the railroad. The most prosperous male in the family is a grave digger.

The Garcías are *compadres* (ritual kin) to the Salas', the second family in this study. The Salas' have always been very poor. Inez Salas, a resident of the area for many years, had acted as a midwife, delivering many babies, and was consulted in matters of illness and curing for many years, teaching one daughter her knowledge. Inez had eight children survive. I know only the nine children of her third son, Guadalupe Salas, who have 50 children of their own. Three of Guadalupe's daughters married the sons of neighbors, and still live in El Jardín, while the others are nearby and visit frequently.

Guadalupe and his wife, Candelaria, farmed in the area. Both died before Guadalupe's mother, Inez, and are now buried at a nearby mission. The Salas family no longer farms, and like the Garcías, most of the men are construction laborers.

The Terrazas' are the third family in the study, and are related to the Salas family through marriage. At 61, Francisca Terrazas is the oldest. Her parents migrated from Magdalena, Mexico, and she was born in the United States. Married at twelve, Francisca and her husband Ruben were agricultural laborers. Economically they are the most deprived of the four families and are supported by welfare. Because of asthma and heart disease, Ruben was forced to retire from his occupation of making adobes, which supported the family in the 30 years that they have lived in the area. Seven of the 13 children who survived infancy live with Francisca and Ruben in a two-bedroom house. The others are married, living in El Jardín or close by.

Around the corner from Doña Francisca is her friend, Rebecca Fraser, whose paternal great-grandfather came from Scotland, and whose maternal grandmother was a renowned curer. The woman across the street, Dora Hawkins, like Rebecca, has a non-Spanish name. Her husband's grandfather was a veteran of the American Civil War.

The fourth family in my study, the Beltráns, is made up of newcomers to the area. Trini and Fernando arrived two years ago after hearing of a house for sale on the Spanish-language radio station. Trini was born in Chihuahua, Mexico, but lived with her grandmother in Sonora because her health was too frail for the migratory agricultural laborers' life that her parents led. Thus, she was able to complete secondary school, an unusual accomplishment for the child of migratory laborers. Besides being one of the best educated of my informants, she also has an inquiring nature and a lively intelligence. Her husband, born in the Southwestern United States but reared in Sonora, Mexico, works in construction labor – the best job he can find after only two years of formal schooling. Fernando's sister, Faustina, finished primary school in Nogales, Sonora, then met and married her husband, Juan, who had come up from Llano Grande in Jalisco. Although a skilled carpenter, Juan has been able to find only unskilled labor. Faustina and Juan had rented a house in the neighborhood, but now they have bought another house, and cousins from Nogales have moved into their former residence.

Fernando's mother was in the area seeking medical help for her husband at the time that I first began my field work. After his death, she returned to Mexico to arrange formal immigration for herself and her four unmarried daughters. She is now living in a rented house across the street from Fernando and Trini, and she has just been joined by another daughter and her family.

In addition to the four families, another informant whom I visited and interviewed is Petra Lopez, a woman respected in years past for her knowledge and skill in treating all manner of illness. Born in Jalisco, Petra came to the United States after her first husband was killed by Carranza's Army in

1918. She has been living in the El Jardín since she returned from California in 1954 with her third husband. Still another informant whom I visited frequently is Manuela Romo, wife of the brother of Candelaria Salas and *comadre* of Juana Ramírez. Manuela came to the area from Sinaloa when she was 18 to find work. She was illiterate and came here after her entire family had died of smallpox. None of her children lives with her. Now she gardens, helps her relatives, and cleans an empty house.

Although these brief biographies are of individual families who live in a unique barrio in a specific Southwestern city, in certain important ways they are representative of many Mexican Americans. Their culture accommodates two societies, Mexico and the United States. They have suffered official neglect from each country, but are adjusted to both. The people are poor, but they are not starving. Neither physically nor psychologically are they slum dwellers, living in a culture of poverty. Their environment looks like Northwest Mexico. There is visual continuity between the ancestral lands of the people and their present residence. The design of the houses, their furnishings, and orientation on the streets; the flowers and trees that grow on the land; the animals that are corralled outside – all resemble a Sonoran village.

THE LIVING ENVIRONMENT

Home ownership is generally high among Mexican Americans in the city and El Jardín has an especially high rate. Of the four families described, only Candelaria Beltrán, officially an emigrant from Mexico for only a year, rents her dwelling.

The Garcías literally built their own homes. "We even made the adobes ourselves," recounts Maria. Since most of the men are employed in the building trades, they are able to make additions and repairs to their houses. Fernando Beltrán solicited the help of two friends at Easter and together they poured a concrete floor for a new back porch. Although such work parties are common, most of the houses are dilapidated and in need of paint.

Most of the houses are quite small, but since they rest on sites that range from one quarter of an acre to several acres in size, the residential area appears spacious. There are many vacant lots. New houses are constructed from cinder block rather than mud adobe. Typically, a house is set at right angles on the lot, with the interior divided into four rooms. The living room is in the right front with the kitchen directly behind it. Bedrooms are to the left, front, and rear. If there is an indoor bathroom, it is located parallel to the kitchen, on the bedroom side of the house.

The living room is dominated by a large television set, usually black and white, but color T.V. is in one-third of the houses. There is also a living room *juego* (suite) of couch and chairs. The coffee table holds knickknacks, hand-crocheted doilies, and usually an ornate ash tray, because most of the women smoke. The walls are decorated with religious pictures and wedding and restored family photographs. Occasionally examples of the children's art-work from school will be displayed. There are always flower pots, containing plastic flowers. The family altar is usually in the living room in a niche with plaster statues or busts of saints, or there are pictures with votive candles burning in front of them. The floor is made of concrete, which is often covered with linoleum. The most prosperous families have floors of asbestos or vinyl tile, which they installed themselves. The windows are usually screened and always have heavy blinds, either roll or slatted, in addition to flowered drapery made of plastic or cotton fabric. These are usually drawn so that the rooms are kept quite dark. If fresh air is desired, a door is left open.

A small gas heater, resting on the floor against the outside wall, serves to keep the whole house warm. All the houses have some kind of evaporative cooler, installed in a window or on the roof.

The kitchen is generally the largest room in the house. All have running water, porcelain sinks, and most have a gas stove and a functioning refrigerator. Francisca's house, by far the most dilapidated, has only a wood-burning stove, which keeps the house warm in winter. Unfortunately, it serves to make cooking intolerable in the summer. At this time of year, she, as well as women with gas stoves, prefers to cook out-of-doors.

Ideally, there is one bedroom for the parents, furnished with a double bed and dresser, and one bedroom for the boys, another for the girls, each with a separate bed for every child. Actually, the ideal is never attained in this area of "high overcrowding." Often the living room must be converted into a bedroom at night when folding cots and sofas are utilized in every room for sleeping.

Because the houses are so small, many activities are conducted outside. The children play outside most of the day. They especially like to go to Trini's house, because she has an old swing set with two functioning swings. Several families have *ramadas,* areas where the packed dirt is swept clear, and there is a roof made of palm fronds. Here it is safe to play — elsewhere there is broken glass, pop-tops from beverage cans, and feces from dogs and other animals. Outside, too, the women wash clothes, hang them to dry, and bake tortillas.

Next to many of the houses there are *nichitos,* small shrines of rock and concrete that shelter a representation of a favorite saint. One also may commonly see a cross of *sauz* (willow) leaves nailed to the side of the house.

Each of the homes has at least a patch of garden. Here the women grow herbs, such as oregano, coriander, rosemary, rue, and chilis, both as condiments and medicines, as well as vegetables and flowers. Gardening is both men's and women's work. The extent of gardening is limited by the cost of water. Most of the trees owe their life to their size, with roots large enough to tap underground sources. The *piocha* (chinaberry) and the *pina* (tamarisk) grow everywhere.

Along the dirt roads, the arroyo beds, and the banks and dry bottom of the river, there is a prodigious stand of growth. Many of the plants are highly undesirable as allergens, by standards of Western medicine, although they are used medicinally by the residents, particularly *chicura* (ragweed) and *hierba del burro* (burro brush). Other plants known to students of Southwestern flora as mallow, jimson weed, and tansy mustard are known to El Jardín women as *malva, toloache,* and *pamita* respectively. Spurge, the dreaded invader of suburban lawns, is here the useful cure, *golondrina.*

Some of the barrio flora exist only in the memories of long-time residents. The women who remember the area as it was 30 years ago recall gathering many different plants. There was a large variety of greens, victims of drought, that no longer appear today. The desert yielded three kinds of what my informants call "spinach," *patas, choales,* and *quelites,* and *chinitas,* a kind of dandelion. *Vergolabas* (pigweed) grew in the sand when it was damp. Today it is necessary to venture far into the desert to find *tunas* (the fruit of the prickly pear). *Pechitas* (mesquite beans) used to be sweet, but they are very dry now and can't be eaten, according to my informants. Even the fruit of the saguaro is no longer as sweet as it once was. The fruits of the saguaro and prickly pear were formerly used for syrups and jellies, but the women no longer make them. They buy *nopal* (prickly pear pads) in jars for salads. They also used to make *atole* (thin corn pudding) from the *pechita* and also from the fruit of the *tápiro* (elder). *Atoles* are still made, but the flavorings come from the grocery store. These changes in botanical configuration are viewed with alarm for future health.

In the spring, blossoms and green leaves give a fresh look to El Jardín. If there is no rain (and usually the rain is restricted in winter to late January and early February) everything is dry and dusty by June. According to local folklore, the summer rains begin on June 24, San Juan's Day. By July, the hottest month, the rains do begin, and August is sometimes humid by desert standards.

Insects are a nuisance in El Jardín. Because of the cows, horses, pigs, and goats that are corralled near the houses, and the chickens and turkeys that roam the yards, there are always clouds of flies. These flies are seen as carriers of disease by women who don't own livestock themselves. Stagnant water in the arroyo beds and in the river bottom provides a breeding ground for mosquitoes, known to be disease carriers by all. Cockroaches may be seen in the houses, and if the family dog is allowed inside, one may see ticks along the walls. Hay racks shelter field mice, which during cold winter nights may run into the houses.

The greatest problem, according to women living in El Jardín, is dust. "You clean your house and then a car drives by and your work is ruined. We all cough and sneeze from the dirt and dust."

At night the barrio is almost silent. People who rise before dawn retire early. The sky glows in the distance from headlights of cars on the freeway. There are no street lights, and few people walk the lanes, for they will awaken the large dogs that most householders have chained up in their yards. There is no noise from cats, since few residents have cats as pets. No one identifies cats as dangerous to health, just simply "not liked." On the other hand, caged birds are common. Parrots, parakeets, and lovebirds are brought into the country illegally from Mexico. The women know that these birds have been condemned by Western medicine, but they don't believe that birds could be harmful.

The Household

In El Jardín, the term *la familia* refers to the nuclear family, or to the occupants of a household. The conjugal family is referred to as *familia carnal* (blood family) and is made up also of *otros parientes* (other relatives) or *parentesco lejano* (remote kin) such as grandparents and cousins. There is also a *familia política,* "in-laws." Any one of these *parientes* may live in a household, and if so, are likely to be considered part of *la familia.* Once individuals leave to establish their own households, they may be considered as having other families. Thus in El Jardín, residence is an important criterion for assigning family membership.

Nuclear families set up their own homes, although immediately after marriage a new couple may live with the wife's or husband's family for a time, with the wife returning to her mother's home to convalesce after childbirth. The new household may be located close to the husband's family. Four generations of Garcías live on nine adjoining parcels of land. Other El Jardín couples have located near the homes of the bride's original family. Still others, who have chosen their mates within the barrio, continue to live near both sets of parents.

In the extended Mexican family, theoretically, the eldest male is the seat of authority. But when Abelardo García died, "Julia is now at the head of the family. Isidro didn't want it. He couldn't drive a car. And he didn't understand [official] papers."

Within the Mexican household, the man is supposed to be the authority, but again, El Jardín departs from the standard. In the Terrazas family, Inez is the authority, because although her husband is still in the home, Ruben and Inez are legally divorced. Younger wives give the impression that they have to consult their husbands for every decision. But they also have demonstrated that they may make decisions first, and then ask for approval. In certain areas, such as matters of health, the man is likely to defer to his wife's specialized knowledge. On the other hand, many women will explain, "my husband won't let me," to outsiders' suggestions that she go to a doctor, practice birth control, make certain purchases, and so forth. This explanation has cultural sanction and is taken advantage of accordingly.

Marriage Relations

Marriage is a desirable condition and is entered into at an early age. This is so in part because a woman's social status is assigned primarily through her husband. She has no real social role without husband and children. Also, sexual intercourse is allowed culturally only to married people. Several informants married when they were 15, one at 12, and only one as "late" as 25. None had a marriage that was arranged by parents, not even the women who married fifty years ago. If a marriage ended by death or divorce in early years, remarriage occurred promptly, sometimes within a few weeks. More than a third of my sample had had more than one husband. The very young marriages tended to be unhappy ones. A bride of 15 recounted later, "It was my mother-in-law. She worked me from morning to night like a slave, and took my husband's paycheck, too. She wouldn't let me see my mother. One day I put my things in a pillow slip and ran home." Another, not yet 16, said, "My husband was terrible. He was always jealous. Sometimes I would go out to buy something for the children, and my mother-in-law across the street would tell him I was gone all day. Then he would lock me out in the cold." Several admitted to a marriage that was forced by pregnancy, and one gave birth out of wedlock. This event was strongly criticized in the community, especially by two women who were married before their first babies were born, and has caused a permanent rupture in family relations.

Sanctions exist against early initiation into sex. Some mothers still do not permit their children to attend school social events, such as dances, although I know of none in El Jardín who chaperones her daughters on dates, a practice still observed in Sonora.

In one of the four informant families, there is history of delinquency, premarital pregnancy, and poverty. I asked Consuela and her daughter-in-law to define a good marriage. They agreed that it was one where husband and wife live and work contentedly together. They don't fight. The husband is good to his children and does not beat them. He brings his paycheck to his wife. Other women? "Men are like that: they have to do it. Maybe you won't know for a long time, if he is reserved. After you know, it's no use fighting about it."

But for another family, the distinctive characteristic of a good marriage was *comprensión,* by which was meant "understanding." Both husband and wife give orders, although the woman may need to utilize "tactics" in hers. Other women? "If you are a complete woman, he won't need another. A man won't accept such behavior, so why should a woman?"

Names

Kinship is reckoned bilaterally, but male links are emphasized. Upon marriage, a woman takes her husband's name, for example, Mrs. Ricardo Ortiz. This does not conform to the standard Mexican practice, where the woman in question would have become Antonia Magallanes de Ortiz, and continue to be referred to as Antonia Magallanes. She is likely to register her child's name using the maternal patronym as middle name, so he might be called Emiliano Magallanes Ortiz. In Mexico, that child would be Emiliano Ortiz Magallanes. The differences in practices lead to some confusion for migrants, and sometimes for representatives of public agencies, who for example may decide that a mother is not married because she gives her maiden name.

Within El Jardín, other peoples' surnames tend to be unimportant and may be unknown. Women don't speak to strangers – they only interact with relatives and friends. The woman of El Jardín may address another by a kinship term, especially the ritual kinship term of *comadre,* if this applies, by the honorific *doña* attached to the first name, if the woman is older, or by a *sobrenombre* (nickname) if the person is the same age or younger. A woman may be baptized formally as María de Jesús, Teresa or Ester, but she receives a nickname based usually on some event which caused a remarkable physical characteristic. Thus, one girl, whose earliest steps reminded her grandmother of the way a certain bird looks when it walks, is called by the same name, "Pita." Another is "Cherry," left over from a name she received when a mosquito bit her on the nose. A twin, now nearing 40 years of age, is still "Cuata," from the Mexican Spanish word *cuate,* "twin." Often women will know the nickname of another without knowing either the Christian or the surname. Again, a representative from an official agency might have trouble locating a specific individual because he is asking for a Mrs. Juan Romero, and everyone denies knowing a person by that name.

Kinship Terminology

To the layman, the anthropologist's preoccupation with kinship terminology may seem peculiar. Obviously, it is hard to obtain a medical pedigree without a knowledge of specific kin terms. But kinship terms tell us much more. If a particular relationship has a label, it indicates a group of people considered to be significant because there are critical responsibilities toward them, as well as rights. If a kinship status has a label, this suggests a category of persons with whom social interaction is expected.

There are differentiating terms for ego's own generation and the generations immediately above and below. The usefulness of such differentiation is illustrated by the García family, wherein there are five women who frequently interact, all named María. If a García woman speaks of one of these five with the proper kin term, the interlocutor is not confused. María García has one daughter (*hija*) named María, as well as one spouse's sister (*cuñada*), one spouse's brother's wife (*concuña*), and one cousin (*prima*).

In ego's own lines there are kin terms for each of four generations. Her parent's brother is *tío*. After her *padre* (father) is her *abuelo* (grandfather), then *bisabuelo* (great-grandfather), and finally *tatarabuelo* (great-great-grandfather). After her *hijo* (son) is her *nieto* (grandson), then her *bisnieto* (great-grandson) and her *tataranieto* (great-great-grandson). "How can you know who came before your *tatarabuelo?*" I was asked, with the implication that since you can't, you don't need another kin term. Likewise, obituary notices testify to the unlikelihood of even centenarians leaving survivors more removed by generations than a great-great-grandson, a *tataranieto*.

An entire terminological group is added to encompass relations resulting from remarriage. Thus, ego's stepfather is her *padrastro;* her stepmother is her *madrastra;* her stepson is her *entenado*.

Relations by marriage, "in-laws," are quite explicit. There are terms to designate not only ego's spouse, *marido,* or *esposo,* his parents, *suegros,* and ego's child's spouse, *yerno* (*nuera,* f.), but also ego's spouse's sibling, *cuñado,* and ego's spouse's sibling's spouse, *concuño*. There are also terms for ego's parent's sibling's spouse, *tío político,* and ego's spouse's sibling's child, *sobrino político*.

One might postulate that the large number of affinal terms, which make the exact relationship explicit, implies frequent interaction between individuals whose statuses are so labeled. This is the case in the barrio. Here, however, families also interact with neighbors, unlike some other Mexican American communities (see Rubel 1966 for a divergent view of Mexican Americans as neighbors).

Language

The women of El Jardín speak Spanish and English. The older, Mexican-born women use the fewest English words. The younger, American-born women can sustain long conversations in English alone. But all, characteristically, shift from one language to the other, even within the same sentence, such as this mixed utterance of a third-generation Mexican American:

> *Las anginas* get to the point that *se hinchan y uno no puede* swallow *mientras que no están* infected.
> "The tonsils get to the point that they swell and one can't swallow, even though they are not infected."

El Jardín women are speakers of a variant of Spanish which the women themselves call "bad," deprecating their Sonora idioms as *pochismos* (border slang). The lexemic content of their medical conversations is distinctive, both because it is *norteño* and also because like any other lay people, they do not know scientific vocabulary. So when the women talk to medical people about their illnesses, they tend to be laconic, for they believe that both their Spanish and their English is inadequate.

The Daily Life

The day begins early in El Jardín. If a husband must be at his job at 7:00 A.M., the woman rises at 4:30 A.M. to make tortillas for his lunch. Many of the women would prefer to buy bread, but their husbands feel they do not receive proper nourishment without tortillas. In this part of the Southwest, tortillas are large, paper-thin wheat cakes known as flour tortillas, for wheat is grown in Northwest Mexico. Dough or *masa* is made from flour, shortening, and water, mixed together and pinched into egg-sized balls, then flattened and pulled with the hands until the cake is the size of a saucer or a dinner plate. Corn tortillas are made from ground corn meal, which is obtained at a nearby mill. *Masa* is available in "instant" form, but this is not generally used since the resultant tortilla does not have the desired texture. The tortillas are baked on a *comal,* a large griddle without a handle, made of metal today rather than pottery, and purchased in Mexico.

Almost everyone in the Mexican American family drinks coffee. The children, however, are discouraged from drinking it by being told that their skin will turn dark, but they are given it anyway, diluted with milk and sugar. In houses where the living room doubles as bedroom, everyone is up early; otherwise, the children may sleep until the man is gone. The baby may be given a bottle before the other children are aroused – few mothers breast feed for more than a few weeks. The first solid food for babies is usually *maizena,* a pudding of cornstarch. Next, they receive more coarsely ground corn in an *atole*. If they are sick, especially with diarrhea, the children may receive an herbal tea in their bottles or the water from cooked rice or cooked beans. Well children are given *champurro,* a chocolate milk drink flavored with cinnamon and thickened with flour. Baby foods in jars are used liberally.

Men who work at a distant construction project may participate in a car pool. Otherwise, they will use the family vehicle, which is most frequently a pickup truck, to drive to work and back. The younger American-born women drive; the others do not.

School-aged children are dressed in clean clothes and hurried to meet the bus. If the child does not feel well, or cannot find his shoes, or his mother feels lonely, he will be allowed to stay home from school. If the child goes, he is expected to follow the rules and be obedient to his teacher.

Artwork and other school accomplishments may be displayed in the living room, but there is little involvement of mothers (let alone fathers) with the schools. In El Jardín parents remember when they were in school and were punished for speaking Spanish; they would prefer to forget the whole experience. If the child wants to stop his formal education after he has finished grammar school, his family may not urge him to continue. Some parents have felt that a high school diploma has not proved to be greatly relevant to a boy's occupational goals. Parents do not expect a girl to have a career, but rather to help her mother with household tasks.

With the older children gone to school, and the younger ones settled at play, the woman of El Jardín dresses and turns her attention to the house. The floor is swept and mopped daily; dirt on the furniture and walls is generally ignored. The woman is resigned to making little impression on the appearance of her house, *"este cochinero"* (dirty place). She washes clothes in the backyard where the laundry equipment is installed. Antiquated pipes make automatic equipment non-functional. The radio is turned on to one of the two Spanish-language stations. Mother washes and irons while the small children play with little restriction on their activity. The older of the preschoolers may watch the younger, for they develop a sense of responsibility for their younger siblings very early. Small children, especially girls, feed and care for babies. "Little women are very good at that."

The activity of the small children is an ethnic variety of the play of all children. They manipulate play dough, making tortillas with an authentic-sounding "slap, slap." They sing Spanish commercials that advertise soap and beverages. Boys play with toy trucks, and girls play with dolls.

Women visit their mothers every day, if possible, even several times each day, or at least engage them in telephone conversations. Most families have telephones, or the use of those of their neighbors, especially if the neighbor is also a sister. Usually the telephone is not listed in the directory. I was given various reasons for this practice, most frequently that the individuals didn't want to be dunned by creditors. Underlying all the reasons seems to be the attitude that no one is entitled to have access to your telephone number who is not close enough to get it from you.

Family illness may occupy a significant part of the day. A woman may take her sister or mother to the clinic or doctor. She may take her daughter and grandchild to Well Baby Conference. If her mother needs medicine, all other duties are put aside while it is obtained. Employers have been obliged to accept unannounced absences from work because, "I had to take my mother to the doctor."

Visiting is frequent. Among friends a call *"Soy Emma"* is sufficient to gain admission to a house. A stranger must knock on the door and remain standing outside until invited in, which may not occur. Handshakes, marking the beginning and end of a visit, are exchanged only with women who have recently arrived from Mexico. Women who have not seen each other for a time may embrace, pressing lips to cheek.

Visits commonly take place in the living room or kitchen, wherever there is room to sit. If another family member passes through, he will greet the visitor with a casual *"Buenas,"* rather than saying *"Buenos días."* The farewell greeting between young women will be *"Andale"* (get along), or more formally *"Hasta luego"* (until the next time). Older women are likely to qualify, *"Si Dios lo licencia"* (God willing).

At lunchtime a woman and her small children consume a light meal at home. If she has company, she may go to the trouble of preparing *gorditas,* thick tortillas of cornmeal, covered with chili sauce. Or it may be a dish of refried beans, that is, pinto beans which have been cooked until soft in an uncovered pan with a little water and finally mashed and "re"fried with lard until soft and mushy. Or *calabacitas,* a dish of squash, onion, and tomato boiled uncovered on the top of the stove, again until very soft. The ancient trinity of corn, squash, and beans remains the mainstay of the diet. Soft drinks, Kool-Aid, and cookies are eaten regularly. Otherwise, by the standards of Western science, their diets are nutritious, because eggs, meat, vegetables, and cereals are eaten daily by all but the very poor. "Wrong eating" is a primary cause of illness, according to the women.

In the afternoon, the children return from school, first those from Head Start and kindergarten, then early primary grades, then the later elementary grades. The children greet their mothers formally and then run out to play. Outdoor play in the dirt is considered essential for "health."

By 4:30 P.M., the men are beginning to return from work. Some stop at a nearby *cantina* to drink with their friends. Others will buy a six-pack of beer, and still others go directly home for coffee, which their wives will have ready for them.

The drinking of alcoholic beverages is a matter of contention. Both men and women enjoy beer, but getting drunk is only common for men. Although frequent drunkenness may be seen as *una enfermedad moral* (a moral illness), it is not acceptable. Women occasionally have the beverage *tesgüina,* which they make from parched corn, fermented with yeast. Hard liquor is not commonly found in the home.

Now the boys are called in from play, or perhaps, from riding horseback. Many of the residents of El Jardín own animals, commonly cows or goats. The most desired animals are horses, as they symbolize the good life for Mexicans. The women who were accustomed to ranch life as children do not question the considerable cost of feeding and watering horses until their incomes fall drastically. The work of animal care usually falls to the men. The girls help their mothers prepare dinner.

The few women who work outside the home are returning. Only women without husbands or small children want to work. The common employment is housekeeping, nurses' aide, and dishwashing or serving food.

More women would work, but the present practices of using disposable linens, dishes, and sterile equipment has greatly decreased the number of jobs available. Private domestic work is considered least desirable, and is also difficult to arrange, because the potential employers live on the other side of the city. Some of the women worked as salesclerks in little shops before marriage, and enjoyed the social contacts, but their husbands are opposed to their continuing work. "We want the things that money buys as much as anyone else, but not enough to neglect our families," they declare. So, although almost all of my informants worked at one time, few are employed today.

There are many things that families do at the same time and at the same place, but not together. Mothers may observe their children's play, but do not play with them. They do not read or tell stories to small children. Husband and wife may attend a social event, but once there, they spend the time in separate, sex-specific groups.

After early childhood, there seems to be little generation gap between the women in El Jardín. The longest separation between mother and daughter is while the girls are attending school. If a mother feels ill, or even feels lonely, she considers it completely appropriate to keep her daughter home from school. At home, mother and daughter do the same things. For example, when Dolores came home from the hospital with her new baby, she handed him over to the care of her 17-year-old daughter, Beatrice. Beatrice took care of four of her younger brothers in this way, too, and really looks like she enjoys such work. Beatrice's apparent satisfaction would corroborate what many writers (Tuck 1946; Heller 1966) have noted about the Mexican American girl, i.e., that she has fewer conflicts about her ultimate role in life, because she is consistently enculturated in it from an early age.

Beatrice dropped out of high school last year, as have almost all of the younger women of El Jardín. She said it was because she hated walking to school and worrying about the carloads of boys who followed her. Her cousin, Linda, dropped out because she failed English and general science. "We had pronouns and nouns every year. It gets so tiresome. And what was I going to use science for? But you have to have it to get your diploma. Me, I got married."

Education is inversely correlated with age among El Jardín matrons, but a high school diploma is altogether rare.

RELIGION AND ETHNOMEDICINE

The women are Roman Catholic in their fashion. The Church has never been a single system of ideas and practices, so it is not surprising that the specific form of worship of Spanish-speaking people in northwest Mexico-southwest United States has its own unique stamp. An especially deviant form is known as "Sonora Catholicism" (Spicer 1964: 28). The term generally refers to Indian syncretisms that developed in conjunction with Jesuit, and later Franciscan guidance. This form of Catholicism, although officially rejected by the Church, has affected more orthodox worship forms in Sonora and southern Arizona.

In this section we will examine Spanish, Mexican, Indian, and American influences on the religious customs of El Jardín. The calendrical cycle of events in El Jardín will be discussed, followed by a description of *compadrazgo,* a system of ritual relationships, life crisis rites, and finally health-related religious activities. We will see that some of their Spanish religious forms have changed. Certain customs (primarily Indian) have been rejected; other customs are being rediscovered and revitalized (Mexican), and still others (generally Anglo-American) are being added to their repertoire of behavior.

The new combination of religious customs in El Jardín provides a model for considering illness behavior. Some disease concepts will be persistent survivals or newly emphasized Mexican folk beliefs. And many concepts and practices will have come from standard American folk medicine, others from Western science.

Annual Events

The annual calendar in El Jardín is an interesting combination of Mexican and American holidays. These include New Year's Eve, Good Friday, Easter, *Cinco de Mayo,* Mothers' Day, *El Día de la Santa Cruz,* the Feast of St. Francis, *El Día de los Muertos,* Thanksgiving, and Christmas. These events commonly are celebrated by individual or groups of families, with men preparing the sites of activity and women cooking the food. The first holiday is New Year's Eve, celebrated with drinks and *menudo* (a soup made from tripe), and, because of the especially late hour, it is the one event that usually excludes children.

One would expect any Catholic community to celebrate Easter, especially one that was heir to the teachings of the Jesuits and Franciscans. But until recently, there had been no celebration marking either the start of Lent or its end, neither a "carnival" nor a Holy Week observance. Now the traditional *El Via Crucis* (The Way of the Cross) ceremonies are conducted. They begin on Good Friday and are culminated with Mass on Easter morning. Holiday dishes include a lenten *capirotada,* a casserole of bread, cheese, fresh and dry fruit, brown sugar, onions, and coriander for flavoring. After Easter *pozole,* a stew of hominy and meat, such as chicken and pork – especially the head of the hog – is served, topped with raw radishes, onion, and parsley or chili. Picnics are a popular recreation, with food such as fried chicken obtained from restaurants.

El Cinco de Mayo, a Mexican patriotic holiday, is celebrated by a carnival at the public school. The mothers of the school children make Mexican foods and organize games, even as they would for the school *kermés* across the border.

Mother's Day, officially recognized in Mexico on May 10, is celebrated on the second Sunday in May in El Jardín, as it is in the rest of the United States. The women cook ham or turkey or make tamales. It is hoped their children will make cards or presents at school, and those children who are grown and gone also will remember to send a card. Women expect also to hear from their godchildren.

El Día de la Santa Cruz, the third of May, is an important home religious day. The night before, women walk over to the *bosque* (wooded area) to gather *sauz* (willow). They form the branches into crosses of about one foot in size. The crosses are taken to Mass to be blessed, and then they are hung on the house. The ones from the previous year are supposed to be burned the day before, although one may notice some old ones hanging beside the new one. Mass on this day is dedicated to the problems of the home, illness, and "juveniles," i.e., delinquency. Popular celebration of the Day of the Holy Cross is common in Mexico, where the cross is the patron of masons and bricklayers, common occupations in El Jardín.

Father's Day in June is reported to get the same attention as Mother's Day, but I saw no evidence of this. And less attention is given to the Independence Day of the United States than to the Mexican one of September 16, when there are picnics in the nearby city park.

On October fourth, the feast of St. Francis is celebrated. This is the time when everyone wants to go to Magdalena, Sonora, for the festivities there. Some families go every year, others go only if there are special reasons, which may range from "asking the blessing of San Francisco on a new car" to recovering from illness.

Halloween is observed by the children at school. Mexican families, however, celebrate All Soul's Day, *El Dia de los Muertos,* on November 2. They visit the cemetery where relatives are buried, and place fresh or plastic flowers on the graves. They also may have a family picnic.

The American holiday of Thanksgiving is celebrated by everyone in El Jardín, even the new immigrants from Mexico. Commonly, the family feast of turkey or ham is served in the home of the oldest or most respected woman. Pumpkin and mince desserts may be prepared as pies or as *empanadas* (fried turnovers).

Christmas is also celebrated American style. The houses are cleaned, refurbished, and decorated with plastic Santa Clauses and real trees. On Christmas Eve, many families observe the Mexican practice of serving beer and tamales as the family holds the *velar al niño.* "It's like staying up for the birth of the Baby Jesus." Other families may travel to observe the day with relatives in Mexico, going to Cananea, Agua Prieta, Hermosillo, or Santa Ana. Christmas is seen as a family celebration for the children, and the women start early in the fall to make presents, not only for all of their children, but also for all of their nephews, nieces and godchildren.

Compadrazgo and Life Crisis Rites

When a woman in El Jardín faces a major turning point in her life, she looks to those closest to her for support. This general human tendency has been institutionalized throughout the Catholic Spanish world in *compadrazgo* (ritual kinship). In El Jardín, *compadrazgo* strengthens already existing bonds of kinship or friendship. When a woman gets married, baptizes her baby, confirms it to the church, or dedicates it to a saint in gratitude for the child's recovery from illness, she turns to people who are already close to her. These people, as we have shown in the previous chapter, are most likely to be relatives who are also friends.

Godparents are chosen for a variety of events. The most common occasions are marriage, baptism, confirmation, and illness. In each case, the godparents for these events are formally referred to as *padrinos* (*madrina,* f.), and informally addressed as *ninos*. The godchild is called *ahijado*. Sponsors and parents refer to each other as *compadres*. It will be noted that the terminology derives from kinship terminology, and also has gender marked by -o and -a suffixes. Let us now look at the principle occasions for selecting godparents.

MARRIAGE

When a couple wants to marry, the young man sends his father to petition for the hand of his sweetheart. If he has no father, his baptismal *padrino* may be asked to serve in the same capacity.

Couples are usually married by religious ceremony. (In northwest Mexico, as in much of Latin America, a civil ceremony occurs first.) Following a reading of banns on three preceding Sundays, marriage is consecrated in church. For this wedding, there are four kinds of marriage *padrinos: padrinos de matrimonio,* also called *padrinos de honor; padrinos de lazo,* the sponsors who place the silver cord that joins the kneeling couple during the rites; the *madrina de ramos,* who holds the wedding bouquet; and *padrinos de arras,* the sponsors who carry the wedding rings, symbolizing family wealth. The *padrinos* are usually the sibling of either bride or groom and the sibling's spouse or *novio* (sweetheart, fiancé).

Marriage *compadrazgo* has changed in El Jardín. *Padrinos de matrimonio* were once considerably older than the couple they sponsored. This was when their advice and support was expected to be useful. Today, marriage sponsors are commonly chosen from age mates. Also, not all the people marry in church. Some have had civil ceremonies, especially divorced women or pregnant brides. With civil services, only one pair of *padrinos* are witnesses.

BAPTISM, CONFIRMATION, HOLY COMMUNION

Baptism has always been the most important Catholic rite because at this time the child's soul is given to God. Should death occur early, the passage of the soul to heaven is assured. At this time the infant is also named, a recognition of his individuality. All El Jardín babies are baptized, but the sacred aspects of this ceremony appear to have become less important than the social, and there is even a de-emphasis of baptism as a social occasion.

Ideally the infant is dressed in beautiful new clothes, purchased by the *padrinos,* who also hold a party in honor of the baby after the ceremony. El Jardín residents often pass the baptismal clothes from one child to the next. The party, too, is becoming rarer, according to some because of the cost involved, and, according to others, because it has occurred to them to wonder, "What can the party mean to the baby?" So parents and *padrinos* simply take the baby to the church when there is a mutually convenient date for all.

The choice of Christian name appears to be an indicator of culture change. Girls born in Mexico are often given names as María de Jesús. Jesús as a name is discouraged by priests in the barrio, so children more commonly have been named after the saint with whom they share a birthday. But with increasing use of English in speech, parents pick nonreligious names, such as those made popular by television and movie personalities. Jesús has become Jessie.

Confirmation, a sacrament which helps prepare one for adulthood, is the next religious ceremony. It is commonly scheduled when the child is still very young. At under two years of age, a child is too young for the occasion to have meaning, according to local priests who have opposed the practice to no avail. The practice of infant confirmation was established in the 18th century to take maximum advantage of a rare episcopal visit. The custom continues in the diocese of this Southwestern city even though this rationale no longer obtains. *Padrinos* are selected for confirmation, too.

There are no *padrinos* for the first Holy Communion. This ceremony follows a prescribed amount of religious education for both the child and his parents and is conducted with more family recognition of the child. Eight and nine-year-old children get new clothes for this occasion, and they are frequently taken to Mexico for portraits in their white dresses and veils, or white shirts and new suits. The fact that there are *padrinos* for baptism and confirmation and none for the first communion supports the idea that in El Jardín, the social value of *compadrazgo* to the adults is greater than the religious value.

Padrinos for baptism and confirmation are most commonly chosen from among relatives. Grandparents are often godparents for their grandchild, although such a selection is frowned upon. "How can you tell your child that his grandmother is also his *nina?* It isn't right." It would seem that this choice is inappropriate because it confuses the paramount relationship of mother and child. The *compadre* relationship is one of deference between peers. For this reason, it is better to select a lesser relative. One chooses someone for whom "respect" is felt already, and the *compadre* relationship increases this respect. As Trini said, "I asked my younger brother to baptize Fernando, because he has always been very respectful and well-mannered to me." For baby Lupita's baptism, Trini has asked her husband's older brother and wife, to be formally arranged when they can travel to the city. In some cases, such as with Consuelo, she is *nina* to all five of her sister's children. Sylvia, however, has asked a friend to sponsor the baptism of her eighth child. Sponsors must be Catholic and have been married by Catholic rites.

In selecting (or being selected by, for women often ask "to confirm" a child) ten or more *comadres,* a woman picks from among her many relatives those on whom she feels she can rely. From these *comadres* there is further selection of individuals who prove to be most supportive. This relationship is most likely to be activated in times of illness. The *comadre* helps the mother seek treatment. If the *comadre* "has a little knowledge" of cures, so much the better. Many people in El Jardín related seeking the advice of *comadres* in curing. And they also spoke of being treated by their *ninas* when they were ill.

When a sister or aunt serves as *madrina* to a child, she is no longer addressed by the kin term, but by the term *comadre*. Sylvia and Linda, aunt and niece who are neighbors, always address each other as *comadre*. There are only two ritual kinswomen of my informants (who are also *cuñada* to each other) who simply use first names. "We've known each other since we were babies. I just can't get used to calling her *comadre*."

Contacts between parents, *compadres* and *ahijados* are also dependent upon proximity. "Olga never sees her *ninos* because they moved away." Some give up the relationship. "It's no good anymore. Kids don't have respect today. They won't listen to you." *Comadres* can then commiserate with each other.

DEATH

The only time that the entire kindred is brought together as a social unit is at the time of death. Adults, upon their death, have one or more ceremonies. After death, the body is taken to a commercial mortuary. At the mortuary, the body is placed in recumbent position in the casket and prepared for viewing, somberly dressed with rosary entwined in the hands. At a scheduled time, a service called the Rosary is held in the chapel of the funeral home. Visitors dressed in black and wearing veils or hats arrive over a four-hour period. They sign one of the guest books, and then file up to look at the body. The bouquets that friends have sent are displayed behind the casket. The visitor then passes to the section where family members are seated. Relations who are closest to the dead – parents, children, or spouse – sit in the front row. Other lineal relatives and their collateral and affinal kin are seated behind. All are greeted, embraced or hands shaken, and regrets expressed.

After a time, the formal ceremony begins. The entire service is in Spanish, including the eulogy and the recitations of the rosary. Not only the kindred, but also friends, attend this service in large numbers to repeat the *Ave Marías* and *Pater Nosters*. Even small children attend. The next day, the body is buried in the Catholic cemetery. Burial may occur as much as four days after death.

On the first Monday that follows death, *novenarios,* nine consecutive prayer services, are conducted on nine consecutive evenings. In El Jardín, *novenarios* are held at home where someone in the community who is used to leading prayers may be hired to lead the recitations of the rosary.

Families are "in mourning" for six months to a year, during which time they dress in black and restrict their social activity. The length of this period is dependent upon the closeness of the relationship. For example, Trini, who spent her childhood years reared by her grandmother, mourned her death almost as long as she would her own mother's death.

RELIGION AND ILLNESS

The people of El Jardín see themselves as Catholics, though few other than old women go to church. Recently priests have been trying to bring the Church to its people. Many Masses were said in the homes, whenever requested, sometimes almost nightly. Some Masses were arranged simply because of the devotion of individual people.

> Manuela is devoted to St. Jude. In her garden she has a three-foot statue. He came to all of us. There were nine days of Masses, held every nine days. Father Ricardo gave a Mass at Manuela's, and then we took the statue to Carmen's house, then to Beatrice, then to Norma, then to Margarita, then to Linda, then to Laura, then to Ignacia. On Wednesday we will have Mass here, and then take San Judas to Anita. When it is hot, we have Mass outside, at night. Now it is too cold.

The devotional occasion was frequently in response to an episode of illness, with the Mass said in payment of a *manda* (vow). One home Mass to which I was invited was arranged some six months after Consuelo had recovered from abdominal surgery at the county hospital. It had been postponed until her husband had obtained steady employment on a construction project. It was scheduled for 7:30 P.M. one August evening, to be said by a priest from a local church, in the family *ramada*.

At the appointed time, the men of the family improvised an altar by placing a large piece of plywood on the television table. Then the men left to sit on a pickup truck and drink beer. Meanwhile the priest, who spoke in a rich Irish brogue, heard confessions in the house. He then came out, and with the help of three boys of his parish, unpacked two cases of altar cloths, vestments, chalices, candles, and other religious paraphernalia. The boys passed out booklets with the service in English. The brief service was read to the hatted or veiled women and children, most of whom received communion. The priest made a few remarks about the absence of the men, the great strength of the family, and reminded the children to be ready for the Saturday morning bus which would take them to catechism classes.

Besides Masses of this kind, there are other religious activities which are performed in association with illness. Castillo de Lucas (1958:137-8) refers to simple prayers, small personal sacrifices, donations, the adoption of religious habits, and pilgrimages. Mexican Americans practice all of these religious activities. They are all offered to God, usually to that aspect of Him conceived of as the Sacred Heart of Jesus. According to official doctrine, God may be considered as a Holy Trinity made up of Father, His Son, and the Holy Ghost. In El Jardín, the Trinity is usually envisioned as the Family of Jesus, Mary, and Joseph, which is not officially correct. I also have seen a picture of the Holy Trinity in which it was presented as three identical pictures of Jesus.

Most students of Mexican culture note the importance of the Virgin Mary, especially as the Mexican Virgin of Guadalupe. In El Jardín a few houses have posters glued to their front windows which declare in Spanish, "We are Catholic. We do not admit Protestant or Communist Propaganda," and are illustrated by a picture of the Virgin of Guadalupe. (These same posters can be seen over much of Mexico.) Other saints are more commonly used for intercession in health matters, however. The function of these saints, an informant explained, is that of a lawyer. They already have been forgiven for their sins, and will take on your case. There are a few general favorites, especially St. Francis Xavier, St. Martín de Porres, and St. Jude.

St. Francis Xavier has been a valued supernatural for the people of this entire region since Father Kino named the mission that he established at Bac for this saint. The personage that is revered, however, is not the historical St. Francis Xavier, but rather a simulacrum that combines the attributes of St. Francis of Assisi, on whose date the feast of St. Francis Xavier is celebrated, and Father Kino, with some of the characteristics of St. Francis Xavier himself. One of the most important days of the year is October 4, the feast of St. Francis, when people from all over Sonora and Arizona make a pilgrimage to the church in Magdalena. At this church, Father Kino's remains are buried. The tradition of pilgrimage has been a long one, preceding the replacement of the Jesuits by the Franciscans, and was lively even before Arizona's separation from Sonora with the Gadsden Purchase. According to one Mexican writer, people saved their money for this event during the entire year, because if an individual vowed to go and did not, St. Francis would "send the bill back with calamities" (Zamora 1944:104, my translation). Here they see the saint, pay their vow, beg his pity and pardon of their sins, and implore that their needs be met. However, in true Sonoran style, the pilgrimage has always been combined with recreation, a time of fiesta, camping, and picnicking.

Such church fiestas are common throughout Mexico, but the one for St. Francis has a unique emphasis on curing. This stress is demonstrated by the extensive commerce in folk medicine visible at the fiestas. There are many stalls for merchants of herbs who come from all over Sonora and from as far away as Vera Cruz. Besides medicinal herbs, which are packaged in brown paper sacks or plastic bags in kilo lots, there are cans of ointments, dry starfish and sea horses, and amulets such as iron filings, beads, and *ojos de venado* ("deer's eyes," actually brown seeds). All these items are labeled according to the diseases that they cure. Merchants also sell religious articles, such as pictures and prayers of special saints associated with cures, and have racks of *hábitos* (habits), which will be discussed later. Women may be seen helping themselves to water just blessed by the priest, or buying eyeglasses or sunglasses. Roaming around the fiesta are men called *merolicos* (charlatans), who with histrionic skill and pseudoscientific demonstrations, urge the purchase of some patent medicines. The audience for *merolico's* pitch is almost entirely men – women scorn his products. Proprietors of the small herb stores in Sonora and Arizona are able to get supplies of all their merchandise during this fair.

When the trip to Magdelena is a pilgrimage made in fulfillment of a *manda* (vow), several elements are involved. They include prayers, a sacrifice, and sometimes equipment, such as special costumes and an effigy. These same elements are important in smaller pilgrimages, too. The prayer is not prescribed, but the women pray extemporaneously, repeating what is in their hearts. They promise to honor a saint in return for the recovery from illness of a loved one, especially a child. When the child is well, he may be taken to church with a godparent selected for this occasion in the traditional garment, which is often a copy of the religious habit of the saint implored. The godmother on this occasion is the *madrina de hábito,* and may be anyone asked by the mother, "Do you want to put the habit on my child?"

El Jardín women commonly acknowledge their gratitude for recovery from a major illness by a walk to a local mission. It is no small sacrifice to walk over 12 miles, especially in the heat of the desert summer. The mother precedes her walk by a trip to a shop selling religious articles. There she purchases a model of that part of the body that is affected by the illness. This effigy is called a *milagro* (miracle) in Arizona and Sonora, *exvoto,* elsewhere. For example, Lupe bought a head, because her dehydrated infant was receiving many intravenous feedings through scalp veins. The effigy is then deposited beside, or attached to, the image of St. Francis. The supplicant also attempts to lift the statue, to learn if her prayers will be answered. With catastrophic illness, the same elements are utilized, but the walk may be made all the way to Magdalena.

St. Martín de Porres, the half-Indian saint of Lima, Peru, has great appeal for the Mexican Americans, both because of his dark color and his American origins. St. Jude, the patron of lost causes, also is valued in El Jardín. Many of the women have persuaded their husbands to construct shrines in their yards to house favorite saints. These are usually kept clean and bright, with flowers or Christmas-type decorations for elaboration.

In Spain there are many saints who are patrons of a certain illness or a part of the body which may be afflicted by disease. The patron saint may be chosen because he was born in the region, or his image had appeared in a certain site there, or because of the type of martyrdom he underwent, or the analogy of his name or role could result in his association with a particular affliction.

In comparison to Spanish women, the El Jardín women have a very slim repertory of such saints. They invoke San Juan, especially when a cure from *caída de la mollera* (fallen fontanel) is sought. (San Juan is also supposed to make it rain, which makes his association with a disease of dehydration an interesting coincidence.) Men named Juan are reputed to be natural curers, and the only effective ones for children named Juan. San Roman *Nonato* (unborn – he was in Shakespeare's words, "untimely ripped") is petitioned at childbirth. St. Jude's statue on a nearby street also is visited after an illness. A few women petition the saint on whose feast day they were born. Most women do not pay particular attention to their saint's days, other than receiving radio greetings broadcast on one of the Spanish-language radio stations. The usual petitions are to the Sacred Heart of Jesus, San Xavier, and San Martín, in that order.

Although women pray to God for cures, they deny that He sends illness. It is true, they say, that God does everything, and for His own reasons, so He *is* the ultimate Cause. But none of my informants in El Jardín could accept vindictiveness as an aspect of their deity. They quote the saying *Dios no castiga,* God does not punish. Also, we must note that Mexican Americans are not especially fatalistic. (See Edmonson 1968, Madsen 1964:16, Lewis 1960:91 for differing assessments of world view and Samora 1961 for divergent beliefs of the role of God in illness.) Generally, women in El Jardín adhere to the saying, *¡Ayúdate y Dios te ayudará!,* "Help yourself, and God will help you."

How did the women of Sonora develop their way of relating religion and health? They learned it from the priests. A history of the missionization of Sonora shows that it was Jesuits who were the first to come to the region in the late 17th century. Jesuits accommodated the beliefs and practices of the Indians that they sought to convert (Spicer 1962), incorporating their ideas wherever they could. The resulting contact cultures have been only partially documented, however. We know all about what missionaries told the men, but nothing about what they must have told women. Nothing has been written about an amalgam of the culture of Indian women with that of European women. But we have seen that many of the religious customs that relate to health have European Catholic roots. Foster (1953:204) points out that priests helped the sick and suggests that they were the vehicle for bringing Spanish scientific medical thought to Mexico. However, the Jesuit priests who came to northwest Mexico were more commonly German-speaking natives with names like Pfefferkorn, Mittendorf, Nentuig, Och, and Kino. Their common source of medical knowledge, according to Pfefferkorn (Treutlein 1940 passim; 1949:279) was the *Florilegio Medicinal* of Johann Steinhöfer, S.J. Juan de Esteyneffer (1712), as he was known in Spanish, wrote a "brief compendium" of 522 pages for the missionaries of the Company of Jesus assigned to the remote provinces ". . . of Topia, Sinaloa, Tepegüanes, Tarahumara, Sonora and Chihuahua." His first edition of the compendium lists patron saints for every disease. All of the ethnomedical disease concepts and treatments followed today in El Jardín may be found in the *Florilegio Medicinal* (Kay 1976), where both European and indigenous medicines are listed.

An interesting example of priests' effects on medical theory comes from the *Rudo Ensayo* (Unknown 1951:45), written by a Jesuit in 1763. Here one learns how women may have decided that they should never bathe during their menstrual periods. The priest wrote of women dying ". . . choked by the stopped blood" of menstrual disorder because they "go into the water and bathe at all times, without regard to the injuries that may follow, and this is the cause of the disorder." Today the idea is firmly fixed in ethnomedicine that bathing is dangerous during the menstrual period. Father Nentuig's essay is filled with his concepts of the cause and treatment of illness, ideas which we shall see reaffirmed in the following sections.

After the Jesuits were expelled in 1767 by the decree of Charles III of Spain, they were followed by Franciscan missionaries, sent from the Holy Ghost Province of Queretaro. The Franciscans also collected information about indigenous cures and planted herbal gardens in the missions. The Franciscans were then turned out after the new Mexican government decreed general expulsion of Spaniards in 1826. There were few regular sources of European medical thought coming to northwest Mexico thereafter. New ideas were filtered from Mexican and then later American medical doctors. The *Florilegio Medicinal,* last reprinted in 1887, may have remained a strong influence.

DISEASE CLASSIFICATION

When a child does not feel well, he goes to his mother and tells her he is sick. She questions him closely, feels his forehead, and looks at the place where he says it hurts. She thus decides what *enfermedad* (illness or disease) she thinks is the diagnosis. She knows many names for illness, and she decides what is the correct one by her interview and examination of the *enfermo* (patient). Limited to those illnesses that she has experienced or observed in her family, she will ask expert help when the illness is beyond her knowledge.

In this section we will consider a long list of illnesses discussed by the women of El Jardín. The list was obtained by asking women how a person felt when he or she was sick, and what were the different kinds. The reader should remember that the English translations given below represent the *thought* of the informants about a disease and may not correspond with a physician's interpretation of the condition. After I wrote down the names that labeled illnesses, I asked the women to classify together those names which were in some way similar, and then learned what criteria they used for their classification. They classified illnesses in an orderly way, because the women were accustomed to considering methodically the signs and symptoms that characterize each deviation from health. Interestingly enough, the women did not know how orderly their own data collection was, because they do not have a set of rules written down or otherwise put into words that describe the processes of making a diagnosis. But after I copied down what the women said about each illness, and how they differentiated one disease from another, they verified what they had said and recognized the logic dictating the order.

In Figure 3.1 we see the underlying order as the women's knowledge of physical illness is arranged into a taxonomy. The taxonomy is a classification in which items are grouped according to the women's ideas about disease. Each group, called a "level," includes increasingly fewer signs and symptoms or "features" that distinguish one condition from another. Thus some features belong to any disease, other features occur only with specific types of disease, and still other features may belong only to one condition.

The symptoms of any *enfermedad* (illness) may include *cansancio* (fatigue), *debilidad* (weakness), *incapacidad* (incapacity), and *tarantas* (dizziness). Any of these symptoms means illness and excludes health.

There are two principal kinds of disease, *enfermedad corporal* (illness of the body) and *enfermedad emocional* (illness of the emotions). The specific symptoms of *enfermedad corporal* (illness of the body) include *calentura* (general fever); *calentura local* (local fever); *dolor* (pain); *basca* (nausea or vomiting); *pujo* (griping); *moco* (mucus) or *tos* (cough); *cambio de color* (change in color); and *erupción* (rash). One or more of these conditions

Fig. 3.1 — Classification of Physical and Emotional Illness

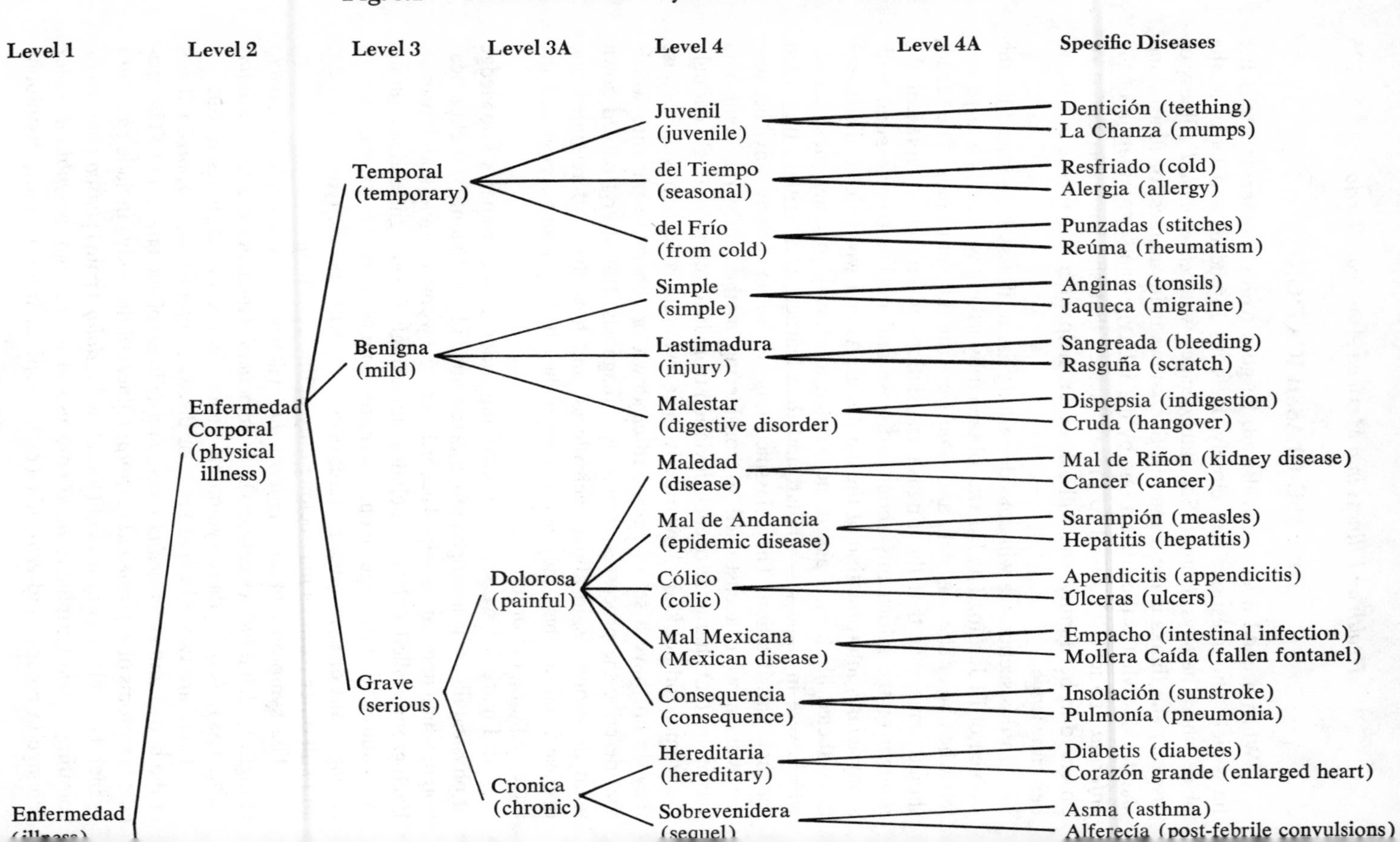

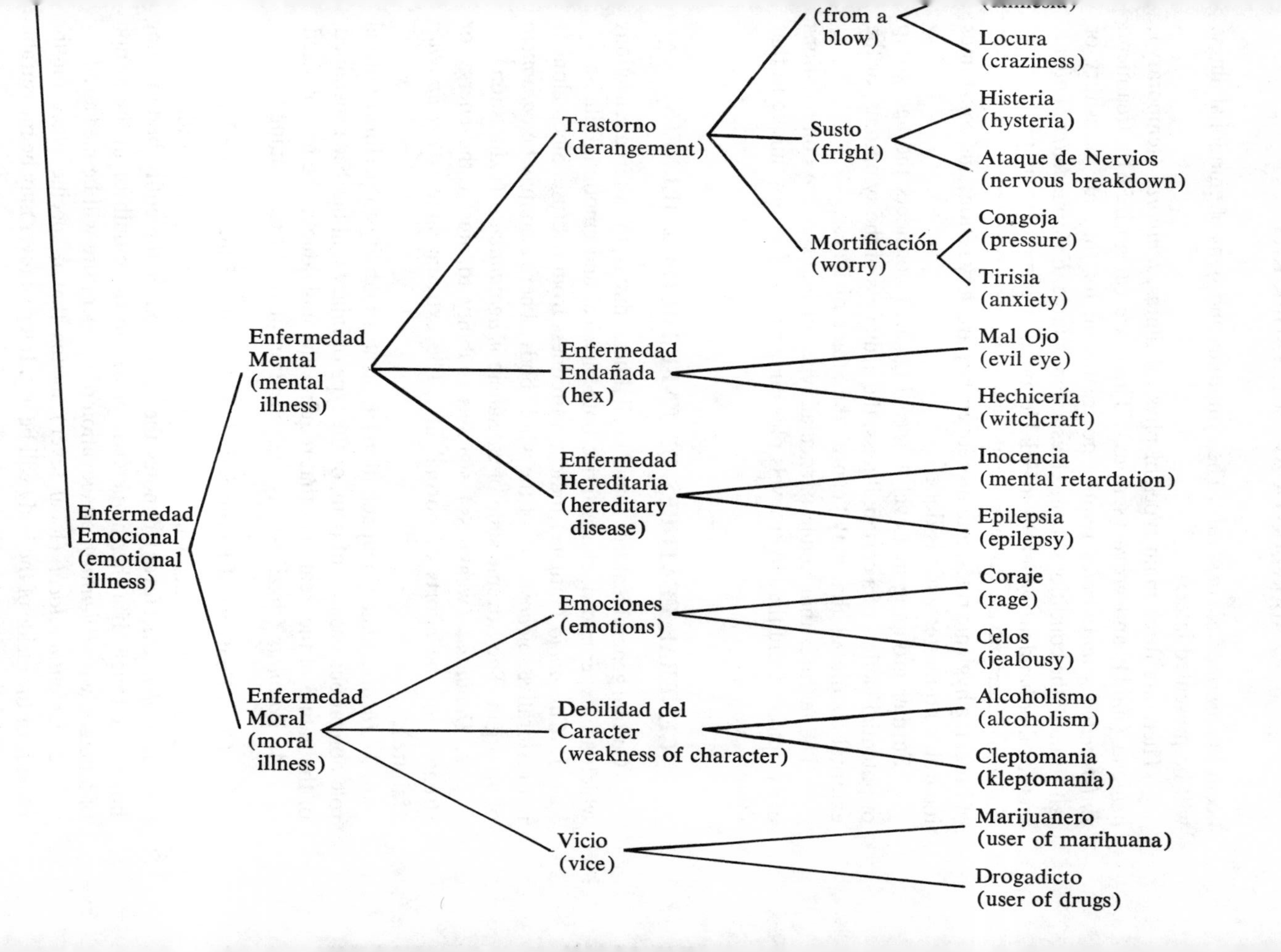

Enfermedad Emocional (emotional illness)
Enfermedad Mental (mental illness)
Enfermedad Moral (moral illness)
Trastorno (derangement)
Enfermedad Endañada (hex)
Enfermedad Hereditaria (hereditary disease)
Emociones (emotions)
Debilidad del Caracter (weakness of character)
Vicio (vice)
(from a blow)
Susto (fright)
Mortificación (worry)
Locura (craziness)
Histeria (hysteria)
Ataque de Nervios (nervous breakdown)
Congoja (pressure)
Tirisia (anxiety)
Mal Ojo (evil eye)
Hechicería (witchcraft)
Inocencia (mental retardation)
Epilepsia (epilepsy)
Coraje (rage)
Celos (jealousy)
Alcoholismo (alcoholism)
Cleptomania (kleptomania)
Marijuanero (user of marihuana)
Drogadicto (user of drugs)

occur in *enfermedad corporal.* (The symptoms and signs of emotional illness will be presented later.)

There are three main types of physical illness, *temporal* (temporary), *benigna* (mild), and *grave* (serious). These are categorized by treatment. *Enfermedades temporales* require no treatment, for they are transitory or self-limited; the conditions themselves are inevitable. *Enfermedades benignas* on the other hand are generally avoidable, but they respond to simple therapy. *Enfermedades graves,* however, cannot usually be explained as the results of breaking hygienic rules, and moreover they are very serious and sometimes incurable no matter what is done.

Further grouping at Level 4 (see Fig. 3.1) considers the age group of potential victims of a certain illness, the acuteness of the symptoms, or the external conditions that may "cause" the attack of illness.

The features that define particular types of illnesses are combinations of symptoms from the larger levels plus one or more features unique to that illness.

GENERAL FEATURES OF ENFERMEDAD (ILLNESS)

Certain general features found in all illness, that is, the altered sensations which are experienced, characterize both physical and emotional illness.

1. *Cansancio* (fatigue) indicates tiredness from overuse. Sleep alone is not restorative to *cansancio* of the whole body. There also may be *cansancio* of an organ. The extreme state of cansancio is *agotamiento* (exhaustion).

2. *Debilidad* (weakness) signifies inability to muster the energy or strength for the efforts of normal life. The extreme state is *decaimiento* (failure).

3. *Incapacidad* (incapacitation) indicates inability to perform normal role obligations because of pain, or the type of injury that has been sustained, or the nature of the treatment that requires the individual to be immobilized.

4. *Tarantas* (dizziness) is the sensation of the head spinning.

Class Features of Enfermedad del Cuerpo (Illness of the Body)

Signs or symptoms which occur in the category of physical illness are:

1. *Calentura* (fever) denotes the condition of the entire body feeling hot to the touch. If a thermometer is placed in the mouth or in the armpit of a person with *calentura,* an elevation of temperature will be measured.

2. *Calentura local* (local fever) means that a specific place on the outside or the inside of the body will be hot. Internal fever may be measurable by a rectal thermometer.

3. *Dolor* (pain) indicates various kinds of pain or alterations in tactile sensation. First comes *cosquillas* (tickles) and *congestion* (congestion), pain in the least degree. The next kind of pain is "numbness" or *tener adormecido.* With *hormigeo* (tingling), one feels as though many insects are moving over

a part of the body. *Piquetes* are "stinging pains" and *picadas* are "stabbing pains." *Un escozor* is a "smarting pain." *Punzadas* (stitches) are feelings of pressure on one or more places, especially the eye or the side of the chest. *Ardor* is "burning pain." *Un dolor necio* is characterized by its persistence. A "strong pain" is *dolor agudo.* The most severe kind of pain, *el dolor más fuerte,* is called *un dolor clavado.* A "cramp" is *un calambre.* "Scratching" is *la rasquera,* and "itching" is *una comezón.* None of these particularly descriptive words is commonly employed; informants simply use *dolor,* and expect the interlocutor to know which kind is meant. Pain is closely related to fever.

4. *Basca* (nausea) denotes both the sensation of nausea and the act of vomiting. Vomitus is *la deposición.*

5. *Pujo* (griping) corresponds to the medical term *tenesmus.* It refers to the desire to move the bowels without necessarily doing so. If there is a bowel movement following this symptom, the feces commonly contain mucus and sometimes blood. Then the condition is known as *disenteria.*

6. *Moco* (mucus) is the secretion of mucous tissues. It may be clear, *moco cristalina;* white, *flema;* or yellow, *moco amarillo.* If there is a mucous secretion from the nose, it is often accompanied by a cough, *tos.*

7. *Ponerse pálido, azul, rojo, amarillo* (to become pale, blue, red, or yellow) refer to changes in the appearance of the skin.

8. *Erupción* (rash) refers to the appearance of various kinds of lesions on the skin. *Llaga* (sore) subsumes various kinds of these lesions, although it applies specifically to one kind.

Enfermedades Temporales (Temporary Illnesses)

The class *temporal* (temporary), also called *pasajera* (passing), is defined by its temporariness or self-limitation of the condition, which is in itself inevitable. Its first subdivision includes those conditions which "must" come in the early stages of human development; they are known as *enfermedades juveniles.* The first of these is *dentición* (teething). *Dentición* includes the features of runny nose, diarrhea, and fever and is distinguished from other conditions that include similar symptoms by the defining features of excessive salivation and discomfort in the gums.

The second *enfermedad juvenil* is *tos ferina* (whooping cough). This term translates as "whooping cough" in the dictionary (a condition caused by the *Hemophilus pertussis*), but in El Jardín the condition is not that specific; it is the spasmodic coughing that "children get in winter." It contrasts with *garrotillo* (croup) for some informants, with the latter cough producing more mucus.

La chanza is translated by informants as "mumps." However, they do not speak only of swelling of the parotid gland. *La chanza* also may refer to prominent swelling of any throat glands, especially those of the external cervical chain. Another departure from Western scientific nomenclature occurs with the next class, *viruela*. This term translates as "smallpox" in all dictionaries, but my informants mean "chicken pox" when they use the term, and *viruela* encodes the same features.

Sarampión de tres días (three-day measles) is recognized as a mild disorder with the features of general fever, and also local fever of the skin where it becomes flushed and then erupts into red spots. Again, more is included than the specific disease of rubella (German or three-day measles). All children are prone to various *sarampiones* (measles), especially at the time that "they go around." All the above conditions are recognized by other societies in the Western medical tradition. Science would take issue with the inevitability of these diseases – but the concepts of El Jardín women reflect their experiences.

Enfermedades del tiempo (seasonal diseases) are an important category in El Jardín, containing the lexemes most frequently elicited: hay fever and *resfriados* (colds), plus *catarro* (runny nose) and *alergia* (allergy). All conditions have the general feature of fatigue, but *resfriado* and *alergia* add incapacity, since sufferers from these conditions must go to bed or limit their work. Similarly, all conditions have the class feature of mucus in the nose. The term *jey fiver* (hay fever) encodes the features of red and itching eyes, a feeling of something like dust in the eyes, and pain in the bone under the eye. Hay fever contrasts with *resfriado* (cold) in that the latter occurs from chilling. The class feature of fever demonstrates infection, and the defining feature becomes the generalized aching of the bones. Informants are agreed that *jey fiver* "comes from" plants, trees, and grass, but the pathological processes are not defined. One says that the soldiers brought it from Korea. It also comes from *humo* (smog), also called *aire sucio* (dirty air), which may develop into *alergia,* the final class member which encodes more features, adding *ronchas* (hives), which are locally "hot."

The dust and pollens (noted in the previous discussion of the living environment of El Jardín) are thus closely attended to and responded to in the lexicon of disease, as are the rapid diurnal temperature changes, important "causes" of respiratory illness.

One group of *enfermedades temporales* was omitted from the taxonomic key to *enfermedad* because of lack of consensus among informants. This class contains those conditions which normally are cyclic in women. Some informants insisted that *el embarazo* (pregnancy) is definitely an *enfermedad* because one suffers from *mareo* (nausea and dizziness), *alta* or *baja presión* (high or low [blood] pressure), and *coraje* (rage). Other informants stated that these were not distinctive features of pregnancy, but illnesses in their own right, from which not every pregnant woman suffers. Mainly, they argued that pregnancy is a natural condition, however uncomfortable, and thus did not qualify as an *enfermedad*. In the same way, *la regla* (the menstrual period) is seen as an *enfermedad* by some women and not by others. We shall return to this problem later.

A final group in this class is a category that really lacks a single word to label it (Berlin, Breedlove and Raven 1968), but *del frío,* "from cold," comes close. It includes those conditions which are caused by rapid environmental change, usually from hot to cold. With such change, it is said, *frío agarra el cuerpo* (cold seizes the body). All of these conditions are uncomfortable but entirely harmless unless their victim persists in exposing himself to more of the same conditions. There is first, *frío de la garganta* (throat cold), a passing pain in the throat that comes from drinking iced fluids. To avoid it, very cold drinks are eschewed by most informants. Similarly, it is "known" that if an individual steps into the wind with an unprotected head, he may get *temblor de ojo* (tremor of the eye muscles), *punzadas* (stitches), or *dolor de nervio* (pain in the nerve). From breathing cold air, there may be pain in the chest, identified as *ataque de viento* (attack of gas), or *aire en el corazón* (air in the heart). Finally, there is *reúma* (rheumatism), pain in a joint, which may come when an individual has overheated a part like his hand in some household task, and then plunged it into cold water.

Enfermedades Benignas (Mild Illnesses)

Enfermedad benigna is a major level, including all the conditions which are *molestias* (annoyances) but which yield to uncomplicated treatment. *Enfermedad benigna* is characterized: (1) *sin temperaturas altas* (without high temperatures); (2) *no encamadas en los hospitales* (not hospitalized); (3) *se puede aliviar* (one can get over it).

ENFERMEDADES SIMPLES (Simple Illnesses)

The first kind of *enfermedades benignas* are *enfermedades simples* (simple illnesses), conditions which cause discomfort or mild pain (*dolencia*) that may be treated by aspirin or other home remedies. These include *anginas* (tonsillitis), *jaqueca* (migraine) and *sangre débil* (weak blood). There also are many conditions of the skin, which often have none of the other general features of illness, excepting that "something isn't normal." *Piel* is the general term for skin, and *cutis* refers to the skin of the face. Skin lesions are differentiated by what they look like, where they occur on the body, or by cause. A *grano* is a skin lesion of any kind. A *grano enterrado* or *granujo colorado* (boil or furuncle) is a skin lesion that goes below the surface of the skin and is infected. The appearance of *granos* over large parts of the body is an *erupción* (rash), also called *una salpicada* (a sprinkling). An *ampolla* (blister) is a lesion filled with clear liquid that commonly appears on the hands or feet from rubbing, such as would occur with manual labor. If the *ampolla* becomes infected, and the fluid is thick and yellow *materia* (pus), the lesion is a *llaga* (pustule). When open, it is an *úlcera* (ulcer).

A *bola* is a lump. One kind of *bolita* (little lump) is a small lesion that swells up and then disappears, a *roncha. Ronchas* may be caused by ant stings (*picadas*) or those of another insect, and also can be caused by plants;

thus, the best translation is hives or wheals. Hives are characterized by *comezón* (itching) so the condition also may be called *una comezón. Una erupción de muchas ronchas* (a rash of many hives) is a *sampullido* (urticaria). The cause and also the closeness of the lesions differentiates *piel de gallina* (chicken skin), known as 'goose flesh' in English.

Mal de ojo (pinkeye or conjunctivitis) is mildly incapacitating because "it hurts to look at the light." The affected eye or eyes are red, sore, and crusted in the morning.

LASTIMADAS (Injuries)

The second kind of *enfermedades benignas* are a result of the active play of children in which they incur small *lastimadas* (injuries). They are all incapacitating to some degree, if only briefly. A *sangreada de la nariz* (nosebleed) follows the contact of the hand of one preschooler with the face of another. There may be a *rasguño* (scratch), *herida* (wound), or *cortada* (cut) which may become *infectada* (infected). A *quemadura* (burn) occurs from touching something hot, like the stove on which mother makes tortillas. A fall from a horse may occasion a fracture (*una quebradura de un hueso*), sometimes so severe that *se salió el hueso* (the bone broke the skin). There are also *descomposturas,* "painful joints where something is out of place" and *torceduras* (sprains). A tooth may become decayed, *muela podrida,* or there may be an abscess of the gum, *postemilla.* One may get *una espina* (a cactus sticker) in his finger or *una astilla* (a splinter). Excepting for quite severe degrees of the above, all are *enfermedades benignas,* cared for by the housewife.

MALESTARES (Digestive Disorders)

Many of the *enfermedades benignas* belong to a third category, labeled *malestares*. These are digestive disorders for which there are a variety of terms. Disturbances of the *estómago* (stomach), which includes the entire gastrointestinal tract from the lower esophagus down, may be caused by not eating, or eating something that does not "fall" well. (1) *Algo te hizo daño* (Something hurt you); (2) *Se cayó de panza* (His stomach was upset); (3) *La comida no le cayó bien* (The food did not agree). In older people, bad teeth can cause *enfermedades del estómago* (stomach illnesses).

Eating something that did not agree with the victim is the *post hoc* factor identified in more illness diagnosed by El Jardín women than any other. Almost all *malestares* (digestive disorders) are characterized by *tarantas* (dizziness); some are incapacitating; some cause weakness. The class feature of all is nausea. *Acedías* (heartburn) is defined by a sour taste and intense pain in the center of the chest, at *la boca del estómago* (the mouth of the stomach). *Falta de digestión* (inadequate digestion) is defined by a feeling of fullness and has the class feature of general pain, which contrasts with *ataque de viento* (attack of gas), wherein the pain is also in the center of the chest but lacking the *agrura* (bitter or acid) taste in the mouth. *Ataque de viento* also may be confused with something more serious, for the pressure of the gases may make the individual complain of pain in the heart. Diagnosis is made if there is successful belching or, if necessary, vomiting, to help the *ataque de viento* to pass. *Cruda* is the *malestar* that follows too much drinking. *Puerco del estómago* (dirty stomach), also called *estómago sucio,* has similar features, but with overindulgence in food as antecedent, and constipation as the defining feature. *Dispepsia crónica* is the frequent occurrence of indigestion.

If *enfermedades benignas* are neglected, the conditions become more serious and lead to new diseases with new names. The home pharmacopoeia, or *remedios caseros,* is especially rich in treatments for various types of *malestar de estómago.* These will be discussed more fully later.

Enfermedades Graves (Serious Illnesses)

Enfermedades graves are defined as serious and perhaps incurable. The majority are classed as *dolorosas* (painful). These are further divided into subcategories.

The first of these classes may be labeled *maledades* (diseases), and includes those illnesses that are named according to the location of the *dolor* (pain) and called *dolor de X* or *mal de X*. Thus there is *mal de riñón* (kidney disease), defined by painful or frequent urination. One form is called *riñón recargado* (overloaded kidney) which manifests itself by the desire to urinate without being able to do so. Any pain in the back is thought to be kidney pain.

Other *maledades* are *dolor de oído* (earache), *dolor de hiel* or *vesícula,* or simply *bilis* ("pain in the gall bladder"), *mal de corazón* (heart disease), *ataque de corazón* (heart attack), *estroc* (stroke), and various kinds of *cáncer* (cancer), and finally *mal de hígado* (liver disease). These diseases all feature fatigue, usually to the point of *agotamiento* (exhaustion), weakness, and incapacity. The class features are poorly defined. In the case of *mal de corazón* (heart disease), defining features are not known. "That's why one goes to the doctor; he knows," I was told. If someone is reported as dying suddenly, the first assumption made in El Jardín is that death was caused by *ataque de corazón.* Death may be preceded by pain in the chest.

MAL DE ANDANCIA (Epidemic Disease)

Some *enfermedades graves y dolorosas* are considered to be contagious, *maledades de andancia,* also known as *enfermedades contagiosas.* The most common of the serious infections is *sarampión malo* (hard measles). It is the one childhood disease that is a member of this category, because the child is so acutely ill and because of the complications that may follow inadequate care. The important features are high fever, cough, and severe headache.

Hepatitis (hepatitis) is also recognized as an *enfermedad contagiosa* when it is in "advanced" stages, with many specific features cited. But the other *maledades de andancia* are vague to informants. They list *polio, meningitis, difteria* (diphtheria), *paludismo* (malaria), as well as other lexemes for communicable diseases known to Western medicine. But the women do not know how these diseases "start," because "they don't go around any more." Some of these *enfermedades contagiosas* are identified only by their English names. "Scarlet fever" occurs when one has high fever and drying skin. With "valley fever" (Coccidiodomycosis), "one has a spot on the lung. One needs rest or it will turn to TB, and then they have to take the lung out." Since these diseases can be diagnosed only by medical doctors, any defining criteria are unknown in El Jardín.

COLICOS (Colics)

When individuals have had personal experience with a disease, they will remember the symptoms that concerned them and the explanation that was given by the official diagnostician. Most informants have suffered *cólico* (pain in the abdomen). *Cólico* is a disease name, and is also a class of *enfermedades graves* that are related because they are characterized by *calambres* (acute cramps). The first disorder is *inflamación del vientre* (inflammation of the belly), also called *frío en el estómago,* which comes from neglect of conditions such as *dispepsia crónica,* described earlier. *Inflamación del vientre* may be inflammation of the stomach, intestines or uterus. *Inflamación* is synonymous with *frío* (cold). It contrasts with *infección* in that the latter is caused by *un microbio* (a germ). When the uterus is the affected part of the belly, and the victim has *frío de la matriz,* "cold of the womb," the condition may manifest itself actively by uterine cramps, or silently, by sterility.

Other *cólicos* include *piedras* (stones), which may occur "in" the gall bladder or the kidney. Sharp pain in the upper part of the abdomen is usually credited to *úlceras* (ulcers), caused by too much acid in the stomach. Ulcers may progress from the stages of *gastríticas* ("stomach"), to *quemantes* (burning), to *heridas* (wounds). *Apendis* (appendicitis) is defined by acute pain in the lower part of the abdomen, and *mal de ijar* (flank pain) is intermittent pain in the same area, which can become *apendis.* "Some people have *apendis* for years until it is operated on. It is full of pus and can kill you." Finally, there are *parásitos* (parasites), worms that may inhabit the intestines. The most common type is the *soltaria* (round worm), but pinworms and *ameba* (amoeba) also are frequent. The *merolicos,* who sold patent medicines at the Magdalena Fair, had elaborate displays of worms preserved in bottles to impress potential customers.

"MEXICAN" DISEASES

There is an entire group of *enfermedades graves,* which informants describe also as characterized by digestive disorder and which they further call "Mexican" diseases, since Anglo physicians do not tend to recognize them. Not all El Jardín informants recognize these diseases either, as will be discussed later. These *enfermedades* include *empacho* (indigestion infection), *latido* (cachexia), *tripa ida* (locked intestines), and *pujo* (grunting), and are identified wherever Spanish is spoken, with regional modifications.

Empacho is the *enfermedad* caused by the adherence of undigested food, which molds in some part of the gastrointestinal tract. *Le pega algo de la comida en los intestinos. Se enmohece.* (Some food sticks to the intestines. It molds.) This causes an internal fever which cannot be observed, but betrays its presence by great thirst, and abdominal swelling that is caused by drinking water to quench the thirst. Children, who are prone to swallow chewing gum, most commonly suffer this *enfermedad,* but its incidence is not restricted to any age group.

Latido (cachexia) is a form of *debilidad* which is diagnosed by great weakness accompanied by the pulsating of the "stomach." This condition is most likely to occur in adults, especially aged ones.

Tripa ida is a severe, generalized condition that is the result of a *susto* – a "fright" or "trauma", as my informants translated it. A very disturbing experience, such as observing an automobile accident, can cause the intestines to lock (Hrdlička 1908 re *tripide*).

Mollera caída (fallen fontanel) is a condition of infants whose fontanels have not yet closed. Most attention is given to the anterior fontanel, the diamond-shaped "soft spot" at the top of the head, although especially knowledgeable informants state that there are also several *molleras* in the back of the skull. The fontanel is felt to be vulnerable to depression, which is mechanically caused by a fall. The fall may not be witnessed, but such an episode is conjectured when a baby fails to suck efficiently. The fontanel also may drop if a nipple is jerked rather than gently pulled out of the baby's mouth. Symptoms of this are crying, fever, vomiting, and diarrhea. Medical doctors note the correspondence of these symptoms with those of dehydration, so many informants see *deshidratación* (dehydration) or *carencia de agua* (lack of water) as synonymous with *caída de la mollera.*

Pujo as a lexeme stimulates disagreement among informants. Their translation is "grunting." According to some, it is abdominal griping, best translated by the medical term *tenesmus*. Others say it refers to an umbilical hernia, magically caused by permitting a menstruating or recently delivered mother to handle someone else's new baby. It is also seen as *diarrea en extremo* (severe diarrhea), to which different causations are imputed, such as teething or disagreeing foods. *Le pega a uno cuando está comiendo cosas que no le caen bien* (It attacks one when eating foods which disagree). Thus, *pujo* is a homonymous lexeme, as is the following disease.

Pasmo (infection) is a Mexican disease without digestive features. It is an infection stimulated by rapid chilling of the body. Luisa spoke of her son, "My youngest son went and got *pasmo*. He was sick from his teething, and I bathed him and then took him out. *Pasmo* then struck him in the cheek."

Pasmo is the name of another disease which occurs in newly delivered mothers. It also can happen to other women:

> I had it three years ago. Well, it was a real hot day, and I went to my sister-in-law, and I was sweating a lot. She told me, did I want a beer? So I had one. Then I got a rash on one arm and then on the other. The eyes swell. I went to the clinic. They just gave me calamine lotion. But from inside, I thought I was burning.
>
> I like to drink beer when I make tortillas. I was breaking out with blisters, and I thought it was the soap, you know, the detergent you wash the dishes with. My sister-in-law told me to buy Yerba De Pasma. I drank it, and washed my hands with it for three days.

When the women of El Jardín are trying to decide if a condition is *alergia* (allergy) or *pasmo,* recalling the event as one of rapid temperature change suggests the latter diagnosis. Both conditions feature warmness of the affected parts, for a skin eruption nearly always predicts local fever.

CONSECUENCIAS (Consequences)

The final class of painful illness groups those conditions that follow some unwise action. Since each is spoken of as *consecuente a* (resulting from) certain events, I am labeling the class *consecuencias*. The first is *almorranas* (hemorrhoids), caused by sitting too long in a hot car. The next is *rotura de la aldilla* (rupture of the groin), which follows lifting something heavy, and *desombligado* (umbilical rupture), which is consequent to an improperly bound navel in early infancy.

Insolación (sunstroke), also called *resolación,* comes from absorbing too much sun. It is an especially dangerous condition for children. The adult who is in the direct sun when temperatures are 90-98°F. for a period of time will have headache and malaise. Some individuals can stand more sun than others; the alcoholic is especially vulnerable. Taking ice water when working in the sun, walking swiftly, or otherwise rapidly cooling the body are all dangerous and can lead to *insolación*. One can become *insolado* indoors if one sits where the sun passes through glass. As described earlier, curtains are drawn in the house, because of the hazards of *insolación*. If children play out-of-doors, they do so under the ramadas. All general features of disease – weakness, fatigue, incapacity, and dizziness – obtain. The defining features are faintness and profuse sweating.

Next come the conditions that may follow a neglected *resfriado* (cold). There may be sinusitis, also called *catarro constipado* (sinusitis), *bronquitis* (bronchitis), and *pulmonía* (pneumonia), also called *numonia. Sinusitis* is defined by headache and "yellow mucus" from the nose. *Bronquitis* affects *los tubos* (the tubes), making it hard to breathe, and *pulmonía* the lungs, making it painful to breathe – the symptoms are the defining features.

Finally, informants list *enfermedades venéreas* (venereal diseases) as consequent to extramarital affairs. Neither general features nor class features could be elicited for these conditions. It was thought that there is a skin eruption with *enfermedades venéreas.*

Enfermedades Cronicas (Chronic Illnesses)

A second major category of *enfermedades graves* ('serious illnesses') is *enfermedades crónicas* (chronic illnesses), and contrasts with *enfermedad dolorosa,* "painful illness," in that the former do not occur suddenly and cannot ever be cured.

The first sub-type is *enfermedad hereditaria* (inherited disease) which comes *de la herencia de la familia* (from the inheritance of the family). Most commonly known is *diabetis* (diabetes), related to gaining too much weight. There are four kinds of *diabetis,* differentiated by treatment and severity, but all are defined by sugar in the urine. The most severe kind requires daily injections of insulin. Milder forms may be "cured" by vitamins or other medicines.

Another common disease is *corazón grande* or *crecimiento de corazón* (enlarged heart). The feature of incapacitation increases, and the *enfermedad* is ultimately fatal. There is also *corazón débil* (weak heart), defined by the fact that "the heart beats too much." *Riñón grande* (enlarged kidney) is an exotic disease, known in the area because a local resident receives hemodialysis therapy. *Alta presión* (high pressure), too, is known in many older patients. Pallor, headache, and dizziness define this disease.

The second sub-type of *enfermedades crónicas* is *enfermedades sobrevenideras* (sequential diseases), which classifies those diseases resulting from neglecting a *pasmo.* There are three kinds of *artritis,* one in which the whole body hurts, another which twists a part of the body, such as the hand, and a third called *reúma seca* (dry rheumatism) or *siática* (sciatica), when pain moves up and down from the knee. The condition may come from the regular practice of overworking, and the neglect of *reúma* (rheumatism). *Se le cuajan los nervios* (The nerves clot).

There is also *anemia aguda* (severe anemia), diagnosed by noting *falta de glóbulos rojos* (lack of red blood cells) in a laboratory test. It is the result of not eating, so that the body does not have enough "vitamins," such as iron. Tuberculosis, called *tisis* by older informants, is a member of this class. Tuberculosis is the result of neglecting *resfriados* (colds) and *sangre débil* (weak blood). It may be suspected by observing that the ear lobes and fingertips are blue, rather than the normal pink in color, but diagnosis is dependent on a skin test and X-ray. *Asma* (asthma), which results from hay fever, is defined by great difficulty in breathing – "One chokes."

Alferecía (post-febrile convulsions) is the dreaded complication of diseases that feature high fevers, such as *sarampión* (measles). *Alferecía* is characterized by convulsions and mental retardation. Only fevers from infections can cause *alferecía;* those caused by *empacho* and other "stomach" disorders cannot, for the latter are local fevers. If an *empacho* is neglected, however, the consequence is *peritonitis* ("severe constipation"). Death can follow the cessation of bowel movements.

The entire list of physical illnesses reflects many disease concepts that are common in other systems of folk medicine. Grattan and Singer (1952) have suggested that folk medicine was formerly official medicine, with scientific principles misinterpreted and misapplied. El Jardín ethnomedicine diverges from official medicine in those ways that represent old-fashioned ideas. Possibly the greatest difference lies in the emphasis given to diseases of the "stomach."

Let us now turn to the other major category of illness, *enfermedad emocional.*

ENFERMEDAD EMOCIONAL (Emotional Illness)

The *enfermo* (patient) who suffers from *enfermedad corporal* can point to an external lesion or a place where it hurts inside. The *enfermo* who has *enfermedad emocional* (emotional illness) is told of his condition by others, who make their diagnosis according to his behavior. There are two kinds of *enfermedad emocional: mental* (mental) and *moral* (moral). Both refer to conditions *de los nervios* (of the nerves). The category of *enfermedad mental* is characterized by its non-volitional qualities. The patient cannot help getting sick. He is a victim of circumstances. These circumstances are next grouped into categories that help to explain the process, such as *trastornos* (derangements), or *daños* (witchcraft). *Enfermedad moral* (character disorder) is the patient's fault. Finally the names of specific diseases are given.

Features of Enfermedad Mental (Mental Illness)

The following signs and symptoms, or features, may occur in *enfermedad mental:*

1. *Mortificación* (worry) or *miedo* (fear) signifies dwelling on unpleasant events, possibilities, or problems of life.
2. *Desequilibrio* (lack of equilibrium) refers to confusion or disorientation.
3. *Tristeza* (sadness) characterizes habitual depression, accompanied by tears.
4. *Coraje* (rage) is an angry, hostile feeling.
5. *Desvario* (delirium) is unrestrained irrational action.

6. *Desmayo* (fainting) is temporary loss of consciousness.

7. *Ataques* (convulsions) are episodes of loss of consciousness together with jerking movements of the body. The term also is used interchangeably for 'delirium.'

8. *Alucinaciones* (hallucinations) connotes seeing and perhaps talking to the dead.

9. *Pequeños olvidos* (forgetfulness) refers to memory loss.

TRASTORNOS MENTALES (Mental Derangements)

Trastornos mentales (mental derangements) group a variety of situations in which behavior is uncontrollable. This category includes mental states that are caused by a specific episode such as a *golpe* (blow) to the head. There may be a brief *amnesia* (amnesia) when the victim does not know his identity, or a more lasting *locura* (craziness). *Locura* is defined by unpredictable, irrational actions.

Un susto (a shock) may result in varying degrees of disturbed behavior. It occurs *de alguna sorpresa* (from something unexpected). There may be physical effects, discussed above under *tripa ida*. With *histeria* (hysteria) one feels heavy and sore in the neck and cries uncontrollably. In *ataque de nervios* (nervous breakdown), the defining features of *histeria* are intensified. There may be agitation, crying, or scolding. The victim faints. His nerves "stick out like balls along the back of the neck." There is swelling over the left side of the chest "where the heart is."

Too much thinking, or dwelling on morbid thoughts, may cause *enfermedades emocionales de pensar* (anxiousness). Such illnesses include *congoja* (pressure) defined by shortness of breath and a feeling of being squeezed in the chest. *Tirisia* (anxiety) is a more severe degree of *congoja,* which is defined by a sorrowful mien and lack of appetite. It is common in toddlers when their mothers are absent; adults, similarly, suffer the loss of loved ones. Note: *tiricia* is an archaic form of *ictericia* (jaundice).

DAÑO (Damage)

Enfermedad endañada (witchcraft) is illness which is *puesto* (put on) for *daño* (damage). Most patients hospitalized for mental illness consider themselves victims of *daño*. It is defined by a wide variety of physical symptoms which persist despite medical treatment, and whose occurrence cannot otherwise be explained. *Mal ojo* (evil eye) may be cast by someone because of her envy of something you have, which is projected onto that which is envied. Typically, a beautiful child is envied and becomes gravely ill as a result of the unfulfilled desire to hold the child by the person who admires it. Twins are more likely to cast a lesser evil eye, especially if they are denied a request. "If your twin wants to taste the soup, and you don't let her, then the soup will be spoiled."

Pets and plants may die from this power, which is distributed to both sexes. "I guess if that person can't have it, he doesn't want anybody to have it." In El Jardín the *envidia* (envy) that is due to the jealousy of others is known only by name.

Hechicería (witchcraft) is used to refer to a condition that occurs in adults, especially an unfaithful lover. Class features of confusion and memory loss combine with a variety of physical symptoms. This *enfermedad* may be expected from an episode of unfaithfulness.

ENFERMEDADES HEREDITARIAS (Hereditary Diseases)

A final category of *enfermedad mental* is comprised of *enfermedades hereditarias* (hereditary diseases). It includes *inocencia* (mental retardation) and *epilepsia* (epilepsy), conditions which are due to prenatal events which are not the fault of the sufferer. The occurrence of disease that is inherited is duly noted by individuals in El Jardín because ". . . it will burn itself out in five generations." Presence of inherited disease does not appear to be a deterrent to marriage.

Inocencia is characterized by incapacity and memory loss, although women tend to lack consensus about both features. For a sizeable number of individuals in this barrio have been relegated to "special education" classes during their schooling, leading the women to ask if mental retardation is especially common in El Jardín or if the educational system is at fault. Drawing on their experiences, the women ask how deficient is a man who is labeled "mentally retarded," but who can read and write, can do geometric calculations required in construction labor, and supervise the work of others? But there are no names to reflect these varying degrees of ability. *Así es él* (he is that way) denotes *inocencia*.

Epilepsia (epilepsy) is characterized by convulsions. It contrasts with *alferecía* (post-febrile convulsions) by defining features; the convulsions are not related to any previous illness.

Enfermedad Moral (Character Disorder)

Enfermedad moral (character disorder) contrasts with *enfermedad mental* at Level 3 in that the former occurs because the individual "wants to be bad." At best, he is deficient in "will power." First there are *hábitos* (habits) or *emociones mal controladas* (poorly controlled emotions) such as *coraje* (rage), *celos* (jealousy), and *envidia* (envy). Homonymous with the *envidia* of witchcraft, El Jardín women almost always use the term *envidia* to mean "envy of possessions," which affects the person who does the envying. Another class is *debilidad del caracter* (weakness of character). Some people get the support that they need to bolster their weak character from drinking and thus suffer the *enfermedad* of *alcoholismo* (alcoholism). Others get into the habit of stealing and become *cleptomanos* (kleptomaniacs). Overeating demonstrates weakness, with *gordura mala* (obesity) the result.

Vícios (vices) are indicative of *un caracter duro* (a hardened character), the end result of uncontrolled habits. Such *enfermedad* cannot be treated. Notable victims of *vícios* are *marijuaneros* (users of marihuana) and *drogadictos* (addicts of drugs). Barrio dwellers have had personal experience with these vices.

CURES AND CURERS

Once the illness has been named, the barrio woman considers treatment. She thinks in terms of three kinds of medicine, depending upon who prescribes the treatment.

A classification of cures was arrived at by the same processes outlined earlier. At the first division are the *remedios caseros* (home remedies) which consist of herbs or kitchen vegetables. The second kind is *recetas del medico* (doctors' prescriptions) such as antibiotics and various *capsulas* (capsules) and *cucharadas* (spoonsful), liquid preparations prescribed for various *enfermedades graves*. The third category consists of *remedios de la farmacia* (proprietary drugs). These are the medicines which the women of El Jardín may buy at the drugstore after hearing them advertised on the radio or on television. This class contains pills and powders, such as aspirin and Alka Seltzer, and various topical treatments, such as *pomadas* (ointments) and *gotas* (drops), often patent medicines.

One may obtain all these medications at a pharmacy. Herbs, prescriptions, and patent medicines may all be purchased at *la botica*. But the source of authority for which medication is given differs.

Remedios caseros (home remedies) are prescribed by knowledgeable housewives, *recetas* (prescriptions) are given by the doctor, and the druggist recommends the proprietary medicine. Since the other two classes are authorized outside the home, by specialists, the housewife knows little about them. For example, she states that antibiotics "are to cure viruses." She has more information about the first category, that of *remedios caseros,* and her information is highly standardized. The bulk of this chapter will be devoted to the herbal remedies known in El Jardín, the sources of information that have made their use uniform, and the folk specialists who know their use.

The reader is now referred to Table 3.1, which presents herbal remedies used in El Jardín today. The first column gives the common name of the herb in Spanish, next in English, then the Linnean name, next the mode of administering the herb, followed by the *enfermedad* for which it is used.

Folk medicine makes extensive use of herbs, which of course were almost the only medicines available until modern technology made chemical

TABLE 3.1

Remedios Caseros — Home Remedies in El Jardín

Spanish Common Name	English Common Name	Linnean	Preparation	Use
Herbal remedies:				
Añil	bluing	Indigofera suffruticosa	crushed	empacho (indigestion)
Anis	anise	Pimpinella anisum	tea	cólico (pain in the abdomen)
Azahar	orange blossom	Citrus aurantium	tea	corazón (heart)
				nervios (nerves)
Boldo	bold	Peumus boldus	tea	falta de digestión (inadequate digestion)
Borraja	borage	Borago officinalis	tea	la tos (cough)
Brasil	brazil wood	Haematoxylum braziletto	solution	tirisia (anxiety)
Canela	cinnamon	Cinnamomum zeylanicum	tea	la tos (cough)
Canutillo	mormon tea	Ephedra trifurca	tea	sangre débil (weak blood)
Chicura	ragweed	Ambrosia ambrocoides	solution	lavado vaginal (vaginal douche)
Chilitipin	chili	Coriandum sativum	tea	atrasos de la regla (late menstruation)
Cilantro	coriander	Capsicum baccatum	fried	dolor de oído (earache)
Cocolmeca	sarsaparilla	Smilax mexicana	tea	dolor de riñón (kidney pain)
Damiana	damiana	Turnera diffusa	tea or douche	frío en la matriz (cold in the womb)
Epazote	wormseed	Chenopodium ambrosoides	tea	dolor de estómago (stomachache)
Estafiate	wormwood	Artemesia mexicana	tea	cólico (pain in the abdomen)
Golondrina	spurge	Euphorbia maculata	tea	diarrea (diarrhea)
			application	mesquinas (warts)
				llagas (sores)
Hediondilla	creosote	Larrea tridentata	tea	riñón (kidney)
				cólico (pain in the abdomen)
				pasmo (infection)
Granada	pomegranate	Punica granatum	tea	cólico (pain in the abdomen)
			solution	anginas (tonsils)
Hierba colorada	dock	Rumex crispus	solution	anginas (tonsils)

Hierba del burro	burro bush	Hymenoclea sp.	solution	artritis (arthritis), cortadas infectadas (infection from a cut)
Hierba del Indio	desert milkweed	Asclepias sp.	tea	riñón (kidney)
Hierba del manzo	swamp root	Anemopsis californica	tea	estómago (stomach)
Hierba del pasmo	spasm herb turpentine bush	Haplopappus larincifolius	tea solution	pasmo (infection)
Lanten	plantain	Plantago mayor	tea	disentería (dysentery) garganta (throat)
Malva	mallow	Malva parviflora	enema	fiebre (fever)
Manzanilla	chamomile	Matricaria chamomilla	tea	cólico (pain in the abdomen) dólores de parto (childbirth pains)
Marihuana	marihuana	Cannabis sativa	tea	nervios (nerves)
Naranjo	orange leaves	Citrus sp.	tea	cólico (pain in the abdomen)
Nogal	walnut	Juglans regia	douche	sangreada (hemorrhage)
Yerba buena	mint	Mentha spicata	tea	cólico (pain in the abdomen)
Maiz	corn tassel	Zea mays	tea	riñón (kidney)
Negrita	elderberry	Sambucus mexicana	tea	cólico (pain in the abdomen)
Orégano	oregano	Origanum vulgare	tea	la regla (menstruation), resfriado (cold)
Pamita	tansy mustard	Descurainia pinnata	tea	empacho (indigestion infection)
Pionillo	croton	Croton coresianus	tea	cólico (pain in the abdomen)
Romero	rosemary	Rosmarinus officinalis	tea	atrasos de la regla (late menstruation)
Sangre de drago	limberbush	Jatopha cardiophylla	tea	sangre débil (weak blood)
Saúco	elderberry flower	Sambucus mexicana	tea	sarampión (measles), fiebre (fever)
Sauz	willow	Salix gooddingii	tea	fiebre (fever)
Rosa de Castilla	rose	Rosa sp.	tea	purga (purge)
Ruda	rue	Ruta graveolens	emulsion in lard	dolor de oído (earache)
Tlachichinole	—	Kohleria deppeana	douche	lavado vaginal (vaginal douche)

TABLE 3.1 (cont.)

***Remedios Caseros* — Home Remedies in El Jardín**

Spanish Common Name	English Common Name	Linnean	Preparation	Use
Vegetable remedies:				
Ajo	garlic	Allium sativum	suppository	tripa ida (locked intestines)
Harina	flour	Triticum aestium	toasted	quemaduras (burns)
Papa	potato	Solanum tuberosum	poultice	dolor de cabeza (headache)
Tomate	tomato	Lycopersicon esculentum	poultice	dolor de garganta (sore throat)
Mineral remedies:				
Azufre	sulfur flowers		dissolved in alcohol	pasmo (infection)
Carbonato	soda bicarbonate		solution	indigestion (indigestion)
Animal remedies:				
Cagada del burro	burro dung		tea	aire (gas)
Telaraña	spider web		poultice	cortada infectada (infected cut) sangreada (hemorrhage)
Proprietary drugs:	Use:			
Anacin	Pain			
Aspirin	Pain			
Alka Seltzer	Indigestion			
Compound W	Warts			
Don Enriquez	High blood pressure			
Gotas de oído	Earache			
Mejorana	Purge			
Mr. Bell	Infection			
Peptobismol	Indigestion, diarrhea			
Vick's Vaporub	Cold			
Baby Percy	Purge			

synthetics possible. Many herbs that are used by the women of El Jardín are the same ones used and known since ancient times. Of the remedies summarized in Table 3.1, approximately half were introduced by Europeans after the conquest of Mexico. These are some of the 400 Galenic "simples" known to Egyptians and Grecians, some valued because of actual therapeutic value, others because of the doctrine of similarity (yellow brews for urinary complaints, red for the throat or for blood disorders), still others from the doctrine of contraries (cool brews for fevers). These are all part of the home pharmacopoeia wherever this combination of ancient and Arabic medicine was introduced. Many remedies derived, for example, from oranges, pomegranates, and chamomile, are cultivated so extensively that it is hard to remember that they did not always flourish in the New World. Some have escaped the garden and grow wild all over – mallow, for example. It will be noted that the herbs that were introduced include anise, orange blossoms, borage, cinnamon, coriander, pomegranate, dock, plantain, mallow, mint, chamomile, oregano, rosemary, rue, and the rose (Kearney and Peebles 1969; Martínez 1969; Henkel 1904; White 1948; Standlee 1961; and personal communications of Charles Mason, curator of the Herbarium, University of Arizona). Wheat and garlic were also introduced by the conquering Spaniards; the latter especially has been utilized for alleged medicinal properties from ancient times.

The other half of the *remedios caseros* summarized in Table 3.1 originated in the New World. Some are herbs indigenous to Sonora, where the value of leaves, roots, and flowers was noted by missionaries to northwest Mexico. As stated by Fr. Nentuig (Unknown 1951:43), one of the Jesuits referred to earlier:

> Divine Providence has enriched this Province, destitute of skillful physicians, surgeons, and apothecaries, with such excellent medicinal products in the way of herbs, trees, roots, gums, fruits, minerals and animals, that no such collection will be found in any of the botanical gardens of the whole of Europe.

In the *Rudo Ensayo,* a description of the Province of Sonora in 1763 just before the time of the Jesuit expulsion, Fr. Nentuig lists 79 plants and minerals "already known in medicine," and then goes on to describe "those medical productions whose virtues seem not to be known in other countries, which have been discovered either by the Indians of this land, or by the old Spanish women who have either set themselves up or have become in the natural course of events the College of Physicians of Sonora." He then selected 35 plants and minerals to identify in Opata and describe their uses, many of which are known today in El Jardín. These include at least anise herb, spasm herb, manso grass, swallow herb, cocolmecate, estafiate, damiana, mugwort, temitzo. It would appear that the descendents of this "College of Physicians of Sonora" have continued in this tradition, selecting some of the Sonora herbs and some of the European herbs.

Local plant ecology dictates a few exceptions. Otherwise, the same herbs are used for the same conditions by Spanish-speaking people from Spain to Puerto Rico to Mexico to California. How is this possible? This stability is maintained by pharmacopoeias that may be found in every herb store, or in the larger houses that supply the little *Expendidos de Yerbas Medicinales* at fairs, such as the one for San Francisco in Magdalena described earlier.

Women get their herbs from many places. Some grow them in the garden. Eva and María have wormwood plants which they share with their neighbors. Alicia has wormseed. Doña Luz grows rosemary, rue, plantain, wormwood, wormseed, elder blossom and pomegranate, and is the best source for most of her neighbors. She places a sheet under flowering trees to collect blossoms, and uses every surface in her kitchen to dry the herbs when they mature. Marihuana sources are not discussed.

Other herbs are collected at the bottom of the river (burro bush, spurge and mallow). Some are collected during mountain excursions, like limberbush, swamp root, and chamomile, and others are found in swampy areas, such as wormseed and dock. Some women feel that it is preferable to be assured of a fresh supply of herbs by collecting them themselves, for "stores sell *old* medicine." However, most women are not so particular and purchase their herbs at certain drugstores. "Certainly you can collect your own *pamita,* but those tiny seeds are a lot of trouble." Women go to one of three pharmacies. One of these has an extensive mail-order business and lists more than 300 herbs. Across the border in Mexico there is a convenient *Expendido de Yerbas,* which sells the same herbs at greatly lower prices, and also offers amulets such as "deer's eye" and iron filings to be used against *mal ojo,* and cards with pictures of saints who are associated with illness. It is at these special drugstores that the women are told what herbs are efficacious for which disorder. The vendors get their information from the folk pharmacopoeias and pass their instructions on to the purchaser.

Referring again to Table 3.1, it will be noted that the vast majority of remedies are for treating mild illnesses, and that in most cases, the herb is prepared as an infusion or as a tea. Digestive disorders are commonly treated by mint tea. More severe conditions such as colics may require anise, rosemary, or orange blossoms. If it is a simple *ataque de viento* (gas), two or three cups of mint tea should relieve the cold. *Boldo* also is used. *Congestión* (congestion) is usually provoked by overeating, or something that disagrees, and may be soothed by one of the teas, or by Alka Seltzer or Peptobismol. *Té de manzanilla* (chamomile) is used to treat digestive disorders and colics. Nausea may be treated by flour and water solution, flour and lemon juice, or cornstarch mixed with a little ground *añil,* which is laundry blueing prepared commercially into balls. Diarrhea is "cured" with *epasote* (wormseed), a ferocious treatment!

Estómago sucio (dirty stomach) is the result of eating something which is too highly seasoned or simply overeating. It is treated by removing the offending material. Laxatives are employed frequently, even weekly, by the ladies to treat all of the family, including the children. Persistent symptoms will be treated by an enema, perhaps prepared with one of the herbs listed for digestive disorders, now often purchased in disposable equipment by the young women. For small babies, *calillos* (suppositories) are used. Severe *aire* (gas) may be treated by a tea made of burro manure.

Tonsillitis is prevented by never walking barefoot, especially on cold concrete. But when the children grow older, they take off their shoes as soon as they come home from school. So, when the seasons change, and there may be daily temperature variations exceeding 50°F., sore throats are common. Hot tea, especially *lantén,* may be given, or gargles of *hierba colorada* (dock) or salt water may be offered. Or a poultice of chopped potato and tomato may be applied to the throat.

Treatment of *catarro* (cold) is directed primarily to prevent complications, especially of the cold "falling" to the chest. To prevent or treat pneumonia, hot cloths are applied. Some recommend poultices of creosote. Most popular by far is the use of Vick's or some other *mentolato*. Two informants had heard of *ventosas* (suction cups) but none had experience with this venerable therapy.

Dolor de oído (earache) is a frequent complication of the common cold. The herb of choice is rue pulverized and held near the auditory canal with a bit of cotton. Most homes have patent eardrops containing rue. Trini's mother once applied the following remedy to Fernandito when the patent eardrops had been left behind: three or four chiltipines, the tiny and exquisitely hot variety of chili, were fried in lard until they turned black. Still hot, they were wrapped, without breaking, in a little cotton and placed in the ears. The ears were closed with the hands. A sound like thunder, of air rushing out, was heard; then the cotton and chili were removed. Trini states that after this treatment, the earache did not return.

When children have a fever, they may receive an enema made of an infusion of *malva* leaves ("you wash it and cook it for 25 minutes"). Again, this is given to prevent pneumonia.

Tos (cough) may be treated by a hot tea of orégano. Medicine may be given also *por vapor* (via steam). *Hierba del pasmo* (spasm herb) is too bitter for a child to swallow, so inhalations are prepared instead. Dried leaves of the ubiquitous creosote bush may also be used, especially for bronchitis. A syrup compounded from *yerba del manso* (swamp root), *saúco* (elder blossom), *borraja* (borage), and raisins cooked together is used for persistent coughs.

For *sangre débil* (weak blood), special foods should be added to the diet. One which the Garcías recommended is *morcilla* (black pudding), a sausage made with coagulated blood left over after butchering, and mixed

..n onions and coriander. The spiny twigs of *sangre dedrago* (limberbush), which when boiled make a bright red tea, also enrich the blood, as does *canutillo* (mormon tea), the close relative of the ancient Chinese herb, *ephedra*.

Headache is often treated with aspirin or Anacin, or other frequently advertised proprietary drugs. A few old-fashioned women prepare frontals. *Pionilla* (croton) may be ground and rubbed into the forehead. Or raw potatoes may be sliced and held in the desired place with Vick's ointment. The potato slices simply may be placed on the affected part. When the potato turns black, its rapid oxidation indicates that the fever has been absorbed by the potato and thus lowered.

Conditions of the skin are treated by the ladies in El Jardín. For an infected scratch some recommend that a dog lick the sore. Others will apply grated potato or tomato, especially when you have a *llaga* "with a lot of pus and you want it to bust." Solutions of spurge or burro bush are good for boils and pustules. The itch of chicken pox lesions may be alleviated by applying browned flour. Blisters, as well as the lesions of measles and of less severe skin conditions that come with fevers, are treated systemically. The blossoms of the elder are administered in a tea so that all the lesions will erupt, "*para que se brote*." "Otherwise they will go inside the body and cause severe complications."

Treatment of Enfermedades Graves

Most of the *enfermedades graves* are treated with medical prescriptions. One group that is an exception to this is the *enfermedades Mexicanas* (Mexican diseases), because the distinctive feature of this category is the fact that it consists of conditions not recognized by official Western medicine. One of these conditions, *pasmo,* the infection that follows sudden chilling of the overheated body, was previously a greater risk when there were no indoor facilities for bathing. The treatment that was recommended was drinking *azufre* (sulfur flowers) dissolved in alcohol, or bathing the swollen parts in an infusion of *hediondillo* (creosote). Some state that the condition of *pasmo* is not nearly as bad as the treatment. A more acceptable treatment is drinking tea made from *yerba del pasmo,* and washing the affected parts with an infusion of the herb for three days. The other *enfermedades Mexicanas* will be discussed later in the section on curers.

Mal de riñón ('kidney disease') may be treated by a tea of corn tassels. *Cocolmeca* (sarsaparilla) is Mexico's gift to Europe for kidney conditions. Acute "kidney" diseases, or any disease in the urinary tract, is, of course, referred to the doctor, but putative chronic conditions are alleviated at home. Actually, although *enfermedades crónicas* are commonly given to the ministrations of the doctor, there are usually some attendant symptoms which are treated at home. For example, dizziness may be caused by *alta presión* (high pressure). "Don Enriquez" is a patent medicine frequently employed to treat high blood pressure. *Té de azahar* (orange blossom tea) is taken for the heart whether or not a medical prescription also is taken.

Treatment of Enfermedades Mentales

Of the *enfermedades mentales,* only the benign ones are treated at home. *Tirisia* (anxiety) has several cures, all involving the color red. A child may be dressed in red. Or he may be bathed in water colored by the addition of *Brasil,* which may be purchased at the drugstore. A young woman may wear a gold ring tied around her neck by a red ribbon. Similar uses of red to treat depression are known all over Europe.

An attack of *coraje* (rage) is immediately handled by throwing cold water on the face of the victim. Since the "nerves" and the heart are considered to be closely interrelated, treatment of all nervous conditions is directed to the heart. One informant spoke of alcohol being applied to the swelling that was allegedly visible on the left side of her chest when she had a "nervous breakdown." The doctor prescribed tranquilizers for the condition, but she had to discontinue their use because they made her too sleepy. *Azahar* tea and alcohol applications had no such unwanted effects. A few informants discussed marihuana tea or poultice: "You don't care about nothing." Most disapproved of this remedy.

Curers

For *enfermedades pasajeras* (passing illnesses), few women go outside their own home for advice. "A little whiskey on sore gums, hot compresses for mumps – what more do you need?"

Enfermedades benignas (mild illnesses) require more knowledge. All of the older women in the sample were authorities in the treatment of *enfermedades benignas.* They were consulted by their daughters, daughters-in-law, and god-daughters for their special knowledge. Knowing *enfermedades* was more important to those families who, at some time in their lives, did not have access to care from medical doctors. "When we lived on the ranch, the doctors were too far away to consult, but my mother knew everything," recounted Faustina Romo. "Now I still ask her what to do for my babies. After all, all 11 of her children lived."

For all the *enfermedades graves* (serious illnesses), a specialist is consulted. To learn what is wrong and to get treatment, the women of El Jardín usually go to a doctor. He may be a doctor of medicine or an osteopath. Informants cite different kinds of doctors: surgeons, pediatricians, obstetricians, dermatologists, specialists in heart disease or allergy. "Some diseases can't be cured, but only a doctor can know what disease you have."

For "Mexican diseases," a folk curer is frequently sought, even though such illness is *grave* (serious). Lowest in status of folk curer levels is the *sobador* (f. *sobadora*) (massager). This status is usually occupied by a woman who has learned from her mother or grandmother. She gives "therapies" rather than medicines. The *sobadora soba un dolor* (rubs a pain) – *es para descomposturas* (is for unfixed joints). She is particularly needed in cases of *empacho* (indigestion infection), to diagnose the location of the adhering food, and also in cases of *mollera caída,* for lifting the 'fallen fontanel.' If you are new to the neighborhood and don't know someone skilled in these techniques, you ask around for *un fulano* (some Joe) who has this skill. Consuelo's husband went to Mexico to find a *sobador,* and others go to chiropractors in the city.

A *curandero* is competent not only in *sobando* (rubbing) but also knows much more about herbs than the usual housewife. None lives in El Jardín, but there are two who are not far away. One is the boarder of Inez Otero's sister. He is a part-time curer who is available to help sick people in the afternoons. "He knows how to cure *mollera, empacho, descomposturas,* everything! He has a special cure for *almorranas* (hemorrhoids), and is especially gentle with *mollera* (soft spot)."

There are several ways to treat *mollera caída* (fallen fontanel). Most people who just dabble in curing will exert pressure for at least two minutes on the palate to elevate the fallen fontanel. This pressure causes pain, and the infant will cry long and hard. The *curandero* is more likely to use gentle measures involving holding the baby by the ankles, and then moving the little body in cruciform motions over a pan of water. Poultices of various materials – eggs, salt, or rue – may be applied to the scalp after the pulsating "soft spot" has been sucked by the curandero.

Several of the younger women suggested that the term *curandero* could be synonymous with "witch doctor" because: *El conoce enfermedades dañados* (He knows illnesses of witchcraft). Other informants objected that a "witch doctor" was really a *brujo,* distinguished because *"Es malo"* (He is bad); *"El pone daños"* (He harms).

Linda went to see someone she identified as a witch doctor in English, and a *curandero* in Spanish, a few years ago when medical doctors failed to treat her "nerves." She had a course of treatment which included massages with oil, prayers, and lengthy explanations of how "your nerves can make you sick." He offered no herbal remedies, usually the special knowledge of the *curandero*. This man, who is a Black, not Mexican, has, together with his mother, a large clientele among Spanish-speaking people. Many El Jardín women have consulted him, although they are usually embarrassed to admit needing such care. Consulting Frank, who "has a license, so you know he isn't a quack," is less humiliating than consulting a psychiatrist, according to Linda. His license is from a school of Swedish massage.

Many women discount *curanderos*. "Doctors can't understand cancer and leukemia. What can you expect from a poor *curandero?"* scoffed one. Perhaps no other topic elicited more disagreement among informants than the role of the *curandero* and the validity of his treatments. Many of the young women are simply ignorant of the treatments of previous days. I was interviewing Rebecca Hawkins about folk diseases one morning. Her daughter, Dora, found the entire discussion both interesting and novel. *"Múy* interesting," said Dora sincerely, "I never heard of that before." Yet, Dora's maternal grandmother had been both a *curandera* and a *partera* (midwife). And Evangelina recounted a time when her grandmother told her to give her baby enemas for *empacho* (indigestion infection), and then it developed that the child's fever was really caused by pneumonia. "I might have killed Felicia."

Ignorance or disdain for folk curers changes, however, when there is an episode of illness that the medical doctor cannot handle. According to many investigators of medical behavior, summarized in Weaver (1970), the illness referral system is commonly as follows. If folk curers are consulted, it is always before official scientific doctors. Folk curers are consulted after the individual has exhausted the resources of his family. Then, only after the folk curer fails, the medical doctor is sought. In El Jardín, the folk curer is consulted after the official system has been utilized without alleviation of the condition. When diarrhea strikes an infant, his mother usually seeks official advice.

> I took Ruben to Dr. Valdez. He gave him pure skim milk and medicine to cut the diarrhea, and also antibiotic injections. After a week, Ruben still wasn't well. My *concuña* was visiting, and she told that Rubenito had *mollera*. When her husband came home from work, they took me to Arsenio so that he could lift up the *mollera*.

It seems likely that women in El Jardín have departed from the sequence found in the "classic" referral system because of forcefully directed cultural change. Specifically, the doctors scold mothers severely when a baby is brought in for treatment "with salt glued to his scalp and the palate a mass of bruises."

Mal ojo, the evil eye, is included among the beliefs of most peasant societies. It gets little attention in El Jardín. However, one informant believes firmly that her children survived their early childhood despite many episodes of *mal ojo* only because of her curing skill.

> I take an egg, very fresh – one that hasn't been in the refrigerator or bought in the store. Now the child with *ojo* has a terrible headache and can hardly open his eyes. I put him down on the bed and *lo persigna.* I make signs of the cross on him using the egg. I begin with head. And I pray while I am making the signs of the cross, ten Padre Nuestros and ten Ave Marías, all over his body. I do it for three days, in the morning still fasting, *en ayunas.* It is the same with *empacho* excepting that one needs *pamita* and *añil* and olive oil to give. And also one has to rub under the ribs.

Tripa ida (locked intestines) is cured by garlic, heated in olive oil, and used as a suppository. *Latido* (cachexia) is treated by tying bread and onions around the waist. Again, not all informants know these cures.

Women prefer not to talk about the possibility of witchcraft. One informant considered witchcraft only after repeated hospitalization failed to provide her with an adequate explanation of her symptoms. She was monolingual in Spanish, and her diagnosis in Western scientific terms was of a rare and fatal disease (disseminated lupus erythematosus). She was convinced that her husband's former girl friend had caused the symptoms and was planning to consult a Yaqui *curandero* in Cuidad Obregon, Sonora.

The *partera* (midwife) had previously played an important role in the health of Spanish-speaking women. In 1952 the Arizona Legislature passed a law requiring literacy in English or Spanish for licensing midwives (otherwise the midwife could not register the birth for an official birth certificate). This regulation immediately reduced the number of midwives in the area. At the same time, hospital benefits began to be included in the contracts of the construction workers' unions to which the men of El Jardín belonged. So the wives of these workers began to give birth in hospitals. In their last years of practice, the two midwives in the area had ever-decreasing numbers of deliveries. With advanced age (one at 88, the other at 84), the two finally retired. Today, the status of *partera* has all but disappeared from the area.

CHILDBEARING AND HEALTH

We have seen that certain *enfermedades temporales* occur in women. In this section we will consider the life cycle, with emphasis on reproduction. The Mexican American women in El Jardín believe that vulnerability to illness is influenced by age, or stage in the life cycle. The stages are labeled as follows:

Criatura: This is the only term that is used commonly for a fetus and a newborn baby. The term extends to any creation of God, and thus even applies to animals, like its cognate, "creature."

Bebe, or *bebito:* baby. This is a child under three years of age. A boy baby is a *varón*.

Niño (f. *niña*): This is a small child, from 3-15 years of age. He also may be called such tender pejoratives as *mocoso, indito,* and *chipilyate*. Translations which convey similar sentiments in English are respectively, "snot-nose," "little savage," and "cry baby."

Muchacho (f. *muchacha*). This term is usually reserved for children 15 years and over. Synonyms are *chamaco* and *buqui,* the latter term commonly used by Sonorans and other *norteños* and derived from the Cahita language.

Joven: A youth, aged 18-21.

Juvenil: Also a youth, but the term usually refers to a delinquent adolescent.

Señor: An adult; applied to any male after 21 years of age, whether married or not. The unmarried adult woman is *señorita,* although the term is also formally applied to the married woman who is more correctly called a *señora.*

Viejo, viejito, viejecito, anciano, señor grande: These terms refer to the aged. These terms are rarely applied to persons under 70 years, or to those who have not yet retired.

A young woman in El Jardín may look forward to many years of fecundity. Menstruation may commence from the eleventh to the seventeenth year, with the secular trend towards earlier menarche reflected by many younger women. Almost all have menstruated by age 14.* *Cambio de vida* (change of life) is usual by 50 years. 'Menstruation' is called *el período* and *la regla;* 'to menstruate' is *reglar.*

A delayed menstrual period is cause for concern and many home remedies are given to treat this problem. The women list wormseed, oregano, coriander, and rue teas "to bring down menstruation." One informant candidly states that these medications also are useful to provoke abortions. Most women report incapacitating pain during menstruation. The most severe discomfort, *dolor de ijar* (flank pain), may be alleviated by drinking chamomile, oregano with cinnamon or mint teas. These same herbs are used in European folk medicine to soothe abdominal and menstrual cramps: the putative abortifacients have had the same reputation in Europe.

After each menstrual period and also following cessation of post partum bleeding, a vaginal douche is indicated. *Chicura, tlachichinole, damiana,* or rue may be used "to clean everything out." The first three of these herbs are indigenous to the New World. The practice of vaginal douching has been common in folk medicine everywhere and has been given commercial encouragement by drug firms. Heavy bleeding is treated by a douche made from a solution of boiled nut shells or leaves.

During menstruation, foods which are "acid," such as lemonade, or "fresh," such as cucumber, tomato, and watermelon, must be avoided. Older women describe these same foods as harmful because they are *muy frío, muy helado,* "very cold." They will demonstrate to the observer that foods like lemon juice are astringent to meat. Similarly, if acids are ingested, the menstrual "blood" may be congealed, later to reappear as cancer. Taking a bath in the presence of vaginal bleeding is similarly dangerous.

Pregnancy is suspected as soon as a menstrual period is missed. A woman who *está gorda* (is fat) or *está con familia* (is with family) may be pampered during her first pregnancy. She is more likely to experience

*Hrdlička (1906) gives similar findings for Ópata and other Sonorans in 1904.

antojos (cravings), which must be catered to or the baby may be marked. She is also supposed to influence the formation of her baby by having pleasant experiences, thinking nice thoughts, and listening to lovely music. *Defectos de nacimiento* (congenital deformities) may occur. Although women know that the first three months are crucial for the formation of the fetus, they feel that care should be taken during the rest of the pregnancy, too. Quarrels with your husband, not attending Mass, and permitting *coraje* (rage) to smolder can tie knots in the umbilical cord and kill the unborn baby.

The young woman goes to the doctor, *va con el médico,* for diagnosis. Some women experience complications such as elevated blood pressure, prolonged *mareo* and *basca,* dizziness and nausea, or *mal de riñón* (kidney disease). These women report promptly and regularly for medical supervision. In the absence of such *enfermedades,* women avoid official prenatal care as long as possible. The pelvic examination is dreaded as painful and unnecessary and is simply unknown to the Mexican immigrants. A few husbands are said to resent such intimate examination by another man. The El Jardín woman who does not report for prenatal care is usually one who owes money to the doctor. All the women take the prescribed vitamins and minerals faithfully, for they impute great importance to these supplements.

Much behavior of the pregnant woman is culturally prescribed to assure an easy delivery. It is thought that the prospective mother should be active, not sleeping too much, or the baby will stick to the uterus. Further, she should not gain too much weight, for that would cause a large baby. A large baby or one that "adheres to the sides of the womb" or a slow labor will necessitate extraction *con hierros,* "with irons" (forceps). Such deliveries are thought to be injurious to the baby, perhaps causing orthopedic deformities. The mother should continue with sexual intercourse until labor is imminent "to keep the birth canal lubricated."

The position of the baby must be attended to during pregnancy. The *partera,* the folk midwife, always saw her patients several times for treatments during each pregnancy *para que se componga,* "in order to fix." This is a type of massage, mild or vigorous according to the operator. Abdominal manipulations of this kind are not commonly given by obstetricians, so some of the women have received them from others among them who know how to do it. Francisca Salas always has given this service to her daughters and daughters-in-law.

During the last month of pregnancy, some women take *té de manzanilla* (chamomile) nightly. When uterine contractions, *dolores,* commence, more *manzanilla* is taken. "If it is true labor, *manzanilla* makes the pains stronger. If your time hasn't come, it makes the pains go away."

Women are taught to keep active as long as possible during labor, because that causes the baby to be born quickly. The distinctive characteristic of a good labor is its rapidity, not the amount of pain suffered. Strong uterine contractions are described as "good ones." Some women stay at home as long as possible during early labor, because they have learned that they will be put to bed as soon as they are in the labor suite of the hospital.

Menstruation may be referred to when a woman says she *anda enferma,* (is sick). When pregnant, she may be *enferma con niño* (sick with a child). Delivery may be called *sanarse* (to be healed). These linguistic cues would suggest that such women see the whole process of pregnancy and childbirth as pathological. But many have a more positive attitude toward their reproductive functions. Several women told me that they like being awake for their deliveries, so they can see what is going on. These women refer to delivery as *parto.* They, and others who are more squeamish about watching, claim that childbirth really isn't all that painful and prefer not to be given the pain medication as is common in the hospital. These medicines are considered disagreeable because of the mental confusion they cause. "The *partera* never gave you anything more than *manzanilla.*"

La dieta is the period of convalescence following delivery. Precautions to be taken during this time may include the same menstrual taboos, such as avoiding bathing and eating foods which are "too acid." Most women who have delivered in the hospital have become used to bathing within a few hours after birth. There are still some who "because my mother so accustomed me" will go into the shower room, turn on the water, but avoid getting wet. Thus they satisfy both the hospital staff and their own sociocultural pressures. Once safely home, they continue with such precautions. Sexual abstinence is considered the most important aspect of *la dieta.* Indeed, sexual intercourse when there is bleeding is always abhorrent to Mexican American women. The newly-delivered mother is considered particularly vulnerable to infection. Formerly she was "required" to rest for forty days following delivery. Such a holiday is not possible in El Jardín today, and no one imputes ill health to a mother's resuming some activity. "Of course she shouldn't be mopping the floor barefooted now," explained Jovita.

The most serious immediate result of transgressions from *la dieta* is the condition of *pasmo.* This term is another homonymous lexeme, referring to various conditions of which some have already been discussed. In connection with childbirth, *pasmo* has features similar to those of tetanus, kidney disease, and septicemia. As a diagnostic term, *pasmo* is well known by the older women. Young women speak of having the diagnosis made on them when visiting in Mexico, the distinctive feature apparently being an appearance of swelling around the eyes and ankles. Even in the absence of this condition, the older women prophesy dire fates to the young women who refuse to observe the precautions of *la dieta.* Today, only those young women who are directly under the supervision of their mothers or mothers-in-law follow customs of *la dieta.*

Delivered mothers wear a *faja,* which is a wide band made of *manta,* a heavy cotton fabric, to bind their abdomens for a given period after delivery. Some women have replaced the *faja* with an elastic girdle. The function of such support is supposedly to restore the figure to the condition it was in before pregnancy. Younger women pursue this objective in a more active fashion, by exercises, again to the dismay of their older mentors. Failure to wear the *faja* or observe *la dieta* results in *frío de la matriz,* externally visible by a fat belly.

If the newborn is breast fed, the mother avoids certain foods in her diet which are thought to affect her milk. The first milk (colostrum) is thought to be bad for the baby, and babies are given olive oil, *aceite de comer,* or even castor oil, to promote evacuation. Breast feeding is considered best for the baby by both mother and father, so most mothers attempt to nurse. *Grietas,* the name given to the cracks on the tender nipples, may appear as a result of breast feeding. Older women say insufficient covering of the back or taking acid foods causes breast infections. Most infants are soon on the bottle and are commonly given commercial formulas. Waters from cooked beans and rice are also given to the newborn. Breast feeding may continue to be given at night to the infant who sleeps with the mother, often past a year of age.

The *ombligo* (navel) is "cured" with *aceite de comer* (olive oil), and the abdomen is firmly wrapped in a smaller version of his mother's *faja.* This practice is thought to prevent umbilical hernia. When the stump of the dessicated cord falls off, it is casually discarded. The baby is kept warmly dressed during the early weeks of his life, firmly wrapped in blankets that come up to the armpits. Diapers, locally called *zapetas,* are changed frequently. On the rare occasion that the baby is taken outside, his head is usually covered. He also wears the religious medal that his mother wore while she was carrying him.

A baby is bathed frequently unless he has a runny nose. Then he is cleaned with baby oils and lotions, even up to school years. Toilet training is casual and usually complete within the second or third year. Discipline seems to vary a great deal, depending upon the mother's convictions. Most women are reluctant to have their infants receive immunizations before they are school age. As Angela said, "my children never had shots from a doctor. I cured them myself as my mother told me." They state that the fevers that follow baby "shots" are dangerous, and besides "my husband won't allow it." The age at which a baby is brought for immunization to the serious communicable diseases of childhood is the best single indicator that the writer has found for acculturation to Western scientific medicine.

Practitioners of Western medicine urge that baby boys be circumcised, but most families do not consent. The results are considered disfiguring to the baby's *cosita* or *weenito.* The older women are firmly opposed to the practice because they believe that when the child grows up and gets married, he will inflict pain to his wife if he is circumcised.

Fertility and Its Control

In the sample of women who were interviewed intensively, it was found that all women over 50 years of age who were fertile completed families of at least 11 children. One woman was pregnant 18 times, another reported 22 pregnancies. For in El Jardín childbearing is the appropriate role of a woman, as these statements from four different informants show:

> When I got married, I knew it was to have children.
>
> There were nine years between my second and my third child. I used to cry at night, why don't more children come.
>
> I have many vexations with the children, to feed them and take care of them. All the same, I want as many as the Lord will send.

The woman who decides to limit the size of her family faces disapproval, primarily from her mother:

> My mother says, how can you say you don't have enough to take care of more children? Your enough for four is so much more than we ever had for our ten.

Only one woman in the sample who was over 50 years of age had ever attended a Planned Parenthood Clinic, and this was after she had six children. Another woman in this oldest age group had each of her four pregnancies end prematurely with a stillbirth. A third had only one live birth. She herself had been one of five survivors of her mother's 14 pregnancies. One young woman had five girls, then six spontaneous abortions when she kept trying for a boy.

Women with such a history of pregnancy wastage, that is, many spontaneous abortions or stillbirths, understandably felt strongly that it was wrong to practice contraception. Those who found themselves with ten children while they were still in their thirties sought sterilization, the most common method of family limitation among Spanish-speaking women in the New World, prior to the development of the contraceptive pill.

Previously, especially fertile women attempted to space their children by prolonging lactation, having learned that menstruation is delayed by many months in the breast-feeding mother. Their husbands "took care of them," that is, practiced *coitus interruptus*. Other women tried the diaphragm, but found it repulsive.

> They put that thing in me. I felt like the whole world could see it as I walked. As soon as I got home, I took it out and threw it away.

Contraception is becoming common today, but the woman who follows this practice does so with misgivings. She has to hide contraceptive materials from her mother. Her priest may not absolve her for this sin. She has no idea of how oral contraceptives work, but uses them anyhow, even though she dislikes side effects such as weight gain and deposition of pigment on the face, called *paño*.

The women are modest in comparison with their contemporaries in other societies. For example, very little girls are taught never to undress completely: they even bathe with their panties on. Children are taught that "touching yourself" is very wrong, so contraception using mechanical means is difficult for adults. In no other area of health practice has there been more rapid change than in the widespread adoption of the contraceptive pill.

The El Jardín woman's knowledge of anatomy and physiology is rather vague. None was told about menstruation before her menarche, and it is still a mysterious subject. They are not sure what organs are involved, just that it "has something to do with the *matriz*." *Matriz* and *vientre* appear to be used synonymously for 'womb' or 'uterus.' But careful feature analysis shows that *vientre* refers to "all the female organs down below," especially in the pregnant state. *Matriz,* on the other hand, refers to the mature but empty womb. A girl who has menstruated has a *matriz;* so does a newly delivered mother. Sterility is called *frío en la matriz* (inflammation or cold in the womb). Their inadequate knowledge of reproduction has ultimate effects on the sterilization practices common to Mexican Americans. After a rapid succession of pregnancies, women may elect to have their tubes tied. They say that the men refuse vasectomy, ligation of the sperm ducts, because this surgery is thought to make them lose interest in sex – *No pueden alborotar* (they can't be aroused). On the other hand, some women believe that they can avoid pregnancy by not permitting orgasm. These women may learn to enjoy sex after they are no longer fertile.

Taught little about reproduction, women in El Jardín are taught less about sex. Sexual instruction has heretofore been left to the husband. Here, too, there is rapid culture change. Recently an informant was asking about the use of the new "adult" films for sexual instruction. It is difficult to make generalizations that would apply to every woman of the four families, for the gap between the young and the not-young is wide in this regard. Such differences touch upon the problem of consensus in all of the taxonomies.

ETHNOMEDICINE AND EFFECTIVE HEALTH CARE

These taxonomies of illnesses, cures, and curers are composites of the taxonomies of the women in El Jardín. The women ranged from 19 to 78 years of age, and were either born in Mexico or were first, second, or third generation American born. Each gave only some of the disease names. When they were asked about lexemes given by other informants, the individual woman would either agree that such words did describe a specific disease, or that she didn't "believe in" such a category. So each informant had a unique list of illness terms. She also had her own way of ordering these disease names, although differences did not reflect opposing principles of organization. These factors might account for different classifications:

1. There is a difference in the opportunity available to learn about the dominant system of Western medical science, either in Mexico or the United States. It may be a matter of exposure to formal education, roughly measurable by years of schooling. Different knowledge of scientific medicine may occur with participation in Western medicine, because of insurance through unions, age-specific programs like Head Start or Medicare. There are also individual differences in experience with illnesses that demand crisis care in modern hospitals.

2. There is a difference in the reinforcement of an ethnomedical system, for some women have more contacts with people who know herbs and curers. Recent immigrants and those who visit relatives in Mexico frequently tend to know more ethnomedicine.

3. There are differences in individual patterns of enculturation – sometimes the result of the proximity of the mother and the mother-in-law, and the degree to which their ideas are sought and adhered to.

4. There are differences in the ability to perceive relationships, as demonstrated by elaborateness and explicitness of categories. Some informants particularly enjoyed, or were better at, the game of "how does x differ from y."

Beyond such variations, what does this ethnomedical study imply? I should like to consider these questions. What are the major ideas of the ethnomedicine of El Jardín and how do they converge with the theory of Western medicine? How do they converge with other ethnomedicines, especially the ethnomedicine of other Spanish-speaking people? Finally, given such differences, what are the implications for the delivery of effective health care?

El Jardín women believe that some illnesses are transmitted which are categorized as *maledades de andancia* (epidemic disease). There are variances in understanding of just how disease may be carried, as these statements from five different informants illustrate:

> The river carries illness through its water. People die, the bodies are washed, and when they throw the water away, a little red animal leaves the body and gets into the water. This filthy water carries the illness.

> After the wind passes over a dead thing, it next attacks the back of someone else, giving him *sarampión, viruela, difteria,* or *influenza.*

> The wind may carry sickness from as far away as Viet Nam where there are so many dead.
>
> The dirt carries a virus. The cooler moves the dirt from different places, also the water in the cooler may be dirty.
>
> Flies go to excrement, and then walk on your food.
>
> Viruses, which can be seen only by special microscopes, cause many diseases. You get sick when your body is attacking the virus.

Western medicine has not been entirely successful in dealing with the question of why one person gets sick, and not another. Its theory includes the germ theory, that some illnesses have specific microorganic causes, and that these microorganisms are spread by vectors such as flies and mosquitoes, and can be transmitted through the air, water, and food. In the ethnomedicine of El Jardín, the more observable of these factors are stressed.

In El Jardín *"hacer desarreglos,"* roughly "to break the rules," is frequently cited as a cause of illness. The person who disregards hygienic rules is likely to get sick. The rules that are invoked are often rules that are recognized transculturally in all ethnomedical systems that share roots with present scientific thought. Scientific medicine grew from a tradition (see Sigerist 1961; Inglis 1965) that was first recorded in Babylonia, from where it went both to Greece and India. The Indian interpretation spread eastward to China and Japan, where illness was seen to be a disturbance of yang and yin. The Greek theory, conventionally credited to Hippocrates, diffused westward to Rome where it was systematized by Galen. In the Middle Ages it was deflected through Arab physicians, such as Avicenna, who brought it to Europe. From this medical tradition came ideas of how to preserve health and prevent illness that are transcultural.

A widespread rule is that one must be careful about what he eats. So in El Jardín, women impute much illness to eating the wrong foods. One of the largest categories of illness is that of *malestares* (indispositions), which come from the ingestion of foods that disagree with an individual. Most of the *maledades Mexicanas* (Mexican diseases) affect the gastrointestinal tract, as do the various *cólicos* (colics). Throughout the world there is enormous variety in beliefs about which foods or food combinations are good, and which are dangerous. Culture almost alone determines what is utilized as food from what is available, and beliefs about food are transmitted to the individual early in his life.

Another widespread concept is that it is dangerous to change the environment to which the body is accustomed. In warm climates, illness is ascribed to absorbing additional heat, and in cold climates, danger is noted in getting colder. So in El Jardín one is told that one will get *almorranas* (hemorrhoids) from sitting on heat, such as in a hot car, particularly on plastic seat covers. The same condition is caused by sitting in the snow, or on cold cement, in northern states, according to folk physiology.

There are also ethnomedical rules against exposing oneself to rapid change in temperature, for this is considered dangerous. Sudden chilling by bathing when one is overheated or when generally feeble or weak from illness is courting trouble. When taking a bath, one should provide for gradual temperature change by letting at least one hour elapse before leaving the house. Bathing should be avoided entirely during the menstrual period, and when suffering from fevers. The individual who is complaining of heat on a summer's day must avoid drinking iced fluids; tepid water is safe. Standing in a draft in the winter or sleeping under an evaporative cooler is unwise, since it usually leads to illness. Of course, many of these illnesses are merely *temporal* (temporary discomforts).

Today we often read about scientific studies in which experimental groups are exposed to cold and wet conditions and then examined for respiratory infection. In neither case do chilled subjects develop more infections than non-chilled subjects. But El Jardín women would never accept such findings; they "know" better. Likewise, no followers of a folk medicine that is heir to Western thought would believe that temperature change is not pathogenic. Why are these ideas so persistent?

It seems to me that the underlying principle is the belief that change is dangerous. This principle is found in most explanations of pathology. It derives from a concept of disease that is found transculturally, the concept of "balance." One of the primary paradigms which scientific medicine uses to explain pathology concerns change and bodily adjustments to achieve homeostasis. Pathology is demonstrated when intracellular fluid shifts to extracellular paths, and when the chemistry of the blood is outside the narrow range of balance between acid and alkaline, due to metabolic or respiratory alteration. The same explanations have been used by systematists throughout millenia. Thus Grecian humors, Chinese yang and yin principles, American color-directions, and twentieth-century fluids and electrolytes must remain in balance, or there will be illness.

Foster (1953:202-3) sees this explanation for such ideas, the transmission of humoral theory by the Spaniards:

> The Hippocratian doctrine of the four "humors" – blood, phlegm, black bile ("melancholy"), and yellow bile ("choler") – formed the basis of medical theory. Each humor had its "complexion": blood, hot and wet; phlegm, cold and wet; black bile, cold and dry; and yellow bile, hot and dry. As the three most important organs of the body – the heart, brain, and liver – were thought to be respectively dry and hot, wet and cold, and hot and wet, the normal healthy body had an excess of heat and moisture. But this balance varied with individuals; hence

> the preponderantly hot, humid, cold, or dry complexion of any individual. Natural history classification was rooted in the concept that people, and even illnesses, medicines, foods, and most natural objects, had complexions. Thus, medical practice consisted largely in understanding the natural complexion of the patient, in determining the complexion of the illness or its cause, and in restoring the fundamental harmony which had been disturbed.

Since Foster's article was published, it has been accepted in all analyses of folk medicine of Spanish-speaking people that there is a level of contrast in disease categories between hot and cold diseases, for according to Foster (1953:204) "there is surprising homogeneity from Mexico to Chile."

Because the hot/cold contrast is ascribed by so many anthropologists of Spanish-speaking people, I tried to elicit evidence of this contrast from my informants. The women were asked about hot/cold diseases and hot/cold herbs (nothing was known of hot/cold foods). No woman under 30 could make such distinctions or seemed to be aware of this system of classification. Petra Lopez, the aged lady from Jalisco, was able to explicate a contrast. *Hierbas frías* (cold herbs) are those which refresh, which bring down fever. They include *saúco* (elder blossom) and *rosa de castilla* (rose). *Hierbas calientes* (hot herbs) are those which bring heat to the chilled person or organ. These herbs include *manzanilla* (chamomile), *romero* (rosemary), *chicura* (ragweed), *hediondillo* (creosote), *canela* (cinnamon), *yerba buena* (mint), and *estafiate* (wormwood). *Enfermedades calientes* (hot diseases) are those in which fever attacks, and *enfermedades frías* (cold diseases) are specified by diarrhea or dysentery, and are caused, "If you sit on a cement bench, you will catch cold. Or if you go around inadequately covered. Or if you don't wear the kind of clothes that warm the stomach."

Other informants did little with this contrast. They used *frío* (cold) interchangeably with *inflamación* (inflammation). Their consensus was that *all* herbal teas are hot, because you cannot brew the infusion without boiling water, and cold teas don't taste good. What the majority of women relate then is not Foster's classic humoral theory. Their fragmentary adherence to a system of hot/cold classification today simply reflects old-fashioned ideas, perhaps taught by the medical doctors that once practiced in El Jardín. They are not survivals of a specifically Spanish version of medieval medicine. Everybody used to think that chills brought illness, and fever was a disease. The use of leeches and blisters to bring out heat, and laxatives and enemas to lower fevers, the soaking of the feet in hot water to prevent or treat pneumonia were all recommended until recently. These concepts of disease are no longer a part of Western science, but at one time they were, passing later into folk medicine. That English vocabulary has terms like "caught a cold," "the cold went to the chest," "he has chills and fever," etc., suggest that when temperature change is cited either as a cause, or as a disease, such identification is not peculiarly Spanish. Much folk therapy everywhere is designed to draw "congested blood" or "air" out of the lungs – by hot baths, fomentations, or poultices which will bring heat to the chest and lungs. Other therapy is directed to warm the insides, by douches or hot drinks.

One should note that it is not uncommon for an infection to be first evident by a sensation of chill. The chill is followed by a fever. The prodromal chill is then interpreted as the cause of the disease. The physiology is universal; its misinterpretation is common.

There are other aspects of El Jardín ethnomedicine which are also in conflict with the current ideas of Western science, although they represented the best of medical science until recently. El Jardín women express beliefs that colds should be allowed to run; that rashes should erupt; that diarrheas should not be checked; that ulcers should continuously drain. The philosophy underlying their beliefs is that these processes are natural phenomena which provide for the draining off of "dirt." If the stomach aches, it does so because something wrong was put into it and should go out. So vomiting or eructation are encouraged, or "neutralization of acid" is promoted by administering patent medicines or herbs "known" to have the desired properties. Diarrhea may mean that the body is trying to "throw off" the "poison," and the process should not be discouraged. (This particular concept is being reviewed by Western medicine.) Constipation is feared not only because it is uncomfortable, but because "the dirt" is being reabsorbed by the body. Thus there is much emphasis on herbs that are purgatives. Children should be purged regularly, and if the medicine doesn't work, an enema must be given. These ideas occur in many different ethnomedicines, and were part of Western medicine at one time.

There are some differences between El Jardín ethnomedicine and that of other Spanish-speaking people which are not immediately evident from looking at the lexemes that are names of diseases, cures, or curers. Let us look briefly at some terms which, in Kany's (1960:8) words, "although outwardly appearing intact have shifted their semantic values." Just because a common folk term is still used, it does not mean that the word still encodes the same features for all users. For most of my informants, *envidia* (envy) is not a disease. It is not a form of witchcraft unconsciously inflicted on the sufferer as it is for Rubel's (1966, 1969) informants. *Envidia* is simply a word that is synonymous with *celos* (jealousy), and indicates poor mental habits which are widespread but not seriously pathogenic. If it causes illness, the disease is a neurosis in the individual who feels this emotion, not one that is projected on to the one who is envied. *Aire,* studied by Redfield (1930), Adams and Rubel (1967), and Madsen (1964), to name only a few, as a volitional wind causing disease, is now thought of as "gas" best treated by *yerba buena* or Alka Seltzer. *Fiebre* (fever) once signified a disease. Now it is seen as a feature of many, if not most diseases. The meaning of *dieta,* which used to refer to post delivery practices of seclusion, food taboos, bathing taboos *et cetera,* has been narrowed to sexual abstinence only. *Curandero* has degenerated to mean "witch doctor." *Susto* is hyperbole now. The former meaning was a great shock, which was also an illness, but the present meaning is only "an unpleasant surprise"; at most, "trauma."

In some cases, old familiar disease names are elevated to scientific status. *Bilis,* which Aguirre Beltrán and Pozas (1954:234) found to be the single most widespread condition in Mexico, is still seen as a condition that has emotional pathogenesis. The disease is caused by anger in the individual, which acts on the gall bladder. But the cure is now surgical, or a low fat diet, just as cholecystitis, or gall bladder disease, is treated scientifically by removal of the gall bladder or by decreasing the dietary stimulation of the organ. *Mollera caída* (fallen fontanel) is recognized as a disease, but it is seen by many informants to be caused by dehydration, which is best treated by administering fluids.

Finally, there are some concepts which appear to be shared with Western science which in fact are not. The specific disease lexemes for which features could not be elicited suggests that the women do not recognize these conditions. They accept illness labels without sharing in the scientific concept of causation or having a precise grasp of pathology. Thus blood clots are "known" to cause strokes, but the origin of the clots is not understood. The women speak glibly of "viruses" and "antibiotics," but assume that the second is used to treat the first, which is not so.

This study indicates that women know a great deal about minor illnesses, how to distinguish them and how to treat them. The taxonomic key lists seven different kinds of stomach aches, and four kinds of runny nose. The symptoms are treated with therapies that are common to the ethnomedicines of western Europe and Mexico. It is only in the United States where all diagnosis and treatment is in theory funneled through the physician. In practice, mild and passing disorders are usually cared for by housewives even here. With serious illness, the women of El Jardín consult people with special knowledge. When it has become economically possible for them to get care from institutions of Western scientific medicine, they are quick to take advantage of this care. This suggests that economic changes in the delivery of health care are more successful than direct assaults in changing health culture.

The many differences in the ethnomedicine of El Jardín from those described in other ethnographies of Mexican Americans show how quickly culture can change. Even old women can be taught new ideas. This teachability should be exploited. At present there are various booklets printed in Spanish for intended use in teaching. Most of these aids are misleading because they use technical words which are incomprehensible to lay people in either English or Spanish or they are otherwise culturally incorrect. Also, few American-born Mexican Americans can read Spanish.

Meanwhile, there can be some accommodation of Western medical practice to local ethnomedicine. Since diseases are defined at one level by symptoms, there should be real effort to treat symptoms. Otherwise, the client will seek other practitioners. For example, a fever will dehydrate feces, so that the excrement is hard, small in volume, and perhaps also difficult to expel. The patient is more likely to concentrate his attention on the inadequate defecation and seek treatment of *empacho* (indigestion infection) if the health practitioner notes only the fever and concentrates only on finding the cause of it.

Also, Mexican Americans feel very defensive about the category "Mexican disease," which is defined as "illness that the Anglo doctor does not recognize." The retention of these concepts should not be disparaged. Alternative diagnoses may be suggested in a nonthreatening manner. The entire expected course of the disease should be outlined, so that quick cures from diseases like *mollera caída* (fallen fontanel) won't be expected.

Herbal remedies are used extensively. Practitioners should be familiar with the pharmacological properties of these herbs and incorporate them in the therapeutic regime if they are desired by the patient. Since a sick infant will be given a tea, it can be calculated into the diet. Dangerous herbs such as *epazote* (wormseed) should be recognized and discouraged.

Health practitioners should spend enough time in the neighborhoods where their patients live and work to become familiar with the environmental characteristics. It has been demonstrated that women attend to the physical environment when considering a disease. But some of this consideration is not verbalized, sometimes because of limited acquaintance with other environments and how theirs is different. In other cases, the woman is all too aware that her surroundings are different from those of her practitioners, and she does not want to mention her outside privy, her lack of beds, etc.

In El Jardín, the world of the women is still mostly a kin-bound world. Role behavior is strictly prescribed by sex. More work needs to be done in order to give appropriate advice in marriage and family planning.

It is important to ask what a woman has already done in a case of illness, and whenever possible to commend her. If she is utilizing a *curandero* (curer), collaboration should be attempted. It was noted that Mexican Americans consult practitioners, such as *curanderos,* more commonly if their experience with Western medicine is unsatisfactory. Incorporation of manipulative therapy, if there is any therapeutic justification for it at all, may make Western medicine even more acceptable.

Since a category of supernaturally caused disease is not recognized, religion should not be seen as competing with science in curing. Prayers, vows, and pilgrimages, which anyway take place following a cure, should not be disparaged. It also should be noted that there is little stress on witchcraft. Now it is altogether possible that witchcraft is more important than the taxonomy of disease indicates. For a variety of reasons the women may be reluctant to admit to such beliefs, or to behavior which would evoke such retribution. In any case, witchcraft is a last resort in diagnosis, an explanation to be used only when others fail.

This study has demonstrated that it is not advisable to apply data from one group of Spanish speakers to another, or from one ethnographic present to another. Does it follow then that every health practitioner need be an anthropologist? Such a recommendation would be impractical. But there are specific attitudes and techniques that can be learned from anthropology. This study has stressed the methodology of ethnosemantics, which is designed to make descriptions in culturally relevant terms. It suggests that questions be designed so that nonscientific concepts may be reflected. It also suggests that health practitioners overcome their glottocentrism and learn to communicate in the language of their patients.

Disease and Curing in a Yaqui Community

Mary Elizabeth Shutler

Disease and Curing in a Yaqui Community

Mary Elizabeth Shutler

THE YAQUI INDIANS OF SONORA, MEXICO, have been in contact with European culture since the seventeenth century when Jesuit missionaries came and gathered them into large villages to teach them Christianity. As a result of this contact, the culture of the Yaquis grew to be a fusion of Indian and Spanish elements. In the last decade of the nineteenth century, following military defeat at the hands of the Mexicans, some Yaquis left their homeland and settled in various other parts of Mexico. Some even migrated to the United States. One of these displaced Yaqui communities is located in the Southwest.

The Yaquis came to the Southwest with a set of beliefs and practices about health and disease which represent a mixture of Indian and Spanish traits. Since they have been living there, the Yaquis have lost some of these practices and adopted in their place some customs of their Anglo-American neighbors. However, other Yaqui-Spanish health customs have been retained and still flourish today.

In 1958* the settlement of Navidad had a population of approximately 400 people clustered into about 50 households. Each household consists of one or more dwelling houses made of adobe brick, corrugated iron, and scraps of salvaged building materials. For each household there is also a ramada used extensively during the summer and household fiestas. The yards are neatly raked and separated from neighboring yards by a fence. A wooden cross erected in each yard is the focus of family rites. The houses face dirt

---

*Note: Although the data for this study were collected in 1958-59, curing methods and beliefs in the Yaqui community had not changed markedly as of publication.

roads laid out in a grid pattern. Only a few houses can boast such luxuries as running water, electricity, window screens, and concrete floors. Most cooking and heating is done on kerosene or wood-burning stoves; candles and kerosene lanterns provide most of the illumination. The rooms of the houses (and many have only one) are small and crowded with stove, tables, metal beds, and personal possessions. In summer the beds are dragged out-of-doors and most activities take place in the shade of the ramada. A few houses wired for electricity have electric lights and radios, and a few refrigerators and television sets can be found in the village. Those families who can afford running water, which more often than not comes from a spigot in the yard, raise trees and flowers. Families without household water draw it from a faucet in the plaza. Groups of children can be seen during the day going back and forth pulling small toy wagons filled with buckets and cans in which they transport the family water supply. To do the family washing, water is boiled in large metal tubs, often over open fires in the yard. Dogs and cats roam the village, and some families keep chickens. Many old cars in various stages of disrepair rust in the yards. Those that still run are used for transportation to and from work and are gone during the day, and taxis sometimes have to be called in an emergency. The bus routes and schedules make trips downtown or to the county hospital inconvenient. Small grocery and drugstores nearby supply most of the family necessities.

The center of community activities is the village plaza. Standing at one end is the small church of San Ignacio and at the other the fiesta ramada, locale of *pascola* and deer dances. These dances performed by masked dancers are an important part of Yaqui ceremonies and fiestas. On one side is the kitchen building where women prepare food for the fiestas. Facing the church and the fiesta ramada are wooden crosses. On Holy Saturday and Easter and during the feast of San Ignacio at the end of July, the plaza is crowded with Yaquis and tourists. Piñatas are swung for the children on the fiesta of San Ignacio and booths selling soft drinks and tacos are set up by Yaquis and Anglo and Mexican vendors. On hot afternoons the plaza yard is deserted; children play by the water faucet, and men sit in the shade of the surrounding trees drinking and gossiping.

The settlement is not isolated geographically from the rest of the city. On one side it merges with a Mexican residential district. Here is located a Catholic chapel where Yaquis attend a monthly Sunday Mass with other people of the area and where their children attend catechism lessons on Saturday mornings. On another side is located the public school which serves not only the Yaqui children, but also the nearby Mexican children. A busy highway lined with motels, trailer courts and stores cuts near the plaza, forming a visible link with the city's urban life.

Villagers support themselves by working outside of the village, primarily as unskilled laborers in agricultural or construction work. Some women do domestic work in homes and motels. The population of the village fluctuates during the year as individuals and families move away to take advantage of seasonal work on the Southwest's farms and ranches and move back again to take part in the ritual life of the village.

Most households are composed of extended families of loose composition and no consistent pattern of residence. Spanish kinship terms are commonly used (see discussion in Kay's chapter). The ritual kinship system is extremely strong. Godparents are acquired at baptism, confirmation, and marriage, as well as upon joining the religious societies. Duties of mutual cooperation between *compadres* (godparents) are important.

Most children attend school fairly regularly. Many attend high school. Although Yaqui is still the ritual language, it is losing ground to Spanish as the household language. All but the aged speak at least some English (Barber 1952).

FIELD PROCEDURES

Data were gathered for this report from June 1958 through July 1959. Most of the information was collected during formal interviews with three informants: a curer, Carlos; a midwife, María; and a layman, Pedro. The informants were paid for their time and notes were freely taken. An interpreter, Carmen, was used with the curer and the midwife and information was given partially in Yaqui and partially in Spanish. With the layman, interviews were conducted in English without the presence of the interpreter. Permission for the study was given by the "chief" of the village, who without holding formal political authority has assumed the task of liaison between the village and representatives of the city's Anglo community.

Carlos refused to talk to me about curing while in the village for fear that other people would listen and steal his secrets, so I interviewed him in an office at the University. Interviews with Pedro also took place at the University. Since he was a single man living with relatives, there was no convenient place where we could talk in the village. María was interviewed in her home. Additionally, interviews were held regularly with Carmen at my home to compare my understanding of the data with hers, and to allow her to contribute what new information she could.

I became friendly with four other people in the village, three women and one man. These people I visited frequently and from them I gained considerable information. Though they were never formally interviewed, they were aware of my purpose of "studying Yaqui ways of healing" and were interested in discussing my study with me.

Attendance at fiestas and ceremonies gave me the opportunity to see people wearing bandages, *hábitos* (garments representing in this case the habit of Franciscan monks), or other outward marks of curing and to meet and talk with other Yaquis. Since polite Yaqui conversation begins with an earnest inquiry into the health of the speakers and each member of their families, some information about curing could be obtained by simply meeting a person for the first time.

Finally, several Anglo-Americans were interviewed about Yaqui curing practices: three public health nurses, the principal of the school, a teacher, and the pastor of the Catholic church.

Several techniques of gathering data were not employed due to the nature of the study. Yaquis believe that their native methods of curing are illegal in the United States, "practicing medicine without a license," so naturally refuse to discuss them with strange Anglo-Americans. They know that Anglo-Americans do not ordinarily believe in witches, so they usually disclaim any knowledge of witchcraft upon first acquaintance. They are most reluctant to reveal the identity of their curers. Holden (1936:82) noted this to be true in Sonora, Mexico, as well.

I had originally intended to conduct a door to door survey asking a random sample of respondents about their beliefs concerning disease and the treatments they had sought. It soon became apparent that this step would engender much suspicion and might endanger future anthropological field work in the community, and I was advised not to attempt it. Because of the secretiveness surrounding native curing, Carlos did not allow me to accompany him to observe his treatments. He felt that his patients would object strongly to my presence. I did, however, get an account of each of the cases he dealt with during the course of the year. Each curer guards his individual secrets of curing. Since Carlos had taken me into his confidence, I could not interview other curers without risking the loss of his friendship. Because I did not wish to jeopardize the faith my informants had placed in me, I did not visit any of the public health clinics. I interviewed the nurses away from the village. I was not allowed to examine the records of the public health nurses or the county hospital to see which and how many Yaquis had come for treatment. Anyhow, I was told, these records do not identify Yaquis as such.

For these reasons, I interviewed intensively only a few informants; perhaps in the future, data can be gathered from a wider range of villagers. Such an extensive survey would add much to our knowledge of Yaqui curing.

The Informants

Carlos was my principal informant. I had meetings with him at least weekly during most of the year. He was a man in his sixties, a member of a very conservative* Yaqui family, and a musician for the deer dancer as well as a curer (see Painter 1962, Spicer 1940). His mother and mother's brother also had been curers. Born in Cocorít, Sonora, he had lived most of

---

*Social workers in the village tend to label individuals and families as progressive or conservative depending upon whether or not they accept their programs.

his life in Navidad, although he had traveled much as a seasonal farm laborer in the Southwest. He spoke Yaqui and Spanish. Carlos shared willingly with me his vast knowledge of Yaqui herbal medicines. He gave me an account of all the cases he treated during the year and recounted past cases. Indeed every aspect of Yaqui curing was discussed at one time or another.

María, a midwife, was interviewed mainly about childbirth, the care of young children, and the treatment of the diseases of infancy. She refused to discuss witchcraft with me. A woman in her sixties, she had been born in Hermosillo, Sonora, and had come to the Southwest as a child. She lived at that time of our interviews in a second Yaqui community in the city, but also had lived in Navidad where she had many friends and relatives and where she had come often to treat patients. Interviews were held for several hours a week in María's home during a two-month period. She spoke Yaqui and Spanish.

Pedro, some ten years younger than Carlos or María, had lived since infancy in the village, although he was born in Magdalena, Sonora. He had traveled fairly widely in Mexico and the United States. Unlike Carlos and María he spoke English as well as Yaqui and Spanish and had attended public school in the Southwest through the second year of high school. Though holding no position in the ceremonial organization of Navidad, he was respected by the villagers as a savant of Yaqui ways. He was interviewed during a month's time on all aspects of Yaqui culture.

Carmen, my interpreter, was present during the interviews held with Carlos and María. She was also regularly interviewed by me during the year. We discussed what the other informants had said; her own beliefs about curing; the illnesses she and her family had had, and what treatments had been sought. Carmen was a high school student, tri-lingual, and her family was regarded as progressive in the village. Her father had been a *chapayeka* dancer in the Easter ceremonies for several years.

The friendships with four additional persons permitted gathering information in casual conversations. All of these people had refused to be interviewed, but were aware of my study and more or less interested in it. No notes were taken on their remarks until after I had left their homes. I visited with Jaime and his wife frequently. He belonged to the Judas Society, a religious organization concerned with the performance of certain ceremonies at Eastertime, and his wife was the daughter of a *maestro* or lay minister (Painter 1962, Spicer 1940). They were known to social workers as progressive. Jaime was interested in the course of my research and contributed additional information on his beliefs on curing, witchcraft, and the identities of curers. His wife and I discussed childbirth, child care, and the diseases of children. Carmen's mother told me of her knowledge of herbal medicines and home remedies. Teresa, a member of the church group, told me of her family's illnesses. All of these people had been born in Arizona and spoke English as well as Yaqui and Spanish.

Orthography

The transcription used for Yaqui words in this report is as follows:

1. The vowels are in Spanish.
2. The consonants are the same as in English.
3. Long vowels and consonants are indicated by a double symbol.
4. ' represents the glottal stop.
5. The plural is formed by the suffix m.

DISEASES

The Yaquis of Navidad recognize a number of common diseases and symptoms by their Spanish or English names. These do not have Yaqui names as well. Frequently mentioned to me were: asthma (*asma*), *cáncer,* colds (*catarro*), chicken pox (*viruelas locas*), *diabetes,* epilepsy (*alferecía*), heart trouble (*latido de corazón*), insanity (*manía*), measles (*sarampión*), mumps (*paperas*), pneumonia (*pulmonía*), *polio,* rashes, (*sarpullido*), rheumatism (*reumatismo*), sores (*granos*), *tuberculosis,* ulcers (*úlcera*), and venereal diseases.

A few illnesses are known by Yaqui terms: *hoktia* (whooping cough), which Holden (1936:61) writes *hooptia; namukia* (drunken, but also used to describe the behavior of a person with rabies); *sawaria* (possibly jaundice); *siavivitek* (fever or other illness transmitted to a baby through his mother's milk); *sihonium* (prickly heat); *sivori* (any sickness due to witchcraft); *taiweche* (fever); *tasia* (coughing fit, probably from the Spanish, *tos*); *tisikwa* (a feeling of weakness and pain pervading the body and said to occur when the blood stops circulating); *tomtium* (small pox); *vostia* (diarrhea); and *helktia* (hiccups). Bleeding, fainting, vomiting, and weakness are all regarded as dangerous symptoms.

A number of Spanish American folk diseases are known: *mal de ojo* ("evil eye"); *susto* ("fright" – the alternate term, *espanto,* was not recognized in Navidad; this condition also has a Yaqui name, *womtia*); and *pujos* (a rash with a straining cough). *Waiwina* is a Yaqui term said to mean "jealousy sickness," a concept which can be paralleled in many Spanish American communities. My informants denied knowledge of *bilis, chincual, chucaque, mollera caída,* and *pasmo,* Latin-American folk diseases. Concepts about *mal aire* and hot and cold diseases are very feebly developed, if at all, as compared to the Mexican American community.

Mamkotila means "a sprained or broken arm or hand" (*maman* means "arms or hands"). *Wakotila* refers to either "sprained or broken legs and feet" (*wak* means "legs or feet"). *Taba'tila* means "broken or loose teeth."

But by far the most common way in which illness was described to me was by "pain" in the leg or arm or whatever, naming the appropriate part of the body. Two Yaqui words are each said to mean *both* "pain" and "sickness," *ko'okwa* and *wantia.* Though they can be used interchangeably, *ko'okwa* seemed to me to be used more to describe pain or illness in general and *wantia* in naming a specific complaint. Thus *kova wantia* means a headache; *naka wantia,* earache; *tam wantia,* toothache; *toma wantia,* stomachache or any illness of the stomach.

Although quite a few "scientific" diseases are known to the Yaquis, the extent of the knowledge about these varies considerably. Thus the curer, Carlos, had never heard of polio, while Carmen had. She had no idea what it was, but recognized the name because the students had been given polio "shots" at school. Very frequently magical concepts can be attached to a "scientific" disease name. Thus Carlos felt that when his daughter got the mumps, the glandular swelling was caused by the intrusion by a witch of a magical bug into her neck.

DISEASE CAUSATION

It is extremely difficult to discuss Yaqui ideas of disease etiology in a manner that seems orderly to a Westerner. The same set of symptoms called by an English or Spanish name perhaps, can on one occasion be due to purely natural causes and on another occasion to magic. One may catch a cold, for example, because when overheated one sat in a stiff breeze; another time the cold may be blamed upon the spell cast by an evil person, or be regarded as a punishment for sin. Certain causes, conversely, may upon different occasions give rise to quite different symptoms. The Yaquis are not, of course, unique in thus attributing multiple causes to specific symptoms. The Anglo layman may say of his sniffles and headache that it is due to one or more physical causes, "a draft," or "caught it from somebody," or even that it is due to magical causes, "not living right." Even scientifically trained physicians may differ in assigning causes to particular symptoms. Throughout Yaqui lore concerning health and illness there is found the blending of Indian and medieval-Spanish ideas, concepts derived from the folk medicines of modern Mexico, and scientific and folk ideas drawn from the Anglo culture of the Southwest. I have, therefore quite arbitrarily divided Navidad theories of disease causation into five categories: natural causes, emotional causes, sin, witchcraft, and other magical causes.

Natural Causes

Overexertion is frequently given as a cause of sickness. Pedro said, "To work hard can cause many illnesses," and Carlos related, "I helped a man with a heart attack. He worked too hard." And again, "Bertola was sewing from morning to night. She tried to get up and fell. She was too weak to stand and was trembling. They thought she had worked too hard. Rafaela said that she felt pains throughout her body. I told her she was working too hard."

This reaction is perhaps to be expected among a group of people who support themselves by hard physical labor. Incidentally, my informants (both male and female) thought the daily housework and child-minding of the women much more physically exhausting than the daily work of the men. Too much physical exertion continued for too long a time can weaken the heart, causing pain in the chest and feelings of extreme weakness and heaviness in the body. Diffuse pain throughout the body or localized pain, a feeling that the body is heavy and difficult to move, weakness, and trembling are all attributed to overexertion. Though exercise is considered good for a pregnant woman, too hard work, stooping, or carrying of heavy objects is thought to harm the fetus or turn it in an undesirable position and can make labor more difficult. María said of a pregnant woman, "She can do anything she wants. Work is good. But when standing or working, she shouldn't bend down too much or the baby will get in the wrong position. Picking up heavy things is not good."

Overexposure to the sun also can have deleterious results. Rashes, feelings of weakness, fainting, and headaches are all blamed on working or even sitting too long in the heat and light of the direct sunshine. Blindness also can occur if one is out in the bright sun repeatedly for long periods of time. It is not believed that the intensity of the light harms the eyes, but that the heat goes into the eyes causing a gradual loss of vision. For example, "Headache is caused by the sun, by the heat of the sun. A person should not work too long in the sun. The heat can go into your eyes and make them weak and slowly the person begins to go blind." And, "Heat from the sun causes rashes. . . . If you sit too long in the sun, you may be weak and faint."

Alternate exposure to heat and cold also is dangerous. Pedro said, "If a person goes from a hot room to the cold, he might get sick." Carlos said at different times, "If you are very hot, you should not drink something cold. You should cool off first." And, "If you work hard in the sun and sweat, you should not sit in a cold place or in the wind." Again, "If you leave a warm house in winter, you should put on something, or it will be too cold." María added, "When a baby is in a warm place and is taken out into the cold, it will get sick." A person who is overheated from exertion or sitting in the sun should not cool off suddenly by sitting in a breeze or drinking cold liquids, but should cool off slowly. It is equally bad in winter to move from a warm house to the cold winds out-of-doors without being warmly dressed. Babies, being weak, are especially susceptible to cold and are always snugly wrapped up when taken out-of-doors in cold weather. Going too rapidly from hot to cold temperatures is thought to cause a number of different disorders. It can weaken the heart, cause feelings of lassitude, headaches, earaches, and fever. This concept of disease causation seems somewhat similar to the idea of *mal aire,* reported from a wide range of communities in Spanish America (Adams 1957:103, 481; Beals 1946:205; Foster 1948:267, 1953:209; Gillin 1947:158; Kelly 1956:71-5; Lewis 1951:280; Parsons 1936:118; Redfield 1930:162-5; Redfield and Redfield 1940:61-3; Saunders 1954:148). Usually the cold wind is conceived as an evil spirit, magically causing disease.

The night air is thought to be especially dangerous. The Yaqui belief seems to be simply that a cool wind is *naturally* dangerous for an overheated person. Navidadeños show no fear of the night air, sleeping out-of-doors in summer. Margaret Clark (1959:173) reports that the Mexican belief in San Jose, California, is that danger to health from the weather lies in the too rapid transition from hot to cold and not in malice inherent in the wind, as does Kelly (1956:93) from Vera Cruz. The San Jose belief in the result of such exposure is thought to have native parallels in Inca culture.

Mechanical injuries – sprains, broken bones, cuts and scratches, bruises, burns and the like – can be caused by preternatural means but can also happen purely by chance, by accident or carelessness. Thus when Carmen tripped and cut her ankle, Carlos thought it was due to witchcraft, but about other cases he said, "There was a young lady who had a sprained ankle. I rubbed it. There was no evil thought. She just fell down. There was also another man in the village who hurt his ankle. I did the same thing." A blow on the head is thought to be particularly dangerous as it is capable of causing insanity.

A number of plants, especially *datura,* are known to be poisonous, causing illness if they are eaten inadvertently. "Bad" meat, which has begun to rot, will cause sickness if eaten. Simply eating too much food is likely to cause nausea. *Empacho* (surfeit, "clogging") is a common Spanish American folk disease. Overeating of certain foods causes them to stick together in a ball in the stomach (Adams 1957:103, 212, 363, 481; Clark 1959:179; Foster 1953:206; Kelly 1956:91; Parsons 1936:77; Redfield 1930:160). My informants did not describe the sticking together of the food or use the term *empacho,* although Nichols' (1961:15) Yaqui informants in Guadalupe, Arizona, did.

Displacement of bodily parts is often reported in different parts of Spanish America as a cause of disease (Foster 1953:210-1; Gillin 1947:134-5), but it is a rare concept in Navidad. One of the most common of these disorders is *mollera caída* (fallen fontanel) in infants (Adams 1957:483, 602; Clark 1959:170; Foster 1948:226, 266; Kelly 1956:92). Again, although this condition is diagnosed and treated by the Yaquis of Guadalupe, Arizona (Nichols 1961:17), my informants did not know it. They did believe that after childbirth a woman should bind her abdomen tightly so that "her organs will return to the right place" Foster 1960:118; Lewis 1951:359). If a person is habitually tense and nervous his bones may get "too close together" and have to be separated by massage or pain will result.

The condition of a person's blood may affect his health. It is commonly believed in Spanish America that a person must have a lot of blood to be healthy (Beals 1946:202; Clark 1959:181; Humphrey 1945:256; Saunders 1954:148). The Yaquis believe that too much blood in the veins will make a person itchy and irritable. "He will think that ants are walking in his veins."

Too little blood will cause a prickly feeling in the extremities and weakness. More serious symptoms can result if the blood stops circulating. Knowledge of blood circulation is probably a recent introduction to Yaqui learning, but the Navidadeños add the belief that blood can circulate very sluggishly or cease altogether, causing illness but not necessarily death.

Dirt can cause illness. Dust, for example, may get into a person's throat and make it sore; the illness can then spread through the body. Because the illness is caused by a "dirty throat," strong gargles, straight peroxide for example, are taken to cure it. A "dirty stomach" can result in sickness. Clark reports in San Jose: "Men, women, and children are thought to get 'dirty stomachs' from time to time. A strong physic is usually administered to each family member two or three times a year to 'keep the stomach cleaned out' " (Clark 1959:180; Saunders 1954:148). Similarly dirt can get into ears to cause earaches and into cuts and sores to make them fester. The concern with dirt as a source of disease is at least reinforced by modern American ideas of sanitation, which are stressed in the hospital, at the clinic, and at school. Germs are thought to be "the little things in dirt that make you sick." Tooth decay is said to be caused by dirt and germs on the teeth, and they must be brushed two or three times a day to keep them clean. Babies must be kept very clean at all times to keep them healthy. Finally it is believed that a sick person should be isolated, and no one should eat from his dish or his sickness will spread.

Emotional Causes

Strong feelings can cause a number of different illnesses. Extreme rage, surprise, jealousy, and fear can result in weakness and trembling, diarrhea, aches and pains, or even high fever and convulsions. Carlos reported, "You can get sick from a great fright. You might get this fright from seeing a ghost." About jealousy he said, "When a baby grows inside, the old baby knows and is jealous. Sometimes he will become sick." María said, "When a person gets frightened, he gets *womtia*. It can be caused by anything." And, "Some children get sick with jealousy of a new baby because they want to be nursed by their mother. . . . It can harm the baby if the mother gets very angry or frightened. Anyone can make themselves sick by being too angry or upset." Foster (1953:211) has indicated that the common Spanish American belief that emotions can cause diseases is Indian in origin rather than Spanish. Parsons (1936:494) points out "the concept of sickness from fright, *espanto*, is known to be an Aztec concept." Gillin (1947:130) says that illness due to fear was also an Inca medical idea. The illness which results from fear is called *susto* (from *asustado*, the past participle of *asustar*, "to frighten") in Navidad as well as in many Spanish American communities (Adams 1957:213, 366, 483; Beals 1946:204-5; Clark 1959:175; Foster 1948:267; Gillin 1947:130-3; Kelly 1956:66-70; Lewis 1951:282; Nichols 1961:16; Parsons 1936:494; Redfield 1930:160-1; Saunders 1954:149). The alternative term for *susto, espanto,* was not used by my informants. More frequently used however is the Yaqui term *womtia;* the fact that a Yaqui term exists may indicate that the concept is native to Yaquis. The description of the condition and its treatment in Navidad can be duplicated in many communities. Unless an attempt is made to calm the frightened person by keeping him quiet and giving him warm water with sugar in it to drink, extreme nervousness, weakness, trembling, fever, or diarrhea may result. If a pregnant woman is badly frightened, her baby may be born with *susto.* Foster (1948:267) has said that in many part of Mexico, illness due to soul loss from fright may have once been a popular belief. The treatment of *susto* includes calling the patient's name, which suggests that the illness is due to the fact the soul has wandered or been stolen away and must be induced to return to the body. This treatment is reported from Mitla in Oaxaca, Mexico (Parsons 1936:121) and San Jose, California (Clark 1959:178). No such custom was recorded in Navidad, but other Yaqui ideas do suggest an ancient belief in soul loss. For example, Yaquis never like to awaken a person suddenly for fear of causing *womtia.* It is best that a person awaken from sleep by himself; if he must be awakened, it should be done gently. Such customs have traditionally been thought to be due to a fear of soul loss (Tylor 1871:436-8). Beals (1943:63) thinks that illness due to soul loss may have been an aboriginal Cahita belief. Curer's souls leave their sleeping bodies to fight witches. Witches are thought to feed their animal familiars on the souls of their victims. Some mothers wrap their babies tightly so they won't be frightened by suddenly touching themselves. *Womtia* is incidentally the only illness that ghosts can bring. A person seeing a ghost would probably be frightened into a case of *womtia.*

Among the Yaquis anger is thought also to cause unpleasant symptoms. They do not recognize the Spanish term *bilis,* which is sometimes used to denote illness brought on by anger in Spanish America (Clark 1959:175) and sometimes has other connotations (Foster 1948:267). Nor do they recognize *mohina,* or *muina,* a disease resulting from anger and envy reported from many parts of Spanish America (Beals 1946:203; Kelly 1956:92; Lewis 1951:295; Parsons 1936:140; Redfield 1930:160).

Jealousy is most likely to cause sickness in children. An older baby frequently becomes so jealous of a new baby in the family that it sickens. Stomachache and fever often attributed to this condition called *waiwiwa.* Sores in the baby's mouth can be caused by his jealousy if he sees others eating things near him without offering him a bit. Older children are cautioned always to give the baby a taste of whatever they are eating. Parents holding even a tiny baby at the table at mealtime offer him a little bit of everything.

Foster (1953:215) also lists "desire, imagined rejection, embarrassment or shame, disillusion, and sadness," as causes of illness in Spanish America. These were not mentioned to me by my informants. They did not know the term *chucaque* used in some parts of Spanish America to denote illness due to shame (Gillin 1947:138).

In Navidad strong desires on the part of one person may cause illness in another. *Mal de ojo* is the commonest form of this kind of illness. In the Yaqui community, a young woman is thought most likely to inflict *mal de ojo,* or "evil eye," and the victims are usually young children. The illness results from an unrequited desire on the part of the young woman to caress the child. The identity of the one who caused the illness, which is characterized by fever and crying, can be seen in the yolk of an egg. The one who caused the illness is then required to massage the child to cure it. Carlos told of a case of *mal de ojo* in Navidad:

> It is bad for the baby if a woman comes to the house and says "Oh, how beautiful!" but doesn't touch or get him. I saw one time three ladies come, and one was tempted to touch the baby but didn't do it. The baby was sick. So they broke an egg on a plate, and an eye appeared on the egg, the eye of the guilty lady. Then they went to the lady, and she gave him a rubdown.

Mal de ojo is one of the most common folk diseases of Spain and Spanish America; called variously *mal de ojo, mal ojo, el dano,* or *ojeo,** it is caused inadvertently and usually strikes children. Incessant crying is frequently given as a symptom. Diagnosis by examining the yolk of an egg, and treatment by massaging with an egg are characteristic curing methods in Spanish America but not in Spain (Adams 1957:104, 212, 264, 481, 598; Beals 1946:205; Clark 1959:172; Foster 1948:267; Gillin 1947:135; Kelly 1956:64-5; Lewis 1951:282; Nichols 1961:16; Parsons 1936:135; Redfield 1930:161-2; Redfield and Redfield 1940:64; Saunders 1954:149).

A rash or fever, together with a straining cough ("the baby tries to pick himself up") may be caused when a pregnant woman wishes to pick up the baby but does not. The condition is called *pujos.* Dysentery (*pujoz*) is not a symptom. *Pujos* is cured by a man named Juan wiping the baby with a soft cloth and throwing the cloth into the fire. The name is evidently related to the verb *empujar,* to "strain" or "push." Foster (1953:205) said that in El Salvador it is believed that a man entering the room from the street, perspiring, or having recently had sexual contact must pick up any child in the room to neutralize his humors or the child will fall ill of *pujo. Pujo* causes swollen testicles in boys. Gillin (1947:134) reports for the village of Moche in Peru, "It (an umbilical hernia) is believed to be caused if either a pregnant

---

*In Navidad *mal de ojo* means evil eye. *Mal ojo* means a diseased eye. There is great variation in the specific form the name of a disease takes in Spanish-speaking communities. Indeed I have observed variation between individual speakers in the same community.

or menstruating visitor to the house picks up any child in her arms. This will product *empuje,* a straining and coughing of a particular type which induces *quibradura* (umbilical hernia)." *Pujo* is reported from Central America by Adams (1957) meaning dysentery (*ibid.*:103, 364, 599), constipation (*ibid.*:212), or infant diarrhea (*ibid.*:418).

Sin

Sin can cause disease. The villagers believe that sin is not only punished by God in the next world but may be punished in this world as well by sickness or misfortune. "God can send sickness as a punishment that nothing can help but God," said Pedro. Frequently illness is the punishment for breaking a vow or *manda.* Pedro and Carlos commented on this point, the first saying, "In case a *matachini* doesn't want to dance and doesn't, maybe he will get sick again." Carlos said, "My brother was sick and made a *manda*; he started to get well so he didn't keep it. Then he got worse and died." The punishment of illness may fall not only on the sinner, but also upon his child or grandchild. Birthmarks and congenital deformities are thought to be a punishment for the mother scoffing at a person similarly afflicted. Said Carlos, "If a pregnant woman sees a person with a deformity and says or thinks, 'Oh, how ugly!' without feeling pity, her baby will be the same. . . . It would be very bad for a pregnant woman to make fun of a disfigured person." María agreed, "A woman laughs at a deformed person and her baby has this mark." Parsons (1936:86) reports this belief is held in Mitla. Also in Mitla deaf-mutism is thought to be due to parental sin. Insanity is often considered to be a punishment for the sins of the sufferer's parents or grandparents. No treatment can cure disease which is a punishment, "It comes from God and only God can cure it. All one can do is pray." If the punishment has come because of a broken *manda,* the illness can not be cured until the vow has been fulfilled. Although the belief in sickness as a punishment of sin seems Spanish Catholic in content, it is interesting to note that the concept is also found aboriginally among some American Indian groups, the Aztecs, for example (Driver 1961:491).

Witchcraft

Some of the illnesses that befall the villagers are attributed to sorcery. Carlos said, "There are people who can make you sick . . . many persons know different ways to hurt." Pedro remarked, "It is understood that there are those with power to hurt others in many ways — make blind, deaf, cripple — then the *hitevi* (healer) must cure." Navidadeños believe firmly in witchcraft; they believe that evil powers reside in some men and women, called *mooream,* "witches," and that this evil power can be manipulated by its possessors by certain acts to cause sickness and death. The sorcery can cause illness and misfortune of all conceivable kinds. Because of a spell cast by the witch, the victim may suffer an accident, contract a cold or fever or an ache somewhere, sores, tuberculosis, lose his job, have his house burn down and so on. Sorcery is suspected when the usual treatments do not cure the disease in a reasonable length of time. Carlos said of Bertola's illness, "It has been five months and nothing can help her. An evil person has done this." Witchcraft is suspected when a person falls ill shortly after having quarreled with another. Carlos told me of treating Luisa, Delefina, and Rafaela. All fell ill after a quarrel, and witchcraft was suspected in each case.

Finally, an illness is thought to be due to witchcraft if it is accompanied by unusual or frightening dreams. Carlos said, "A sick person may have a dream. It would be a strange one. He would call the doctor to interpret it, and he would find the witch." Both Luisa and Carmen told Carlos of dreams they had had when ill which made him suspect sorcery. The suspicion is confirmed when the curer dreams a particular kind of dream in which he sees the witch.

Bohannan (1963:352) has observed that generally societies which possess belief in witchcraft have only vague ideas of how it is implemented.

> . . . [W]e can see another constant attribute of witchcraft; the unsureness of just how the dirty work is done. The reason is easily apparent: when nothing is actually done, there must be some mystical explanation if the belief is to be maintained. Everyone will profess ultimate ignorance about how these things are done not just because to do otherwise would make one appear to know too much about it, but also because one actually does not know.

In Navidad, however, there are a number of current beliefs on the technique of sorcery. One of the most common of these is the belief that the witch can stick pins into a doll made to look like the victim and cause sickness and pain at the point impaled by the pin, a form of imitative magic. Carlos told me about one of his cases:

> Luciano came to me with pains in his heart. I saw his father in my dream. He was in a little room sticking pins in a doll. The doll resembled Luciano. . . . To make such a doll you would have to do something of the person in it, like a hair. . . . He put in about three pins and then took them out. If he hadn't taken them out Luciano would have died. I put medicine over his heart, and I prayed. I made the sign of the cross. The pins pushed themselves out. I picked them up with two pieces of mesquite like a tweezers and put them into a jar. I took the jar three miles from the house and buried it, three feet deep. If you do this the witch will die. Luciano's father got sick and died.

This method of sorcery, *envoûtement,* is well known in the folklore of Mexicans and Anglos alike in the Southwest and may be a recent introduction. The method was common in Europe (Davies 1947:13). Numerous ethnographers have recorded the custom among American Indian tribes, but most have assumed that the idea was introduced by the Spanish. Among the Indians of the Rio Grande Pueblos, images were made of deer skin, cloth, wool, or clay mixed with the victim's urine, named for the person it represented and stuck with thorns (Dumarest 1919:165; Hawley 1950:146; Parsons 1927:127, 1939:110-1). Hawley (1950:146) remarked, "This specific use of imitative magic is so similar to that of Europe that its derivation from Spanish American neighbors seems rather certain."

The Navajo custom of causing sickness by stabbing thorns or shooting points into a doll is also thought (Kluckhohn 1944:32) to be Spanish derived. The Pomo of California are reported to bathe dolls with poison to cause the death of the victim (Loeb 1826:330). The use of dolls in witchcraft occurs sporadically throughout Spanish America (Beals 1946:157; Gillin 1947: 128; Kelly 1956:77; Parsons 1936:140). Morss (1954:55-6) however suggested the possibility that this type of sorcery may be native to the New World as well as to the Old. He has noted that clay figurines stuck with thorns or otherwise mutilated and dating from pre-Spanish periods are occasionally found in Southwestern archaeological sites in areas where *envoûtement* is practiced in modern times. Morris (1951:33, 38; figs. 24b and b^1, 26i and i^1) illustrates two figurines from the Prayer Rock district of Basketmaker III age which are pierced with numerous cactus spines. Steward (1931:128) suggested that witchcraft was perhaps an explanation for some of the Kanosh, Utah, figurines.

From Hohokam territory in southern Arizona, Haury describes a clay figurine decorated with black and white paint and having a "well formed quartz pressed into the clay on the front side at about the heart position" (Haury 1950:361). Some clay figurines of Hohokam type have been found in Sonora (Morss 1954:51), and early explorers have credited the Yaquis with owning and using images and fetishes. The Inca so used dolls in witchcraft (Gillin 1947:128). There is therefore at least the possibility that the Yaqui belief that witches stick pins in dolls to cause illness is ancient and the expression of a widespread pre-Columbian American concept.

One of the most powerful techniques of the Yaqui witch for causing disease is through the use of the *chooni* fetish, an Apache scalp. It is believed that some witches possess these, and that they come alive at night when they appear to be furry little animals; then the witch can send them out to attack his victims. The scalps are thought to derive from ancient battles between Yaquis and Apaches when the Apaches were raiding in Sonora. A person who has *seataka* (supernatural power) – and considerable courage – may upon meeting a *chooni* wandering about the village at night approach it, speak softly to it, stroke and feed it, and keep it as "a pet." It will then leave its old master and serve the new one. It it a dangerous feat, however, for if the *chooni* is on a mission of evil, it may attack the intruder. Besides doing harm, the *chooni* guards its master and averts danger from him. The old

Yaqui war parties are believed to have used *choonim* to go ahead of them and warn of the presence of the enemy.

Carlos reported that *choonim* are frequently heard and less frequently glimpsed during the night in the village. He, himself, one night heard a scratching sound on his roof. When he climbed to the top of the house, he saw nothing and was convinced it had been a *chooni* sent out to harm him. He recited the *Salve Regina* and thus averted the danger. Scalping of enemies is reported from almost every area of North America. Frequently supernatural power was believed to be acquired in this way (Driver 1961:340-535). Some Pueblo groups are reported to have kept and fed Navajo scalps in the kivas, underground chambers where secret ceremonies are performed. They were believed to cause and cure certain diseases (Goldfrank 1962:48). Apparently related to this idea is the belief that the witch can take several Apache hairs (whether these are thought to be taken from a *chooni* I could not determine), braid them, and dip them into oil. The hairs are then unbraided one at a time and fly out through the night to entangle themselves about the victim's throat and strangle him. The neck of a corpse so murdered will bear a purplish mark.

The witch is thought to have familiar spirits in the shape of small reptiles and insects, which he can send into the body of the victim to make him suffer. This belief in the intrusion of magical things or beings as a cause of illness is extremely widespread throughout the Americas (Adams 1957:104; Driver 1961:503; Kelly 1956-62; Parsons 1927:107, 1936:135). Beals (1932:128) says that the intrusion theory of disease was general in northern Mexico and considers it part of aboriginal Cahita culture (Beals 1943:63). It is reported specifically for the Opata (Johnson 1950:32). It is said by some Yaquis that the animal spirits of the witch must be fed by souls, and for this reason the witch must kill to obtain souls; if he stops, the spirits might kill him. The possibility of an ancient Yaqui belief in illness through soul loss has already been mentioned. About these familiars of the witch, Pedro said:

> The animals that run out of the execution fire (of the condemned witch) are those used by the bad witch to hurt people with. She uses animals to carry evil. This is what the *hitevi* sucks for. She has them in her captivity. They are not actually animals; some say they are the lives of the witch. They are human-eating creatures and must be fed. . . . When the witch keeps from doing harm, he gets sick. It is the ill-fed animals that make him sick. . . . They do not actually eat human flesh. They eat the souls of those the witch has hurt.

Hair combings of the victim can be useful to the witch in causing sickness. I did not, however, determine just how these were thought to be used other than to be placed in a doll. Using something of the victim to cause his sickness, contagious magic, is also a common idea. Parsons (1927:109) says, "It's believed in Zuni and Taos, and probably elsewhere, that witches can use hair cuttings in their black magic, so hair cuttings are burned or thrown into the river."

The witch also can pray for sickness or misfortune to strike his victim. My informants said that the witch would not pray to God, because what he asks is evil, but he could pray to a saint, one whose protection he felt sure of. Parsons (1936:206) says of Mitla, "San Esquipula sends sickness; San Marcial, earthquake. It is well known at Mitla as elsewhere that the saints may work harm." This is reminiscent of American Indian concepts of the guardian spirit who can be called upon to aid and protect its devotee in specific ways regardless of the morality of the situation (Driver 1961:470-2). Beals (1943:59-60) postulated that a belief in guardian spirits was one of the features of Cahita religion. In spite of the fact that it was denied that God could be prayed to to cause evil, I did hear a story where this was purported to be the case. Carlos recounted that one day while he was walking through a vacant lot near the village he came upon a man (well known to him as a neighbor, a *hitevi,* and suspected by him of being a witch) lying full length, face down on the ground. His arms were outstretched so that his body formed a cross. Candles were burning at his head and feet and at each hand. He was praying to God in a loud voice not to forgive a certain person and to cause him misfortune. When he became aware of Carlos watching him, he jumped up in confusion and ran away, forgetting his candles. Beals (1946:157) reports that candles are used in witchcraft because of their association with the dead.

Witches are believed to be able to change into animals to work their mischief. "The witch can turn into any animal she wants. Maybe one time a wild cat or a rattlesnake and the next time a wolf," said Carlos. Pedro said, "The bad witch appears to be an animal. He changes from time to time so as not to be recognized." This is a concept of European witchcraft (Davies 1947:26) which is also found in Spanish America (Adams 1957:104, 601; Beals 1946:157; Foster 1948:275; Gillin 1947:1288; Kelly 1956:73; Lewis 1951:279; Parsons 1936:132) and elsewhere in North America (Driver 1961:496) as among the Navajo (Kluckhohn 1944:26) and the Pueblo Indians (Parsons 1927:106). Beals (1943:63) considers the changing appearance of the witch to be an aboriginal Cahita belief. If anyone dreams of a witch it generally is seen as an animal.

The witch also can harm people through the sheer strength of his own power. He can think "evil thoughts," and his victim will suffer "because his hate is so strong."

Other Magical Causes

Lunar eclipses are feared and are thought to cause birthmarks and deformities in the baby if the expectant mother stays out-of-doors during one. This is a belief generally found in Spanish America (Kelly 1956:105;

Lewis 1951:357). Frequently a key or a red sash is worn about the waist to neutralize the moon's influence (Beals 1946:165; Foster 1948:224; Kelly 1956:359; Parsons 1936:72; Van der Eerden 1948:9). This latter custom was not known in Navidad. Foster (1948:224) suggests that the fear of the eclipse is pre-Spanish and native to the Americas. Staying out-of-doors during a solar eclipse is thought to turn a person's hair to snakes.

The Yaquis believe that a supernatural power, which they call *seataka,* is inherent in the animals and plants of the wilderness. If a person stays too long alone in the *Monte* (any wild and uninhabited spot), the power may become too much for him and make him sick or insane. "Those who are alone in the desert become wild, just like animals who get rabies; they are insane. It comes from the bewitchment of the desert. There is a power there that is too strong," said Pedro.

To summarize, the beliefs about diseases and their etiology represents a mixed tradition composed primarily of Yaqui and Spanish elements. Some diseases widely recognized by modern Europeans are known to them: colds and smallpox, for example. Other diseases they list, such as *mal de ojo,* pertain to the folk cultures of Spanish America. Other sets of symptoms are known only by Yaqui terms, as for example *sivori* (sickness due to witchcraft) and are presumed to be aboriginal concepts. As for the causes of disease, they attribute illness to natural causes, such as accident or exposure; to emotional causes, such as strong feelings of fear or jealousy; to God's punishment of sin; to sorcery; or to the malevolent power of the lunar eclipse or the wilderness.

DISEASE TREATMENT

The Yaquis of Navidad list five means of curing illness. These are *seataka,* prayer, medicine, diet, and massage. No one of these can be said to be more effective than the others. Any one of them may be used alone, or all may be employed during the course of an illness.

Seataka

Seataka is an archaic Yaqui word of rather obscure meaning. It can be literally translated as "flower-body." It is the innate and mysterious power possessed by an individual which enables him to cure. *Seataka,* however, is not limited to curing power. It is thought to pervade all of nature, occurring in greater concentration, as it were, in certain individuals, animals, plants, and places.

The concept is not clearly thought out in Navidad, and my informants found it difficult to define. They did agree that *seataka* is an inborn power. It is either present in the baby at birth or it is not, and if it is absent, it can never be acquired. Carlos thought that it might be inherited from one's parents; Pedro thought not. Pedro believed that all humans (or at least all Yaquis) possessed *seataka* to some degree. He compared it to intelligence, saying that although everybody has some, only a few exceptional persons have a great deal.

Seataka in the individual expresses itself in a love and concern for all other people, animals, plants, indeed, all of nature. The person possessing *seataka* is friendly and helpful to other people and is well liked in return. He volunteers to help in time of trouble and illness. He likes to play with children and tell them stories. He is kind to animals, giving them food and water and never harming them. He is fond of flowers and other plants, tends them in a garden, never breaks off their blossoms, leaves, or twigs wantonly. He has a keen appreciation for the beauties of nature. He dreams vividly during his sleep, and his dreams are meaningful in foretelling the future and revealing the machinations of witches. He is clairvoyant, able to see things happening at a distance. He is able to manipulate fetishes. He learns things "naturally"; "he just knows" without having to study.

The Navidadeños say that *seataka* is an ancient Yaqui power. They believe that before Christ came to Sonora, the Yaquis wandered about hunting and growing their food. They knew which plants could cure. One powerful chief had a lake he could roll up and take with him wherever his people went. "They lived by *seataka*." Today only a few Yaquis are believed to have this power.

The power of *seataka* is recognized even in children who seem especially good and happy, but particularly seem able to cure. Carlos, for example, thinks that his five-year-old daughter may have *seataka* because she was so concerned when some of their chickens became ill. She mashed some leaves with water and fed them to the chickens, and the chickens recovered. Usually some unusual circumstance attends the birth of a child who has *seataka*. When Carmen was born, a bit of organic material somewhat resembling a scorpion was caught in her hair. I was unable to ascertain just what this might have been, but it was thought by all who attended the birth to be an indication of her *seataka* and has been carefully saved by her mother. Twins are believed to have *seataka*.

Seataka is most commonly used to cure illness. To be a curer, a *hitevi*, a person must have this power. However, *seataka* is not limited to curers. Yaquis say that great leaders have *seataka*. They have love for their people, and the desire to help them, which are attributes of *seataka*.

The deer dancers, *pascolas*, and the musicians who accompany them also possess *seataka*. Pascola and deer dancers dance and sing for the entertainment of others, "for the good of the village." The members of organized societies such as the *matachinis*, dance and work "for themselves." The members of these societies have pledged their services as a result of a vow taken in return for a cure. The deer and *pascola* dancers and their musicians do not take such a vow. Almost all the *hitevim* (living or dead, of whom I heard about) had been or are deer dancers, *pascolas,* or their musicians. Carlos said that this was not by chance, that all *hitevim* had an obligation to further serve the community by participating in these dances. However, though all male *hitevim* are connected with the performance of deer and *pascola* dances, some of the deer and *pascola* dancers and singers are not also *hitevim.* Others besides *hitevim* may take part in the rituals. Since there are no roles for women in the *pascola* arts, female *hitevim* are excluded from taking part in these performances.

Yaqui fiestas and ceremonies are accompanied by dancing and singing of various groups of men. Masked *chapeyekas* and colorfully costumed *matachinis* usually dance in the village plaza. These dancers belong to organized societies. Their costumes, music, and dances reflect Spanish influence. Deer and *pascola* dancers are also found performing at Yaqui fiestas and ceremonies. The *pascola* dancer, masked and accompanied by his own singers, dances in a special ramada at the edge of the plaza. In the ramada the deer dancer, wearing a deer's head, dances alternately with the *pascola.* The deer dance, imitative of the motions of the deer, is accompanied by its own musicians and singers. The *pascola* and deer dancers and their musicians do not belong to any society. Their performances are evocative of pre-Spanish Yaqui ritual.

Animals possess *seataka,* but most especially the deer itself. The Yaquis say that the *seataka* of the deer is manifested in the fact that it is the only animal to have a leader, that through its hooves it can perceive approaching hunters, that it can blow its breath at them to cause them injury or misfortune, and that when thirsty it can suck water from its rear hock joint. The rituals associated with deer hunting and deer shamans of aboriginal Yaqui culture already have been mentioned. Certain parts of the deer have supernatural curing power. For example, pieces of deer hide are used in Navidad to bind broken or sprained bones. Deer hide is extraordinarily effective because of the *seataka* of the deer. Toor (1937:55) says that Yaquis attribute curing powers to the tail of the deer, which they hang up in their houses. My informants said that the deer's tail brought success in hunting but not in curing.

Seataka exists in the plants and rocks of the *Monte,* the Yaqui term for any wild place, or more particularly the mountainous area north of the Yaqui River in Sonora, Mexico. For an ordinary person to wander alone in the desert would be to court danger and illness, because the *seataka* of the wilderness would be overpowering to him. Unbaptized and invisible people are said to live in the *Monte* and to be the source of *pascola* music and dances. Especially skillful dancers and musicians are believed to have learned their music from the people of the *Monte. Pascolas,* when they first appear at a fiesta, act in a strange way as though they were coming from another world (Spicer 1954:122).

Two plants, in particular, have supernatural powers above the natural powers of plants to nourish or cure. These are *hu'upa* (mesquite), and *hiyakvivam* (tobacco). *Hu'upa* grows both in Sonora, in the Yaqui homeland, and in Arizona, and although all *hu'upa* has natural curing powers, only the *hu'upa* which grows in sacred Yaqui territory has mysterious power to detect and vanquish witchcraft. A piece of *hu'upa* will protect its owner against witches, especially if it is cut in the shape of a cross. The *hu'upa* wood, moreover, will glow at night to warn of an approaching witch. Beals (1943:20) lists mesquite beans as one of the most important wild foods gathered in former times by the Yaquis. A Yaqui myth tells of a "talking stick" of mesquite wood which foretold death to all people baptized as Christians. Those who nevertheless wished to be baptized burned the stick. Those who wished to remain unbaptized became enchanted and went to live, undying and invisible, in the *Monte* (Spicer 1954:123).

The Navidadeños today do not cultivate *hiyakvivam*. The ash and smoke of any cigarette can be used in curing ordinary illness, but *hiyakvivam* grown in Sonora and made into a corn husk wrapped cigarette has added power to cure, to strengthen the deer singers so they can sing all night, and to warn of and combat witchcraft. The presence of a witch, Carlos said, can be detected at night by placing a lighted cigarette near the ramada. It will be seen to glow redly as the invisible witch, lurking in the dark, can not resist smoking from it. Sometimes the cigarettes of the *hitevi* and the witch can be seen fighting in the air at night. While smoking a cigarette, the *hitevi* can become clairvoyant. Pedro said that during the wars with the Mexicans, *hitevim* accompanied war parties and smoked to spy out the movements of the enemy. There does not seem to be any suggestion of a trance involved with this clairvoyance. I saw Carlos do this, and he simply smoked a rather strong homemade cigarette and coolly told me what he saw. Smoking tobacco is mentioned by Beals (1943:37) as a component of pre-Spanish rituals and curing, and reports that contemporary Cahitans use tobacco ritually and in curing (Beals 1945:45).

Flowers, themselves a part of the word *seataka,* figure prominently in modern Yaqui-Catholic rituals and in the deer and *pascola* dances (Painter 1962:4; Spicer 1940:105, 180, 195, 207, 242; 1954:116, 117, 132, 153, 195). Parsons (1936:496) has said: "The formal or ritual use of flowers in general among the Zapoteca and other Indian-speaking peoples is largely of pre-Conquest origin."

There are interesting connections between these diverse manifestations of *seataka.* The deer and plants of the *Monte,* the home of ancient, unbaptized people, all possess *seataka.* The *Monte* is the source of *pascola* music and dances. The *pascola's* hair ribbons are called "flowers." The *pascola* dances with the deer dancer who mimes the powerful deer. The deer singers smoke *hiyakvivam* to strengthen themselves and the *pascolas* distribute cigarettes to the crowd. The ramada in which they dance and sing has a cross of *hu'upa* wood facing it. All the performers possess *seataka* and may themselves be *hitevim,* who are able to cure. The *hitevim* frequently use *hu'upa* and *hiyakvivam* as medicine.

Seataka, which can be conceived of as a power for good, has an opposite force, a power for evil; or *seataka,* itself, can be used for evil. My informants disagreed on this point. They agreed, however, that some people in the village have unusual power which can cause misfortune, sickness, or death. These people, called *mooream**, are witches characterized by their hatred of their fellow man, animals, and nature, and their delight in discord. "This person says to little children, 'Kill, kill, kill! Throw a rock at that dog!' He makes dogs fight each other." These people can cure and sometimes accept patients, but are very likely to make the patient sicker through sheer malice.

Carlos told of a woman who came to him with an earache. She had previously sought aid from another woman who occasionally did some curing. The earache became more severe, and she suspected that the curer was making it worse. Carlos' dreams revealed that this was, indeed, the case. The techniques the *moorea* employs to cause sickness have been discussed earlier.

Pedro thought that two different powers were involved, *seataka,* a power for good, and an unnamed power for evil. He did not believe that the *moorea* had *seataka* because: "The person with *seataka* wants to do good so much that he just couldn't do bad things." Though once he stated, "The *moorea* can make sickness through hate because of his powerful *seataka.* Weaker persons can hate, but not cause illness in doing so." When questioned he said that he had, after all, not really meant *seataka* exactly but just power. Carlos, a *hitevi* himself, felt that it was the same power used differently. He claimed that he could do evil if he wanted to. Indeed, some people in Navidad believe that Carlos is a *moorea.* The dualism of *seataka* is indicated by the belief that one of a pair of twins will be a *hitevi* and the other a *moorea.* Yaquis often translate *hitevi* and *moorea* into English by the terms good witch and bad witch (Giddings 1959-70). Beals remarks that in pre-Spanish Yaqui culture a "feeling of duality of good and evil was attached to the curers and wizards" (Beals 1943-63). Parsons (1936:497) noted that: "Generally in Indian society whoever sends or causes disease, whether spirit or shaman, can also cure disease, an identification of cause and cure which sometimes renders the doctor's life very precarious."

---

*The singular is *moorea.* This pronunciation Carlos used consistently. Other students of Yaqui culture have heard instead *moria'a* (Spicer, personal communication).

Seataka is thought either to be inherited from one's family or to be a free gift from God. *Hitevim* do run in families, the younger members of the family learning curing techniques from their elders. Again Beals' (1943: 60-1) reconstruction of ancient Cahita culture offers a parallel. He mentions the presence of shamans possessed of curing powers partially inherited and partially gained through visions of guardian spirits.

Seataka figures in curing in many ways. The *seataka* of the *hitevi* is what enables him to learn curing techniques, to diagnose illness, and to effect the patient's recovery. Its possession enhances every medicine he may give, every massage he performs, every prayer that he offers, and renders them more effective. Sometimes the *seataka* is so powerful that the presence of the *hitevi* alone will cure. The *hitevi* has "healing hands" and sometimes can cure by merely touching the patient. His *seataka* enables him to know the cause of the disease and what course of treatment to follow, or if he is capable of curing the patient at all. Sometimes a *hitevi,* even before he treats a patient or during the course of treatment, will recommend that another *hitevi* be called. If he does not, and the patient continues to fail, he may be accused of being a *moorea* and of causing the illness.

The *seataka* of the *hitevi* empowers him to dream meaningful dreams which diagnose illness due to witchcraft or warn of coming evil. Beals (1943: 63) believes diagnosing by dream to be an aboriginal Cahita belief. No special techniques are needed to induce these dreams; they simply come while the *hitevi* sleeps, but Carlos recommended saying nine prayers, any nine, before going to bed at night. I collected a number of accounts of these dreams and most of them follow the same pattern. The *moorea* appears in the form of an animal and engages in a fight with the *hitevi.* Carlos said that the soul, *ánima,* of the *hitevi* actually leaves his body and fights with the soul of the *moorea.* Though the *moorea* is expected to appear in animal form in the dream, Carlos recounted one of his dreams in which the *moorea* appeared as an airplane, which Carlos killed by knocking it out of the sky with a stick. When the *hitevi* has vanquished the *moorea,* either by killing or hurting his animal form, the *moorea* reassumes his normal appearance and is recognized by the *hitevi.* The true body of the *moorea* does not suffer and does not bear marks of this conflict. If the *hitevi* were to be beaten, he himself would sicken. When the *hitevi* awakes, he knows that witchcraft is involved in the case he is concerned with and who the *moorea* is, and he can suit his treatment to this fact. The patient is then given more magical treatment than in the usual case: prayers to God to hinder the *moorea* (Carlos thought the *Salve Regina* to be particularly effective), and the use of the cross, mesquite, tobacco, and the saliva of the *hitevi.*

Besides having dreams to diagnose illness due to witchcraft, the *seataka* of the *hitevi* allows him to interpret dreams the patient may have had, which seemed meaningless to the dreamer. Two of Carlos' cases indicate this sort of diagnosis.

After trying home remedies unsuccessfully, Luisa came to Carlos complaining of running sores on her legs. Carlos treated her for a number of days, giving her an herbal infusion with which to bathe her legs, but without success. Suspecting witchcraft because the sores were not cured by a remedy which on previous occasions he found effective, Carlos asked Luisa if she had recently had any unusual dream. She admitted that for a number of weeks she had repeatedly dreamt of a small animal like a cat which had crept onto her bed and scratched her legs. Carlos was then convinced that she was being bewitched and that the animal she saw in her dreams was either the *moorea* in animal form or an animal-spirit companion of the *moorea* sent to harm her. A few nights later Carlos, himself, dreamt of a cat with which he fought and which when wounded appeared to be Luisa's mother. Carlos then told Luisa that she was being bewitched without telling her who the *moorea* was because he "didn't want to cause trouble in the family." Carlos advised her to pray to God for protection. He also prayed. The herbal wash was continued as well. I learned that a few weeks before two of Luisa's brothers began to fight violently in her yard. Luisa called for the police who took them both to jail. Her mother was extremely angry with her "for getting her own brothers into trouble." They quarreled about it on several occasions, and the whole incident was known to Carlos before Luisa came to him for treatment.

Carmen, my interpreter, had tripped on her doorstep and cut her ankle. The wound had become infected and was being treated by the high school nurse. Carmen was disturbed because the sore did not seem to be healing, and in my presence asked Carlos to look at it. Carlos removed the bandage and examined the wound carefully. He then asked Carmen if she had dreamt recently. She said that the night before she had cut her ankle she dreamed that while she was coming out of her door, a rattlesnake had bitten her on the ankle. Carlos assured her that the dream indicated that a *moorea* had caused the accident. He admitted that he did not know who the *moorea* was, but said that he could cure the sore without that knowledge. He said the *Pater Noster* and the *Ave María* in Spanish while holding her ankle and traced the sign of the cross on the sore very rapidly three times with his finger wet with his saliva. He then told Carmen to put the bandage back on, and the sore would be healed in a week. Carmen continued to see the school nurse, but attributed the cure (by the end of the week) to Carlos. Later Carlos said he dreamt of a snake with whom he fought, and that it was the *moorea,* a man, who had hurt Carmen. He did not tell her who he was.

Finally, the *seataka* of the *hitevi* permits him to "just know things." When Carmen and I were wondering on what day school would open in autumn, Carlos "just knew." Carmen was quite impressed when she checked the calendar and found that he was right. Carlos attributed his knowledge to his *seataka*. He said that some things he didn't have to stop and think about, he just knew. Sometimes he told me about the weather in Sonora, whether it was raining or fine, and what the people were doing, working in the fields, sitting and resting, or getting ready for a fiesta. He said that if he sat and thought about it, he could sometimes see them by his *seataka*. He also, at times, "just knew" that danger threatened. He stopped me one day as I was about to drive him back to Navidad. We first had to say three *Ave Marías* because he felt that at that moment a *moorea* was "thinking evil thoughts" about us because he was teaching me "how to cure," and that we would have an automobile accident.

Although Foster (1953:213) has reported that there are in Spain, as in America, curers with supernatural powers, the Yaqui concept of *seataka* seems to be aboriginal. The extreme importance of dreams and visions in curing is not typical of Spanish curing, although it has been postulated to be characteristic of aboriginal Yaqui curing (Beals 1932:141, 213). A fight between the witch and the curer is reported from Cheran (Beals 1946:158). The concept of impersonal supernatural power, *mana,* occurs, of course, sporadically, all over the world. *Seataka* can be defined as *mana*. It occurs in certain people, animals, places, and things. It can not be purposefully gained or increased. It can be manipulated for good or evil purposes. It is dangerous for persons without *seataka* to come into contact with objects, animals, or places with it. Among the Navidadeños, today, the primary use of *seataka* is in healing disease.

Prayer

Prayers to God or to the saints are the constant accompaniment of every phase of curing among the Yaquis as among other people elsewhere in Spanish America (Adams 1957:105; Saunders 1954:149). From the time that leaves and flowers of healing plants are gathered in the fields, to the successful completion of a cure, prayers are offered along every step of the way.

Prayers are offered along with every other sort of treatment. God and the saints are implored to strengthen the power of the *hitevi,* to render the medicine effective, to steady the hand of the surgeon in the county hospital. Frequently prayer alone is trusted to effect a cure.

With one exception, all the prayers offered are Spanish and Catholic. The exception is that while collecting medicinal herbs, the prayers are not made to God, but are offered to the plant, explaining the necessity of picking the leaves, and asking that they may cure. Presumably the apologies and prayers to the plant represent an ancient Yaqui practice. Beals (1943:17, 19) has suggested that pre-Spanish Cahita may have had customs of explanations and prayers to fish and animals before they were killed.

Prayers are offered by the *hitevi* as he gathers and prepares medicines, before going to the patient's house, and as he walks between his house and the house of the patient. He prays again before examining the patient and while he gives him medicines or a massage. The *hitevi* is expected to remember his patients in his daily prayers. He prays before he sleeps at night, asking God to protect him and his patients from witchcraft and that he may receive a dream of a *moorea* if one is causing illness. The *hitevi* asks God that he may diagnose the sickness properly, that he may decide upon the correct treatment, and that it be effective in curing the patient. When the patient is healed, the *hitevi* must pray again to thank God.

The patient too is enjoined to pray for his own cure. Carlos told me twice of treating his co-workers. He thought it important to point out to me that since they were not Catholics, he did not tell them to pray, but that he prayed especially hard for them. The friends and relatives of the patient also are expected to pray for his recovery.

The prayers offered vary between the formal prayers of the Catholic Church which Yaquis memorize as children and spontaneous orisons made up for the occasion. I repeatedly asked my informants for specific prayers for specific situations, but they invariably replied, "Just say any prayer you know or make one up." Carlos usually said either the *Ave María* or the *Pater Noster*. A prayer, called by Carlos, *Niño su oración,* was said by him to be particularly effective in curing. *"Elevada sea dulcísimo nombre de Jesús, María, y José* (repeated three times). *Del poder de Dios me valga la fuerza de su fe por su limpia concepción de Nuestra Señora la Virgen María que fué conservida sin mancha sin pecado original por siempre jamás. Amen, Jesús, María, José."* Carlos frequently told me secretively of a prayer that he had found to be very strong in guarding against witchcraft. He recited it each night and whenever he felt that he or a patient was in danger. On our last interview, he taught it to me as a great favor. I was vaguely disappointed to discover that it was the common Catholic prayer the *Salve Regina* he had mentioned previously. The sign of the cross, the words of the usual blessing accompanied by tracing the form of a cross with the right hand, precedes and ends all prayers. The gesture and the words are used to bless all medicines. The sign of the cross is frequently traced on the patient. Medicines may be applied in the form of a cross or massages begun and ended by rubbing in the shape of a cross.

Besides these formal and standard Catholic prayers, improvised prayers are offered continually. "May this medicine help," said while preparing a medicine; "May even this little bit of medicine heal him," said while giving the patient a dose; or "May drinking this medicine help me," said by the patient, are all examples of improvised prayers that were given to me.

The lighting of candles or placing flowers before representations of the saints may be done as a prayer for a cure, in the home informally before small statues or holy pictures, or in the little Yaqui Church of San Ignacio, or the nearby Church of Santa Rosa. Spicer (1940:277) also reports ". . . the occasional offering of a candle to a deity with the expectation of help in curing. . . ." Sometimes the giving of candles or flowers to a saint is the result of a formal vow or *manda* as will be discussed below.

Prayer not only accompanies all ordinary curing but is intensified when the illness is thought to be due to witchcraft. The power of God is considered to be a vital force in hindering the evil of the *moorea.*

Prayer is the final resort of the patient when all other treatment has failed. "When the case is hopeless, only God can cure." Prayer is relied upon exclusively when the illness is recognized at the outset to be incurable. Illness which is thought to be punishment for sin, congenital malformation, and insanity are usually so diagnosed.

The Catholic hagiology has attributed to certain saints particular interest in and power to cure specific diseases. Thus the intercession of Saint Blaise is implored in ailments of the throat, because legend tells that he miraculously extracted a fish bone caught in the throat of a child; Saint Agnes is the patroness of diseases of the breast; Saint Dymphna is prayed to for cures of mental disorders; Saints Raymond and Gerard are prayed to for safe pregnancy and childbirth, and so forth. The villagers do not seem to share the Catholic lore about the saints which is found in much of Spanish America (Foster 1953:213, 1960:103). My informants said to pray to any saint no matter what the illness. They had not heard of the custom of praying to particular saints for cures of particular illnesses. Carmen had heard of praying to Saint Blaise (*San Blas*) for a sore throat, because she had attended service at the Catholic Church one year on his feast day when throats were blessed. Carlos said that prayers for any intention addressed to Jesus and Mary, to Saint Anthony of Padua, and to Saint Francis Xavier were especially effective. Spicer (1954:178) has reported that in Potam "Jesus is honored specifically in Lent as a great curer, and curing power is attributed to him more explicitly than to any other supernatural; but also . . . it is clear that all three of the major supernaturals have curing power." My informants did not feel that Jesus was more specifically to be called upon for cures, but rather, that God or any of the saints would answer any prayer "if it is the will of God."

The *manda* or vow to perform some stated service in return for a cure is a form of prayer of special significance in Yaqui communities (Spicer 1940:130-1, 1954:68, 91, 93). It has been observed that in the village the members of the religious societies are usually recruited to join that society because of a *manda* made when ill. The *manda* is made, judging from the few cases I collected, when a person has been chronically ill, or when the sickness has not yielded to other treatment. For example, one of Carlos' brothers was promised as a *matachini* when he was a small boy. The *matachini* are a society of boys and young men who dance at fiestas and ceremonies. He was always weak and sickly, and his mother promised him "so that he would live to grow up." The taking of a *manda* is a serious decision. It is made by the parents for a child or by an adult for himself. In either case the matter is discussed with the rest of the household. Carmen said, "When my father was in the hospital, he made a *manda,* but all the relatives agreed that it was right." Usually a *maestro* is called for his opinion and to witness the *manda.* The pledge to join a religious society is usually made for life, but may be made for a specific shorter period of time. Three years was, outside of life, the only figure mentioned to me. Though the one who does the service is ordinarily the recipient of the cure, I did hear of a case in which a man promised himself as a *chapeyeka* for three years in return for a cure of his aged and ailing father.

Once taken, the *manda* to join a society can not be lightly ignored. This does not mean that the member must forever take part in every ceremony. A member may be excused from ceremonies by the head of the society, and he is not expected to appear if he is working far from town. After a man has taken part faithfully for a number of years, it is considered that he has fulfilled most of his *manda,* and he may appear less regularly in ceremonies. A man pledged to two societies may choose the one with which he is going to dance. Spicer (1940:141) notes that the men's societies are roughly and informally age-graded. *Matachinis* tend to be young, *fariseos* middle-aged, and *maestros* and *temastim* old. Many men dance with one society when young and work with another later on in life. If, however, a member who is able consistently refuses to take part in the activities of the society, punishment from God is thought to be sure to follow: sickness, bad luck, or even death. I was told of a *matachini* who began to refuse to dance when called. He began to drink heavily and to miss more and more dances, because he was always drunk until he finally died. Carlos and Carmen believed that his death was clearly a punishment from God for having broken his *manda.*

Occasionally a person will join a society simply because he wants to. He is then a full-fledged member, but he may quit at will without fear of punishment for a broken *manda.*

Spicer (1940:53) has indicated how important membership in the religious societies is for winning prestige. In addition, upon "confirmation" into a society the novice receives another set of godparents, and he and his family extend their ritual kinship ties further through the village in accordance with the *compadrazgo* system. These factors must surely be of influence when the decision to make a *manda* to join a society is considered.

A *manda* may take other forms than joining a society. Often a person pledges to give a fiesta, a *fiesta de promesa.* These fiestas usually are promised to be held during the Lenten season on three consecutive years, though occasionally another date may be chosen. If the vow has been made to Jesus, the *fariseos* are present; if to Mary, the *matachinis* dance instead. As at every fiesta, the *pascolas* dance. The giving of a fiesta is an expensive affair. The religious society which dances and the *pascolas* must be fed as well as anyone else who may choose to attend. The participating society helps by clearing the yard for the dancing and by gathering wood. Just before the fiesta, the participating society conducts a *limosna* (the word means "alms" in Spanish) through the village. Participants go from house to house begging for contributions of food and money to help defray the cost of the fiesta.

Pilgrimages may be taken as a result of a *manda*. The longest one I heard of was the pilgrimage to the annual fiesta in Magdalena, Sonora. Easier pilgrimages are to light a candle or to take flowers to a saint in the cathedral in the city, or to the local mission. Attendance at the fiesta of San Francisco Xavier at the local mission is frequently promised. Again these pilgrimages are usually undertaken on three consecutive years.

Sometimes a pilgrimage and a fiesta are promised together. "This man made a *manda* to go to Magdalena and to give a fiesta when he came back for three years. He had heart trouble. He did this to get well, and he did."

A form of *manda* which seems to be dying out is the wearing of an *hábito*. In 1940 Spicer (p. 98) reported that: "The resort to the *hábito* penance is frequent . . . for both males and females of all ages." In 1958 and 1959 I could find only two little girls wearing *hábitos,* and unlike the former custom which was to wear the garment until it wore out, these children appeared to be wearing it only at fiestas and ceremonies. They did not wear their *hábitos* to school. The *hábito* worn here is a brown cotton dress with a white rope sash made to look like a Franciscan habit *(Catholic Encyclopedia* 1908 Vol. 6:291). Wearing of *hábitos* is a custom reported occasionally from other Catholic countries (Meyers 1954:114). At Navidad the *hábito* is assumed at a ceremony with a male and female sponsor at the small Yaqui church or at the local mission. The person who has made the *manda* assumes the *hábito* before the altar in the presence of his sponsors. The school teachers disapprove of this custom, considering the *hábitos* to be dirty and ugly. Children who have worn them to school in recent years have been sent home to change.

Taking a vow or pilgrimage in return for a cure is a widespread Catholic practice found in all Catholic parts of the Americas from Brazil (*The Catholic Encyclopedia* Vol. 12:94) to Quebec (*The Catholic Encyclopedia* Vol. 1:539-40; Miner 1939:100).

Medicine

The giving and taking of medicine is an important part of almost every cure. The *hitevi* is expected to have a great knowledge of medicine and to be able to recommend or supply the correct ones to his patients. I was told, "A *hitevi* should know 69 ways to use every herb." The very word *hitevi* implies an association with medicine: *hitoa* means "medicine"; *hitoata,* "to give medicine"; and *hitone,* "to cure."

From Carlos I obtained a list of some 70 herbs that he used in curing. I believe that this list in no way contains his entire knowledge of medicines; until the last week I interviewed Carlos, he was from time to time reminded of another plant or medicinal recipe that he had forgotten to give me. Only about a dozen of the herbs that he used regularly are of European origin. The rest grow wild in or near the Yaqui River region. Some of the herbs I was completely unable to identify; the villagers knew them only by their Yaqui names; Carlos and the stores selling herbs had only small bits of their leaves, stems or roots, or powders ground from them so they could not be identified. The herbs most used by Carlos in curing were: *hiyakvivam* (tobacco); *huchasko* (brazil wood, also used as a medicine by Mexicans in Sonora and Arizona); *hu'upa* (mesquite, which the herb stores do not sell as a medicine); *huvakvena* (*Bursera laxiflora*); and *wasarako*. The herb stores in the city do not know this last herb; an herb store in a town in northern Sonora bought it from the Yaquis living along the Yaqui River in southern Sonora to sell to the Yaquis living in northern Sonora and southern Arizona. The proprietor of the herb shop said that *wasarako* is native to Sonora and has no Spanish name.

This list of herbs used by Carlos is surprising because of the large proportion of native plants used. Foster (1953:207) has commented that, in spite of the interest shown by the early Spanish physicians in New World plants, Spanish American medicinal herbs are mainly European in origin, saying, "In view of the many efficacious native American herbs, this predominance of the Spanish testified to the force of the impact of Spanish medicine in the New World." Various lists of Spanish American medicinal herbs (Adams 1957:105; Broadbent 1952:4-9; Clark 1959:167; Foster 1953:207; Gillin 1947:139-42; Saunders 1954:154-5) show how popular certain European plants are. *Alhucema* (lavender), *ajo* (garlic), *canela* (cinnamon), *clavo* (cloves), *límon* (lemon), *manzanilla* (chamomile), *naranja* (orange), *romero* (rosemary), *ruda* (rue), and *yerba buena* (mint) are frequently listed. Navidadeños know most of these substances, but do not use them as medicines. Of medicinal herbs popular with local Mexicans only *manzanilla* (chamomile); *chuchupate,* called *pawis* by the Yaquis (wild parsley); *saúco* (elder); and *yerba buena* (mint) are much used for curing in the village. I collected lists of medicinal herbs known to Pedro, to Carmen and her mother, and to María. None of these knew the uses of more than a dozen herbs, and unlike Carlos' list, about half of the herbs they knew were popular with local Mexicans.

A certain amount of ritual accompanied the gathering of herbs. My informants said that long ago in the Eight Towns of the Yaqui, herbs were gathered early in the morning by the *hitevim,* who knew plants' habits of growth. The leaves, blossoms, roots or whatever part of the plant was gathered, were taken only from the side of the plant touched by the rays of the rising sun. These sections of the plants were believed to have especially powerful curing properties. Before the *hitevi* touched the plant, he prayed to it, explaining the necessity of picking its leaves and apologizing to it.

There was no particular season for gathering herbs. Some medicines were made of the flowers or fruit, others of the bark or roots. Flowers or fruit had to be gathered during the proper time of year, which varied from one plant to another. Leaves were plucked when they were fresh and green; bark and roots when they were needed. The *hitevi* tried to keep enough herbs on hand to supply his patients' needs, making the herbs up into particular medicines as they were required. Wagner (Holden 1936:86) reports that the "medicine man" at Torim said that it took a lot of work to keep up his collection of herbs. He said that he had to go as far as 300 miles for some of them. Lay people who had some knowledge of herbal medicines also gathered what they needed for home use, approaching the plant from the east and praying to it. I was not able to get any information on whether or not herbs were obtained by trade from outside the Yaqui territory.

Carlos and Pedro said that when Navidad was first founded and during the '20s and early '30s, men used to come to the village with horse-drawn carts, selling herbs, holy pictures, candles, artificial flowers, and various other items. They were in those days the principal sources of herbs in the village. One of these men was well known to Carlos. He lived in another town and bought many of his herbs from growers or gatherers in Sonora and traveled through Arizona, selling them in Mexican communities. I was unable to determine if this man was a Yaqui. He was, at any rate, well acquainted with Yaquis in Arizona and knew the Yaqui names of the herbs. Some plants which grew nearby continued to be gathered. Visitors to Sonora frequently returned with herbs given them by friends and relatives.

Today Navidadeños seem to consider it extremely difficult to find the proper medicinal herbs. Carlos was constantly complaining that he could not obtain the herbs that he needed. His meager supply was kept in a quart mason jar, and he rationed out medicines to his patients very grudgingly. Indeed, he used such minute quantities of his herbs in teas and washes that any curative value that they may have had must have been much diluted. Carmen's mother, a housewife, also told me how difficult it was to find herbs, and María, the midwife, said that the Mexican drugstores simply did not sell Yaqui herbs. All agreed that herbs were very expensive; that one would pay two or three dollars for an ounce or so. Actually, I found that herbs were easy to buy in the city and in Sonora and was able to buy an ounce or two of a couple of dozen different herbs for five dollars. The difficulty seems to be that the villagers are not sure of the Spanish names of many of their herbs, and the herb dealers do not recognize the Yaqui names. In addition some of the Yaqui medicinal herbs are rarely if ever used as medicines by other Mexicans and so are not carried in the herb stores.

There is a very large drugstore in the city which specializes in selling herbs and Mexican home remedies. They advertise their wares over the radio, and all of my informants knew of the store. Yaqui customers at this store tend to buy common Mexican herbs, because they find it difficult to get Yaqui herbs, and because the store through its advertising and salespeople tends to "push" well-known Mexican remedies and herbs, such as chamomile, rue, and mint. Besides this store, there are a number of other drug and grocery stores in Mexican sections of the city that have limited supplies of medicinal herbs for sale. There is said to be a drugstore in another Southwest town, where they sell "Yaqui" herbs. Navidadeños who are doing agricultural work near this town stock up on herbs there. This store was Carlos' main source.

In a Sonoran town, there is a large shop dealing exclusively in herbs. This shop was not known to my informants. They eagerly copied down its address, because they found themselves frequently in that town. The husband of the proprietor of this store takes an annual trip through Sonora and adjacent states buying herbs. He said that some of the herbs are grown by farmers, and others are collected wild by a few families, both Mexican and Indian. The markets also usually have some herbs for sale. Many kinds of herbs are bought directly from Europe by the store proprietor's wife. The "best" chamomile comes from Europe although some is grown in Mexico. The people who own the store not only retail the herbs in their own shop, but they also sell them wholesale to other herb dealers in Sonora and Arizona. From what I could determine, they are probably the major supplier of herbs to this part of the Southwest.

The villagers have a fear of being cheated when buying herbs. They told me that *huchasko* (brazil wood) was likely to be any stick painted red. I was told to soak a bit of it overnight to see if the red color washed off before trying to use it as medicine. Other herbs should also be tested by soaking, because "real" herbs are thought to retain their odor even in an infusion. The characteristic fragrance of the different plants is evidently an important way of identifying them, for whenever I showed fresh or dried plant materials to Yaqui they invariably sniffed them first.

Some herbs are still gathered wild; *hu'upa* (mesquite) and *kovanau* (creosote) are both plentiful in the southern Arizona desert and are much used Yaqui curing herbs. *Kwapaim* (milkweed) and *saúco* (elder) were other plants which Carlos still gathers himself. Carlos still follows the custom of gathering herbs at dawn from the side of the plant first touched by the rays of the sun and praying to it. Plants that grow in sacred Yaqui territory are thought to be much more effective in curing than plants which grow elsewhere, especially mesquite and tobacco. Navidadeños visiting in

Sonora therefore try to bring a few herbs back with them. One plant though, a variety of creosote, is said to be rare along the Yaqui River and Sonoran Yaquis visiting in Arizona usually take some back with them when they return home.

Not many herbs seem to be grown in the village. I examined most of the gardens in the village. Outside of a few trees, the majority of the plants were flowering annuals. The only herbs I saw: carrots, parsley, and dill seemed to be intended for kitchen use. One garden did have some mint growing in it, and Carlos had a pomegranate tree in his yard. He used the fruit medicinally. Most of the plants listed by Beals (1943:10) as grown aboriginally by the Cahita-speaking Indians of Sonora are food plants. Only one of them, tobacco, was used as a medicine. Evidently Yaquis prefer gathering their herbs wild to growing them.

Certain other substances are used by the villagers as medicines: saliva, occasionally urine, beef lard, mashed insects, and certain types of sea shells, red clay, salt, and baking soda. Patented medicines are also becoming popular. Aspirin, cough syrups, Kaopectate, Bromo-Quinine, Vick's Vapo-Rub, alcohol, and peroxide were frequently mentioned to me as remedies. These remedies are widely advertised on the radio and television, are known to Navidadeños, and are easily obtained not only in drugstores but in most grocery stores in the city. Many villagers now procure treatment for minor illnesses by going to a drugstore and asking the clerk which patent medicine to buy. The remedies are usually used for the purpose for which they are intended, but I collected some exotic uses of common patent medicines: straight peroxide used as a gargle, for example, or Vick's Vapo-Rub applied to insect bites.

The *hitevi* not only recommends herbal doses to his patients, but usually supplies the medicine. Carlos usually prepared and mixed the medicine himself, giving it to the patient or leaving instructions with his patient on how to take it. More rarely he would simply tell a patient what herb to use for a specific complaint. Carlos was asked for such advice often during casual conversations. He was somewhat annoyed by the amount of free advice he was expected to give. Sometimes Yaquis would come to Carlos' house asking to purchase a quantity of some particular herb, evidently when they had run out of it and couldn't obtain it elsewhere. On these occasions Carlos sold them the herb, if he had it, without inquiring why it was wanted or suggesting how it should be used.

As has been mentioned, different parts of various plants are used as medicines so that the preparation of a particular medicine depends to some extent on whether a piece of root, bark, leaves, or blossoms are to be used. In the village almost all herbs are used dried, evidently not through preference, but because they were bought that way, or because a freshly picked supply dried out in storage. Flowers, leaves, and small twigs are usually reduced to a powder before use, grinding them against the side of a small bowl with the back of a spoon, or if a very small amount is wanted, simply by rubbing them between thumb and forefinger. Fresh leaves or bigger leaves are cut up into a cup or small bowl and mashed with the back of a teaspoon. Pieces of roots, bark, or branches are scraped with a knife to obtain a powder. Holden (1936:80) reports this practice for the Sonoran Yaquis. Some herbs are toasted before use by holding them near the fire or putting them into a hot oven. The purpose seems to be to dry them out so that they will be easier to grind.

Teas are probably the commonest way medicinal herbs are used. The herb is boiled for a time in water after having been ground. If several different herbs are to be used in the same tea, they are ground and mixed together in a bowl before being placed in the boiling water. The tea is cooled off and drunk when lukewarm. Navidadeños believe that hot medicinal teas are stronger than cool teas and may be harmful to the patient. Pedro said that the tea was always cooled by pouring it from one cup to another and that "this is frequently seen at the patient's bedside." It is never blown into to cool it. "Germs would ruin it." The tea sometimes is cooled off completely and used as an external wash. Often the same batch of tea is used both ways, the patient drinking part, and using the rest to bathe the afflicted part of his body.

For other medicines, the herbs are not boiled but are simply steeped for several hours in a glass of cool water before being drunk or used as a wash. Sonoran Yaquis also use herbal infusions as medicines (Holden 1936:79).

The dried powder of the herbs is often sprinkled onto cuts and bruises or used rather as talcum powder when the patient is massaged. Sometimes the herbal powder is first mixed with olive oil or lard before being massaged into the patient's skin.

Emetics and purges are considered to be helpful in a number of illnesses and are frequently prescribed by Carlos. A number of quite different herbal teas are said to induce vomiting; most contain enormous quantities of salt.

Poultices are much used by the Yaquis. The herbs are moistened with water, urine, saliva, or lard and stuck to the painful spot; often a cloth bandage also is used to help keep them in place. It is usually recommended to leave the poultice in place until it falls off by itself. Poultices of herbs, cloth, or paper are frequently used in Spanish America (Beals 1946:203; Foster 1953:206, 214; Johnson 1950:32; Parsons 1936:451; Saunders 1954:149). Their use is reported from the Yaqui River by Holden (1936:79). In Navidad and in Sonora poultices are a common remedy for headaches. Giddings (1959:55) recounts a *pascola* story from Sonora in which a poultice of watermelon seeds is used on a horse.

Diet

The *hitevi* is expected to advise his patient as to the diet that should be eaten during the course of the illness. The concept of "hot" and "cold" foods so prevalent in Spanish America is only vaguely known in Navidad. Foster and Rowe (1951:1) have stated:

> Ethnologists have found in many parts of Latin America that important ideas concerning health and sickness are based on the Graeco-Roman concept of "hot" and "cold" qualities innate in nature; for example, certain illnesses are believed to be inherently "hot" and are treated with "cold" remedies, while other illnesses are "cold" and are treated with "hot" remedies. Food also is so classified, and the maintenance of health requires care to avoid the mixing of incompatible dishes. The qualities of "hot" and "cold" in this system have nothing to do with physical temperature and nothing necessarily to do with physiological effect; from a scientific viewpoint, the attribution of a substance to one or the other of these categories may be purely arbitrary. Honey, for example, is almost always "hot," while pork is by nature "cold."

My informants knew that some foods are considered to be "hot" and others "cold"; only Pedro, however, was able to give me a list of hot and cold foods. He listed as hot foods: apple, banana, beans, cantaloupe, chili, figs, and prunes. As cold foods he mentioned: apricot, cabbage, grapes, grapefruit, lemon, lettuce, orange, peach, pear, tomato, and watermelon.

The Redfields (1940:64) in Yucatan got from one informant the following list of hot and cold foods. Hot: steer-beef, sweet potato, other potatoes, peas, eggs baked in ashes, atole, chicken, black pepper, salt, and honey; cold: pork, cow-beef, orange, lime, certain imported beans, papaya, and *quana* beans.

Clark (1959:166) collected an extensive list of hot and cold foods from Mexicans in San Jose, California. Very hot: chili, garlic, crackles, white beans; hot: onion, capon, fish, goat's milk, pork, turkey, barley, wheat bread, beans, chick peas, white and sweet potatoes, rice, sweet rolls, wheat tortillas, wheat, honey, brown sugar, and salt; temperate: goat, pinto beans, and white sugar; cold: green beans, beets, cabbage, carrots, cauliflower, coriander, parsley, peas, pumpkin, radish, squash, turnip, beef, boar, lamb, mutton, rabbit, cow's and donkey's milk, red beans, lentils, corn tortillas, and vermicelli; very cold: cucumber, pickles, purslane, spinach, tomato, hen or pullet, and human milk.

From Panama, Adams (1957:105) lists pineapple, watermelon, oranges, and papayas as cold foods and corn as a hot food. From Honduras he (*ibid.*:601) gives coconuts, pork, fish, bananas, and salt as cold foods and oranges and beef as hot foods.

As can be seen, the lists do not correspond exactly. Probably in each community there are local ideas as to which foods are hot and which cold.

Carlos consistently recommends a diet of meat, meat broths, rice, and noodles for his patients no matter what disease they may have. He said that these foods are heavy, *pesado,* and hence strengthening to the person weakened by illness. The Redfields (1940:64) reported that in Dzitas, Yucatan, the word *pesado* implies a dangerous condition and is applied to cold foods. Carlos and Pedro said that oranges eaten when one has a cold are curative. They are warmed a while on the stove before being eaten. Usually in Spanish America oranges are thought to be a cold food and would not be eaten if one were suffering from a respiratory infection, a "cold" disease. The Redfields (*ibid.*) point out, though, that an orange warmed for a moment in the ashes is no longer regarded as a cold food. María advised women recently delivered of a baby not to eat acid foods, believing that "while the womb is bleeding, acid can get into the blood." Menstruating women also avoid acid foods. Nursing mothers do not eat chili as it is thought to get into the milk and cause diarrhea, stomachache, or rash in the baby. Clark (1959:122) reports that in San Jose, California, expectant and nursing Mexican mothers do not eat chili for fear their babies will get diaper rash. María recommended that nursing mothers drink a lot of soup as it would increase their milk.

Massage

Massages are given to the patient during the course of many different illnesses. Judging from the cases of which I heard, the patient is massaged if he is suffering from aches and pains, weakness, nervousness, or diarrhea; for a high fever, the patient is bathed with a cool herbal tea or infusion as he is massaged. Olive oil, water, liquid herbal medicines, herbal powders, and alcohol can all be used as a lubricant during massage. Navidadeños believe their *hitevim* have great skill as masseurs, skill which is unequaled by Anglo chiropractors to whom they compare them. Some Yaquis who do not put much faith in the medicines of the *hitevi* go to him for massages. Jaime said to me, for example: "I don't believe in these old medicines. I don't use them for my family. We buy medicine at the drugstore. But some of these old women know how to massage good. When the baby had diarrhea, we took him to an old woman. She rubbed his stomach with some leaves, and the sickness went right away."

Broken bones are massaged into position by the *hitevi* and then are bound tightly with strips of hide. The midwife massages the abdomen of an expectant mother to assure that the child will be in the right position, and during labor to help expel it.

Since I could not accompany Carlos when he treated the patients, I have very little idea of just how the massaging is done. Carlos did massage me one time when one of my arms was aching. He said the *Ave María* three times in Spanish, made the sign of the cross, three times each on the inside of the wrist and elbow of my right arm (the one that was sore), on my forehead, and on the inside of my left elbow and wrist. He then began to rub my right arm briskly with hard, rapid movements of his fingers. He seemed to probe out and follow the position of each of the bones. He massaged up my arm, across the back of my shoulders and neck, and down along the left arm. He finished by picking me up under my arms and dropping me heavily on my feet three times. The arm did feel much better thereafter.

Massage is said to be a common element of Spanish American folk curing (Adams 1957:105; Gillin 1947:132; Parsons 1936:130; Saunders 1954:149).

The Navidadeños do not know any surgical techniques and greatly fear those of the Anglo-Americans. They seem to believe that surgery is the first curing technique attempted in the county hospital and that operations frequently result in death. "They want to operate right away there. The Yaquis do not cut people up. Their curing is the natural way." Indeed, my informants did not have very exact ideas of human anatomy. Most of them knew only Spanish terms for the internal organs, could not remember all of them or their functions, or contradicted each other. The following list represents the total knowledge of Carlos, Carmen, and Pedro. None of them knew all of the organs and their functions.

The heart in Yaqui is called, *hiapsi;* "It makes everything work." The blood is *chovo;* "It carries food to the body." *Toma* means the stomach; "It is the storehouse of the body." The lungs (*pulmón*), the womb (*matriz*), and the brain (*sentido* – sense), are known only by Spanish names. "Air goes into the lungs when you breathe." The womb is "the house of the baby." The brain is "the seat of thought." *Sikupuriam,* an unidentified internal organ, was thought by Pedro to mean the kidney (*riñón*) and by Carmen to mean the appendix (*apéndices*). Carlos did not really know; he thought probably one or the other. He said, "When you are sick in this, there is always blood in the urine." Although they named it, none of them were sure what the *hayman* was; there is no translation for the word. Carmen thought perhaps it is the liver. Carlos said that all the blood veins are attached to it, and if it is hurt or sick, the blood will not circulate.

Cupping (*ventosas*), a common folk remedy in Spanish America (Clark 1959:169; Foster 1948:267, 1953:205, 213; Redfield and Redfield 1940:71), is not done in Navidad.

CURERS AND PATIENTS

The Hitevi

The *hitevi* is the principal Yaqui medical specialist. He is a professional curer and is paid for his services. He has undergone a lengthy though informal period of training and apprenticeship. Most important, he is the possessor of supernatural power which enables him to diagnose and to cure disease.

Both men and women can be *hitevim*. Most women *hitevim* (all whose names I learned) also practice midwifery, which is not ordinarily among the duties of male *hitevim*. A female *hitevi* does not seem to be in any way restricted in her curing activities because of her sex. Pedro suggested that a woman might not attempt to cure while menstruating, but Carlos said that it would not make any difference.

The means used by *hitevim* to cure illness have been discussed earlier, but to summarize briefly here: The *hitevi* diagnoses the illness of the patient, recommends medicines or massage, and usually administers them. He may suggest foods the patient should eat or avoid. He invariably prays for the patient and often advises the patient to pray. His supernatural power, *seataka,* enables him to guess if witchcraft is causing the illness, to confirm his suspicion, and to thwart the witch in his dreams and by the use of other magical techniques.

The most important requisite for a *hitevi* is that he be born with *seataka,* with innate power to cure. The Navidadeños recognize that a *hitevi* works hard to learn the medicinal properties of different herbs. They believe that the medicines can cure by themselves, since they do take medicines (home remedies) without consulting a doctor. They know that the *hitevi* has acquired skills of massage to ease aching muscles, and that he frequently calls on supernatural powers greater than his own by praying to God and the saints to aid him. But the Yaquis feel that all of this knowledge and skill is enhanced, indeed made possible in the first place, through his *seataka*. Carlos said, "Anyone can go to a *hitevi* and try to learn to cure, but if they don't have *seataka,* it is no use." Pedro said, "The American doctor must study hard with books. He learns many things, but the Yaqui doctor learns and knows things the natural way. He knows through his own power. His power helps him."

Though curing knowledge and skill is thought to be hard to obtain even for those with *seataka* (I asked Carlos why none of his brothers or sisters were *hitevim,* and he replied "It is too much work to watch and learn, not many want to."), success in curing is considered to be impossible to obtain without power. The *seataka* of the *hitevi* gives extra strength and efficacy to his medicines and massage. Pedro remarked that "there are some with power so that when they give even a little medicine it cures, even though another might give the medicine and it might make worse." And again, "It has been told that there are some with healing hands, so that they cure merely by massage. It is their touch that cures." And Carlos recounted that when Nick had a heart attack, and the boy's father ran to get Carlos, he had the medicine already prepared to take to him because, "I thought someone might need it so I made some up." Because the *hitevi* is good and powerful, God is more likely to heed his prayers. Pedro said "A *hitevi* is naturally kind and good-hearted. He feels sorry for people who are sick. He prays for them and God listens."

To become a *hitevi* a man or woman must have some indication that he has *seataka.* These indications seem to take a variety of forms. To have one's birth accompanied by unusual circumstances, to be a twin, for example, is one such indication. To have, as a child, sympathy for the sick and some luck in their cure is another. Carlos' daughter gave sick chickens mesquite leaves to eat, and they recovered. He felt this was surely a sign that she had *seataka* and would be a *hitevi.* Pedro said, "They can cure even as little children; they are sorry for sick people and try to comfort them." Evidently the *seataka* of one person can recognize it in another. One day while we were discussing *seataka,* Carlos peered intently at Carmen and felt the pulse in her wrist and her forehead. He said that he felt by her pulse that she had a good heart and power, that she could do anything she liked and could become a great healer. This excited Carmen exceedingly, and she began at once to tell Carlos that her mother thought so too, about the thing caught in her hair at birth, and about how vividly she dreamed.

Dreams are probably the most important indication of *seataka.* To dream frequent and unusual dreams suggests the presence of *seataka,* especially if the dreams foretell the future. Carlos felt that he had *seataka* when he was a young man, because he dreamt frequently of flying like a bird. Carmen thinks that it is significant that she dreams of volcanoes erupting and that sometimes other dreams that she has "come true."

Carlos also said that, in addition, most *hitevim* have, before they start to practice, a dream in which they see God and in which He asks them to start to cure. Carlos said that they are given certain medicines, prayers, or skills at this time, and a magical number. His own number is three, and he usually repeats treatments and prayers three times. This dream is, of course, reminiscent of the guardian spirit quest, in which the supplicant receives certain powers and directions as to how to use them from a vision of some supernatural (Driver 1961). Beals (1943:59) postulated that a feature of aboriginal Yaqui religion was a belief in guardian spirits who conferred power when they appeared in dreams. It was unclear to me whether in the dream God conferred or confirmed the curing power. Presumably the *hitevi*-to-be already has *seataka,* having been born with it, and *seataka* usually implies a power to cure. There seemed to be a similar haziness about some aspects of *seataka* in the minds of my informants as well.

On a more practical level it is extremely helpful to the aspirant *hitevi* if he has a parent or other relative who is a *hitevi.* Carlos emphasized that although the novice can go to any *hitevi* and ask to learn, it is much easier to learn from a *hitevi* in the family: "When he lives with you, you watch him all the time. You see all the medicines. It is very hard to learn from someone else." There is also a vague feeling that *seataka* may be partly inherited. Carlos said once, "I got my power from my family and God."

There were many *hitevim* in Carlos' family. His mother, Juana, and Ignacio, her brother, who always lived with his sister's family, were both *hitevim.* They started curing in Cocorit, Sonora, where Carlos was born and continued when the whole family moved together to the Southwest. They were among the first residents of Navidad. Carlos said that his uncle especially was a famous *hitevi.* Many Yaquis living around the city had known him or heard of him in Sonora and came to consult him in Navidad. He lived to be a very old man in Carlos' brother's home and kept on curing right up to the end. Carlos' stepfather was also a *hitevi* and a musician for the deer dancer. He taught Carlos to play his rasp when he was very small. There are two other relatives of Carlos who are *hitevim.* One is Joe, a cousin of his stepfather, and the other, Leonardo, is the younger brother of his uncle Ignacio. Leonardo now lives in another Yaqui community in the Southwest.

Even as a young boy, Carlos learned something about medicines from his mother, uncle, and stepfather. He says, "I used to watch through holes in the walls when my mother was massaging patients." And "I would sit and watch my father make medicines. . . . My uncle sent to Sonora for all his medicines. He used to show them to me and tell me their names."

Though he recalls that he dreamt much as a boy, especially of flying, which he now regards as a sign of *seataka,* Carlos did not decide to become a *hitevi* until he was a grown man. "I was about 32. I was married." It was at that time that Carlos had the unusual dream that he considered to be a divine call to cure.

> One night I dreamed a dream. I was in a strange place with no people. There was a steep hill with a cave where God lived. I asked him for water, and Christ handed me just a little water, about four or five drops of water. I didn't want to take it, because there wasn't enough, and I wanted God to take it. God said to drink my fill so I did, and my thirst was quenched even with just a little. Then I asked God for power and some medicine. *Wasarako, houvakvena, pawis* – God handed me sticks of these. So after I got the medicine, I said I was going, and God told me to come back. So I dreamed it for three nights. On the third night, I dreamed that I visited God again, and God invited me into the cave where there was a waterhole, very deep. God told me to jump in, and if I didn't fear, I wouldn't drown but spring up. I was afraid, but God told me not to be. So I did it three times. After I did this, I had to wash my face with the water and drink. God gave me the power to cure. I had *seataka* before, but it was not enough.

Carlos later said that if he had been afraid and left the cave in his dream, God would have let him go without harm, but he would not be able to cure. Because he was told to jump into the pool three times, he repeats prayers, treatments, and doses three times.

After this dream, Carlos went to his uncle Ignacio and asked permission to watch and learn. He said that he watched him prepare medicines and watched how he treated all the patients who came to the house. He also went with him when he went to call on patients. Carlos also watched his mother when patients came to be treated by her. After several years of watching (Carlos does not remember exactly how long), never actually helping, the people in the village began to come to him for treatment, when they could not find his mother or his uncle. As he was successful, people told each other, and more patients came.

A *hitevi* from Torim, Sonora, who was curing in Navidad for several weeks in 1959 had with him a young man who accompanied his teacher everywhere and who was always present when he was with a patient. I was told by a number of people in the village that he was a young *hitevi* who was still learning.

Once a man or woman is known as a *hitevi* by reason of having cured a number of people, he must watch his behavior carefully to avoid becoming known as a *moorea*. It will be recalled that there is a feeling in Navidad that those who can cure illness can also cause it. Even Carlos stated that if he wanted to, he knew how to do much evil. There is an uncanniness about the *hitevi* who dreams, who "knows things," who can fight witches, and an uneasy feeling that he might after all really be a witch masquerading as a healer. Carmen told me that her friends thought she was brave to work with Carlos. They were afraid of him because many in the village thought he might be a *moorea*. Even Pedro who disagreed with Carlos in saying that *seataka* and evil power were quite distinct remarked, "The *moorea* can cure when in danger of being exposed. He can cure by evil. He caused the illness, so he has the capacity to remove it."

The unsuccessful *hitevi* is very likely to be suspected of actually causing the illness he is pretending to cure. "If a person said he was a *hitevi* but couldn't cure, they would think the person was really bad and making people sick." Carlos once cured a woman of an earache. He said she foolishly had sought treatment from another woman in Navidad who had actually caused the illness and who made it worse while she pretended to cure it. To protect himself from having too many unsuccessful cases, the *hitevi* can refuse to take the case in the first place. "One man may not have a good hand for everyone. He can tell if he is good for this patient. If he is not, he will tell him." This is the only reason a *hitevi* can give for refusing to treat a patient. Since by definition a *hitevi* is kind and full of sympathy for the sick and longs to help them, any other refusal would immediately label the *hitevi* as a *moorea*. Also if the treatment is not going satisfactorily, the *hitevi* can recommend that the patient consult another *hitevi*. During 1958-1959 two of Carlos' patients were sent to him by another *hitevi* who had failed to cure them.

A *hitevi* must continue to cure. If he stops, it will be thought that he is devoting himself instead to witchcraft. Carlos said that no *hitevi* ever stopped curing. "God would not punish him if he stopped curing, but people would not like him anymore; they would think he was bad." Carlos' mother and uncle continued accepting patients until they died. All the *hitevim* about whom I specifically asked had continued to cure until their last illnesses.

The *hitevi* also must indicate to the community that he is curing for "love" and not because of the fees. He can do this by volunteering his services, by offering much free advice, and by never discussing his fee with his patient.

My informants (see also Beals 1945:197 and Toor 1937) said that in ancient times a suspected *moorea* was accused before a council of the leaders of the town societies. When questioned, the *moorea* would reveal himself by cursing God and boasting of his powers. He was then burnt alive in a crib made of green wood. The evil little animals who were his familiars would run out of the fire and had to be caught and thrown back in to destroy them. Pedro claimed that his uncle had witnessed such an execution. The execution of a witch by burning alive might well derive from Europe (Davies 1947). I heard of only one *moorea* who was openly accused in Navidad. During the 1930s, a woman was accused by a villager of bewitching his daughter and making her sick. She was forced by the man and his supporters to massage the girl and thus remove the spell. The girl eventually recovered and the woman was ignored and avoided by her neighbors until her death.

Although the *hitevi* expects to be paid for his services, he is in no sense a full-time specialist. During the year that I interviewed Carlos, his fees were low and must have formed only a fraction of his total income (small though that was). I estimated that he received about twenty dollars in cash and the value of about sixteen dollars in other gifts. He did not buy any medicines while I knew him. He had a full jar of herbs which he showed me in August 1958, and which he used sparingly until the next July.

In addition to curing, Carlos has always worked at either construction or agricultural work. He and all other Yaquis with whom I discussed the matter repeated that no *hitevi* had ever supported himself solely by curing, neither in the Southwest nor in Sonora, in the present or in ancient times. Indeed, Navidadeños seem to prefer to believe that the *hitevi* cured solely from a desire to do good. They always refer to the *hitevi's* fee as a "present," and insist that it is given freely in gratitude for a cure. It is quite true that Carlos never discusses his fee or "present" with his patients; they give him whatever they feel is suitable, either cash or goods. The "present" seems usually to be given to the *hitevi* a few days after the cure in the course of a ceremonious visit to the home of the *hitevi* to formally thank him for his help. But it is also true that Carlos fully expects to be paid for his services, and he spoke angrily of the very few times a patient had omitted to give him a present. His income from curing, though small and irregular, did provide him and his family with a few luxuries they much appreciated. The only occasions when the patient did not expect to pay was when he was merely given advice without actually receiving a medicine, massage, or other tangible treatment. Carlos several times said that he felt that he should be paid for his advice too, since it was hard to learn about medicines, but that "is not the Yaqui way." He treated both his son and his grandson during the time I knew him and was paid in each case. Carlos said that the *hitevi* should be given a larger fee if medicine was given to the patient, because he had to buy the herbs or go to the trouble of collecting them. Occasionally being a *hitevi* can be more profitable. During the weeks the Torim *hitevi* and his young apprentice were in Navidad, they treated many cases. I visited the house they were living in three times in the evening, during their stay and each time found about ten people waiting to consult them. Others I questioned, both Yaqui and Anglo, who had been in the house during this period, gave me similar esimates.

There is considerable evidence that *hitevim* from Navidad do not limit their curing activities to their own village. Nor do Navidadeños consult only their local *hitevim*. Five non-villagers were treated by Carlos during the year I worked with him. He said that in the years he has been curing, patients have come to him from "many places . . . from many places." He also said of his uncle Ignacio, "He was a famous doctor, many people came to him from all over."

A woman from Navidad, Bertola, was said to have consulted a *hitevi* in another town. This *hitevi* was well known in Navidad. A public health nurse told me of a little girl who had been taken by her parents to be treated by "some quack in Sonora," a *hitevi* in Vicam, I learned later. Vakot Pahkola, also from Vicam, was known as far away as Navidad. "He was the first [i.e., most powerful] of all *hitevim*. He could cure people on the point of death. Many people went from the Southwest to see him. He died not too long ago."

A famous *hitevi* may be invited to visit another village. Pedro said, "It is said that in old times in Sonora, they used to send a horse and wagon to get a doctor from another village to cure someone, if their own doctors could not help. He stayed there for awhile curing. He did not move there. He went home again." The *hitevim* from Torim originally were invited to Navidad by a man whose nephew suffered from epilepsy. He evidently had frequent seizures in spite of the fact that he was receiving Anglo medication. The *hitevim* lived and ate with their host while in Navidad. I did not meet them because they were afraid of being deported from the United States and would not speak to me. They seemed to be an immediate sensation in the village. The house where they were staying was crowded each evening from the time people got home from work until about ten o'clock with people waiting to consult them. Jaime told me that people came from several Southwest Yaqui communities to see them. Carmen said that three of her young friends had gone to them. The two *hitevim* stayed in Navidad from the middle of February until almost the end of March. Carlos went to visit with them. He was much downcast because he felt that all of his patients were going to them; actually he had as many patients consult him during this period as any other during the year. Carmen and Pedro attributed their popularity to the belief that *hitevim* in Sonora have greater power than those in Arizona. Carlos said their success was due to the good supply of medicines they brought with them; medicines he said were hard to get in Arizona.

The *hitevi* works completely independently of all other *hitevim.* He is not a member of a curing society, nor does he work under the compulsion of a vow or *manda* he has taken. Unless the *hitevi* is accompanied by a student-assistant, he visits and treats his patients alone. If a second *hitevi* is to be called in, the original *hitevi* must first give up the case. *Hitevim* never work together on a patient. In fact, they seem to be quite competitive. Carlos was quite annoyed at the business that the Sonoran *hitevim* did in Navidad, and he once said, "If a *hitevi* got a good medicine, he would never tell anyone, but keep it so he would get all the patients." One great difficulty in finding out anything about Yaqui curing was that all the *hitevim* keep their medicines, prayers, and techniques closely guarded secrets. When the *hitevi* dies, none of his medicines or paraphernalia is buried with him. "There is no need of medicines or *hitevim* in *Loria* (heaven)."

A connection between the deer and *pascola* dancers and *hitevim* has been mentioned above. All are thought to possess *seataka,* and Carlos said that all *hitevim* should also serve the village by acting as a deer or *pascola* dancer or as a musician. Spicer (1940) has pointed out that neither the deer nor *pascola* dancers are organized into a society; they do not take a *manda.* Connections between these dances and curing are few. The personnel of the rituals, which may include *hitevim,* possess *seataka.* Curers and dancers draw upon a common body of lore about the plants and animals of the *Monte* and their mysterious powers. The dances themselves are often performed at fiestas, which are given in fulfillment of a vow taken when ill. But the dances themselves are not thought to have curing power, and the performers are not necessarily curers. If as Beals (1943:69) suggests, Yaqui curers were ever organized into dance societies, these must have broken down under the impact of Christianization, and the curers have become loosely attached to the surviving animal dances because both retained a fairly large body of pre-Christian religious beliefs. It is, of course, possible that the connection is entirely coincidental. Just as curing skills seem to be handed down in families because of the ease of instruction, so it might be that deer and *pascola* dances and songs are similarly taught mainly to younger members of the family. Through the years, the two sets of skills might have been united in certain families. It will be remembered that it was Carlos' stepfather, a *hitevi,* who taught him to play the rasp for the deer dancer.

I was never able to determine just how many *hitevim* there are in Navidad. Carlos said about 40 but this seems to be too high an estimate. It would indicate that almost one in every ten people is a curer. Pedro said, "There used to be many, but the power is diminished; there are not many who have this power now." Carmen knew of only three curers in Navidad.

I learned the names of only three *hitevim* active in Navidad. One, of course, is Carlos. The second, Loretta, was also a midwife. She is the *hitevi* who recommended two patients to Carlos the year I was working with him. Josefina also was mentioned to me as a *hitevi.* She also is thought to be a *moorea* by some of my informants. There is a Mexican woman living in Navidad who dispenses love potions and does some curing. Carmen said that she was told that she sucks to cure. My informants regarded her as a witch, a *bruja,* but said that she was not a "Yaqui witch," neither a *hitevi* nor a *moorea.*

Of former *hitevim,* Hilario Pascola was said by Carlos to be the first *hitevi* to come to Navidad. He was, as his name implies, a *pascola* dancer. He is dead now. Juana and Ignacio, Carlos' mother and uncle, and his stepfather already have been mentioned. Ignacio was a *maso,* a deer dancer, and a deer singer. Carlos' stepfather played the rasp for the deer. Another *hitevi,* Antonio, died when Carlos was about 40 years old. He was a coyote dance musician. Still another man named Carlos was a *hitevi* and thought to be a *moorea.* He was the man Carlos found lying on the ground surrounded by candles, casting a spell. He was a deer musician and is dead now. Francisca was a *hitevi* and midwife in Navidad. During the 1930s she was accused by a man of making his daughter sick. The case was variously reported by the newspapers at the time, but Carlos said: "The girl's father called the police, and they made Francisca rub her with ashes in the sign of the cross. The Mexican cops said they would shoot Francisca with a gun. Two months later the girl got well, but Francisca died. (The implication here is that a defeated witch dies.) People just ignored her and wouldn't speak to her. Her grandson may have this power today." Spicer (unpublished field notes) lists Angel, a brother of Carlos, as a man who was "consulted when the son of Chico was bewitched." Angel was unable to help him. Carlos denied that Angel was a *hitevi,* though he had learned quite a bit about curing from his mother and uncle. Spicer's notes also list a woman named Carmen as a curer and midwife. I was unable to get any information about her.

Outside of Navidad I learned of Carmen's "somehow aunt," María, who is a *hitevi* and lives in a different Southwest Yaqui community. Her brother is a *pascola,* and Leonardo, Carlos' uncle, who is a *hitevi* in still another Yaqui community, "sings for the deer." I got no information on Carlos' stepfather's relative, Joe, other than he is a *hitevi* and does not live in Navidad. The two *hitevim* from Torim may be added to the list. Both are musicians for the *pascola;* Vakot Pahkola, mentioned before, who lived in Vicam until he died recently, was said by Carlos to be the most powerful *hitevi* of all, and was a *pascola* as his name indicates.

This list undoubtedly does not contain all the names of *hitevim* active now or in the recent past known to the villagers, and probably reflects the Yaquis' reluctance to discuss their curers. Though Carlos was willing to talk about his curing with me, I found it difficult to get specific facts about other curers from him or from any of my informants.

The *hitevi* acquires a patient when he is called to the bedside of a sick person, or if the patient is able to walk, he comes to the *hitevi* to ask for help. More rarely, the *hitevi* may go to the home of a person he knows has been ill for some time and offer his services.

The *hitevi* examines his patient, looking at the site of the pain, the wounds or sores and sometimes probing them, asking questions, and feeling for pulse and fever. Carlos said that he determined the rate of the heart beat by holding the right wrist of the patient in his left hand with all the fingers save the thumb on the palmar side, while placing his right hand on the patient's forehead. Illness, especially heart trouble, is suspected if the pulse is particularly strong and fast, or conversely slow and weak, or if the *hitevi* "feels something moving in the head." Beals (1945:192) describes a similar custom practiced by the Mayo Indians in Sonora.

Depending upon his diagnoses, the *hitevi* may prescribe medicines, or massage, or both, and may take magical steps against witchcraft. If the *hitevi* has to make up a special medicine, he will go home to make it and return later to administer it to the patient. Sometimes, though, he has the proper medicine already made up, and it can be given immediately to the patient. Indeed, upon a number of occasions, which Carlos told me about, he seemed to give the patient whatever medicine he happened to have left over, regardless of the symptoms.

If the patient is well enough to come to the *hitevi,* he is given a bottle of medicine with instructions on how to use it. Carlos advises taking a medicine on three successive days, or sometimes three times a day until it is gone.

If the *hitevi* goes to the patient's house, either because the patient is bedridden or because he requested the *hitevi* to come to him, the *hitevi* prepares the medicine at home and takes it to the patient in whose presence he cools it. The *hitevi* then administers the medicine personally to the patient, giving him some to drink from a spoon or a glass. Surplus medicine is left with the patient with instructions on how to take it, or the *hitevi* may administer it himself on his next visit. Pedro said that only the one who made the medicine could give it to the patient. Carlos agreed, but said that if the patient was strong enough, he could help himself to the medicine. An exception was noted in a few cases Carlos told me about where the mother of an infant was given a medicine and directions as to how to give it to her child.

Massages are given either at the home of the *hitevi* or the patient, whichever is the most convenient. In any event, whatever the treatment and whenever it is given, the *hitevi* must call upon or inquire about his patient daily until he is cured. In a very serious case, the *hitevi* is expected to stay with his patient day and night until some improvement is seen.

As noted above, if the *hitevi* feels that he cannot cure the patient, he should tell him so and advise him to seek aid elsewhere. Frequently he recommends a specific *hitevi*. Loretta recommended Carlos twice during the year I knew him. If the patient is dissatisfied with the treatment, he should tell the *hitevi* and ask him to recommend another. Though Carlos, Carmen, and Pedro all said this should be done, none could think of an actual case where it had been. I heard of a number of cases where the patient had gone to a second *hitevi* without the permission of the first. I would guess that if the patient feels that he is not getting well, his *hitevi* may possibly be a witch, and it is better to go quietly to consult another without telling the first one. Carlos did tell me of three cases where a patient came to him accusing a *hitevi* of making them worse while "pretending to cure them."

When the patient is cured, he should come to call upon the *hitevi* to thank him for his aid and to give him a present. The present can be anything that the patient thinks is correct. Money was mentioned to me most frequently. Oddly enough "a new pair of pants," but never any other article of clothing, was mentioned to me by all my informants as a suitable gift for a *hitevi,* and Carlos did receive trousers twice in payment for a cure while I knew him.

During the year I worked with Carlos, I was able to get a current account of the cases he was treating. Although details of some of these illnesses have been given already, the entire list is recapitulated here. Carlos had difficulty remembering on just what day an event happened, so the cases are given only by month. Though I feel that the list is reasonably complete, it is quite possible that a few incidents escaped his memory.

Patients' Cases

In August, 1958, a Black with whom Carlos was working on a construction project complained to him that his feet were swollen and painful. Carlos showed him *taykonauwia* (datura), *chamiso* (cane), and *kovanau* (creosote) growing nearby and advised him to pick and mash the leaves, to boil them together, and to wash his entire body with the tea. Carlos said that he prayed very hard for the man that night. He did not tell him to pray for himself, because since he was not a Catholic, Carlos was not sure that he knew how to pray. The next day the man reported to Carlos that his feet felt much better. He did not pay Carlos for his advice.

In September, 1958, a man named Juan, who lives in Navidad, ran to Carlos' house in the middle of the night to beg him to come quickly to treat his mother, Delfina. Carlos found that she had been suffering from sharp pains in her neck and head since the afternoon, and they had suddenly worsened. Carlos immediately asked her to whom she had been talking and who had visited her recently. Delfina replied that that afternoon Josefina, who was thought by some to be a *moorea,* had come to her house and offered to sell her a watch. Delfina had refused to buy it, and Josefina had become very angry before she left. A few minutes later, Delfina began to feel pains in her head. Carlos made the sign of the cross with his saliva on her throat and forehead and said some prayers. He then returned home, and when he fell asleep, he dreamt of an airplane, which swooping low tried to kill him. Carlos dreamt he knocked it from the air with a stick, and it changed its form to Josefina. A few days later, Delfina called upon Carlos to thank him for curing her and gave him two dollars.

Later in the month, a Mexican boy, who lived in the Southwest in another town, was brought to Carlos by his parents, who hoped that he could cure his broken kneecap. Loretta, the *hitevi* from Navidad, had tried to help the boy when she was living temporarily in his home town, but had failed. She suggested that his parents take him to Navidad where they could consult Carlos. The parents brought the boy directly to Carlos' house. He probed the kneecap with his fingers while praying and pushed it into place. He said that no bandage was necessary to hold it. The boy's parents immediately gave Carlos five dollars.

In October, Carlos treated a village woman called Lorenza. Unfortunately I have no information on this case. I list it simply to indicate that Carlos saw at least one patient each month during the year.

In November, the man whom Carlos had treated in August fell from a building under construction and "broke" his back and knees. He was taken to the county hospital for treatment and released the same day. He still complained of the pain while walking, and that evening he came to Carlos' house to ask for help. Carlos massaged him "to put the bones back in place" on that same night and on the following night and prayed for him. The third day, the man felt well enough to return to work. He paid Carlos one dollar at work that day.

In December, while Carlos was attending a fiesta in another community, a Yaqui girl who lived there suddenly fainted. Though the crowd thought she was dead, someone ran to call the ambulance to take her to the county hospital. Carlos at once volunteered his services. He felt her pulse at the wrist and forehead and decided by reason of its fast and irregular rhythm that she had suffered a heart attack. He massaged her chest about the heart and prayed, and she revived before the ambulance came. Carlos mentioned that he thought her condition was probably due to overwork. He did not know her and did not remember ever seeing her before. He was not paid for the treatment.

In January, 1959, a Navidad man, Tomás, sprained his ankle and sent one of his children in the evening to ask Carlos to come to his house. That night and the two following evenings Carlos went to his house, prayed, and massaged the ankle "to get the bones together." A few days later Tomás came to Carlos' house to thank him and gave him a new pair of cotton trousers as payment.

In February one evening Rafaela, a Navidad woman, came to Carlos complaining of an earache. She had recently quarreled with Josefina, the reputed *moorea,* and was afraid that she was being bewitched. Carlos prayed, made the sign of the cross with *hu'upa* (mesquite) ash on her ear and blew *hiyakvivam* (Yaqui tobacco) smoke into it. In his dreams that night Carlos saw Josefina sending bugs into Rafaela's ear. When in his dream, she perceived Carlos watching her, she vanished. Rafaela called on Carlos some days later to thank him and to pay him two dollars.

It was in February one evening that Luisa came to Carlos wishing to be cured of sores on her legs. Carlos gave her an herbal infusion with which to bathe her legs. When this failed, Luisa told him that she had dreamt of a small animal that climbed on her bed at night to scratch her legs. Some time later, Carlos himself dreamt of a cat with which he fought and which turned into Luisa's mother when wounded. Carlos then prayed for her and advised her also to pray to God for protection. The wash continued. Luisa was evidently unsatisfied with the treatment, because she consulted the visiting Sonoran *hitevim* about the same condition. Carlos felt that she had not acted fairly in going to these *hitevim* without telling him. He said that if the *hitevim* had been local people, they would have known that she was his patient and would have never treated her without his permission. He was never paid by Luisa.

On a Saturday morning in February, a Yaqui woman who had recently moved to Navidad from another town came to Carlos' house to ask him for medicine. She complained of painfully swollen legs and feet. Carlos did not know her; again Loretta, failing to cure her, had sent her to Carlos. He mixed together *avachonda* (unidentified), *vaykanau* (caltrop), *huchasko* (brazil wood), *wasaraka* (unidentified), and *huvakvena* (*Bursera laxiflora*) and boiled them in water while she waited. Carlos then gave her the tea in a bottle and told her to drink a third of it once a day for three days. She returned to his house some days later, thanked him and paid him one dollar.

In the same month a young woman, Juanita, sprained her ankle. Her mother called upon Carlos and asked him to treat it. He returned with her the same evening and massaged the ankle and prayed. He went back to massage it again the two following evenings. On the third evening he was given some packages of cigarettes as payment.

A few days later a woman, the daughter of Rafaela who in the beginning of the month had been cured of an earache, came to Carlos asking him to take as patients her father, Antonio, and her daughter, Lucía. Antonio and Rafaela lived in the same house with their daughter and her husband and their unmarried, though grown, granddaughter. Lucía had been crippled since she was 16 years old and had recently begun to suffer from severe pains in her legs. Carlos went to the house and massaged her and prayed on three consecutive evenings.

Antonio, Lucía's grandfather, complained that his eyesight was "cloudy." He couldn't see at a distance. Carlos felt that probably he had been working too hard and perspiring in the cold air. He told me that he had seen cases before where this sort of activity had impaired the vision. When Carlos went to massage Lucía's legs for the first time, he brought Antonio a bottle of strained tea of *huvakvena* (*Bursera laxiflora*), *azafrán* (saffron), and *huchasko* (brazil wood).

On the last night Rafaela also consulted Carlos. She told him she felt pains all through her body. Carlos told her that she had probably been working too much. He returned the next day, a Saturday, bringing her a bottle of tea of *wasarako, huvakvena, machaho* (unidentified), and *yerba del golpe* (*Alfilerilla lopezia*). He massaged her with some of this twice a day for three days, prayed, and gave her some to drink. On the third day, he left her a bottle of it so she could drink some of it three times a day until it was gone.

Several days thereafter the entire family called upon Carlos to thank him and present him with a new pair of cotton trousers, a carton of cigarettes, and five dollars.

In March, Carlos told me that he was planning to volunteer his services to Bertola, the wife of a *maestro*. During the previous October, she had been at work "night and day" sewing, when she fell over and coúld not get up again. Several months later, she was still very feeble and unable to work. It was believed at first that her illness was due to exhaustion, and a *hitevi* from another community was called to treat her. He was unable to help her. Her family had been urging her to go to the county hospital, but she was afraid and would not go. Carlos said, "She is old; she sticks to the old ways." Since she had been nearly five months without a cure, Carlos was beginning to believe that witchcraft was involved. Just before Carlos was to call on her, he learned that she had gone to consult the *hitevim* from Torim. He therefore did not offer his services to her. He was rather piqued that Bertola had not come to him, going first to a *hitevi* in another town and then to those from Sonora.

In the same month Lauro, a brother of Tomás who had come to Carlos for treatment in January, came to Carlos' house. He said that he had had a fever and chills for a long time and nothing seemed to help. Carlos told him to mix *saúco* (elder) and *manzanilla* (chamomile) in water, to boil it, and drink the tea. He was not paid for this advice.

Also in March, a man named Juan met Carlos at the church door one evening and asked him what he should do for fading vision. Carlos recommended that he should bathe his eyes with *hu'upa* (mesquite). Again, he was not paid.

In April, Ramón came to Carlos' house at night to ask what he would suggest for poor eyesight. Carlos again said *hu'upa.* He told me that Ramón – who is not known to be either a *hitevi* or a *moorea,* but who is old and said to know many things – was probably testing him to make sure that he was not a *moorea.* Ramón did not pay Carlos for his advice.

Later in April, Tony called on Carlos and asked him to come and examine his daughter-in-law. She complained of pains about her chest and felt dizzy, and (Carlos thought because) her menstrual periods had stopped. She had been treated by someone in the family with home remedies. Carlos visited her the next evening and asked her what medicines she had been taking but received no answer. He boiled up a tea at home of *pasote* (*Chenopodium incisum*), *huchasko, huvakvena, wasarako, manzanilla,* and *saúco* and returning the next evening gave her some of it to drink, using the rest to massage her, and prayed. That night he dreamt of a large dog whose belly was slit so that the entrails were dragging on the ground. Carlos saw himself standing with a knife in his hand. He made the sign of the cross, made the dog stand up, and struck it on the back with his hand. The dog instantly changed into Josefina and at her side was standing a man, Luis. Carlos said that everyone knows that Luis is good and has "no power" and that the *moorea* probably "took him into the dream" to confuse Carlos and make him think that Luis had caused the illness. Carlos returned the next evening to his patient's house to massage her again. In the course of the massage, he struck her with the flat of a knife blade, because he had seen the knife in his dream. Immediately upon the first blow, the young woman said that all the pain had left her. He returned on the third night to give her a final massage. Carlos told the girl that she had been bewitched, but did not tell her by whom "because it would frighten her, and the *moorea* can't hurt this girl now because I am curing her. Maybe later, five years from now, she could." Carlos said that the person in her family who was trying to cure her failed because he had no *seataka* and could not know the *moorea.*" Carlos was paid one dollar on the third evening he visited the girl, and she later called on him to thank him and to give him a gift.

Finally, in April, Carmen tripped and cut her ankle at her doorstep, as described previously. The wound did not heal in spite of the daily treatments by the school nurse. Carmen mentioned the sore, and Carlos examined it one afternoon in the course of an interview. Carmen said that before she hurt herself, she had dreamt of coming out of her door and being bitten on the ankle by a rattlesnake. So Carlos guessed that a *moorea* had caused the accident. He prayed and traced the sign of the cross on her ankle with saliva. He later told Carmen that he had dreamt of the *moorea,* a man, in the form of a rattlesnake, but he refused to tell either Carmen or me who the *moorea* was though he advised her to pray for protection. As far as I know, Carmen did not pay Carlos for the treatment.

In May, Micaela (said by the public health nurse to be the very model of a "progressive young mother") brought her baby to Carlos. The baby had been crying incessantly and had a fever which would not go down. Micaela had taken the baby to the Well-Baby Clinic, but the condition had not been relieved. Carlos gave the baby a tea made of the same eight ingredients he gave to Tony's daughter-in-law (he had some left over) and massaged the baby and prayed. That night Carlos saw Juana, whom he believed had bewitched Micaela's baby, in a dream. He struggled with Juana while she laughed and taunted him. Finally he knocked her down. Carlos said that she appeared in her own form because the illness wasn't serious, and she wasn't frightened. He said that Juana hardly knew Micaela, and "she hated the baby for no reason. She is just mean." The next morning Carlos actually did meet Juana standing in front of her house. She asked him how Micaela's baby was, but Carlos refused to speak to her. Then Carlos said, "She was scornful and said the baby was just pretending to be sick. Then she went into her house." He did not tell Micaela that Juana bewitched her baby, but prayed for it and went to Micaela's house for the next two nights to massage it. Micaela called on him later to thank him and gave him $1.

In May, Carlos massaged my arm, which was aching as described previously. He said after feeling the arm, "The bones are too close together." I called at his house a few days later, thanked him, and told him my arm felt much better, and gave him a carton of cigarettes.

Carlos' son Luis, who lives on the opposite side of Navidad with his wife's family came to him one evening in May saying that he had noticed blood in his urine. Carlos gave him a tea of *akivea* (fruit of the organ pipe cactus), *huchasko, wasarako, huvakvena, saúco, pasote, manzanilla,* and an unidentified root. He told him to drink some and to bathe with the rest, three times. His son later gave him some packages of cigarettes as payment.

A few evenings later Carlos' married daughter brought her baby son to him. He also had blood in his urine. She had taken the baby to the county hospital five days before. She said that the doctor had given him an injection and some medicine to drink, but he still was not well. Carlos gave his grandson some of the same medicine he had given his son. First, he gave him a little to drink and bathed him with more and told his daughter to repeat the treatment on the two following days. His daughter called on him later to say "Thank you" and brought him some fruit as a gift.

Also in May a Navidad woman, Antonia, came to buy some *nautoria* (unidentified) to use as a medicine. Carlos sold her some without inquiring how or why she intended to use it. I don't know how much he was paid for the herb.

In June, Antonio, whose family Carlos had treated in April, went to Carlos' house in the evening to have Carlos massage his legs because he was having pains in them. Carlos massaged him and prayed for three nights. On the second night, he gave Antonio a bottle of medicine and told him to drink a bit of it and use the rest to wash himself all over. The medicine consisted of *wasarako, huvakvena, huchasko, vaykanau,* and *babis* (*yerba del manso*) boiled together.

During the course of his treatment, Antonio said that his wife, Rafaela, was feeling badly. Her body felt heavy "as though pine cones were sticking to her like needles and dragging her down." Carlos went that same evening to see Rafaela, massaged her, prayed, and gave her to drink some of the same medicine he had given Antonio. Two days later, he went again to her house to see how she was and found her much improved. Antonio called on Carlos later to thank him and to give him two dollars.

In July, Carlos met Manuel at church. Manuel complained that he had difficulty urinating and asked Carlos for some medicine. Carlos asked him to come to his house that night and the next two nights. He massaged him, prayed, and gave him some of the same kind of medicine he had given to Antonio and Rafaela to take home and drink "because he also feels heavy and pains in his body." Antonio had suggested to Manuel that he consult Carlos. Manuel paid Carlos the usual call later and gave him some packages of cigarettes.

Late in July Carlos heard of a woman in Navidad who had "a hole in her head and worms are in it"; in the opinion of her family and friends, she was being bewitched. Another *hitevi* had tried to help her without success. Carlos called on her, volunteered his services, prayed for her, making the sign of the cross on her forehead with his saliva. Just before I left town, he was expecting to dream of the *moorea* troubling her. I did not learn the outcome of this case.

From these stories we see that Carlos dealt with 28 different cases during the year involving 24 people. His Black co-worker and Antonio were each treated twice, and Rafaela was treated three times. All but five of his patients were from Navidad. All were friends or acquaintances of his except the girl to whom he administered first aid.

The Partera

The Yaquis consider childbirth to be a medical problem requiring the assistance of a specialist. The midwife is called the *partera,* a Spanish term. Only one of my informants, Carlos, could think of a Yaqui equivalent for *partera* and then only after several weeks' thought. The term he volunteered was *yeyokekechame,* "the one who stands people up." *Parteras* are no longer active in Navidad. They ceased to practice in accordance with Arizona law. The following information concerns the recent past.

The *partera* was always a female. She was not necessarily a *hitevi,* although all the female *hitevim* whom I heard about also had practiced as *parteras.*

The duties of the *partera* were to give advice and medical aid to the expectant mother, to assist in delivering the baby, and to treat any illnesses that might befall the new mother and infant. To fulfill these duties, the *partera* prescribed a few herbal remedies; her knowledge of medicines was not as extensive as the *hitevi's.* She was a masseuse and knew the proper diets for mothers and babies. Finally she was acquainted with a few magical techniques and prayers to safeguard the mother and the child. The *partera* was paid for her services and competed with other *parteras* for patients. Never would she share knowledge of a new medicine or technique with other *parteras.* My informants disagreed as to whether the *partera* possessed *seataka.* Unlike the *hitevi,* the *partera* was under no obligation to help all those who came to her. She would accept only as many cases as she wished. It was also her right to stop practicing altogether without fear of being a suspected *moorea.*

To become a *partera,* a girl or woman dreamt of herself in that role. An especially vivid dream or a recurrent dream in which one sees oneself performing particular duties is thought to be a supernatural call to that role. To ignore the call would be to court illness or bad luck. To become a *partera,* the woman started by watching an accomplished *partera* go about her duties. This observation might start casually before a dream has called her to the profession or after she has dreamt of herself as a *partera.* Because a girl will have a close association with her older female relatives, most of the *parteras* of whom I heard were the granddaughters, daughters, or nieces of *parteras.* It was not necessary, however, for the prospective *partera* to be related to a *partera,* nor did the daughter of a *partera* have to choose that profession. If a young woman who wished to learn midwifery had no one in her family to observe, she might go to any *partera* and ask permission to watch and assist her. The *partera* might or might not accept the student. She agreed to train her or not as she wished. The student did not pay the *partera* for her education. Training never started before marriage because unmarried girls were not allowed to be present at childbirth. Unmarried girls were supposed to be ignorant of sex and childbirth. As she observed the *partera* ministering to her patients, the student learned the proper medicines and procedures for the care of mothers and babies. When she had observed for a while, the student started to assist the *partera* with her duties. However, she did not have to accompany her teacher each time the *partera* was called. The *partera* and her student ought to have had complete confidence in each other and special devotion, one to another. The people of the village knew that a young woman was learning midwifery, and when an expectant mother was confident enough, or desperate enough, to call her, and the student was sure enough of her own abilities to agree to help, she was a *partera*. If she was successful, more patients came to her. If she was unable to help her patient, no one else would turn to her. I did not obtain exact information on how long the training period of a *partera* was likely to be. My impression is that it would vary considerably from a few months to many years.

María, my *partera* informant, is the daughter and granddaughter of *parteras*. As a child she frequently saw herself in dreams as a *partera*. She listened casually to her mother and grandmother discussing their cases at home and thought that she would probably be a *partera* one day. When she married in her early teens, she started to accompany her mother when she was called to deliver babies and to watch and listen when patients came to her mother's home. María and her husband lived with her mother. Through observation, she learned the uses of various medicines, how to massage, and other practices and beliefs. María was soon able to help her mother treat a patient or to deliver a baby. Her mother was willing to teach her, more because she wanted someone to help her than because she wanted to perpetuate her art. During the time she was in training, María repeatedly dreamt of herself as a *partera*. It was not until her mother died, about 1938, when María was about 40, that she began to practice midwifery on her own.

María remembers her first case well. She was called to attend the labor of a woman late one evening. The woman knew that María was inexperienced, but no other *partera* was available. María said that she was a little nervous, but was reassured by the fact that the woman's sister-in-law and female friends were all present and ready to give María aid and advice if she needed it. At the successful completion of this first case, more patients came to María. María claims that she had not worked as a *partera* since the State of Arizona has required a license for midwives. Since she cannot read or write, she is ineligible to receive a license.

Navidadeños believe that all pregnancies last nine months. This differs from the common Mexican belief that a first pregnancy lasts only eight months (Foster 1948). María said that in Sonora, medicines are known to help a woman conceive. These medicines are not known to the Yaquis of Arizona. They know of no way to insure that a boy or a girl will be born, and of no way to determine the sex of the unborn child. María, like all of my other informants, vehemently denied that Yaquis know of any way to prevent conception or to cause abortion. They said they regarded both as very sinful acts.

The expectant mother herself chose which *partera* to consult. Some women came to the *partera* in about the third month of their pregnancy. The patient either called at the *partera's* house or asked the *partera* to come and see her. The *partera* palpated the patient's abdomen to determine if the baby was in the correct position. The fetus was believed to be right side up in a sitting position until it was eight months old, then it turned upside down. If the *partera* believed that the baby was in the wrong position, she would try to turn it by massaging the mother's abdomen. Besides this examination, the *partera* offered the patient advice on her diet and behavior.

It was thought that an expectant mother should not eat heavy foods, such as butter and cheese, in the evening. It was believed that these would stick together and harm the child. Beans and chili were to be avoided at all times. Rice, spaghetti, and jerked meat were especially good for her.

Though the pregnant woman could continue with her usual work, María advised that she should avoid picking up heavy objects. She said that too much stooping and bending might move the child into the wrong position. If the child turned upside down too early, the mother would feel sick and have a more painful labor.

The mother also had to be careful in her behavior or the child might be born with a birthmark or a more serious deformity. Staying out-of-doors during an eclipse of the moon (*mukila,* "death of the moon or sun") was particularly dangerous for an expectant mother. If she did stay out, her child might be born without fingers or toes, with a limb missing, a cleft palate (*hauri,* the term for any facial deformity), or some other serious disfigurement. Drums, tin cans, and plates are beaten during an eclipse of the moon in Navidad, partially to warn pregnant women to get indoors, partially to awaken the dead moon, and because everyone, especially the children, has such a good time making the racket.

Pedro said that the moon is female and has more influence over women. He said that a lunar eclipse indicated that many women would die during the following year. A solar eclipse is said to turn the hair of those exposed to it to snakes. It warns that many men will die, as the sun is thought to be masculine. The Yaquis are said to have worshipped the sun as a god and the moon as a goddess aboriginally (Beals 1943: 1945) and similar beliefs about eclipses are generally held among Sonoran Cahita speakers. Spicer (1954:125) specifically records the belief in Pótam, a Sonoran Yaqui village, that during a lunar eclipse the moon is struggling with the sun. Johnson (1950) reports that the Opatas also venerated the sun and the moon. During a lunar eclipse, the Opata woman had to run around her house three times or her child would be born with a part missing. The Opatas believed that the eclipse was caused by the moon hiding herself from an enemy, and a great noise was made by the people to frighten the enemy away. Avoidance of a lunar eclipse by pregnant women is also reported from Mitla (Parsons 1936) and from Mexicans in San Jose, California (Clark 1959). If a woman scoffed at a crippled person, her child might be born with a birthmark (*hisovawam* or *hisowam,* distinct raised spots; or *tatayriam,* diffuse markings "like a rash"), or if she fell or was struck by something sharp her child also might be born deformed. If the mother was in poor health, the child might be sickly or weak or deformed in some way. A woman had to abstain from sexual relations for two months before the child was born to avoid injuring it.

An emotional shock to the mother could injure the unborn child, a common belief in Spanish America (Foster 1953; Clark 1959; Parsons 1936). If the expectant mother became very angry or frightened, it was thought likely that the child would be born unable to hear or to speak. An agitated mother was urged to drink sugar and warm water to calm herself and so protect her child. Warm water also was given to pregnant women to drink to cure nausea.

The father was under no restrictions during the pregnancy of his wife. Because he did not bear the child, Navidadeños believed that his behavior could not injure it. All of these beliefs about the diet and behavior of pregnant women were not known exclusively by the *partera,* but were common knowledge in the village.

After first consulting the *partera* at about three months of pregnancy, a few women returned several times during the following months so that the *partera* could check the position of the baby and the general health of the mother. Many women, however, did not call the *partera* at all until labor started. In such cases, the parturient had to be content with whichever *partera* could be found. If she was unable to indicate which *partera* should be called, her husband, relatives, friends, whoever was present, would call one. If no *partera* could be located, an older woman, usually a relative, who had had several children, would take charge. Carlos was once called to deliver a baby when no *partera* could be found.

María said that she kept a supply of clean cloths and herbs on hand to take with her when she went to deliver a baby. When she arrived at a patient's house, she would find the patient's female relatives and friends gathered there. Sometimes, though not invariably, the father would be present. All other males were barred from the house as were the unmarried girls. María insisted that some member of the family be present with an automobile to take the patient to the hospital if María's skill was exhausted.

Upon arrival, María prayed that God would help her deliver the baby successfully, washed her hands, set out clean cloths, and heated water. She then bathed the parturient mother. The mother would walk around until her pains became more severe, then she would lie down on the bed or on a mat on the floor. María preferred to have her patients lie on the floor, "because it is harder and makes the mother try to help herself more." She boiled *manzanilla* (chamomile) in water to make a tea which the mother drank to ease her pain. Bits of *anhenhible* (*jengibre,* ginger) dropped into this tea made it even more effective.

During labor, a woman was not allowed to eat, but she could have a little water to drink if she was thirsty. María also boiled strips of cloth and laid them hot on her patient's back to help relieve the pain. She kept boiling more and renewing them as they cooled off. The patient's abdomen was rubbed to force the child into the correct position if it was not already there. María said that long ago she had heard that ashes were rubbed on the patient's stomach to hasten delivery, but that she herself had never seen this done. She had never heard of smoke being blown on the parturient, a custom Johnson (1950) reports for the Opata. At birth the mother either knelt on the floor or lay on her back in bed or on the floor. María preferred the lying position. She thought kneeling was very old-fashioned, although it was still done in the village while she was practicing. Two other informants, Carlos and Pedro, thought that kneeling was best with the mother clinging to a length of rope tied to the ceiling. María helped by pushing down on the mother's abdomen from behind, while watching for the baby to appear. If a competent helper was present, María would have them push, while she watched for the baby. During this time, the only restriction on the father was that he should not kill a chicken or take a bath, lest the mother suffer dire consequences. Beals (1946) reports that in Cheran, if the father kills any animal during this time, it will enter the child through the nose or the mouth and the child will be born dead.

When the baby was born (*yototine,* "to be born") and the placenta (*asokari;* Beals [1945] gives *asokarali*) expelled, María cut the umbilical cord (*sia*) with a pair of scissors, or with a knife or sharp stick if no scissors could be found. A friend was delegated to bury the placenta far from the house, not through fear that the child would suffer if the placenta was disturbed, but because it would be unsanitary, dirty, to have it nearby. María patted the baby's back or blew on its forehead to start it breathing. If these methods did not work, she would spank it or dip it into cold water. The baby was then cleaned with baby oil (María said that water was used formerly). She dusted it with baby powder or applied baby lotion, whichever the mother supplied, bandaged the navel (*siku*), wrapped a band snugly around its stomach, and dressed it in the clothes that the mother had prepared for it. Some mothers wrapped the baby tightly in a small receiving blanket to prevent it from being frightened by suddenly touching itself. Other mothers omitted the swaddling, believing that the baby would benefit from the exercise derived from moving its arms and legs freely. María said that special care was taken to keep a premature baby warm, and that it was watched more carefully than a full-term baby. No special customs were attached to the birth of twins (*worim*). It was felt that one of them would be a *hitevi* and the other a *moorea*.

After the baby had been taken care of, or during this time if relatives and friends helped out, María bathed the mother again and tied a band around her abdomen to "help her organs to return to the right shape." The use of a tight binder, worn for several weeks after birth, seems to be common among Spanish American women and is found in Spain (Clark 1959; Foster 1953). María gave the mother something to eat, she thought warm soup was especially good, and if this was the woman's first baby, a short sermon. She told her how good it was to be alive and to give birth to a baby. The husband would then speak to his wife telling her to be calm and happy, and how nice it is to have a baby and how happy they would all be together. Older male and female relatives also talked to her, giving her advice on how to care for the baby and telling her how happy she should be to have a child. (Yaquis, incidentally, seem to be very fond of giving and receiving short homilies, not only on important occasions, but also whenever the mood strikes. Interviews with informants were constantly interrupted while one informant or another would lecture to my interpreter and me on some aspect of leading a good life.)

Her work finished, María said a prayer thanking God for a safe delivery, was paid thirty dollars* by the husband, and went home.

The new mother rested in bed for a day or two and slowly resumed her normal duties when she felt strong enough. The baby was given water to drink from a bottle until the mother's milk came. María usually returned after two or three days to see if the mother and baby were in good health. If they were, she did not return again. The mother abstained from sexual relations for 40 days after the baby was born. She ate lightly and avoided acid foods, "because her womb was still bleeding and acid can get into the blood." Menstruating women in Navidad were said by María and Carmen to avoid citrus fruits and other acid foods for this reason. Nursing mothers never ate chili. María believed it would get into the milk and cause diarrhea, stomach-ache, or diaper rash in the baby. Soup was thought to be good to increase the mother's milk. The Opatas are said to have had a 40-day period of seclusion and dietary restrictions for mothers after childbirth (Johnson 1950). Foster (1953) reports that the custom is widespread in Spanish America and in Spain.

The account given by Carlos of the duties of a *partera* during childbirth was much the same as Maria's. He was once called by the father to deliver a baby. The couple were living in a farm labor camp, and no *partera* could be found. Carlos knew what to do, because he had been with his wife when their babies were born, and his mother had been a *partera* as well as a *hitevi* and had discussed her cases with him. Carlos gave his patient *bwasubwila*

---

*This fee, quoted by María, seems to me to be excessively high. None of my informants could offer any other information on just how much a *partera* was paid. Thirty dollars was paid by a neighbor of mine to a licensed midwife in the County. It is a much higher fee than a *hitevi* could hope to earn. Spicer (unpublished field notes) lists a fee of ten dollars paid to a midwife in Navidad in the late 1930s.

(*yerba del Indio*, an *Asclepiadacea,* probably *Gonolobus*) and *esmosgiar* (ground nutmeg) boiled in water to drink to ease the pain of labor. He said that this tea should be taken by a woman who continues to have pain after the baby is born. He also used the tea to bathe the forehead of his patient. To hasten labor, Carlos said that a lock of the woman's own hair can be placed in her mouth. This will cause her to vomit, and the baby to be expelled. This custom is also reported from Spain (Foster 1960). Carlos felt that the husband should stay with his wife, rubbing her back to make her feel more comfortable and talking quietly to reassure her. His presence would keep her from feeling frightened and thus having a difficult labor. Carlos also said, in contradiction to Maria, that a *partera* might call a *hitevi* to assist her during a difficult labor, though he himself had never been asked to help a *partera.* Carlos said that the newly born baby should be washed in water.

Not much information has been published about the ancient and contemporary birth practices of the Yaquis of Sonora. Beals (1943) in his reconstruction of aboriginal Cahita culture has suggested that in pre-Spanish times there were probably few prenatal taboos or beliefs. A pregnant woman did avoid working too much in the sun, lest her child get an eye disease. Delivery took place in the home in a sitting or kneeling position. The child was received on a skin. The mother was assisted by an experienced female neighbor, perhaps a semi-professional midwife who had a male assistant, possibly a shaman. The midwife stood before the mother; the assistant grasped the mother from behind, applying pressure to help expel the child. The midwife cleaned the baby and cut and tied the cord, burning the end with a hot coal. The placenta was buried in hot ashes or hidden in a cactus. It was believed that if a dog ate it, the mother would have stomach pains. When the remnant of the cord dropped off it was buried in a red ant's nest. After birth the child was given a herbal infusion as a laxative. It was nursed by another woman for three days. The child was visited after birth by neighbors, but no menstruating woman or any person fresh from sexual intercourse could come near it, or it would break out in spots. As mentioned above, this condition variously called *pujo* or *pujos* is reported from elsewhere in Spanish America and from Spain by Foster (1953). The father refrained from working for a few days after the birth. The mother rested five days, eating only maize, which was thought to encourage lactation, broiled dried meat, and bone broth. Other foods might kill the child. After five days the mother might go to the kitchen, her face painted with ashes or earth. She stayed at home 40 to 45 days, probably as a protection against witchcraft. At the end of this period, she bathed on three successive days and resumed her normal life, cohabitating with her husband. Children were nursed until they were from two to five years old. They were tightly swaddled as babies and went naked when they began to walk. Their ears were pierced to prevent misfortune. They wore strings of rattlesnake fangs about their necks to aid teething, were placed on animal dung to aid walking, and had liquor rubbed on their gums to aid talking.

Holden in 1936 (pp. 30-31) observed that Yaqui women in Sonora regarded pregnancy as a pleasant experience. The only precaution they took before birth was to avoid lifting heavy objects. When in labor they were attended by a midwife, although a "medicine-man" might be called in on a difficult case. Birth took place in a kneeling position. The placenta was buried in hot ashes or placed high in a tree in accordance with the belief that if it were not disposed of properly, the mother would have trouble with her next pregnancy. The mother rested on a mat from two to six days and observed a 40-day period of ceremonial purification. The baby was given a calendrical name, which he used until he was baptized as soon as possible after birth. The baby was nursed by another woman for six or seven days; the mother meanwhile massaged her breasts to drain them. The Yaquis thought that the mother's milk was not wholesome during that period. Children were nursed from two to four years. From about the age of six months, their diet was supplemented by tidbits of adult food.

Wagner (Holden 1936:80) reported that in Sonora in the 1930s, a Yaqui woman in labor was usually attended by an older female relative, any experienced woman, or by herself. The "medicine-man" was rarely called. After delivery some mothers were up at once, but most rested on their mats from three to five days.

Beals (1945) describes some of the customs of the contemporary neighboring Mayo. He reports that among the Mayo, birth took place in the home. A professional midwife, called the *partera* or *hamut ania asoamta* ("woman helping child receiving") and a male helper, the *tenedor* or *au wikapabwise hiepsipu* ("man holding by the middle very tight") delivered the child. The curer was not called in. The mother sat on the ground or knelt at birth. For difficult births, she might have been suspended from the ceiling by a rope tied under her arms. The baby was received on a sheepskin, its mouth cleaned, the cord cut and burned with a candle. The navel was anointed with oil, the cord with sulphur. The afterbirth and cord were disposed of ritually. The mother formerly was confined to bed 40 to 45 days, more recently for nine days. She observed dietary restrictions, and on the fifth day, ashes or dirt were rubbed on her face to protect her from the wind. She bathed after the confinement period. Beals' (1943, 1945) own researches among the Sonoran Yaquis indicated to him that their birth practices were essentially similar with the following exceptions: The child was washed with warm water after birth. The mother ate only atole and dried cow, not bull, meat for two or three days. During this period, the father could not work. The afterbirth was buried or placed on a bush or cactus; the cord portion cut off and placed in a plant. When the remainder of the cord dropped off, it was placed by some in a red ant's nest.

María's account of childbirth in Navidad describes beliefs and practices functioning during the 1930s and 1940s. They are well remembered by older women, but the young mothers of the late 1950s are not well acquainted with these ideas. Today in Navidad almost all women go to the county hospital to have their babies. The public health nurses seek out pregnant woman and encourage them to do so. Midwives are forbidden by law to practice (unless licensed, and none of the Yaqui *parteras* were eligible). Former *parteras* are known to the local county health officials, because their names used to appear on birth certificates, and they dare not practice illegally. The advantages of the hospital are many according to my informants: The services are free; the doctors are more skillful than the *parteras;* effective drugs to ease pain are available; and the confusion of filling out the birth certificate is taken care of by the hospital staff.

The *parteras,* today as in the past, are called upon to treat the illnesses of infants. A well-baby clinic is held once a month in Navidad, but when babies fall ill between clinic days, the parents may well call upon the *partera.* A *hitevi* might also be called, but my information suggests that when an infant is ill, the parents are more likely to consult a *partera.* Today in the village, the treatment of the illnesses of babies is all that is left of the practice of the few women who are still called *parteras.*

María said that babies are especially susceptible to fever (*taiwechi*) caused when the mother's lactation did not start immediately. Fever and other illnesses also are believed to be transmitted from the mother to the baby through the milk. For this reason María thought bottle-fed babies are apt to be healthier. Illness contracted by a nursing baby from its mother's milk is called *siavivitek.*

To cure a fever, María prescribed a tea of *saúco* (elder) given in a nursing bottle, and Vick's or Mentholatum salve rubbed on the forehead to cool it. Infant diarrhea (*vostia*) is also treated with *saúco* tea or with Kaopectate. A "swollen stomach" (*vaihia*) is rubbed with olive oil, sodium and warm water and salt given to the baby to drink.

When a baby is taken from a warm house into a cold wind, it may develop symptoms resembling an epileptic fit. For this condition María gives the baby *manzanilla* (chamomile) tea, a massage with Vick's or Mentholatum, and then wraps the baby tightly in a blanket to induce perspiration. Massage is prescribed along with medicines for almost all infant ailments. The skill of the *parteras* as masseuses is highly thought of in Navidad. Teething difficulties are treated with medicines obtained from the well-baby clinic or from the drugstore. A bit of onion given to the baby to chew is thought to help the teeth to emerge. Even more than adults, babies are thought to be vulnerable to emotional illnesses. *Susto* or *womtia* (fright) and *waiwiwa* (jealousy) are common infant complaints in Navidad. *Womtia* leaves the baby pale, weak, and trembling. María advised that it should be wrapped up snugly, kept warm, and given liquids to drink. If a nursing mother suffers an emotional shock, the baby should be given cow's milk from a bottle for several days so that the baby will not be adversely affected through the mother's milk. María said that a nursing baby can tell through the taste of the milk when its mother is pregnant and will become sick with jealousy and cry continuously. Carlos said that the baby just senses that a new baby is expected; it does not taste its presence through the milk. If a baby is not offered a bit of everything children or adults around him are eating, his jealousy will cause sores in his mouth. *Mal de ojo* (evil eye) and *pujos* (a rash with a hard cough) are also thought to be diseases of infancy.

Young children have no dietary restrictions. Soup and fruit juices are given to small infants to supplement their milk. After about six months of age, they are thought to be able to eat everything.

Infants are weaned when they are about one year old. If difficulties are anticipated, the child is sent to stay at the home of some relative for a number of days. Navidad children are expected to learn to walk at about nine months to a year and to talk at a year to eighteen months.

A well-baby clinic is held regularly, every month in Navidad. The public health nurses call at the homes of parents of new babies to encourage their mothers to take them to the clinic, and, indeed, most children are taken fairly regularly. The nurses in their talks to the mothers stress the importance of cleanliness and proper nutrition in the care of babies. Babies are weighed and examined, medicines are prescribed if they are needed, and routine inoculations are given. The nurses feel that great strides have been made in the proper care of babies since the clinic was opened in the '40s. They say that babies are cleaner and better nourished and less subject to infections and infant diarrhea.

The Lay Curer

In Navidad a great deal of curing is done by people who are not professional curers, who are "laymen" in the curing institution. I was told that minor illnesses are usually dealt with at home. Professional medical care is sought only if the symptoms do not yield to home remedies, or if they worsen. Carlos said for example, "*Manzanilla, yerba buena,* and *saúco* made into a tea is good for stomachache. This is something people would do at home." Pedro said of colds, "They are called *catarro*. People usually keep medicines on hand to treat them."

Of home curing Carlos said that he thought "most adults know a little bit about medicine. They know how to take care of themselves. . . . People know what medicines to use because someone gave it to them when they were sick." Carmen's mother kept a small stock of dried herbs, aspirin, a patent cough syrup, Alka Seltzer, and Vick's Vapo-Rub ready for medicinal use, and Carmen said that most families would have some medicines.

Lay people obtain herbal medicines mainly from Mexican drugstores in the city. Carlos said that Navidadeños still gather some wild herbs, but I was unable to find anyone other than himself who did. I assume therefore that the practice is rare. Spicer's field notes for the 1930s mention Yaquis gathering elder blossoms in spring to make medicinal teas. The patent medicines used in the home treatment of disease are purchased in drug or grocery stores. Jaime said, "When the children get diarrhea, we get some white medicine for them at the drugstore." Carmen related, "My mother gives us some sweet cough syrup. You can buy it at the drugstore."

Some Yaquis have acquired more than average knowledge of medicine, either through special interest or opportunity, and are frequently consulted by their relatives or even their neighbors. These people are not *hitevim*. They have no supernatural powers, and they are not paid for their advice or treatment. Of such a man Carlos said, "No, Ramón is not a *hitevi*. He does not know many medicines. He always takes care of his family. Maybe his parents were *hitevim*." Jaime's mother also had more than usual knowledge and often prescribed remedies for Jaime and his wife and children.

It is sometimes difficult to distinguish between the especially skilled layman and the *hitevi* through observation of their practice. Carlos' brother, for example, like Carlos, learned much medical lore from his mother and uncle. He usually treates the illnesses of his family and is sometimes consulted by his neighbors. He is, however, not a *hitevi*. He does not claim to have *seataka,* and he never charges for his treatments. The layman, however skilled he may be, does not have the power to deal with witchcraft. Only the possessor of *seataka* can successfully conquer a witch. It will be remembered that Spicer's field notes, quoted earlier, tell that Carlos' brother was "consulted when the son of Chico was bewitched" but was unable to help him. Carlos said that the layman trying to cure Tony's daughter-in-law failed because he did not have *seataka* and could not "know the *moorea*." On another occasion Carlos said, "There is a woman in the village with swollen legs; she goes to the county hospital. The doctor cannot cure her because she is bewitched."

Pedro explained that lay people follow the same customs as the *hitevi* in the preparation and administration of medicines. "It is common that they pray out loud when preparing and giving medicines. . . . The person who makes the medicine should apply it. . . . Boiled medicines are cooled before they are given." But he says, "Medicine leaves you pick or buy are treated this way but not commercial medicines."

Though herbal medicines are still used by many families, various patent medicines are becoming quite popular. Again Pedro says,

> Families keep whatever they can get at hand; the more they have, the better they are. Many just don't have the proper things. You can buy medicines at _____ (a big local Mexican drugstore). They have many

things from Mexico, but they are not like the Rio Yaqui. . . . Some modern families hardly have herbs, and they go buy the commercial medicines.

Though I have no figures, the information given by Carlos, Pedro, Carmen, and María seems to indicate, as stated above, that most minor illnesses, such as colds and coughs, stomach upset, aching muscles, sores and rashes, are treated entirely at home, using Yaqui or Spanish American herbal medicines, massages or poultices, or by the use of patent medicines available without a prescription. In addition, home remedies often seem to be the first treatment applied during the course of an illness; when these fail, professional treatment may be sought. Luisa, Lauro, and Tony's daughter-in-law had all tried home remedies unsuccessfully before consulting Carlos, and Antonia had bought a quantity of a medicinal herb from him, presumably for home use.

It has been mentioned above that most of the lore concerning the proper conduct of childbirth and the care of expectant and new mothers and infants was not the exclusive knowledge of the *partera* but general knowledge within the village.

There is also a body of information in Navidad on how the individual should keep himself well. Germs are recognized, and it is believed that people must keep their persons, clothing, and food clean to avoid disease. Illness can spread from a sick person to a well one. Babies, in particular, being small and weak, must be kept free of dirt. There is, however, also the belief that cold water is extremely dangerous to weak or sickened people. Cold baths should never be taken by small babies, people suffering from any illness, or by menstruating women. Cold water is equally dangerous as a drink and is kept from babies and sick people. Strenuous physical exercise, overexposure to heat and cold, especially alternating heat and cold, should be avoided to prevent illness. There is little that the layman can do to save himself from illnesses caused by witches other than to pray to God for protection and to avoid offending suspected *mooream*.

Laymen, the family of the patient, assist the *hitevi* in his cure by making sure that the patient has proper rest and warmth and is given the medicines and diet recommended by the *hitevi*. It is their responsibility that the patient be kept calm and free from worries. "They should talk to him, telling him not to worry; he will be well soon."

The Lay Patient

The most important right of the patient is to choose for himself what sort of medical treatment he will undergo. He may choose to rely upon home remedies and decide which medicines he will take, or he may choose to go to a clinic of the county hospital, the veterans' hospital, or to a doctor in private practice, an M.D., O.D., or chiropractor. He may go to a Mexican *curandero,* a Chinese herb doctor, or decide to consult a Yaqui *hitevi,* either one from Navidad or from some other Yaqui community in the Southwest or in Sonora. My informants emphasized that only the patient may choose the "doctor." Relatives and friends may make suggestions, and usually do, but no one can insist that a reluctant patient follow his advice. Parents, of course, choose a course of treatment for a child; a husband or other close relative may choose a doctor for an unconscious patient, but, with these exceptions, the wishes of the patient are always followed.

Bertola refused to go to the county hospital in spite of the urgings of her family. Another woman insisted upon being taken to the county hospital in opposition to the pleadings of her family and friends who were afraid that she had been bewitched and advised that she consult a *hitevi.*

What makes one person seek the aid of modern Western medicine, while another calls the *hitevi*? Or why does the same person consult a *hitevi* one time and go to a clinic another time? The statements of Navidadeños are confusing. One says "If the *hitevi* does not have the proper herb, then he (the patient) must go to the hospital," implying thus that the *hitevi* is the first choice. Another says, "If it is a hopeless case, if the doctors cannot help, the *hitevi* takes over. He offers the last hope." Cases can be found to illustrate these different opinions. A man called the *hitevim* from Torim to treat his nephew when modern medical means had failed. Carlos took his daughter once to an Anglo doctor when his herbal remedies did not cure her. If the system of medical practice with which one has started treatment fails, one can always try another.

A number of quite different factors can be seen to affect the choice between *hitevi* and hospital. Treatment at the county or veterans' hospital and at the various clinics is usually free to Yaquis, or less expensive than even the *hitevi's* modest fees. Fear of an operation keeps some people from going to the doctor. Western doctors are known to have powerful pain-killing drugs which cannot be equaled by those of the *hitevim.* Their medicines, while perhaps not admitted by all to be superior to Yaqui medicines, are at least readily available. Yaqui *hitevim* seem to run out of medicines with distressing frequency in Navidad. To those people who wish to appear well-educated and "progressive" in the eyes of the community, adherence to Western medicine is an indicator of their education. Every Navidadeño I met upon first acquaintance told me either that "old ways" of curing were no longer practiced or that he himself did not believe in the *hitevim* and always went to the clinic. In no case did I find this to be true. The people who at first told me they always went to the clinic were active in consulting *hitevim.* They had told me that the old ways were gone to protect themselves from my potential ridicule. Teachers and nurses frequently ridicule Yaquis, sometimes in scathing terms, for believing in witches and herbal medicine.

If, however, witchcraft is seriously suspected to be the cause of the illness, the *hitevi* must be consulted.

The fees of the *hitevi* are said to be smaller than those of any other medical practitioner in private practice in the city: M.D., O.D., chiropractor, Mexican *curandero,* or Chinese herb doctor. Moreover, the *hitevi* can be paid in goods rather than in money. Gifts such as tobacco, clothing, and food stuffs are mentioned as presents given to Carlos as payment for treatment. Some villagers seem to prefer to identify themselves with traditional Yaqui behavior and would so consult a *hitevi* rather than a foreign curer. Of Bertola who refused to go to the county hospital, it was said: "She sticks to the old ways."

Perhaps most important of all is the availability of the *hitevi. Hitevim* live right in Navidad; one can get them at any hour of the day or night without making a trip by car or bus to a hospital, doctor's office, or clinic. The *hitevi* is required to treat whoever calls him. The hospital is overcrowded and frequently simply cannot take some cases immediately. A school nurse told me, "Tonsillectomies are stacked up in the hospital for months; there is hardly any point sending kids there." The hours of the clinics are often inconvenient. Men work during the day; older children attend school; women have the care of younger children and housework; whole families may be out of town for several weeks picking cotton. A *hitevi* can be found in Navidad in the evenings when the men are home from work and are free to seek medical aid, and the women can leave younger children under the care of other adults in the family. During 1958-1959, Carlos treated most of his patients during the evening or on the weekend. The Torim *hitevim* also held "office hours" in the evening. Women *hitevim* are usually to be found at home during the day as well. Navidadeños complained to me that physicians in the city do not often make house calls. The *hitevi* does not fail to attend patients at home if they send for him. They remember well one physician practicing in the city in the 1930s and 1940s. "He always came to Navidad when he was needed . . . he came anytime. He was like a *hitevi.*" This man is mentioned also in Spicer's unpublished field notes.

Yaquis consult medical practitioners other than their own *hitevim,* and M.D.'s, O.D.'s, and chiropractors were mentioned as well as Mexican *curanderos* and Chinese herb doctors. All of my informants denied any knowledge of Papago curers or curing methods though many Papagos live in the city and Navidadeños frequently visit the local mission where there is a Papago reservation. Pedro and Carlos said that Mayos have *hitevim* exactly like those of the Yaquis. They did not know of anyone, though, who had consulted one.

From lists given me by Carlos, Carmen, and Pedro and from casual conversations with Jaime, I gained the names of six "Anglo" doctors consulted by the villagers; four of these were M.D.'s, one was an O.D., and one a chiropractor. All of these were said to be Anglo doctors like those at the hospital. Pedro had met one of the M.D.'s at the county hospital and consulted him later at his office. Carmen's mother had occasionally taken one or another of her children to see a second. And Carlos, himself, had taken his daughter to the third.

Three Mexican *curanderos* were mentioned to me. One lives in the city and was said by Carlos to have great power. He had taken an ailing son to him at one time. The second is the Mexican woman mentioned above who lives in Navidad and is thought to be a *bruja*. The last lives in a nearby city. He is of Mexican descent and a chiropractor, though my informants unanimously claimed him to be a *curandero,* not, evidently, only because he is Mexican. One of the M.D.'s listed as an "Anglo" doctor is also a Mexican American and is said to speak Spanish to his Yaqui patients. My informants regarded these *curanderos* as more like *hitevim* than the Anglo doctors. "They use some of the same medicines, although many are different." "He was like a *hitevi;* he saw right away that an evil person was doing it." My very limited information suggests *curanderos* are consulted when for some reason they are more available than a *hitevi* or when a *hitevi* has failed to cure, but the patient still wishes to avoid modern Western medicine.

None of my informants had ever actually consulted a Chinese herb doctor, though they had all heard of them. Pedro knew a man who had once gone to one in the city to be cured of some skin disease. He said, "They cure with herbs like Yaquis. This patient went to his office, and the Chinese doctor prepared the medicine himself. He gave him the medicine and told him how to take it. He was supposed to go back if the medicine ran out."

An important function of the patient in curing is the decision to make a *manda.* As we have seen, the *manda* is a special form of prayer to God and the saints made to obtain a cure for a disease. The *hitevi* prays for the cure of his patient, but the patient is also expected to pray. Praying by the patient can accompany any other kind of treatment. My informants assured me, moreover, that prayers should be made no matter if one treats oneself at home, or goes to receive treatment from a *hitevi,* the hospital, a *curandero,* or whatever. They said that God and the saints can "strengthen" any kind of cure and will sometimes cure unaided.

The decision to make a *manda* rests with the patient. He may decide to light candles before the statue of a saint at home, in the church in the village, or perhaps at the Franciscan mission. He may pledge himself to make a pilgrimage or to wear an *hábito*. He may promise to join one of the religious societies. Carlos and Pedro said that a person will make a *manda* if they see themselves doing the promised action in a dream, if they have a strong conviction that God wants them to do the service, or if medical treatment has failed. In any case, the decision rests with the patient. Because making a vow is a serious decision and fulfilling the promise cannot be shirked without fear of supernatural punishment, friends and relatives may offer advice and suggestions, but the decision rests with the patient. In the case of donning an *hábito* or joining a society, godparents are chosen, but only after the vow has been made; a *maestro* may be called to witness the *manda,* but he is called in only after the patient has determined to make the vow. Again the father and mother of a child, never the godparents, may pledge him to a service, but this is the only exception.

Medical Beliefs and Practices Among Lower-Income Anglos

Eleanor Bauwens

Medical Beliefs and Practices Among Lower-Income Anglos

Eleanor Bauwens

THE DOMINANT SYSTEM OF BELIEF AND PRACTICE in matters of health and illness in the United States is scientific medicine. However, not all sick persons seek scientific medical care – that which, by methods of science, is systematically developed, disseminated, and practiced by "legitimate professionals" in medical schools, laboratories, clinics, and hospitals (Saunders and Hewes 1953). Therefore, it is necessary to look at that body of alternative medical beliefs and practices that permeate our culture and influence behavior with respect to illness.

The information presented in this study is intended to illustrate the medical system of a group of lower-income Anglos. Beliefs concerning how these individuals view health, the causes of illness, illness itself, and treatment will be described. The information in this study is based on the ethnographic study of this system in a Southwestern town.

The town has a population of approximately 13,000 inhabitants. About 64 percent of these claim Spanish as their mother tongue, 29 percent claim English, and 6 percent other (U.S. Bureau of the Census 1971). Of those who claim English as their mother tongue, 18.9 percent, or about 700 individuals, are below the poverty level as defined by the United States Bureau of the Census (1971). The 50 individuals in the study sample represent 7 percent of the poverty-level Anglo population.

The major employer in the area is a mining corporation, which operates a copper smelter. Although the economy always has been closely related to copper mining and smelting, it has become diversified in recent years.

Increasing numbers of residents are involved in manufacturing industries, agriculture, retail trade, and tourism.

Economically, the town is a shopping center for Northern Mexico. Its sister town in Mexico offers an opportunity for American industry. Manufacturing companies take advantage of the low wage scale in the Mexican town by shipping materials and equipment there for assembly. The assembled goods are then returned to the United States for sale.

The individuals in the study reside in a neighborhood in the northeastern section of the town known as "Sunnyside." This is a heterogeneous neighborhood with the ethnic composition divided among Mexican Americans, Anglos, and Blacks.

Housing is generally old and cheap – makeshift composites of corrugated metal, wood, and adobe. Trailers, mobile homes, Quonset huts, and shacks are interspersed among vacant lots, horse corrals, chicken coops, gardens, and various auto-related structures. Rather well-kept houses are juxtaposed with often unkept yards. One residence is virtually surrounded by a junkyard of old cars, discarded furniture, and empty beer cans. Chain link, wire, or wood fences, many of which need repair, surround nearly all houses. Several porches are used for the storage of such articles as auto tires and parts.

The marginal character of the area can be seen in such anomalous structures as a Quonset hut with an elaborate stone facade and old, dilapidated houses constructed of boards with tar paper roofs that have new brick additions attached.

Cooling is also a problem. Coolers are scarce, necessitating opening windows and doors. Many window screens are torn and have gaping holes, or are absent altogether. Screen doors are lacking in most instances.

Some of the homes present many potential hazards, such as underground electrical outlets and switches near water sources, high sills under almost all doors, and even doors that require some rather fancy dance-like steps before they can be opened. Unvented gas heaters are frequently seen.

Most of the streets are unpaved, and there are few street signs. The streets are not oiled, and dust is a frequent problem. Storm sewers are nonexistent. There are no sidewalks.

Dogs are seen in yards and running free in the streets. Many individuals note that stray dogs are a nuisance and complain of barking dogs. Horses are kept by some residents, creating a fly and odor problem. One resident has a cow in the backyard that keeps the family supplied with milk.

Because the study was concerned only with "lower-income" Anglos, all 50 informants were at the lower end of the economic continuum. All individuals interviewed had incomes under $3800 per year; thus, the sample of individuals in the study was close to the bottom of the present low-income population in the United States. These individuals had little or no cushion to protect themselves from unemployment and had no prospect of economic security in old age except for the federal government's old-age insurance program.

Occupations of the informants tended to be of the type requiring few skills and little education. Informants reported the following occupations: convenience market clerk, handyman, custodian, salesman, railroad laborer, waitress, bar maid, domestic worker, housewife, and mechanic.

Fourteen informants are retired. Three of these were under 65 years and unable to work because of ill health and/or job-related injuries. One male, age 57, was working for a construction company when he fell from a scaffold and sustained serious head injuries. He is unable to work and collects Social Security Disability. One female is only 44 years old, but suffers from diabetes, gout, hypertension, arthritis and other ailments. Her husband is deceased, and she is not old enough to collect his Social Security benefits. She receives public assistance funds. Eight other individuals are public assistance recipients. Another individual is a divorcee with three children, two of them in school. She receives public assistance under the Aid to Dependent Children (ADC) program. Another divorcee also receives ADC for her daughter. Neither of these individuals feels that receiving ADC is unrespectable. They consider it "just a source of money to make ends meet." Bernard (1964:81), in his study of ADC mothers in Boston, found that the use of ADC is a "recognized and accepted aspect of lower-income life."

Thirty-four of the informants have lived in the town for 15 years or more. Only two individuals were recent to the community, having been there only six months or less. The length of time an individual resides in a city is important, because of the light thrown upon his or her possible knowledge of health facilities and services available in the community as a whole.

Thirty-eight individuals have lived in the same residence for five years or more; forty-two individuals have lived in the same residence for two years or more. Only five individuals had resided at their present address less than six months and may have been handicapped by not having had time to form friendships with neighbors. If individuals have continued to live long enough at one address to have "put down roots," they will be more likely to obtain health information and assistance in illness situations from neighbors and acquaintances.

Forty of the informants live in owner-occupied dwellings. These homes, like other structures in the same areas, are old and of low value. Ten live in rental units. Two of these units are run-down and receive little attention from absentee landlords. Individuals living in these units can only afford to pay $25 per month rent and, therefore, have little chance of obtaining adequate housing.

Of the 41 households in the study sample, 22, or 53.7 percent, are headed by women only, i.e., female-headed households. The composition of these households includes women living alone (whether separated, divorced, or widowed), women living with minor children, and one woman whose 50-year-old son lives with her. She considers herself to be the household head since her son is ill and unable to hold a steady job. The youngest female head-of-household is a 31-year-old divorcee. The oldest individual in this category is an 88-year-old widow.

There are five, or 12.2 percent, of the households in the study sample headed by men only. These male informants all live alone; four are widowers and one is separated from his wife. The youngest informant in this category is a 60-year-old man who is separated from his wife. He has not seen her for 30 years. The oldest informant is aged 78 and a widower. He has resided in the town since 1917. He has a daughter and son in a neighboring state who worry about him living alone. The daughter wants him to come to live with her, but he says, "I'm not ready yet! Why should I give up just because I'm 78?"

There are 14, 34.1 percent, households occupied by married couples. Only two of these households include small children. One retired couple cares for a grandchild, while the daughter-in-law works. One husband is confined to a wheelchair with multiple sclerosis. He is completely dependent on his wife. Four other couples are retired.

The average age of the informants is 54. The youngest individual, a woman, is age 31; the oldest, a male, is 90. Koos (1954) notes that needs for medical treatment are related to age, with symptoms being given importance if they occur in a young person but being disregarded in the middle-aged or elderly. The amount of morbidity in a population is also linked with the aging process (Mechanic 1968). In agreement with Mechanic, it was found that the older the informant, the greater was the incidence of illness experience.

The level of formal education attained by informants is somewhat low. The median number of years of formal education is 7.0 for males and 6.7 for females as compared with the national median of 12.1 years for both sexes (U.S. Bureau of the Census 1973).

HEALTH FACILITIES AND SERVICES

Local health facilities and services include the county hospital, which has 144 in-patient beds, a 35-bed community hospital established and run by the local mining company, and a local branch of the county health department. There is a nursing home which opened in 1972. The home has a bed capacity of 17 and is approved for Medicare patients.

The location of the county hospital presents a problem to the medically indigent and to those individuals with low incomes because it is located about three miles from the northern city limits. Since public transportation is not available in the town and most of these individuals do not own or have access to an automobile, they are without transportation to the facility. The local taxi service is said to be undependable and expensive. It is not unusual to see these individuals walking or hitchhiking along the highway to the county hospital.

There are 12 physicians residing and practicing medicine in the town. There are no gynecologists or psychiatrists. In addition, there are 63 registered nurses and 27 licensed practical nurses, one optometrist, four dentists, and one chiropractor in the town. From a major metropolitan area over a hundred miles from the town, a number of specialists visit at regular intervals. As in most small cities, many health services are not available and patients needing special health care are sent to the two major metropolitan areas in the state.

Since health cannot be viewed out of the socio-economic aspects of daily living, local problems reflect the low wages prevalent in the area. Many families have multiple problems – health, finances, and the like. Koos (1946:24–25) eloquently portrays the marginality of living in such families:

> Only the things that must be done managed to get done. There are no sheltered reservoirs within which man can store up his surplus thoughts, energies and products – and not surprisingly, because for people living under these conditions there are no surplus thoughts and energies and products. They need all their energies and every cent they earn in order to meet the day-by-day demands . . . upon them whichever way they turn. Life under such conditions takes on a nip-and-tuck urgency that belies our culture's middle-class ethos of a reasoned calculation of one's future.

Families whose economic well-being is marginal are more vulnerable to health problems. Periodic surveys of morbidity in the general population, based on information collected by the National Center for Health Statistics, show marked differences in the number of disability days in relation to income.

The major causes of death in this town are heart disease (30 percent), cancer (15 percent), and respiratory disease (8 percent). About 4.5 percent of mothers do not receive antepartal care (Weaver 1973).

CAUSES OF ILLNESS

Informants believe that one has to work at it constantly to have good health and that how we take care of our bodies is important. Eating "right" is also important. If one has no identifiable symptoms of illness, it is possible to conclude one's health is good.

The causes of illness are diffuse and generalized – climatic changes and impurities being the most often mentioned. There is little understanding that specific microorganisms cause specific illness, that the chicken pox virus causes chicken pox, or that the measles virus causes measles, for example.

Climatic Changes

The cause of illness mentioned by many individuals is exposure to the elements, such as cold air or drafts. Commonly, illnesses caused by exposure to drafts and by entry of cold air into the body are respiratory infections, such as colds and pneumonia. Many of these illnesses are considered the result of carelessness, i.e., failing to take proper health precautions. Exposure to cold air when overheated is considered dangerous and foolish. For example:

> Getting into a draft will cause colds. Like riding in a car with the wind blowing over your shoulders or go into a store where they got refrigeration on and then come back in that heat.
>
> (Sam) could have a cold because he's hot and sweaty, and the air cools him off blowing on him. That's pretty dangerous to do.
>
> I think Sam took a cold from cooling off too quick. That would give nearly everybody a cold.
>
> Yes, he's taken a cold, and he's laid himself in a good position to get pneumonia, letting that air cool him down too fast. Why, you don't even do that to horses!
>
> Sam shouldn't cool off by letting wind blow on him when he's hot and sweaty. That's foolish.

The belief that when you fail to protect yourself from cold air, it causes illness is held by several informants.

> A cold, exposure can cause that. Say I strip myself down, and think I can go outdoors two minutes. You get the exposure to the cold air.
>
> Getting chilled. That's how I got this cold. If I run around barefoot in the winter, it'll give me a cold.
>
> If I got to bed with my hair wet in the winter, I get a cold. In the summer, it's all right. The breeze from my bedroom window will do it in winter – exposure, you know.
>
> Colds – I think a lot of that is carelessness. Running around when it's cold without proper clothing or being barefoot.

Individuals with arthritis referred directly to changes in the weather or the nature of the climate as the cause of the condition. For example:

> My knees . . . get stiff and my joints swell up. . . . I can always tell when it is going to storm.
>
> . . . [A]rthritis all lays with the weather. I can tell you within two to three days if we're going to have a bad storm.

The idea that climate causes arthritis seemed to be based on the individual's observation of the appearance of joint discomfort immediately preceding or at the time of weather change.

Impurities

The second major cause of illness is another vague outside agent, impurities. These impurities enter the body and are responsible for ailments such as various types of skin eruptions, tuberculosis, and diabetes.

Impurities enter the blood and are responsible for skin eruptions such as boils, rashes, and ringworm. Boils are thought to represent poisons in the blood trying to come out. The blood is considered to be affected and is referred to as "bad." One informant notes:

> Boils is good business. They collect the impurities – something in the blood, and they let it come out. They're caused by bad blood. Every one that comes to a head leaves out the bad.

Thus, boils serve as a vehicle for the release of impurities from the blood.

Other cutaneous manifestations such as rashes, ringworm, and urticaria are also believed due to impurities in the body. These manifestations represent the "letting out of poisons"; thus, informants believe that they "purify the blood." External dirt, i.e., "dirty skin," also can result in a "breaking out" of the skin. Some individuals equate filth with "germs" that get into the body through the skin and then must "come out."

Two other conditions thought to be caused by impurities are tuberculosis and diabetes mellitus. One woman notes: "TB, that's just a blood disease; some kind of impurity. Germs enter the blood, and make it unpure." Another woman reports that diabetes is caused by "impurities in the kidneys." One man believes that "some kind of chemical impurities in the food kill the pancreas and cause diabetes." Failure of the individual to eat the "proper" foods can result in bodily impurities, which can cause disease. Another man says, "Too much sweet stuff can build up in your body . . . diet is a controller. . . . It is important to keep yourself cleaned out." Very often the diagnosis is made by reflecting over preceding events. The individual did not eat the proper type of food or overindulged in a particular type of food, such as sugar. As a result, these foods built up and formed impurities in the body.

Contagion

A few informants believe that you can "catch" certain illnesses; that is, that some illnesses such as colds, measles, tuberculosis, and shingles can be transmitted from one individual to another.

One female states that "colds are catching – something in the air people get and they 'pass it around'." Another female notes that "you can catch them [colds] from other people." Other informants make inferences based on past observations of a correlation between the onset of illness and certain situations in which contagion is likely. Measles, for example, are caught by being in contact with someone who has them; ringworm is caught by touching the skin lesions of someone who has it. One individual reports that "you can get shingles from others who have them and from being around somebody with chicken pox." Another is not quite sure whether measles are contagious because when her daughter had the measles, "none of the rest of the family got them and they have not had them – so it's debatable how catching they are."

Most individuals believe that tuberculosis is "catching," but that one can avoid the condition by "taking care of yourself" and "not getting run down." Two informants who have or have had immediate family members with tuberculosis note that they "don't have TB." Also, being exposed to copper dust in the mines is thought to be a cause of tuberculosis. "If your resistance is the least bit down, and you get that copper dust in your lungs, it can cause TB." Only a few individuals express the belief that tuberculosis is caused by a "germ." These individuals do not consider this to be a specific microorganism, but, rather, "some kind of bug." One male states that "TB is inherited." He bases this conclusion on the fact that his father and one brother had tuberculosis, but neither he nor the rest of the family have the disease. As a result, he makes the observation that tuberculosis is not contagious, but inherited. Thus, there is differential belief in contagion as an element of disease transmission.

HEALTH MAINTENANCE

Failure to take proper care of the body also can cause illness. Eating "right," sufficient rest, and moderation in life-style are important in the maintenance of good health. As one male informant, aged 72, states:

> You know, you are what you eat. People eat too much junk food, and the additives and all the stuff like coloring that they put in our food aren't good for you. *If I feel tired or out of sorts, I figure I must not be eating right*. I usually eat foods that are valuable to me.

The oldest informant (age 90) in the study attributes his good health to eating right:

> I watch my food, and I watch that I don't get constipated, because I think that is a very important thing with old people to keep their bowels open and keep themselves cleaned out. *Sluggish bowel can cause fever.* I have cereal every morning and grapefruit. . . . Diet is a controller of what you are.

Special foods such as "health foods" may also prevent illness. Health foods are believed to improve general health and well-being as well as to help with specific health problems. "Good health" is something that must be worked at constantly, rather than a natural thing. The following comments illustrate this point:

> We have a lot of protein through vegetables – just eating health foods, not too much meat, working real hard to find foods without preservatives. We are almost completely macrobiotic, and this is how we have done so much healing. I had some female problems. I've been on the macrobiotic diet for quite a while and have managed to get these under control.

> We find if we stay away from refined sugar . . . we've arrested our daughter's asthma by taking her off refined sugar 100 percent. I buy 15 gallons of raw honey a year. We get it from the bees around here; it's natural.

> Once you get your system cleaned out, if you go full blast into prepared foods and low-priced foods that have a lot of MSG and tenderizers in them, preservatives and so forth, it's just as though you had taken a big dose of strychnine. I became toxic from some of these foods at a friend's house and had to go to the hospital with severe pain.

> We're health enthusiasts. My husband had obesity and all kinds of things. We found this book, *Body, Mind, and Sugar,* and that started us off investigating health foods. We went to other books afterward. We're not so fanatic that we think we can cure ourselves. It's just that there are things you can do to help yourself. If we have a headache, we can cure it as well as a doctor can. Trace back the source of that headache, in other words, what did we eat today? If you really get on health foods solid, you become so attuned to your body harmony, your symptoms, that I could go off and eat a dinner and immediately get this headache. It would be due to chemicals, MSG, or whatever.

> We've found that certain foods will cause you to lose your hair. And we've proved it by eating these foods and then quitting. Quit eating them for a few days and then eat one or two of them and notice the difference in the amount of hair on the bed pillow. I gave this advice to one young man here in town who was almost completely bald, and I told him what foods to go off. . . . He went off them for over a year. He's had a miraculous recovery of hair. He has quit losing his hair and a little has grown in.

Laxative products are also taken to maintain health. All informants believe in using laxatives, and all report using them at some point in their life. If fecal matter is allowed to remain for too long in the body, harm may result. The belief in the necessity for clock-like regularity survives today from early nineteenth century medicine, which regarded "purging" as a standard treatment for virtually all ailments.

> . . . it is important to have a bowel movement every day you know, and if you don't you need to do something about it. . . . I take milk of magnesia. . . .

> It's important to keep bowels open and keep cleaned out. . . . We take a little mineral oil.

Individuals tend not to regard the regular inducement of bowel activity as "treatment," nor do they regard laxatives as "medicine." As one man told me:

> I take milk of magnesia, but I don't think it should be called a medicine.

Vitamins and mineral tablets also are considered of value in avoiding sickness. Individuals also consider them as providing pep and energy. Some individuals also note that they use vitamins as a form of "insurance" against the possibility of some deficiency in the diet that might lead to illness.

Moderation in life-style is important in keeping healthy. Drinking too much alcohol (even consuming small amounts according to some persons) and excessive smoking are thought by most individuals to be "asking for trouble."

WHAT IS GOOD HEALTH?

Perfect health may be viewed as an ideal concept. It is an idea toward which people are oriented rather than a state they expect to attain. Health is ordinarily taken for granted if one is not ill.

Illness, on the other hand, can be defined in terms of symptoms, capacity for normal role performance and feeling states, which fall within the experience of most individuals (Baumann 1961:39–46). While the criteria used to define illness may vary, and the degree to which any given criterion must be present for an individual to be called "ill" may vary, any one individual is relatively certain that illness can be defined with clarity.

Definitions of what is "normal" health vary widely. In general, individuals' evaluations of normality are based on experiences, cultural beliefs, and values, and the particular group context, such as social class. As Mechanic (1968:16) has noted:

> Implicit in all ideas of health and disease . . . is the concept of normal fitness and behavior. But concepts of health fitness and acceptable behavior, as well as those of disease and disability, depend on . . . the social and cultural context within which human problems are defined.

Cultural groups vary in the extent to which they perceive a set of circumstances as constituting health or illness, normalcy or abnormality (King 1962:66). Social class groupings provide a framework of beliefs and values that influence the individual's perception of what is normal and what is abnormal. For example, Koos (1954) finds that variations exist between the highest and lowest social classes in recognition that some symptoms are abnormal. The meanings individuals give to symptoms are the product in some measure of their life situation. Individuals who work long hours expect to be tired, and therefore, may be less likely to see tiredness as indicative of illness. Persons who do heavy physical work are more likely to attribute such symptoms as backache to the nature of their lives and work rather than to an illness condition. Thus, it is possible to rationalize a wide variety of symptoms within a frame of reference other than sickness (Koos 1954). However, it is unlikely that an individual experiencing a high fever will consider himself "normal" and "not sick." And no matter how stoic a person is, a fractured leg is likely to make him seek medical care.

Individuals in the present study tended to identify themselves as being in good health on the basis of: 1) the absence of identified illness symptoms or conditions, 2) the definition of those conditions which had been identified as trivial, or 3) non-impairment of activity.

Those persons who noted the absence of identifiable illness tended to make statements such as:

> Health is very good as far as I know.
>
> Pretty good, I guess. I've never had to go to a doctor since I've been in ____________. I haven't seen a doctor in 13 years.
>
> Good, very good. I'm not sickly–I haven't any signs of anything wrong.

Others assessed their health as good on the basis that their known health condition was trivial. They reported either a past or present experience with a major disability.

> I think it's [health] good. I had my gallbladder removed two years ago, and I have no more trouble with that. I had a coronary thrombosis ten years ago, but its all healed up now, takes medicine that's all. I go out and climb mountains now.
>
> Good. Before I had this spacemaker [pacemaker], I couldn't walk to the store and back to get groceries.

> It's [health] good, all but my knee since this accident. I have arthritis, that's all.

Thus, from the comments above, an individual can be defined as healthy even with a known health condition. The assessed seriousness of the condition was a factor focused on the perceived degree to which life was threatened or physical activity impaired. Informants perceived their health to be "good," because they did not perceive an interference with some physical activity.

DEVIATIONS FROM "GOOD" HEALTH

Individuals designated themselves as deviating from "good" health on the basis of: 1) changes in feeling states, such as pain, 2) bodily changes not accompanied by pain, and 3) interference with normal activity.

The Presence of Pain

For most individuals pain was considered a symptom indicating an altered health state. The experience of pain was sufficient for them to consider themselves sick.

> I have a bleeding ulcer. . . . I've had it about two years. I was hurting so bad. I knew I was pretty sick, and the pain made up my mind.
>
> I had such a terrible pain in my knees, and I finally went to a doctor, and he said it was arthritis.
>
> [I had] a pain in my shoulder. I thought it was a heart attack. I went to a doctor right away – I was sick.
>
> Well, I had this pain in the center of my chest – felt vice-like. I didn't know what it was.
>
> I went to the doctor right away. I was cold and sweaty, and it was a severe pain. Doctor said it was my heart.
>
> I was ready to faint with pain in my stomach. Finally, I couldn't stand it any more, so I decided to go to the hospital.
>
> Pain in the chest is always bad. Pain is something that tells you to get help. I know. I've had it.

The presence of pain was sufficient to decide that someone was sick. If the individual concerned had had some past experience with an illness that was accompanied by pain, he was all the more certain that any pain was a definite symptom of an illness.

Other Body Changes

Some individuals noted that "You can be sick and not have pain sometimes." That is, a change in the biological state of the organism, which does not involve pain, may still be an illness.

> I was constipated, just all the sudden. I was always regular. With something new, a change, it's always a good idea to check and make sure.

For another individual, the fact that a condition was new led to a search for explanation and possible redefining because of fear of possible outcomes. Here newness, that is, change, was a factor; but the fear of outcomes seemed to be the motivating force:

> The first I knew that I had a cataract was when I went to get my driver's license renewed. . . . They said I'd better go to an oculist and see what's wrong. You can scarcely see at all out of your right eye, they told me. About that time, we had those men on the moon. I thought I'd look at the moon and see if I could see anything different about it. My Lord, I seen seven moons. . . . So if you get cataracts, that's the way you'll find out. I was afraid that I was going blind.

Interference With Normal Activity

Another symptom or sign of illness reported was the development of an incapacity to perform normal activities. The activity in question may be occupational or non-occupational. For example:

> I'm not able to do anything. The doctor doesn't want me to even lift a pot or wash a dish. I'm a semi-invalid. The doctor says that I have one small bone holding me together and if that breaks, I'm in a wheelchair.

> I have a back injury. . . . There's no treatment for this condition. I'm totally disabled as far as working. It's difficult for me to walk as the back injury has affected my legs.

> I've had arthritis for the past 30 years. It started in my neck and then went to my shoulders and knees. I've been on crutches or with a cane ever since.

> I used to do housework. I haven't been able to work for five years. I fell and hurt my back, and I haven't been able to work since. I can hardly straighten up sometimes.

The presence of pain, body changes not accompanied by pain, and the interference with normal activities were the criteria that individuals used to decide that there was an altered health state present. Among the individuals studied, pain was the most frequent and most significant indicator of illness.

INFLUENCE OF OTHERS

There is considerable variation in the numbers of people who become involved in the decision-making process in regard to whether or not there is an altered health state present. The individual himself may assess his own state of health and decide on a course of treatment without consulting anyone else. He is both the receiver and the validator of an altered health state. One female decided that she had arthritis:

> My knees would be stiff, and my joints would swell up. This was when I was in Illinois. Since I've been out here, it hasn't been so bad. . . . I never did go to a doctor about it. I just take care of it myself.

One male developed what he decided was dyspepsia attributable to pills he took for tuberculosis:

> I had dyspepsia on and off. I take a little baking soda and it helps. I attribute it to the pills I took. That's the first sign that I had, when I took the pills.

In another instance, another male went on a "drinking bout" after his dog died. He decided his condition was sufficiently serious to warrant medical attention. He was assisted by a neighbor in getting to the hospital.

It would appear, then, that unassisted self-definition of illness occurred for two of the above individuals when the condition was relatively familiar and regarded as not serious. These individuals interpreted their symptoms as those of an illness, but assigned them a low priority, because they did not threaten survival. When aches were classified as "normal," they were not given what might be called priority attention in the individual's value system. On the other hand, the third individual described above assigned high priority to his symptoms of an altered health state and their perceived seriousness directed his action. In the latter example, assistance was sought for treatment, while in the former, self-treatment was regarded as sufficient. This suggests that the interpretation of symptoms as serious depended upon assumed normality or abnormality under a given set of circumstances.

The individual may consult his spouse or other relatives for the validation of an altered health state. He may ask directly for validation or advice may be proffered without solicitation.

Some individuals consulted only with their spouses. In these situations, there was agreement between husband and wife that the symptoms were those of an illness and needed attention. In most instances, consensus was reached quickly on the proper course of action for that problem. The following response was typical of those in which agreement was reached quickly on a course of action:

> When I had the chest pain, I called the doctor after talking it over with my wife. She agreed I should call him. He told me to go to the hospital right away.

In another case, agreement was implied:

> . . . Just as I went to open the icebox door, down I went. I just collapsed right there. [My husband] thought I'd had a heart attack, so he called the doctor and told him what happened. He came out and gave me a shot. . . .

In one instance, an individual disagreed with her spouse as to the significance of the symptoms presented:

> In West Virginia, my husband wanted me to go to the hospital, but I wanted to get back to Arizona. I didn't think it was serious, so I pooh-poohed the idea of going to the hospital and went on. When we got home, I was still sick. My husband got in on that all right. He called the doctor.

In another situation, the informant bowed sufficiently to the decision made by his wife to seek the advice of a physician:

> I went out in the yard to top that big old tree out there. I had a little pain develop, so I come down and sat on the chair. [My wife] insisted that I call the doctor. So he insisted on me going to the hospital. I told him I'd be all right if I just sat down and rested for a few minutes. I ended up out there in the hospital.

While the individuals above decided on their health state in consultation with their spouses, others consulted with their children for validation that there was alteration in the health state. For example, one woman reported her vision getting "bad." Both her son and she discussed the matter:

> I've had this growth on my left eye that I should have taken off, but I haven't. . . . I talked to my son about it, and he seemed to think that I'd have to have it taken off some day. . . . My son bought me a magnifying glass so that I can read.

For another individual, the sensation of pain was a cue to initiate inquiry with her brother into its meaning.

> The first sign I had that I had arthritis was my ankles. My ankles hurt, like maybe I sprained them. My brother said why don't I soak them in hot water with epsom salts. He thought it was arthritis. Then I went to the doctor and had tests. Sure enough, it was arthritis.

In yet other situations friends, neighbors, or co-workers were asked to act as illness decision-makers. The following illustrate the point:

> They usually come and ask me. I had a friend come to my house and ask me what to do for her baby. . . . The baby was having gas and a stomachache, and I said give him soda water. That's what I gave mine.
>
> If I ever get depressed, I know where to go. You need people to talk to, to ask about what's wrong. A friend really straightened me out.
>
> I talk to my neighbor about things. Mostly, I've been urging her to go to the doctor.

Individuals were more apt to consult friends or neighbors in the community when there was disagreement with the spouse's opinion on a course of action, or if the individual had no immediate family or relatives in the town or vicinity.

Individuals also seek out persons who are thought to have special healing abilities to validate that an altered health state is present. These persons may or may not have professional medical training; however, they are recognized by the sick individual as a professional. These healers are widely distributed in American culture in the persons of physicians, osteopaths, chiropractors, reflexologists, health food advisors and the like. The use of such healers appears to be partly determined by the socioeconomic class of the individual and leads to a consideration of class factors in beliefs and reactions toward illness. According to Koos (1954), lower-income Whites are more likely to patronize a chiropractor than are upper-income Whites. In the present study, however, although all individuals interviewed knew about chiropractors, only a few had ever consulted one. Only one individual actually consulted a chiropractor to validate a state of altered health; the others saw him for treatment of illnesses that had already been validated.

Individuals consulted such persons as lab technicians. One informant stated:

> I thought I might have diabetes. I discussed it with a lab technician that was a friend. I just called down to the lab and asked my friend to run a blood sugar the next day when I came in.

The same informant also consulted a druggist:

> I usually talk to the druggist more than I do anybody else. Where you get a druggist that is a friend, they will discuss problems with you. . . .

The services of nurses were also used. For example:

> There's a nurse up the street. So, I usually ask her if there's anything I want to know. She can explain to me what things are. . . .
>
> The health nurse comes here. I have as much faith in her as I do the doctor. She is good at telling what's wrong. . . .

Other individuals obtained advice from books and magazines. Two of these reported:

> I would go to a book before I would go to a person. Like Adelle Davis – she's an authority on nutrition – or Mr. Rodale on macrobiotics.
>
> They describe different conditions in the magazine and what to do. I read that and I know what I have.

When an individual concluded that his illness was serious, he immediately consulted a physician or osteopath for validation. In these cases, the symptoms were generally very obvious, and the individual was incapacitated to some degree. There was no question that the individual was not well.

The amount and source of an individual's income were also important in the selection of a validator. Those individuals who received welfare checks and those with insufficient income are eligible for free care at the county hospital from physicians. They might, therefore, elect to see a physician rather than pay another professional.

Another factor may be whether the individual was reared in an urban or rural area. Individuals reared in rural areas may have had little experience with physicians and, therefore, be less likely to look upon the physician as an accessible source of illness validation. Although both of the individuals in the study who were reared in urban areas consulted with a physician or osteopath to validate health states, it cannot be concluded that this was an effect of urban upbringing, since other individuals consulted physicians and osteopaths, too.

The necessary condition for becoming a patient is the affirmation of an altered health state based on the individual's definition of being "sick." To be "sick" is to play a social role that is learned as part of the content of a culture – to do certain things because it is the "proper" way to act when sick.

Once the individual decides that he is "sick," usually the next step is to consider ways of regaining health. Parsons (1951) has pointed out that the individual is expected to seek cure and that every effort should be made to bring about as rapid and complete recovery as possible. The individual is expected to seek out a competent healer.

TREATMENT MODALITIES

Koos (1954) showed that lower-income individuals differed not only in their definitions of illness, but also in their beliefs about the treatment of illness. One of the major differences occurs in the matter of information about health and disease. Because lower-income individuals tend to be less educated in science, they will tend to be more ignorant of the origins of illness, as scientifically specified, and more likely to hold vague ideas. Individuals in the present study support Koos' hypothesis that education is directly related to social class; therefore, it is likely that lower-income people are less likely to know the causes and effects of illness.

It is also possible that the lack of scientific health and illness information among lower-income individuals contributes to their willingness to use non-scientific healers. So long as a person is uninformed about the etiology, symptoms, treatment, and prognosis of disease as medical science describes them, there is no reason to go to a scientific practitioner. As Blum et al. (1960:41) have noted:

> It is as true of class differences as it is of culture-determined ones, that the nature of the belief about the cause of illness leads to particular kinds of treatment measures.

The Chiropractor

Koos (1954:93-98) found that lower-income individuals considered chiropractors "the poor man's doctor," because the chiropractor was more friendly, gave more time, and explained things in words they could understand. In the study being reported, only five persons admitted ever having undergone chiropractic treatment. One individual noted:

> There's one chiropractor I go to, but I don't care about going to him. . . . He's rougher than an old boot . . . I had a hurting in my neck, and it just stayed. It had bothered me for years. I went down to see him and . . . from that day on, I was better. He said there's a lot of chiros today who can't do that for people whose got pressure there. He relieved it, and I haven't been bothered since. It's been a couple years. . . . Then I went to one in Tucson. . . . A friend told me about him and how he helped him. He hurt his back. He X-rayed him and after four treatments, he released him. That shows that sometimes chiros do some good.

When asked why he had gone to the first chiropractor, he replied, "Because

I thought he could help me." Even though he considered the chiropractor to be "rough," he was satisfied with the benefit received from the treatment. Another individual noted that:

> I did take chiropractic treatments for about two years when I hurt my neck, a whiplash, from an auto accident. But he's so rough. The chiro wouldn't release me, finally I got disgusted and quit going. I couldn't see where he was doing me any good.

Although this woman also noted that the chiropractor was "rough," she continued to see him for treatment for two years. Her decision to stop treatment was on the basis of dissatisfaction, because she could note no further improvement in her condition.

Other individuals had seen a chiropractor for back problems at some time in the past. All felt that there were limits to chiropractic treatment, but that it was "good" for bone and muscle ailments.

The Druggist

Individuals also sought medical advice from the druggist. The druggist played a role in the treatment of illness for which professional care was not sought:

> We asked what is a good ointment to use on a boil that was needing attention. The druggist suggested an ointment. Sometimes you ask them about a prepared medicine – what would be best as far as a cough syrup.
>
> I asked (the druggist) for a cough syrup and something for piles. What he gave me helped.
>
> Yes, a couple of times I've asked this druggist out here which was the best patent [medicine] something or other to use . . . for cough or something like that.
>
> Lots of times you ask him [the druggist], and he'll say, "Well, I got a lot of medicine here, but I like this for that." They know the ingredients of each thing, and what they mean.
>
> The druggist at ____________ [drugstore] is real good in helping you. They know more than the doctors.
>
> Druggist at ____________ [drugstore] is pretty good. I haven't asked him anything personally, but I think I would. They know more than doctors about drugs.
>
> In New York I asked the druggist about something for laryngitis one time. He gave me some throat lozenges.
>
> I have migraines, and I asked the druggist for something to relieve them, and he gave me something. It worked in half an hour.

Further, the druggist played a supplementary role in the treatment of illness being cared for by the physician. For example:

> Doctors are the darnest. You ask them a question, and they look at you as if you were silly to have asked the question. . . . I asked Doctor ______ about tincture of violet for an infection of the knee. He said it was old-fashioned. So I asked the druggist about some.
>
> One time I asked if a pill I was getting for my sister was a tranquilizer. He [the druggist] said, "Yes, and I wouldn't let her take too many."
>
> Oh, whenever I want to know what a certain medication is that the doctor has given me or a different treatment involved in illness, I call the druggist and he tells me.
>
> I always check with the druggist when the doctor gives me medicine to be sure that there's no aspirin in any drug I'm buying. I'm allergic to aspirin.

From the preceding illustrations, it is apparent that the druggist's role is significant. He advised, diagnosed, and recommended treatment for a number of individuals. When the individual was confronted with a choice among several brands of medicine, he asked the druggist for assistance in making a decision. When the individual needed clarification regarding a medication prescribed by a physician, the druggist again was consulted.

Koos (1954:91) also found that lower-income individuals utilized the druggist as diagnostician, prescriber of therapy, and advisor. Although most individuals realized the legal sanction placed on the druggist's role, they still expected him to satisfy their own particular needs.

The Reflexologist

Reflexology is "a scientific technique of massage that has a definite effect on the normal functioning of all parts of the body" (Carter 1972:1). By massaging specific areas of the foot, sick glands are said to be stimulated, and this enables them to return to a healthy state. Areas of the right foot are mapped out to correspond to the right side of the body; areas of the left foot are mapped out to correspond to the left side of the body. For example, the heart is on the left side of the body; the reflex to the heart is in a corresponding area on the left side of the foot.

Informants told me that the nearest reflexologist was in a nearby city, approximately 60 miles away. However, I was able to finally locate three individuals who had practiced reflexology either on themselves or members of their immediate families. These individuals all cautioned me that a person is treading on "thin ice" if he tries to advise anyone. As one individual told me:

> Even with friends, I'm tempted to say try it. But then, I'm not a doctor. What if they had a reaction? I say, Investigate it for yourself, this has helped me. People are funny, they don't really want to hear too many things – just platitudes.

Another individual told me how she had learned about reflexology, and how she has used it. She also included cautions:

> Somebody loaned my husband and I this book, and it showed the connection between the different parts of the feet and the glands in the body. You massage a certain area of the foot. We experimented with it. My husband and I both had a little lung congestion that night, and I did it on myself. You don't play games with stuff like this, or you'll wind up with swollen glands and everything else. If you are going to fool with it, you better buy the book. Study it and investigate it, because this one lady said that it felt so good that she kept it up, and she wound up with a lump in her throat. The book advises you how many minutes to do it for different things.

This same individual told me that she knew a woman who was completely "cancer-ridden." Since the woman has practiced reflexology, she has had no pain.

One female related that she has "no more female trouble" since she has used reflexology. She had gone to the practicing reflexologist in the nearby city and learned the technique from her, and now uses it on herself.

Reflexology is also used to diagnose illness. The individuals interviewed feel that reflexologists are efficient in massaging feet and that they have learned where the reflexes are located in the bottom of the feet; thus, they are able to locate tender spots. Then, by referring to the charts, they will know what gland(s) in the body is in special need of stimulation.

Self-Treatment With Patent Medicines

Self-treatment with patent medicines is fairly common. Patent medicines may be defined as commercially produced preparations available to the public without a physician's prescription and used for the relief of symptoms and/or illness. In addition, such common household supplies as bicarbonate of soda, table salt, and Clorox are used.

It was found that most individuals tended to use self-treatment for such common symptoms or conditions as diarrhea, constipation, sore throat or runny nose, feeling tired all the time, backaches, sinus trouble, allergy, indigestion, arthritis, dizziness, hemorrhoids, and inability to sleep.

Most individuals noted that they would not use self-medication longer than a week; three noted that they would probably use it for as long as two

TABLE 5.1

Number of Individuals Reporting Possession of Specified Categories of Patent Medicines

Type of Patent Medicine	Number
Vitamins	20
Analgesics	20
"Stomach medicine"	20
Cough or cold remedy	13
Mineral tablets	13
Cathartic or laxative	10
Hemorrhoid remedy	7
Allergy pills	6
Linaments or "rubs"	5
Tonics	3
Eye drops	3
Antiseptics	3
"Kidney pills"	2
"Liver pills"	2
Ear drops	1
Nose drops	1

weeks, and one male reported that he would use patent medicines for "feeling tired" for at least a month, and then would consult a doctor only if he was not improving.

Individuals were asked the types of patent medicines kept on hand. These were grouped into categories by the author. For example, aspirin was placed in the category, "analgesic," cough syrup was placed in the category, "cough or cold remedy." It was assumed that the possession of these items indicated their use as needed.

From the data in Table 5.1 it can be seen that there is widespread use by this study's lower-income Anglos of vitamins, analgesics, and stomach remedies. The fact that television commercials constantly urge viewers to use such remedies (always with the promise that well-being will result) probably contributes to their widespread popularity and acceptance.

Some individuals reported using large dosages of particular vitamins in the treatment of specific conditions. For example:

> I take vitamin E in large amounts for my emphysema.
>
> I take vitamin C by the handful. It's awfully good for nervousness. I didn't have a cold all winter. Vitamin C really helps.
>
> Take vitamin C, because I bruise so easily. It helps it.

> We take 600 IU's of vitamin E each day. According to Adelle Davis, it helps varicose veins. . . . My husband's arm was so bad about five years ago that one doctor told him the joint was all rotted out. I was taking vitamin C at the time, so I started feeding him vitamin C by the cupful! His right arm is just fine now.
>
> I use vitamin E for hemorrhoids. It'll take the pain right away. You can just open a capsule of vitamin E and use it for cuts, burns, itches too.
>
> That's [vitamin E] really good for you. I take 600 units a day. I feel tired if I don't.

One male reported that his physician had prescribed vitamin E for the individual's circulation. In another instance, a woman reported that she had talked with a pharmacist:

> I felt like I didn't have any pep at all, so I started taking vitamin E. Several pharmacists told me to take those – that they did. I noted that after a month, I could do more than before I took vitamin E. I think that's a pretty good test.

Other individuals continued using vitamins and related products despite physicians' advice that they were worthless or a waste of money:

> We got vitamins. We take ______ [tonic] all the time. . . . Doctors think they are worthless, but we know people that tonics have helped. If it makes you feel better, you should take it. If it gives you pep, you should take it.
>
> I told the doctor once that I used vitamins, and he said it was a waste of money. But its helped us [her family] and that's proof enough for me.

These individuals continued to use these vitamins and tonics, because they were satisfied with the benefits derived from their use.

Individuals noted that they used analgesics for such symptoms and complaints as headaches, arthritis, and stomach trouble, or "upset" stomach. Most persons reported having aspirin or aspirin-containing compounds in their medicine chests. Mothers frequently reported that they used aspirin to "bring down" fever in their children.

Various patent preparations were considered to be good "stomach medicine." Antacids such as *Maalox* and *Gelusil* were frequently used. Many mentioned *Alka-Seltzer* as a remedy, especially if you knew you had overeaten. The effect of television advertising was obvious in the use of "stomach" remedies. Individuals frequently used soda mixed with water for such things as indigestion and overeating.

Epsom salts were used for soaks for arthritic pain and for various other aches and pains. They also were used as a laxative by some persons.

All informants admitted that they had "doctored" at home with patent medicines at one time or the other. Generally, if the symptoms were relieved or the condition was alleviated, the individuals tended to consider that a "cure" was effected (at least temporarily, anyway), and the incident was forgotten.

When symptoms were severe or did not respond to treatment with patent preparations, a physician or osteopath was generally consulted. When asked by the author if they were taking medication that had been prescribed by a doctor, individuals promptly produced the container(s). Common complaints for which medications had been prescribed were: allergy, arthritis, high blood pressure, diabetes, hay fever, heart, nerves, sleep, stomach "trouble," thyroid, "water" retention, and various antibiotics for infections.

Individuals also used prescribed medicine simultaneously with patent medicines. For example:

> I have a kidney condition. I have to take water pills. I also take those kidney pills that you buy at the drugstore. . . .

This individual had not informed her physician what she was taking, because he would "just laugh at her."

Self-Treatment With Folk Remedies

Knowledge of folk remedies and "old timey" medicines is common among the lower-income Anglos studied. Nearly all individuals who used these remedies explained that they had learned about them from their parents. Knowledge of these remedies was passed down by word of mouth from their parents, or people remembered being treated with them when they were children. The use of folk practices was found to be more frequent among older persons than among those who were younger.

Old timey medicines are used frequently for coughs, colds, as "physics," as "tonics," infections, such as boils, skin rashes, allergies, such as hay fever and asthma, and to relieve pain. Individuals note the remedies they use for coughs:

> I make a cough syrup that my mother used to make with lemon, honey, and eucalyptus.
>
> My mother taught me to make onion syrup for cough. Boil an onion in water with sugar and salt. You can eat the onion, too.
>
> In Texas when I was small, my parents used to put a few drops of kerosene on a teaspoon of sugar, light it and let it burn. Blow it out, and use it as a cough drop.

There is a varied display of folk remedies for colds. Some of these used by informants are given below.

> Horseradish, dry and grated. I make it into a tea. I use it for fever with a cool bath. You can use the horseradish and lotus root together with a little bit of ginger and soy sauce and some salt. This is very good for fever and that horrible feeling that accompanies cold or flu. I might add that tea made from the horseradish is good for dropsy too. It'll flush your kidneys.

> Melt skunk fat to an oil and put it on your chest. Cover with a piece of flannel. That helps a cold to break and helps the chest pain, too.

Some of the older informants believe that the home remedies they learned as children are the best. For example:

> You take a lot of those old time medicines, they work. Better than what we get nowadays. . . . When I was a kid, mom used to make a cough syrup for us. There was something else she made. It was made out of what she called Indian turnips. It's some kind of root that grew in Virginia. Turpentine and lard was good for a chest cold too. I think that if we went back to the old time remedies . . . we'd be a lot better off.

Other persons also mentioned that mustard plasters were frequently used when they had a "chest cold." The heat produced relieved the pain and chest congestion and simply "felt good." Some individuals cautioned against using plasters in young children for fear of blistering the skin.

Individuals are influenced by relatives, friends, and neighbors as well as by television commercials and magazine ads to use various products for "irregularity." The use of patent medicines as laxatives was discussed previously. Persons also proclaim that certain foods have laxative qualities. Rhubarb stewed is said to have laxative properties. Figs, bran, citrus fruits and juices, and fresh fruits also are used as laxatives. Psyllium seeds were mentioned by two individuals as of value, because they added "bulk" to the diet.

Enemas also were used by a few individuals for constipation. One woman attributed her colitis cure to colonic irrigations.

> My mother thought it was colitis; I thought it was a little bit, too. A chiropractor told me I had this stoppage on the left side, and that's where the pain was, too. So my husband went to ______ for colonic treatments. I didn't think I needed the treatment when I took it, but my husband was taking it, and he thought that anything he did, I had to, too. The lady that was giving them said they wouldn't hurt you any, so I went ahead and took them. Why I haven't had anything to amount to anything since. They did find the blockage was on the right and not the left. By taking that colonic treatment, it all cleared up.

Some individuals refer to laxatives as "physics." This term seems to be used interchangeably with the term "laxative" without any definite distinction between the two.

Tonics also are used – especially spring tonics. Various teas are used to purify the blood. Chamomile tea is used quite frequently for this purpose. Comfrey tea also is used as a spring tonic. Sarsaparilla – a popular blood purifier – is used by a few individuals to make sassafras tea. Sulfur and molasses still are being used by a few individuals.

Flaxseeds are made into a paste to be used as poultices for relieving all kinds of inflammation and bringing boils "to a head." Hot water also is used as a soak for inflammation. Sometimes epsom salts will be added to the water. Raw bacon also is placed on inflamed areas and covered with a dressing so as to "draw out the poison."

Various skin disorders, such as rashes, are treated with folk remedies. For example, one woman told me the following:

> My son-in-law had barber's itch, and he went to every doctor around here. Finally a wetback one day came along and knew what he had. He speaks Spanish so he could talk to him. He said to get prickly pear leaf, burn the thorns off, and take the inside and make a poultice all over his face. He did, and in 30 minutes it began to cool off and feel better, in a couple days he was all right. Here, he'd been trying to get rid of it for over a month.

The same individual also related that her husband used to get hives every spring. She related the following experience:

> Sulfur is good for hives. It'll stop them quicker than anything. My husband used to get them every spring. He'd sit in the bathtub for hours. The doctor told him to take epsom salts. Well, you take three or four doses, and you've had it. So one day we was at his mother's and he started to break out. She told him to take flowers of sulfur. She gave him a teaspoonful and told him to wash it down with a glassful of water. So he did. In 30 minutes he was all right. After that, he went to the drugstore and got some.

Various folk remedies are used to remove warts. A few individuals were aware that warts are caused by a virus. Other persons were not sure what caused them and frequently would jokingly say, "Toads. Toads have warts, and if you touch them, you get warts." Magical properties were associated with warts – they go away without any treatment, and then they come back again. Others commented that "things work mysteriously on them." Some individuals found that iodine painted on warts caused them to go away. Others noted that covering warts with a cloth saturated with cooking oil or olive oil would "kill" them. Another woman noted that castor oil will work, too. Another informant said that she "had had them [warts] and a fellow we knew bought them, he gave me a quarter for them. He told me to put the quarter away and not think of it. The warts went away."

One woman who claimed American Indian heritage told about an old Indian belief:

> I had a seed wart, and my dad "powwowed" it off. Some Indian belief. There was Indian on both sides. My dad mumbled some words, and he'd rub it 3 times around and then again. My wart went away then. Dad died suddenly with a heart attack before he could pass it on to my brother.

This woman regrets that the "cure" is now lost.

One man related that if "you rub raw potato on them and then go away and bury it, the wart will disappear when the piece of potato rots."

Various remedies also are used to treat allergies such as hay fever and asthma. For example, one woman discusses her daughter's asthma:

> My little girl has had asthma since she was two and a half years old. She's not on any medicine now and she can do anything. We took her to a doctor way back, in ____, and she was getting shots. We took the sugar away and use honey. We get it from the bees around here – it's natural. Asthma is like diabetes – we found that we've arrested our daughter's asthma by taking her off sugar 100%.

Others believe that their hay fever has been helped by eating honey and using vitamin C.

Honey also is used in conjunction with other ingredients for hypertension and arthritis. One informant relates:

> Well, a neighbor told me to mix up garlic, honey, and lemon and take it. Since then, I haven't had any more high blood pressure.

The woman who used honey for arthritis notes:

> I take hot water, vinegar, and honey for my arthritis. I drink it lots of times for breakfast. It's a good general drink. I try to drink vinegar, we don't get enough of it. . . . You need to use natural honey.

Several individuals noted that it was all right to eat honey if you had diabetes, but that you should not eat refined sugar. They do not appear to realize that honey is a sugar and diabetics cannot tolerate it any better than they can any other sugar.

Alfalfa tea is considered good for arthritis as well as the honey, vinegar, and hot water remedy mentioned earlier. Many individuals also use heat in one form or another, such as hot soaks. Patent medicines which generally include aspirin are used in conjunction with folk medicines.

One informant wore a copper bracelet to help her arthritis. She reported that a friend who had arthritis had been helped by wearing one and she felt she, too, was improved. She also noted that a magnetic bracelet could be ordered from Japan which is supposed to be even better than the copper one for arthritis. Apparently, the old belief that body contact with certain metals has therapeutic value is still prevalent today.

Other miscellaneous folk practices were noted. One man noted that cobwebs were good to control bleeding from a wound or from the nose. He said that on occasion he had used the puffballs from dandelions.

Lard is also used for burns. One man related:

> One time I save a fella's life. His trailer caught on fire. I greased his face, and he was just as greasy. I got an old sheet and wrapped around him. I took him to ______ hospital. They said, "What's a matter with him?" I said he's burned. And that doctor said who ever put that grease on him saved his life. I didn't rub it, I just plastered it on. That fella looked at me and said, "you're a doctor." I said, I ain't either.

Soda also is made into a paste and applied to burns.

One woman noted that if an individual thought he might have diabetes that he should "have tests and be diagnosed." But, personally, after finding out that it was diabetes she would:

> Treat it with diet – pumpkin seeds have natural insulin in them. So do Jerusalem artichokes. You could replace the insulin from the doctor with that plant. You have to be careful that you don't eat too many.

Some individuals felt that diabetes was due to some sort of impurities in the kidneys and that it would be necessary to clear these up in order to treat diabetes. The presence of sugar in the urine was considered as an impurity.

From the preceding discussion it can be seen that folk practices and folk medicine are indeed present in the group studied. Individuals studied are aware that orthodox medicine often minimizes or discredits the value of folk medicines, and, therefore, they note that they generally do not tell the physician about the home remedies they have used.

The Physician

Extended periods of self-treatment were most common for such symptoms and ailments as diarrhea, constipation, sinus trouble, indigestion, and "feeling tired all the time." When complaints were more severe or did not yield to folk practices or patent medicines, a trip to the physician or osteopath ensued.

Practically all individuals who had heart trouble, diabetes, or kidney trouble reported the ailment as being diagnosed and treated by a physician, which was not surprising in view of the widespread awareness of the seriousness of these conditions. However, not all these individuals cooperated with the treatment prescribed. When the treatment regime required modification of personal habits, such as smoking and diet, individuals tended to cooperate the least.

Individuals who tended to use patent medicines and folk medicines most frequently were the most apt to state that they had lost confidence and faith in doctors. Some even considered the local physicians the least desirable of the lot. Inability to pay the fees charged appeared to accompany expressions of lack of faith. For example, one woman related to me:

> We've been through a lot of emotional and physical illness, and we've got to the point where doctors is a dirty word. We've lost faith in the medical profession as such, and we've not been economically able to afford this luxury to go in and have care . . . . We don't think all doctors are crooks, you get all kinds. We know one doctor personally who told us he is going to get all he can. This is why he is a doctor. He's not a good doctor. This I heard from one of his patients. Some tricks he's pulled. In the big city he'd not get away with it. But, we got healthy through not having funds to go get medical advice. We started reading books on our own. We were forced through poverty to improve our health. The wrong eating was one thing that caused our sickness. We eat right now. One of these times we'll probably kill ourselves. In the meantime, we stay away from doctors. We say if we're not bleeding or broken, we can take care of it.

Another individual who considered himself an alcoholic told me the following:

> I don't think doctors know enough about nutrition. I have made an appointment to see the doctor, and then you get out there and you have to wait and wait. Then they see you for a couple of minutes. I don't feel free to ask the doctor anything. They won't tell you. They just prescribe something and won't tell you what it is or what's it for. They never ask you if a medicine doesn't agree with you or not. They had me on Librium for six years. It's harder to get off than drinking. Another trouble with these doctors is that they don't know anything about alcoholics, the worse thing is to give them drugs.

This individual was not only dissatisfied with his treatment, but felt that he could not even communicate with the physician. And all individuals who had been to the county clinic complained that they had to wait long periods in order to see a physician for what seemed to them as only a few minutes.

Another individual compares today's physicians with the family doctors of the past:

> Doctors think you ought to know about things – you know, they get you in and out in a hurry. They don't treat you like the old family doctors, you know, and I think we need more family doctors. You know

> they sit down with you and talk with you and do you just as much good as the medicine, because they could sit down and talk to you. You're scared anyway. I think that's why people go to chiropractors, because they'll sit down and talk to you. They may not know anymore than you do, and they may not do you any good, but then, going to chiropractors helped me. They helped my back.

Again, the dissatisfaction with the lack of communication between patient and doctor was evident. Individuals pointed out that if they understood what the doctor was saying to them, they would have more confidence in him and would be more apt to follow his prescribed treatment. Others expressed dissatisfaction because the physician's definition of their illness did not correspond with their definition; still others felt that their expectations of the doctor's contribution to recovery from the illness were not met. As a result, individuals tended to ignore medical advice for "routine" illnesses and common aches and pains; only serious illness, that is, life-threatening situations, would bring them to the physician.

Reference Material

Bibliography

Adams, Richard N.

1957 *Cultural surveys of Panama, Nicaragua, El Salvador, Honduras.* Washington, D.C.: Pan American Sanitary Bureau.

Adams, Richard N. and Arthur J. Rubel

1967 Sickness and Social Relations. In *Handbook of Middle American Indians,* Vol. 6, edited by Manning Nash, pp. 333-357. Austin: University of Texas Press.

Aguirre Beltrán, Gonzalo and R. Pozas

1954 Instituciones indigenas en el Mexico actual. In *Metodos y resultados de la política indigenista en Mexico,* edited by A. Caso, pp. 171-272. México, D.F.: *Instituto Nacional Indigenista Publicaciones, Vol. 6.*

Barber, Carroll

1952 Trilingualism in Pascua: the social function of language in an Arizona Yaqui village. M. A. thesis, University of Arizona.

Bauer, W. W.

1969 *Potions, Remedies and Old Wives' Tales.* Garden City, New York: Doubleday & Co., Inc.

Baumann, Barbara

1961 Diversities in Conception of Health and Physical Fitness. *Journal of Health and Human Behavior,* 2:39-46.

Bauwens, Eleanor E.

1974 *Medical Decision-Making Among Lower-Class Anglos of Douglas, Arizona.* Ph.D. dissertation, University of Arizona.

Beals, Ralph L.

1932 The comparative ethnology of Mexico before 1750. *Ibero-Americana, Volume 2.* Berkeley and Los Angeles: University of California Press.

1943 The aboriginal culture of the Cahita Indians. *Ibero-Americana, Volume 19.* Berkeley and Los Angeles: University of California Press.

Beals, Ralph L. (*Cont.*)
1945 The contemporary culture of the Cahita Indians. *Bureau of American Ethnology, Bulletin 142*. Washington, D.C.: Smithsonian Institution.
1946 Cheran: A Sierra Tarascan village. *Publications of the Institute of Social Anthropology, Number 2*. Washington, D.C.: Smithsonian Institution.

Berlin, Brent, Dennis E. Breedlove, and Peter Raven
1968 Covert Categories and Folk Taxonomies. *American Anthropologist* 70: 290-99.

Bernard, Sydney
1964 *The Economic and Social Adjustment of Low-Income Female-Headed Families*. The Florence Heller Graduate School for Advanced Studies in Social Welfare. Brandeis University, Boston.

Blum, Richard H., Joseph Sadusk and Rollen Waterson
1960 *The Management of the Doctor-Patient Relationship*. New York: McGraw-Hill.

Bohannan, Paul
1963 *Social anthropology*. New York: Holt, Rinehart, and Winston, Inc.

Broadbent, Sylvia
1952 Home medicines among Spanish Californians in Monterey, California. Unpublished.

Bruner, Jerome S., Jacqueline J. Goodnow and George A. Austin
1967 *A Study of Thinking*. New York: John Wiley and Sons.

Carter, Mildred
1972 *Helping Yourself with Foot Reflexology*. West Nyack, New York: Parker Publishing Company, Inc.

Castillo de Lucas, Antonio
1958 *Folkmedicina*. Madrid: Editorial Dossat.

The Catholic Encyclopedia
1908 New York: Robert Appleton Company.

Clark, Margaret
1959 *Health practices in the Mexican-American culture: a community study*. Berkeley and Los Angeles: University of California Press.

Davies, R. Trevor
1947 *Four centuries of witch beliefs*. London: Methuen and Company,

Dewhurst, Kenneth
1966 *Dr. Thomas Sydenham (1624–1689) His Life and Original Writings*. Berkeley: University of California Press.

Driver, Harold E.
1961 *Indians of North America*. Chicago: University of Chicago Press.

Dumarest, Father Noel
1919 Notes on Cochiti, New Mexico (translated and annotated by Elsie Clews Parsons). *Memoirs of the American Anthropological Association, Volume 6, Number 3*.

Edmonson, Monro

1968 *Los Manitos—A Study of Institutional Values*. New Orleans: Middle American Research Institute, Tulane University.

Esteyneffer, Juan de, S. J.

1711 *Florilegio Medicinal* de todas las enfermedades, sacado de varios, y clásicos authores, para bién de los pobres, y de los que tienen falta de medicos, en particular para los provincias remotas en donde administran los RR. PP. misioneros de la Compañía de Jesús. Mexico. Microfilm at Brown University.

1887 *Florilegio Medicinal* o breve epídome de las Medicinas y Cirujia. La primera obra sobre esta ciencia impresa en México en 1713. Mexico. At the University of Illinois.

Fisher, Edna Marie

1921 Medical knowledge and practice in New Spain during the sixteenth century. M. A. thesis, University of California, Berkeley.

Foster, George M.

1948 Empire's children: the people of Tzintzuntzan. *Publications of the Institute of Social Anthrolopogy, Number 6*. Washington, D.C.: Smithsonian Institution.

1953 Relationships between Spanish and Spanish-American Folk medicine. *Journal of American Folklore, Volume 66, Number 261*, pp. 201-217.

1960 Culture and conquest, America's Spanish heritage. *Viking Fund Publications in Anthropology, Number 27*. Chicago: Quadrangle Books.

Foster, George M. and John Howland Rowe

1951 Suggestions for the field recording of information of the Hippocratic classification of diseases and remedies. *The Kroeber Anthropological Society Papers, Number 5*. Berkeley: The Kroeber Anthropological Society.

Frankel, Barbara

1970 Childbirth in the Ghetto: Folk Beliefs of Negro Women in a North Philadelphia Hospital Ward. Master's thesis, Temple University.

Giddings, Ruth Warner

1959 Yaqui myths and legends. *Anthropological Papers of the University of Arizona, Number 2*. Tucson: University of Arizona Press.

Gillin, John

1947 Moche, a Peruvian coastal community. *Publications of the Institute of Social Anthropology, Number 3*. Washington, D.C.: Smithsonian Institution.

Goldfrank, Esther S. (ed.)

1962 Isleta paintings, with introduction and commentary by Elsie Clews Parsons. *Bureau of American Ethnology, Bulletin 181*. Washington, D.C.: Smithsonian Institution.

Goodenough, Ward H.

1957 Cultural Anthropology and Linguistics. In *Report of the Seventh Annual Round Table Meeting on Linguistics and Language Study,*

Goodenough, Ward H. (*Cont.*)
edited by Paul L. Garvin, pp. 167-173. *Georgetown University Monograph Series on Language and Linguistics, No. 9.*
1963 *Cooperation in Change.* New York: Russell Sage Foundation.

Gordon, Milton
1964 *Assimiliation in American Life.* New York: Oxford University Press (reprinted 1970).

Grattan, John and Charles Singer
1952 *Anglo-Saxon Magic and Medicine.* London: Oxford University Press.

Haury, Emil W.
1950 *The stratigraphy and archaeology of Ventana Cave, Arizona.* Tucson: University of Arizona Press. Albuquerque: University of New Mexico Press.

Hawley, Florence M.
1950 The mechanics of perpetuation in Pueblo witchcraft. In *For the Dean.* Santa Fe: Hohokam Museum Association and Southwestern Monuments Association.

Heller, Celia S.
1966 *Mexican American Youth: Forgotten Youth at the Crossroads.* New York: Random House.

Henkel, A.
1904 Weeds Used in Medicine. *United States Department of Agriculture Farmers' Bulletin 188.* Washington, D.C.: U.S. Government Printing Office.
1907 *American Root Drugs.* United States Department of Agriculture Bureau of Plant Industry. Washington, D.C.: U.S. Government Printing Office.

Herskovits, Melville
1938 *Dahomey, an Ancient West African Kingdom. Vol. 1.* New York: J. J. Augustin.

Holden, W. C., and others
1936 Studies of the Yaqui Indians of Sonora, Mexico. *Texas Technological College Bulletin, Volume 12, Number 1,* Scientific Series Number 2. Lubbock: Texas Technological College.

Hrdlicka, Ales
1908 Physiological and Medical Observations Among the Indians of the Southwestern United States and Northern Mexico. Smithsonian Institution *BAE Bulletin No. 34.* Washington, D.C.: U.S. Government Printing Office.

Humphrey, Norman D.
1945 Some dietary and health practices of Detroit Mexicans. *Journal of American Folklore, Volume 58, Number 229,* pp. 255-8.

Hurston, Zora N.
1935 *Mules and Men.* Philadelphia: J. B. Lippincott Co.

Inglis, Brian
1965 *A History of Medicine.* Cleveland: World Publishing Co.

Jarvis, D. C.
1958 *Folk Medicine*. New York: Holt, Rinehart and Winston.

Johnson, Jean B.
1950 The Opata. *University of New Mexico Publications in Anthropology, Number 6*. Albuquerque: University of New Mexico Press.

Kany, Charles E.
1960 *American-Spanish Semantics*. Berkeley and Los Angeles: University of California Press.

Kardiner, Abram, and Lionell Oversey
1951 *The Mark of Oppression*. Cleveland: The World Publishing Company. First printing, Meridian, 1962.

Kay, Margarita A.
1976 *The Fusion of Utoaztecan and European Ethnogynecology in the Florilegio Medicinal*. Proceedings XLI International Congress of Americanists, September 2-7, 1974. Mexico City, Mexico.
1977 *Southwestern Medical Dictionary*. Tucson: University of Arizona Press.

Kearney, Thomas and Robert H. Peebles
1969 *Flowering Plants and Ferns of Arizona*. Berkeley and Los Angeles: University of California Press.

Kelly, Isabel
1956 *Santiago Tuxtla, Vera Cruz*. México, D.F.: Culture and Health Institute of Inter-American Affairs.

Kiev, Ari
1968 *Curanderismo: Mexican American Folk Psychiatry*. New York: The Free Press.

King, Stanley F.
1962 *Perceptions of Illness in Medical Practice*. New York: Russell Sage Foundation.

Kluckhohn, Clyde
1944 Navaho witchcraft. *Papers of the Peabody Museum of American Archaeology and Ethnology, Volume 22, Number 2*. Cambridge: Harvard University.

Koos, Earl L.
1946 *Families in Trouble*. New York: King's Crown Press.
1954 *The Health of Regionville*. New York: Columbia University Press.

Lewis, Oscar
1951 *Life in a Mexican Village, Tepoztlán restudied*. Urbana: University of Illinois Press.
1960 *Tepoztlán Village in Mexico. Case Studies in Cultural Anthropology*. New York: Holt, Rinehart and Winston.

Liebow, Elliot
1967 *Tally's Corner*. Boston: Little, Brown & Co.

Loeb, Edwin N.
1926 Pomo folkways. *University of California Publications in American Archaeology and Ethnology, Volume 19, Number 2*. Berkeley: University of California Press.

MacDonald's Farmers Almanac
1973 Binghamton, New York: Atlas Printing Co. (unpaginated).

Madsen, William
1964 *The Mexican-Americans of South Texas.* New York: Holt, Rinehart, and Winston.

Mair, Lucy
1969 *Witchcraft.* New York: McGraw-Hill Book Co.

Martínez, Maximino
1969 *Las Plantas Medicinales de Mexico.* Quinta Edicion. México, D. F.: Ediciones Botas.

Mechanic, David
1968 *Medical Sociology.* New York: The Free Press.

Metraux, Alfred
1959 *Voodoo in Haiti.* New York: Oxford University Press.

Meyers, Sister Bertrande, D. C.
1954 *Devotedly yours.* Chicago: Empire-Stone Press.

Miner, Horace
1939 *St. Denis, A French-Canadian Parish.* Chicago: University of Chicago Press.

Mintz, Sidney and Eric R. Wolf
1950 An Analysis of Ritual Co-Parenthood (Compadrazgo). *Southwest Journal of Anthropology, Vol. 6, No. 4,* pp. 341-369.

Morris, Earl
1951 Basketmaker III human figurines from northeastern Arizona. *American Antiquity, Volume 17, Number 1,* pp. 33-40.

Morss, Noel
1954 Clay figurines of the American southwest. *Papers of the Peabody Museum of American Archaeology and Ethnology, Volume 49, Number 1.* Cambridge: Harvard University.

Nichols, Andrew W.
1961 *A proposed manner of introduction of more adequate medical care to a semi-isolated Mexican-Indian community.* Stanford: Stanford School of Medicine.

Oliver, Paul
1960 *The Meaning of the Blues.* New York: Collier Books.

Painter, Muriel Thayer
1962 *Faith, flowers, and fiestas: the Yaqui Indian year, a narrative of ceremonial events.* Tucson: University of Arizona Press.

Parsons, Elsie Clews
1927 Witchcraft among the Pueblos: Indian or Spanish? *Man, Volume 27, Numbers 70, 80,* pp. 106-112, 125-128. London: Royal Anthropological Institute.
1936 *Mitla, town of souls.* Chicago: University of Chicago Press.
1939 *Pueblo Indian religion,* 2 volumes. Chicago: University of Chicago Press.

Parsons, Talcott
1951 *The Social System.* Glencoe: The Free Press.

Pierce, R. V.
1895 *The People's Common Sense Medical Adviser in Plain English: or, Medicine Simplified.* Fifty-sixth edition. Buffalo: World's Dispensary Printing Office and Bindery.

Postell, William
1951 *The Health of Slaves on Southern Plantations.* Baton Rouge: Louisiana State University Press.

Rainwater, Lee
1970 *Behind Ghetto Walls: Black Family Life in a Federal Slum.* Chicago: Aldine Publishing Co.

Redfield, Robert
1930 *Tepoztlán; a Mexican village.* Chicago: University of Chicago Press.

Redfield, Robert, and Margaret P. Redfield
1940 Disease and its treatment in Dzitas, Yucatan. *Carnegie Institution of Washington Publications, Volume 6, Number 32* (Contribution to American Anthropology and History, Number 523). Washington, D.C.

Rubel, Arthur J.
1960 Concept of Disease in Mexican-American Culture. *American Anthropologist,* Vol. 62, No. 5, pp. 795-815.
1966 *Across the Tracks: Mexican Americans in a Texas City.* Austin: University of Texas Press.
1969 Analisis functional y efectos negativos de algunas creencias acerca de la causacion de enfermedades. México, D. F.: *Anuario indigenista,* Vol. XXIX, pp. 269-275.

Samora, Julian
1961 Conceptions of Health and Disease Among Spanish-Americans. *American Catholic Sociological Review,* Vol. XXII, No. 4, pp. 314-323.

Saunders, Lyle
1954 *Cultural Differences and Medical Care: The Case of the Spanish-speaking People of the Southwest.* New York: Russell Sage Foundation.

Saunders, Lyle and Gordon W. Hewes
1953 Folk Medicine and Medical Practice. *Journal of Medical Education,* 28:43-46.

Shryock, Richard H.
1966 The Medical History of the American People, pp. 1-45. *In Medicine in America.* Baltimore: The Johns Hopkins Press.

Sigerist, Henry
1961 *A History of Medicine, Vol. II.* New York: Oxford University Press.

Simpson, Robert B.
1970 A Black Church: Ecstasy in a World of Trouble. Doctoral dissertation, Washington University, St. Louis.

Snow, Loudell
1973 "I Was Born Just Exactly with the Gift": An Interview with a

Snow, Loudell (*Cont.*)
Voodoo Practitioner. *Journal of American Folklore* 86:272–81.
1974 Folk Medical Beliefs and Their Implications for Care of Patients. *Annals of Internal Medicine* 81:82–96.

Spicer, Edward H.
1937 Unpublished field notes. Department of Anthropology, University of Arizona.
1940 *Pascua, a Yaqui village in Arizona.* Chicago: University of Chicago Press.
1954 Potam, a Yaqui village in Sonora. *The American Anthropologist, Volume 56, Number 4, Part 2, Memoir 77.*
1962 *Cycles of Conquest. The Impact of Spain, Mexico and the United States on the Indians of the Southwest, 1533-1960.* Tucson: The University of Arizona Press.
1964 Apuntes Sobre el Tipo de Religion de Los Yuto-Aztecas Centrales. *35th International Congress of Americanists.* pp. 27-38. México D. F.

Spicer, Edward H. (ed.)
1961 *Perspectives in American Indian cultural change.* Chicago: University of Chicago Press.

Standlee, Paul C.
1961 Trees and Shrubs of Mexico. *Smithsonian Publication 4461,* Washington, D. C.: U.S. Government Printing Office.

Stekert, Ellen
1971 Focus for Conflict: Southern Mountain Medical Beliefs in Detroit. In *The Urban Experience and Folk Tradition,* edited by Americo Paredes and Ellen Stekert, pp. 95-127. Austin: University of Texas Press.

Steward, Julian H.
1931 Archaeological discoveries at Kanosh, Utah. *El Palacio, Volume 30, Number 8,* pp. 121-130.

Toor, Frances
1937 Notes on Yaqui customs. México, D. F.: *Mexican Folkways* (*Yaqui Number*), July.

Treutlein, Theodore E.
1940 The Jesuit Missionary in the Role of Physician. *Mid America XXII,* pp. 120-141.

Treutlein, Theodore E. (Translator)
1949 Pfefferkorn's Description of the Province of Sonora. *Coronado Historical Series, Vol. XII.* Albuquerque: University of New Mexico Press.

Tuck, Ruth
1946 *Not With the Fist.* New York: Harcourt, Brace & Co.

Tucson Department of Community Development, City of Tucson
1969 Survey of Social Characteristics in Improvement Areas, Community Development Program. Multilith report.

Tylor, E. B.
1871 *Primitive culture,* 2 volumes. London: Murray.

Unknown Jesuit padre
1951 *Rudo ensayo.* 1763. Translated by Eusebio Guiteras. Records of the American Catholic Historical Society of Philadelphia, Volume 5, Number 2, 1894. Re-published by Arizona Silhouettes, Tucson.

U.S. Bureau of the Census
1971 *U.S. Census of Population: 1970, General Social and Economic Characteristics.* PC (1) – C4 Arizona. Washington, D.C.: U.S. Government Printing Office.
1973 *U.S. Census of Population: 1970, Characteristics of the Population.* Vol. 1, Part 4, Arizona. Washington, D.C.: U.S. Government Printing Office.

Van der Eerden, Sister Mary Lucia
1948 Maternity care in a Spanish-American community of New Mexico. *Anthropological Series, Number 13.* Washington, D.C.: The Catholic University of America.

Vogel, Virgil J.
1970 *American Indian Medicine.* Norman: University of Oklahoma Press.

Weaver, Thomas
1970 Use of Hypothetical Situations in a Study of Spanish-American Illness Referral Systems. *Human Organization, Vol. 29, No. 2,* pp. 140-154.
1973 The Cultural Ecology of a Border Town. Unpublished Paper presented to the Rural Health Conference, College of Medicine, The University of Arizona, Tucson.

White, Stephen S.
1948 The Vegetation and Flora of the Region of the Rio de Bavispe in North Central Sonora, Mexico. *Lloydia, A Quarterly Journal of Biological Science, Vol. II, No. 4,* pp. 229-302.

Zamora, Agustin A.
1944 *La Cohetera, Mi Barrio.* México, D. F.: Estado de Sonora.

Index